America's Emerging Fascist Economy

America's Emerging Fascist Economy

CHARLOTTE TWIGHT

ARLINGTON HOUSE·PUBLISHERS
NEW ROCHELLE, N. Y.

Library of Congress Cataloging in Publication Data

Twight, Charlotte.

  America's emerging Fascist economy.

  1. United States—Economic policy—1961-
I. Title.
HC106.6.T9   338.973   75-30632
ISBN 0-87000-317-8

36196

TO RICHARD TWIGHT

Acknowledgments

I am profoundly grateful to Arlington House for publishing this book, to Richard Twight for unwavering psychological support and endless generosity in devoting time to evaluating the manuscript, and to John D. Eshelman, Chairman of the Economics Department of Seattle University, for reviewing the economic analysis included herein.

Contents

1

Fascism's Economic Tenets

The term "fascist" is an emotionally charged, vituperative label more often mindlessly affixed to one's opposition than dispassionately analyzed. This book has two primary aims: first, to describe objectively the salient economic policies of a fascist state, showing how these policies are necessary corollaries of fascist philosophy's conception of the relationship between the individual and the state; and second, to outline the highly developed structure of United States statutes and judicial decisions adopting similar premises as the foundation of the modern American economic system.

While it is objectively accurate to label the prevailing American economic structure fascist, most Americans do not realize that the economy embodies fascist principles and have not consciously chosen to embrace such a system. With little access to information describing the legal basis, economic consequences, and philosophic implications of the vast powers the government wields over the economy, most citizens are the victims rather than the architects of the economic/legal system outlined in this book.

The book will not attempt to document the actual fascist economic systems that emerged under Hitler in Germany and under Mussolini in Italy. Any reference to those systems will be peripheral, designed only to provide concrete examples of specific characteristics. No detailed historical description will be undertaken, for ample historical analysis is already available in the works cited throughout this chapter. The purpose of this book's discussion of fascist economic policies is more general. It seeks to identify the *economic principles* that *any* fascist state tends to adopt as a logical consequence of fascism's philosophic premises. The distinguishing, paradigmatic economic characteristics of the political/philosophic/economic system called fascism will be explored.

This chapter abstracts the common economic attributes shared by previous fascist systems from the mass of data documenting the laws and administrative structures that characterized these historical examples of fascism. Throughout this chapter, whenever reference is made to a fascist economic policy, it does not represent idle speculation about how some hypothetical fascist economy might behave: an economic policy is so labeled because past fascist economies have in fact adopted precisely the measures described. Although only the general case is described, it can be identified as fascism's economic model only because historical instances of fascism have embodied the economic pattern here outlined.

FASCISM'S PHILOSOPHIC CORE: CAPITALISTIC COLLECTIVISM[1]

The essence of fascism is collectivism, which endows a group or "collective" with rights superior to the rights of the individual. Fascism deems the welfare of the nation to be its paramount concern; if national interest and private interest conflict, fascism forces people to sacrifice their individual desires. The rub implicit in fascism's lofty exhortation to self-sacrifice is in defining this abstract national welfare, in translating the ideal national interest into tangible goals. Like any form of collectivism, fascism empowers an elite to determine the specific purposes that other individuals in the society are compelled to serve.

There are only two philosophic models for political and economic systems, collectivism and individualism. A society that makes individual rights inviolate must choose either limited government or an anarchic structure based on voluntary contractual relationships as its political expression, and private rights to use and disposal of property as its economic foundation. If it desires to maintain its philosophic integrity, such a society cannot allow even the individual's right to vote and to control his property to be used to transgress other people's rights. Without compromising fundamental principles of individual rights, democracy cannot be used by fifty-one percent of the population to enslave the remaining forty-nine percent, nor can individuals invoke private property or capitalism to justify inflicting physical harm upon others. The direction of a nation philosophically committed to protecting individual rights is determined from below and is nothing more than the sum of individual agreements among its citizens. Power flows either from the individual to a government authorized to fulfill only those functions delegated to it by the people, or between all individuals in fulfillment of a complex of voluntary contractual relationships.

Collectivism inverts this pattern. Its political manifestation is totalitarianism, total power (whether or not fully exercised) of the state over every citizen. It may adopt socialism, communism, or capitalism as its nominal economic form, but the rights of those empowered to use and dispose of the means of production are always circumscribed by superior rights conferred upon the collective, whether that collective is the community, the government, or the nation. The collectivity — community or state — is quite literally envisioned as the sole source of value or worth.[2] The individual's primary purpose is to further the welfare of the group by pursuing goals formulated by his superiors in the political hierarchy.

Like any other form of collectivism, fascism requires individual independence to be totally eradicated, for the individual's will must be wholly subservient to whatever the political rulers decree to be the community's interest. The individual is not permitted to question or independently assess the politically sanctioned national interest, any more than an individual cell can question whether its genetically programmed function is the proper means to promote the human body's well-being. The fascist believes truly independent thought to be as ludicrous and detrimental to the welfare of the nation as it would be to the health of a human body whose cells were free to act independently without mental or genetic guidance.[3] Even the language of freedom is redefined by fascism to suit a totalitarian context. Freedom of action in any area (personal liberties such as free speech, as well as economic activity) is tolerated only if the desired action is compatible with the state's official declaration of the national interest. Fascist "freedom" is freedom to do what the state permits one to do,[4] a fundamentally totalitarian concept regardless of its euphemistically libertarian label. Fascism is philosophically committed to totalitarianism; it is the antithesis of limited government and individualism; it uncompromisingly seeks to obliterate individual rights.

To achieve these goals, fascism strives to nullify any distinction between individual and collective interests.[5] The ideal fascist state would be maintained by a psychologically submissive people whose conformity was secured by their *voluntary* dedication to whatever they were told was in the national interest, rather than by storm troopers and physical coercion.[6] In practice, however, fascist states achieve power by augmenting "voluntary" compliance with forceful intimidation.

Fascism is unique among collectivist systems in selecting capitalism as its nominal economic mate, but capitalism is turned inside out in this unlikely union. Fascism embodies an inherent conflict, for its totalitarian political philosophy is diametrically opposed to its capitalistic economic preference. Totalitarianism's recognition of the superiority of group "rights" over the individual is fundamentally incompatible with capitalism's acknowledgment of individual rights as superior to any collective will. Fascism's resolution of this dilemma is simple: it deems itself collectivist first and only secondarily capitalistic. That is, fascism embraces private-property rights only as a utilitarian means to economic ends,[7] the productivity and military superiority of the state. Since private property and the profit motive work effectively as incentives for high production, fascism uses these features of capitalism *insofar as they do not conflict with the national interest as formulated by fascism's political authorities.*[8] But the private entrepreneur is always regarded as a trustee of his property,[9] allowed to use it according to his private desires only if the state has not decreed that his individual purposes contravene the political elite's determination of the state's best interest.

No economic sphere is immune from government control, for any economic activity that allegedly transcends private interests and affects the community at large is deemed a legitimate subject of state control. As Italy's "Program Manifesto of the Fascist Republican Party" openly asserted: "In the national economy, everything that, in scope or function, goes beyond private interests and affects those of the community comes within the State's sphere of action."[10] If a right is defined as a freedom to act which is legally protected from both governmental and private infringement, then fascism tolerates the *form* of private ownership at the government's pleasure, but it eliminates any meaningful *right* of private property. Fascism recognizes an individual's right to use and transfer his property to the same extent that any dictatorship preserves the right to free speech, for each supposed right is tolerated only as long as it does not interfere with the changing purposes of transient political rulers.

Other collectivist systems are more honest about acknowledging where the ultimate economic power lies. Both socialist and avowedly communist countries, for example, empower the state to function as the exclusive owner of the material means of production and distribution of all products, although such systems occupy a spectrum from totally authoritarian, autocratic imposition of central economic planning to relatively more "liberal" attempts to incorporate consumers' views into the centralized decision-making process.[11] Fascism alone pretends to embrace capitalism's recognition of the right of private individuals to ownership of the means of production and distribution. But it is a bogus capitalism indeed, a sham deferral to individual economic rights readily nullified whenever political leaders deem it expedient.

Thus fascism is not *philosophically* committed to the principles of capitalism. Private property and profits are regarded as useful incentives only in areas where the government has not directly usurped total economic control. Fascism espouses capitalism except where its totalitarian political hierarchy dictates otherwise. Fascist capitalism is "regulated" capitalism; it is government intervention in the economy on a massive scale, regardless of how euphemistic the label used to describe it.

FASCISM'S ECONOMIC POLICIES

Although fascism gives lip service to capitalism, a fascist economy is essentially orchestrated from the top by its political authorities.[12] Fascism represents the antithesis of a market economy, for the government's political decisions rather than consumers' preferences ultimately control the nature and quantity of production. In a free market system, a country produces only those goods and services which 1) consumers desire and have the means to purchase, and 2) that country can produce relatively more efficiently than other nations (that is, those goods in which a country has a comparative advantage relative to producers in other countries). Fascism supplants these market considerations with political considerations.

Economic activity can serve either of two fundamentally incompatible purposes. It can work to satisfy consumers' actual demands for goods and services in the least costly way possible, or it can be used to accomplish the social goals of designated political leaders with only perfunctory regard for economic costs or consumers' wishes. The former economic approach makes the consumer's choice sovereign; the latter empowers a political elite to control the goods and services available to consumers. The former approach is implicit in a market economy; the latter is embraced by all totalitarian political systems including fascism. Fascist states' determination of what production is required in the "national interest" is by definition something other than the production that would result from the private market's response to consumer preferences. Like the capitalist, the fascist asserts

17

that his system is vindicated by considerations of "economic efficiency," but unlike the capitalist, the fascist defines economic efficiency as the achievement of the political elite's economic purposes rather than the satisfaction of consumers' desires. Nevertheless, a candid fascist would proudly concede that fascism channels its resources into pursuits that subordinate both individual choice and objective economic costs.

The fascist state initially assumes increased control over a few industries deemed "vital" to the national interest.[13] The list may vary, but it usually embraces agriculture, armaments (national defense), energy, and finance (as a means of engineering the full spectrum of its economic, social, and political policies). Both Germany and Italy acted early to centralize control over the key areas of agriculture and finance, abrogating capitalism to a degree at that time unusual for the budding fascist economies.[14] As the economic effects of government intervention in these few "vital" industries begin to be felt, the fascist government compensates by encompassing an ever-wider sphere of economic activity, and the requisite threshold for deeming an economic realm vital diminishes correspondingly.

Fascism's disregard of consumer demand and increased production costs to promote political goals has myriad consequences, all requiring increasingly strict control over the nation's economy if the fascist state is to remain viable. First it must acquire centralized control over the money supply and banking system, such as that procured in Germany through the Reichsbank. Unless the government creates internal *inflation* by expanding the supply of currency and credit, a fascist nation must either endure substantial unemployment or absorb a serious decline in personal income. Since massive unemployment or drastically reduced personal income would create political unrest of a magnitude wholly unacceptable to the fascist elite, fascist states typically prefer inflation to unemployment. The German Nazis, for example, in spite of the public's still vivid horror at Germany's 1923 inflation, adopted inflationary policies while espousing full employment as one of their chief goals, perceiving their political survival to be contingent upon widespread if nonremunerative employment.[15] So ardently did the Nazis seek full employment that they discouraged or banned the use of labor-saving devices in some industries, desiring to spread the available work as thinly as possible rather than seeking to increase the average worker's economic welfare.[16] Rampant expansion of Germany's credit was accomplished primarily by the government's profligate issuance of short-term government notes, which entered the banking system as a net addition to Germany's money supply and later were converted by political fiat into long-term debt upon which the government ultimately defaulted.[17] The Nazi government's total control of the nation's banking system and its extensive financing of large-scale public-works projects also facilitated expansion of the money supply.[18] This expansion of government debt inflated Germany's money supply because a huge amount of the debt did not "absorb" existing money or credit. Instead, the government merely issued debt instruments called "mefo-bills" or "employment bills" to pay for its armaments orders and public-works projects. These mefo-bills were accepted by all German banks and functioned as part of the money supply, even though they were backed by nothing but the government's insubstantial promise to pay.[19]

Concerned about the inevitable consequences of its inflationary policies, the German government sought to avoid those results by simultaneously absorbing most money held by private interests throughout the economy. Designed to mitigate the effects of inflation, this deflationary "blotter" function enabled the government to expropriate the maximum amount of "hard" currency to finance governmental escapades by reducing citizens' consumption to the bare minimum necessary for subsistence. For example, citizens were compelled to deposit all their "excess" income (as determined by government decree) in state-controlled banks or to "invest" it in government bonds and short-term notes.[20] Banks and corporations, legally divested of any responsibility to investors and prohibited from paying interest or dividends above a low level approved by the government,[21] were "encouraged" by liberal tax rewards, subsidies, and subtle threats implicit in unlimited political control over the economy "voluntarily" to invest all savings and profits in government bonds and short-term notes which never would be repaid.[22] Later, the subtle threats were transformed into overt compulsion, and government bonds were marketed through imposition of government-decreed quotas mandating the purchase of government debt.[23]

Fascism also typically invokes the ubiquitous national interest to justify wage and price controls, designed to obscure temporarily the symptoms of the government's inflation of the nation's money supply by forcing artificially low prices in spite of the decreased value of each unit of currency. In Germany, for example, absolute legal power to fix prices was alternately conferred upon the Minister of Economics and a "National Price Commissioner," who consulted with members of government-imposed cartels through an administrative hierarchy of industrial trade groups within the National Economic Chamber before reaching his ultimate decisions.[24] Similar unlimited power to fix prices was claimed by the fascist government in Italy.

In addition to concealing inflation, wage and price controls benefit fascist rulers by empowering the government to alter the economic data upon which industry normally operates. In a free market, prices mirror consumer desires and tell the businessman what kinds of goods to produce and in what quantities. By tampering with wages and prices, fascist rulers can give false input signals to businessmen, stimulating production that satisfies political demands rather than consumers' desires. For example, by legally setting the price of a commodity artificially high, fascist authorities can cause increased production of that item (provided the government also guarantees that it will purchase the commodity if consumers do not). Conversely, an artificially low price will increase demand for the product, causing demand to exceed supply and necessitating government rationing of the commodity. Ever desirous of concealing high prices caused by inflationary policies while further centralizing governmental economic power, fascist administrators welcome the imposition of artificially low prices, covertly hoping to stimulate public demand for further government control in the form of rationing.

Fascism also installs the *mandatory government license* as a central economic weapon, for compulsory government licensing of businesses allows the political hierarchy to control the nation's economy without the appearance of totalitarian coercion. Italy's fascist regime, for example, by its laws of January 12 and May 15, 1933, explicitly required a government license for the creation of any new factory or the expansion of an existing one, licenses seldom granted without concomitant approval by established businesses potentially threatened by the prospective competitor.[25] Nazi Germany similarly prohibited expansion of any business without a government license, whether the business was an industrial plant or a retail shop.[26] After 1935 a "Masters' Examination" in each craft was made a prerequisite of opening any new German business.[27] By establishing subjective criteria for the granting of these government licenses for the creation, expansion, or cessation of business, fascism institutionalizes administrative arbitrariness, guaranteeing political control over economic decisions. Altruistically phrased, vague licensing standards such as the national or community interest, local needs, or the personal qualifications (reliability, loyalty) of the applicant preserve a facade of justice and due process to conceal unlimited governmental power. Exactly such elastic standards for government licenses prevailed in Nazi Germany.[28]

Fascism's ultimate reliance upon coercion is most clearly revealed, however, through the direct government production decree, and the fascist hierarchies under both Hitler and Mussolini made abundant use of this weapon.[29] Omnipresent quantity and quality controls prevailed.[30] Not only were prices set at artificial levels, but businesses were required to produce specific quantities at the government-sanctioned prices while paying government-ordered wages, even if this forced businesses to operate at a loss.[31] Italy's "Program Manifesto of the Fascist Republican Party," for example, while superficially authorizing private production activities, explicitly ordered producers to "[hand] over to the pools the *quantity of goods fixed by law at the prices established by the controls.*"[32] Germany was able to control the quantity of production by a plethora of methods, including government allocation of raw materials and credit required by regulated businesses.[33] The state told business what and how much to produce, where to produce it, and where to deliver it.[34] In agriculture, where German fascism exercised its most stringent controls, government officials dictated the type and quantity of produce each farmer had to deliver, enforcing such minutely detailed production regulations as that requiring each hen to lay sixty-five eggs per year.[35] A German firm could not even cease production without the government's permission.[36]

Cartelization is another hallmark of fascist economic intervention, a feature which has characterized such fascist economies as Italy, Nazi Germany, and Japan. A cartel is simply a group of businesses that uses nonmarket machinations to procure a monopoly position with its concomitant ability to exclude potential competitors.[37] Fascism fosters cartelization by bureaucratically operated government permit or licensing systems, which confer upon a few select firms the exclusive right to produce specific commodities, schemes often implemented (at least partially) through mandatory trade associations. Both Italy and Germany imposed mandatory trade associations.[38] Nazi Germany was typical. Its active support for cartels culminated in the law of July 15, 1933, which empowered the Minister of Economics (head of the National Chamber of Economics) to coerce firms to join existing cartels or to form new ones.[39] Identical laws had been adopted by Italy in June 1932 and by Japan in April 1931.[40] Cartels are the logical outgrowth of fascism's creation of a government-approved economic bureaucracy, for both government licenses and mandatory government-sanctioned trade associations serve to exclude all competitors except suppliant association members bearing the government's stamp of approval.

Cartels emerge in part because fascism's abrogation of the market in favor of political control over the economy inherently favors big business at the expense of the small entrepreneur.[41] Big business inevitably prevails under fascism because the financial resources of large firms make it easier for a big enterprise to absorb the cost of the administrative red tape that any fascist bureaucracy imposes as an integral part of its political decision-making, while the economic power of a large-scale business enhances bureaucrats' responsiveness to its

21

wishes. In addition, influential political administrators not overawed by a large enterprise's sheer economic power may be persuaded by more tangible enticements, and a big firm's coffers oil more bureaucratic wheels with less strain on solvency than do those of firms with more meager assets. Big business also lures government officials into rendering favorable administrative decisions with promises of plush retirement jobs, while the government seduces corporate executives with promises of lucrative and prestigious government posts, making extensive interchange of positions between ranking civil servants and high corporate executives uniquely characteristic of fascism. Further, taxes imposed to finance a fascist government's social programs exert a much greater strain on small or marginal businesses than on larger firms. Finally, in a fascist economy in which business and government are administratively intertwined, size alone increases the likelihood that a large firm will incorporate enough influential party members to procure a favorable political decision. Quick to perceive its advantages over smaller enterprises in dealing with a fascist government, big business tends to favor the development of a fascist system. In the early 1930s, for example, some of the richest, most influential German businessmen helped to finance Hitler's rise to power.[42] Thus a symbiotic relationship between large corporations and the fascist state emerges, as big business envisions fascism's political decision-making to be a means of excluding competitors without facing the rigors of the marketplace.

As discussed above, one of fascism's chief goals is to eliminate people's consciousness of any collective identity other than the politically approved "national interest" of the fascist state. If a people's fascist consciousness is to be enhanced, awareness of other collective identities must be decreased. Fascism cannot tolerate fractionalization of its people's consciousness; the national interest of the fascist state must totally permeate people's lives as the paramount standard of value. Fascism therefore strives to *eliminate overt conflict between capital and labor interests*, for people acutely conscious of their unique interests as part of an identifiable group called "labor" or "management" are to that extent less subservient to the politically decreed national interest.[43] In Nazi Germany, for example, the government attempted to minimize distinctions between employers and employees through imposition of the "leadership" principle, which gave leaders (management) and followers (labor) the same status while subjugating both to omnipotent government-controlled "Honor Courts" empowered to oust an owner of a business on the basis of a political determination that he had behaved in an "antisocial" manner or had wounded his "followers' " sense of honor.[44] Employees were prohibited from joining any organization that represented their group's interests exclusively.[45] In Italy, the superficial harmonizing of employers' and employees' conflicting interests was supposed to occur as these factions ultimately merged under the umbrella of huge bureaucratic structures called corporations, idyllically envisioned as a utopian union of management and labor.

Fascist economic associations, whether composed of labor or management or both, tend to be organized along trade lines in order to erode the notion that members of one firm have anything to gain through competition with other members of the same economic association. Fascism's slogan might accurately be described as "one nation, one collectivity." Labor must not be conscious of itself as *labor*; capital interests must not perceive themselves as *management*; all must envision themselves only as working in different but equally important ways to achieve the same overriding abstraction labeled the national interest. Thus fascism seeks apparent structural if not actual *equality between management and labor.*[46]

To support the appearance of equality between labor and capital while securing firm political control over the fundamental employment relation, fascism tends to impose mandatory economic associations upon all workers and entrepreneurs. Myriad mandatory economic organizations prevailed in Germany as well as Italy. In Germany, both management and labor were forced to participate in a government-controlled organization deceptively labeled the Labor Front. Although membership in the Labor Front technically was not compelled by law, in reality membership was compulsory because an employee could lose his job for "antinational" attitudes and an employer could lose his position as "leader" if he refused to join.[47] Supplementing the Labor Front in Germany was a complex structure of mandatory government-imposed cartels, coupled with intricate government regimentation of economic activity achieved through a system of "Estates" and national economic groups directed by the Minister of Economic Affairs and the National Economic Chamber.[48] The fascist government in Italy similarly compelled membership in state-controlled economic organizations, opting for parallel hierarchies of mandatory economic associations for employers and employees at the local level rather than integrating them into a single administrative entity. In Italy's case, the melding function was reserved for the national "corporations."[49]

All of these government attempts to fuse management and labor, molding them into a monolithic instrument for achieving whatever government officials decree to be the national interest, serve a dual purpose. First, they establish the *appearance* that all interests are fully represented in the bargaining process, effectively pacifying potential malcontents. Second, the unitary nature of compulsory trade and worker associations facilitates political control of these economic groups. Nevertheless, while strengthening a structure of politically approved economic organizations, fascism simultaneously seeks to *eliminate strikes and lockouts*, as was done in both Italy and Germany.[50] Strikes and lockouts are alien to a fascist system both because they constitute visible evidence of a conflict of interest between management and labor and because they recognize workers' and employers' rights to act independently of the politically approved national economic hierarchy, thus tending to subvert implementation of the government's economic policies. Fascist labor policy represses overt conflict between capital and labor by erecting a bureaucratic facade of economic organizations supposedly representative of the interests of their constituents, while seizing the only tools through which those constituents can implement their own interests. A myth of unity of interest—a pretense of management's and labor's goals coalescing to achieve the national interest—is fostered while the fascist government deftly secures covert but total political control of the nation's economy. The national interest is but a ploy to assuage conflicting interests, inducing a false sense of unity while conferring absolute economic power upon a centrally administered government bureaucracy.

A fascist government's coerced distortions of the domestic economy cannot succeed even temporarily without governmental control over international economic relations as well. Since fascism's internal policies raise production costs above their normal level absent government regulation, consumers must pay more for goods and services, and the entire country fares worse economically—that is, more resources are consumed in producing fewer and less-desired goods and services. Unless the fascist state naturally has a substantial comparative advantage in producing a regulated commodity, government-induced inefficiencies will immediately attract imports of competing goods from other countries. Unwilling to see its domestic policies thus undermined from abroad, fascism's next step is to protect its controlled domestic economy by regulating imports and exports through tariffs, quotas, and subsidies as well as overt prohibitions. While nations generally have sought to maintain an equilibrium between their imports and exports to ensure their ability to finance imported goods, fascist countries use export subsidies and import tariffs and quotas to cheat on the international market by giving their products an artificial edge over those of other countries. Competition between nations for markets is rigged under fascism, and while the fascist government may endure, the consumer foots the bill in the form of higher prices and a

24

reduced standard of living. In Germany, for example, the Nazi government seized total control over imports and exports, requiring prospective importers and exporters to obtain explicit governmental approval of any international transaction.[51] Thus no foreign country could market its products in Germany without the approval of German rulers intent upon artificially insulating the German economy from the international market. Hungry for foreign currency to finance the imports necessary to achieve its politically conceived economic objectives, the Nazi government sought to give German exports an artificial advantage over other nations' goods on the international market both by forcing "private" businesses to contribute governmentally fixed amounts towards an industrywide subsidy of designated export commodities, and by pumping government funds and credit into subsidized export industries.[52]

Fascism's protectionist economic policies in international economic matters further stimulate cartelization. As fascism raises barriers to other countries' products by imposing import duties, national monopolies emerge within the shelter of these restrictions on free trade. Such national cartels or monopolies evolve because domestic firms can price their goods just under the sum of the world market price charged by foreign competitors and the import duty imposed by the fascist government.[53] Thus import duties, particularly floating import duties subject to change on government whim, effectively exclude foreign competitors by creating an artificial (nonmarket) advantage that confers upon domestic firms the monopolistic, exclusionary powers of a governmentally inspired cartel.

But other countries refuse to sit passively by while their exports are systematically discriminated against or excluded from a fascist competitor's territory. All countries need to export, for exports are the ultimate source of the foreign currency necessary to pay for imports. Rather than submit to exploitation by a fascist country using import barriers to shield its internal economic inefficiencies, other nations retaliate by erecting their own barriers to goods imported from the country that initiated the protectionist measures. The fascist nation's efforts at protectionism thus create a constantly constricting circle progressively choking off trade with the rest of the world. As fascism shuts its doors to certain imports, angry competitors become increasingly unwilling to accept fascist exports.

A fascist country facing the international repercussions of protectionist regulation of its international trade will take radical steps to sustain itself. With survival itself at stake, the most desperate maneuvers appeal to an economically threatened fascist government. Using implied threats of physical force as its ultimate stock in trade, Germany desperately grabbed foreign capital by exporting both goods that Germany could produce cheaply (for example, a fifteen-year supply of aspirin) and totally unusable products (such as cameras without lenses) to vulnerable neighboring countries intimidated into trading with Germany, although the so-called trade completely distorted the concept of mutual exchange of value.[54] Further, the German government indirectly confiscated imported goods by paying foreign producers in German currency deposited in the sellers' German bank accounts, a scheme which lasted only until the foreign creditors, upon discovering that German currency could not be used to purchase other commodities desired by the creditors, curtailed their sales of additional goods to Germany.[55]

Progressively deprived of the ability to export its products, the fascist state ultimately becomes unable to import, for exports finance imports. Protectionist policies thus force fascist countries to turn ever inward to satisfy their economic needs, to seek autarky (self-sufficiency) as the only alternative to the foreign trade its policies have destroyed. Autarky was proclaimed to be Germany's national aim in September 1936.[56]

Autarky as a national economic goal has profound drawbacks, however. First, consumers suffer. The country's economic resources are used in a less than optimum manner, with domestic business forced by political dictates to produce substitutes for commodities normally imported. The domestic substitutes are usually more expensive and/or less desirable, often of poorer quality or functionally inferior as replacements for the formerly imported items. Germany's synthetic rubber, for example, was four times as expensive as imported rubber.[57] Autarky implies a lower standard of living both domestically and internationally, because the fascist economy's resources are not employed in producing those goods and services that it can create most efficiently for itself and for the world. Although the citizens of a fascist nation endure the reduced living standard most directly, in a broader sense fascism's economic distortions indirectly lower world-wide prosperity and productivity by inefficient use of a portion of the world's resources. Finally, in most cases autarky is physically impossible. Unless a nation is endowed with natural resources that can at least satisfy its people's basic requirements for subsistence, self-sufficiency implies self-destruction. Indeed, even if willing to accept bare survival as the norm, few countries possess the domestic resources to endure completely severing themselves from all imports.

Physical constraints upon the achievement of national self-sufficiency lead to autarky's ultimate consequence, *war*.[58] If a fascist nation seeks self-sufficiency because of international reaction to fascist protectionism but lacks the internal resources necessary to attain complete autarky, the fascist state naturally perceives conquest of foreign lands as the logical means to expand its resources and thereby further its autarkic ends. Thus one of Germany's predominant goals in conquering new lands was seizure of valuable factories, banks (for their precious foreign currencies), and other resources, action taken promptly after any newly occupied territory was subdued.[59] The less naturally self-sufficient a fascist nation is, the more vigorously it will pursue, as an overriding national policy, forceful acquisition of new territory and resources. Even if a fascist nation possesses the resources necessary to achieve total self-sufficiency, the consequences of implementing a national policy of autarky will be equally disastrous, for the great majority of nations not physically capable of attaining self-sufficiency will understandably rebel at exclusion from markets upon which their survival depends.

THE CULMINATION OF FASCISM'S ECONOMIC POLICIES: ECONOMIC AND PSYCHOLOGICAL DEPENDENCE

To sustain its power and achieve its economic ends, fascism seeks to make its people economically and psychologically dependent on the government. Such dependence both enhances the government's tangible control over its citizens' economic activities and stimulates that intangible psychological support so crucial to maintaining a viable fascist state.

Economic dependence is fostered on many levels. All businessmen are forced to depend on government licenses as a prerequisite of pursuing their trade, making entrepreneurs subject to bureaucratic whim and governmental fiat for their economic livelihood. Since small, independent businesses operate at a disadvantage and often are actively discriminated against in a fascist state, their owners frequently are forced to close them and work instead for large corporations.[60]

The economic survival of corporate workers is dependent upon the corporation's financial well-being, which, culminating a chain of total economic dependence, is in turn contingent upon governmental contracts and political decisions. Moreover, the government's manipulation of the supply of money and credit reduces private citizens as well as businessmen to utter dependence upon the government regarding both the value of their monetary assets and the condition of financial markets. Further, as the fascist government usurps direct control over more and more aspects of the economy in the "national interest," government orders represent an ever-expanding proportion of the nation's total economic transactions, vastly increasing the government's economic leverage over corporations through its power to distribute valuable government contracts. For example, when government orders constitute eighty percent of all contracts, as was estimated to be the case in Hitler's Germany,[61] the government holds life-and-death power over the very existence of most businesses, stimulating a degree of "voluntary" compliance with the government's wishes otherwise highly unlikely.

Wage and price controls also expand economic dependence, for labor and capital alike must look to government bureaucrats who determine their economic fate. Regardless of consumers' demand for a product, a bureaucrat's whim can instantaneously render its production unprofitable merely by raising the costs of the factors of production. Wage and price controls more subtly tighten the government's reign over the economy by causing shortages, producing artificial emergency conditions that encourage an economically naive populace to bestow increased control upon the government to alleviate the shortages by rationing the "inexplicably" scarce commodities. Aloof from and unresponsive to the individual consumer's preferences, bureaucrats formulating government price-fixing and rationing decrees control the products that a dependent citizenry is allowed to purchase.

Government licensing, government contracts, wage and price controls, manipulation of the money supply, rationing — all of these are overt mechanisms creating actual, tangible economic dependence. A more subtle consequence of fascism is to make people psychologically dependent on the government for their economic well-being. As a fascist government increasingly usurps the functions of private enterprise in providing the daily necessities of its citizens such as health care, food, housing, energy, and insurance, the individual becomes acutely aware that his survival is dependent upon governmental decisions that he as an individual cannot significantly influence. Progressive governmental usurpation of market functions creates a docile, disillusioned citizenry, which gradually accepts fascism's implicit premises that individuals cannot succeed by independent action not blessed with the government's approval, that money and political power are the only avenues to favorable government action, and that economic success is victory by one politically potent group in ripping off, with the government's complicity, a less-powerful rival.

Fascism eliminates voluntary risk-taking from the economic sphere, substituting a government bureaucrat's unpredictable decree for the predictable, conscious risk of the market. The risk remains, a risk of greater magnitude because it is controlled by arbitrary political considerations rather than by predictable economic realities, but economic risk is *imposed* on people by the government; it is not consciously and voluntarily incurred by individuals. Fascist citizens do not choose economic risk; they are subjected to it by the government.

Although preventing independent economic decisions and voluntary assumption of economic risk at first arouses opposition, the government's bureaucratic control over the economy gradually becomes imbued with the security of the status quo. Citizens and businessmen become unused to taking known economic risks, and they eventually feel more comfortable attempting to influence government bureaucrats than anticipating the demands of the market. Corporate officials become content cajoling government bureaucrats in covert pursuit of government funds, carefully embellishing their quest with the articulate plea that their pet scheme merits "government" money (forcibly expropriated from the nation's citizens) because it is in the "national interest."

Economic freedom eventually is transformed into an unknown, remote and rather frightening. Resistance to government control over the economy fades as people become content with the hope that they can manipulate the controls to their advantage, free of the objective constraints of the market. Simultaneously, the individual's knowledge that he cannot implement any economic decision without government approval tends to create a psychological sense of helplessness and concomitant dependence on the government as the ultimate source of all "correct" economic decisions. Leaning heavily on the collectivist crutch of the national interest, people increasingly turn to the government for the solution to all economic problems arguably affecting the nation's welfare.

2

Unlimited Federal Power to Control the U.S. Economy

I. THE CONSTITUTIONAL FOUNDATION: THE INTERSTATE COMMERCE CLAUSE

Article I, section 8, clause 3 of the United States Constitution gives Congress the power "To regulate Commerce with foreign Nations, and among the several States, and with the Indian Tribes." Power over commerce *not* encompassed by this provision belongs to the states under the Tenth Amendment, which specifies: "The powers not delegated to the United States by the Constitution, nor prohibited by it to the States, are reserved to the States respectively, or to the people." Historically, the federal government and the states have ardently fought over how much of the economy each is constitutionally empowered to regulate by these provisions. The central government has won this battle, usurping power over all aspects of the economy formerly conceded as areas of exclusive state discretion.

THE ORIGINAL TESTS
The Interstate Commerce Clause was originally understood to be a means of preventing the states from becoming warring sovereignties intent upon establishing economic barriers to trade flowing between

30

the states. This function was reflected in early judicial decisions, which dealt with such isolationist moves as a state's attempt to exclude all but designated licensees from its internal waterways despite Congress' recognition of other persons' rights to use the same waters while pursuing the "coasting trade" between different states.[1] The recurrent theme was (1) that *intra*state commerce (commerce occurring within a single state) was the exclusive domain of the state, (2) that the central government had sole power to regulate *inter*state commerce through federal laws, which typically conflicted with only the most overt state commercial isolationism, and (3) that states could regulate interstate commerce within their borders if no conflicting federal legislation existed.

PRELIMINARY EXPANSION OF THE INTERSTATE COMMERCE POWER
A. National Uniformity Sought
These original tests of the scope of the interstate commerce power have been expanded infinitely in every conceivable direction. The first such expansion occurred when the U.S. Supreme Court prohibited states from regulating anything deemed interstate commerce if *either* conflicting federal legislation existed *or* the subject regulated was deemed to require a *uniform national system of regulation.*[2] That is, state regulations could coexist with federal laws controlling the same areas of commerce only if the national rules were not fundamentally contrary to the state's regulations, and (regardless of whether Congress had enacted legislation) the subject did not require a uniform national rule. Since no litmus test to identify which areas require uniform national rules has ever been devised, this crucial determination ultimately depends on the majority vote of the nine sitting United States Supreme Court justices.

B. Limited Federal Control over Intrastate Economic Transactions
Second, the constitutionally permissible extent of the federal government's regulation of economic transactions physically occurring solely within a given state was significantly expanded. The United States Supreme Court first broadened the concept of interstate commerce to include commercial transportation occurring exclusively within a state provided that the intrastate transport of goods formed one link of a continuous chain that moved goods from one state to another. In other words, the federal government could regulate *intra*state commerce if products transported by a company operating solely within one state were received from or destined for another state.[3] In

its 1871 decision of a case called *The Daniel Ball*, the Supreme Court held:

> The fact that several different and independent agencies are employed in transporting the commodity, some acting entirely in one State, and some acting through two or more States, does in no respect affect the character of the transaction. To the extent in which each agency acts in that transportation, it is subject to the regulation of Congress.[4]

The reasoning of *The Daniel Ball* was reaffirmed by *Stafford* v. *Wallace*, a 1922 decision upholding the constitutionality of federal regulation of local stockyard owners, dealers, packers, and commission men. Although each stockyard necessarily existed within a single state, the Court waxed poetic in sustaining federal control under the interstate commerce power:

> The stockyards are but a throat through which the current flows. . . . Such transactions can not be separated from the movement to which they contribute . . . [S]uch streams of commerce from one part of the country to another which are ever flowing are in their very essence the commerce among the States and with foreign nations which historically it was one of the chief purposes of the Constitution to bring under national protection and control.[5]

The concept of interstate commerce was expanded further in the *Shreveport* case, where the Supreme Court held that the federal government could regulate *intra*state railway rates already approved by the state railway agency merely to assure that *intra*state traffic did not receive more favorable rates than those established by the Interstate Commerce Commission for *inter*state railway lines. Assuming the propriety of the rates set by the Interstate Commerce Commission for interstate lines, the Court concluded that the government's power over interstate commerce encompassed the right to control purely intrastate trade if the absence of federal regulation would cause "discrimination" against interstate commerce — that is, to protect interstate commerce from competition by intrastate commerce. This judicial decision means that whenever the federal government chooses to exercise the full breadth of its constitutional power, states can be prevented from permitting lower rates for intrastate commercial transactions than those set by any federal agency for interstate commerce in the same commodity, for lower intrastate rates would necessarily be deemed to discriminate against interstate commerce by encouraging commerce within the state. Thus a single judicial opinion deftly extended the federal government's power so as to encompass all of a state's internal commercial affairs that were in direct competition with government-regulated interstate commerce. After stating that "it is immaterial, so far as the protecting power of Congress is concerned, that the discrimination arises from intrastate rates as compared with interstate rates," the Court concluded that the federal government's power over interstate commerce embraced "all matters having such a close and substantial relation to interstate commerce that it is necessary or appropriate to exercise the control for the effective government of that commerce."[6] While still acknowledging some area of internal state commerce immune from federal control, the Court declared that Congress "does possess the power to foster and protect interstate commerce, and to take all measures necessary or appropriate to that end, although intrastate transactions of interstate carriers may thereby be controlled."[7]

FRAGILE BARRIERS TO EXPANDING FEDERAL POWER

A. Production, Manufacture, and Labor Relations Not Deemed "Commerce"

The Interstate Commerce Clause of the Constitution originally was interpreted to permit federal control only over *trade* or *transportation* of articles of commerce between two or more states. Neither production nor the employment contract (wages, hours, and working conditions) was subject to federal regulation. Until 1937 the courts quite consistently held that a producer's intangible *intent to export* his finished product to another state did not transform it into an article of interstate commerce while it was being manufactured. Hence the manufacture of a commodity produced exclusively within one state but ultimately destined for export could not be controlled by the federal government, even though interstate commerce might indirectly be affected by such production.[8] This reasoning was explicitly upheld in *Hammer* v. *Dagenhart*, a 1918 opinion which declared unconstitutional a congressional attempt to standardize the states' child-labor laws, where the Supreme Court declared that "the mere fact that [goods] were intended for interstate commerce transportation does not make their production subject to Federal control under the commerce power ... [T]he production of articles, intended for interstate commerce, is a matter of local regulation."[9]

The U.S. Supreme Court enforced this distinction between production and trade (commerce) as late as 1936, regarding it as a fundamental limitation on the cases discussed above extending federal control to *intra*state transportation activities that composed part of an *inter*state distribution scheme. In *Carter* v. *Carter Coal Co.* (1936), the Court concluded that the "flow of commerce" cases did not justify federal control over prices, wages, and hours in the mining industry because cases such as *Stafford* v. *Wallace* "nowhere suggested . . . that the interstate commerce power extended to the growth or production of the things which, after production, entered the flow."[10]

A pre-1937 exception to this rationale appeared in a series of antitrust cases that held the Sherman Act applicable to employers and employees engaged in manufacturing and production.[11] While nominally upholding the distinction between production and trade, antitrust labor cases held that employees on strike from manufacturing jobs nevertheless fell within the federal commerce power if the purpose or inevitable result of the strike was to restrain the supply or to control the price of the manufactured commodity moving in interstate commerce.[12]

Pre-1937 constitutional interpretation also maintained that the employment relation (including wages, hours, and working conditions) could not be controlled by the central government, but rather was a local matter governed by state law. The refusal to permit federal control over the employment relation was really a corollary of the generally accepted proposition that the central government could not control local production activities internal to a state. The Supreme Court made this rationale clear when it rejected as unconstitutional the 1935 Bituminous Coal Conservation Act's attempt to establish minimum prices, maximum working hours, and minimum wages for the coal industry:

> The employment of men, the fixing of their wages, hours of labor and working conditions, the bargaining in respect of these things — whether carried on separately or collectively — each and all constitute intercourse for the purposes of production, not of trade. The latter is a thing apart from the relation of employer and employee, which in all producing occupations is purely local in character. . . . [T]he affect of the labor provisions of the act . . . primarily falls upon production and not upon commerce. . . . [P]roduction is a purely local activity. . . . The relation of employer and employee is a local relation.[13]

B. Indirect Effect on Interstate Commerce Considered Insufficient

Another judicial barrier to unlimited expansion of federal economic power was the accepted doctrine that the central government could constitutionally regulate intrastate commerce only if the intrastate trade had a *direct* effect upon interstate commerce. In *Gibbons* v. *Og-*

den, an 1824 decision which held that a state could not monopolize its navigable waters by excluding interstate trade conducted by federally licensed commercial navigators, the Court recognized a sphere of commerce internal to a state as immune from federal regulation, while interpreting the federal interstate commerce power broadly to encompass all internal state commerce that "affects" other states. The Court commented:

> The genius and character of the whole government seem to be, that its action is to be applied to all the external concerns of the nation, and to those internal concerns which affect the states generally; but not to those which are completely within a particular state, which do not affect other states, and with which it is not necessary to interfere, for the purpose of executing some of the general powers of the government. The completely internal commerce of a state, then, may be considered as reserved for the state itself.[14]

Subsequent pre-1937 Supreme Court decisions interpreted *Gibbons* v. *Ogden* narrowly to permit federal regulation only if the intrastate commerce in question had a *direct* effect on interstate commerce, which until 1937 was construed to denote *trade and transportation,* not production or manufacture. The facts of *Gibbons* supported such a limited construction, for the *Gibbons* Court was judging New York's right to exclude interstate traffic from internal waterways that formed part of a continuous highway for transporting and distributing goods between New York and New Jersey, clearly a paradigm case exemplifying a state's direct effort to restrict interstate transportation. That a *direct* impact on interstate commerce was a prerequisite of federal regulation of intrastate commercial activity was further emphasized in such landmark decisions as *Schechter Poultry Corp.* v. *United States* (1935), which declared certain Live Poultry Codes promulgated under the 1933 National Industrial Recovery Act (NIRA) to be products of an unconstitutional delegation of legislative power as well as beyond Congress' authority under the Interstate Commerce Clause.[15]

The direct/indirect test as a limitation on federal power was expressed succinctly in *Carter* v. *Carter Coal Co.* (1936), in which the Court refused to allow Congress to set minimum prices, maximum hours, and minimum wages in the coal mining industry. The Court noted that all local production of goods intended for interstate sale and transportation has *some* effect on interstate commerce, but maintained that the federal government can regulate such internal manufacture only if it has a direct impact on trade between the states. Insisting that governmental power to regulate intrastate production is contingent upon the *character of the relation* of local manufacture to interstate commerce rather than the *magnitude* of its impact, the Court commented:

> The word "direct" implies that the activity or condition invoked or blamed shall operate proximately — not mediately, remotely, or collaterally — to produce the effect. It connotes the absence of an efficient intervening agency or condition. And the extent of the effect bears no logical relation to its character. The distinction between a direct and an indirect effect turns, not upon the magnitude of either the cause or the effect, but entirely upon the manner in which the effect has been brought about. If the production by one man of a single ton of coal intended for interstate sale and shipment, and actually so sold and shipped, affects interstate commerce indirectly, the effect does not become direct by multiplying the tonnage, or increasing the number of men employed, or adding to the expense or complexities of the business, or by all combined. . . . [The] question is not — What is the *extent* of the local activity or condition, or the *extent* of the effect produced upon interstate commerce? but — What is the *relation* between the activity or condition and the effect?[16]

C. Regulation Does Not Include Prohibition

There were early constitutional skirmishes over whether the central government's power to regulate interstate commerce encompassed authority to prohibit forms of interstate trade deemed undesirable. The issue seemed to be resolved in favor of federal power to prohibit certain interstate commercial activity by the Lottery Case (*Champion* v. *Ames*), a 1903 decision upholding the constitutionality of congressionally established criminal penalties for the interstate transportation of lottery tickets imposed by the Federal Lottery Act of 1895. A felt dearth of judicial precedent or logical rationale supporting the Court's conclusion is revealed by the opinion's constant reliance upon unanswered rhetorical questions and emotionally loaded language in lieu of rational arguments to justify the Court's decision. The Court queried:

> Are we prepared to say that a provision which is, in effect, a *prohibition* of the carriage of such articles from state to state is not a fit or appropriate mode for the *regulation* of that particular kind of commerce? . . . Or may not Congress, for the protection of the people of all the states, and under the power to regulate interstate commerce, devise such means, within the scope of the Constitution, and not prohibited by it, as will drive that traffic out of commerce among the states? . . . If a state . . . may properly take into view the evils that inhere in the raising of money [through lotteries] . . . why may not Congress, invested with the power to regulate commerce among the several

states, provide that such commerce shall not be polluted [!] by the carrying of lottery tickets from one state to another?[17]

Congressional prohibition of commerce also was sustained by later judicial decisions upholding the constitutionality of the Pure Food and Drug Act's proscription of interstate commerce in impure foods and drugs as well as the "White Slave Traffic" Act's prohibition of interstate transportation of women for purposes of prostitution. However, in declaring the Child Labor Act unconstitutional, the Court in *Hammer* v. *Dagenhart* (1918) reversed this trend by stating that the federal commerce power authorizes the central government "to control the means by which commerce is carried on, which is directly the contrary of the assumed right to forbid commerce from moving and thus destroy it as to particular commodities."[18] But the Court's attempt to distinguish the previous cases validating congressional prohibition of commerce was as weak as the original defense of those decisions. Its unconvincing justification was that the lottery, prostitution, and impure food and drug cases entailed the use of interstate transportation as a factor necessary "to the accomplishment of harmful results," hardly an unassailable gem of objective analysis and clearly not intuitively obvious to anyone who deems child labor an evil appropriately eliminated by federal legislation.

D. Taxation Cannot Be Used for Regulation

Prior to 1937 a strong if somewhat erratically imposed barrier to expansion of federal regulation of intrastate commerce was the established principle that Congress could not use its taxing power for regulatory purposes to achieve a degree of control otherwise impermissible under the Interstate Commerce Clause. This principle was clearly expressed in the Child Labor Tax Case (*Bailey* v. *Drexel Furniture Co.,* 1922). Having failed to secure judicial approval of its overt legislative prohibition of interstate commerce in the products of child labor (*Hammer* v. *Dagenhart*), Congress attempted to achieve the same result covertly through taxation. The Child Labor Tax Law assessed a ten-percent tax on the annual net profits of any employer who hired a child under certain specified ages. Finding the statute unconstitutional and deeming the tax a palpable penalty, the Court said:

[A] court must be blind not to see that the so-called tax is imposed to stop the employment of children within the age limits prescribed. Its prohibitory and regulatory effect and purpose are palpable. . . . Grant the validity of this law, and all that Congress would need to do hereafter, in seeking to take over to its control any one of the great number of subjects of public interest, jurisdiction of which the states have

37

never parted with, and which are reserved to them by the 10th Amendment, would be to enact a detailed measure of complete regulation of the subject and enforce it by a so-called tax upon departures from it. To give such magic to the word "tax" would be to break down all constitutional limitation of the powers of Congress and completely wipe out the sovereignty of the states.[19]

Despite this consciousness of the issue, the Court's opinion has occasionally vacillated. Such ambivalence is evident, for example, in the Court's 1904 decision upholding a federal Oleomargarine Tax Act, which imposed a one-fourth-cent-per-pound tax on uncolored margarine while assessing a ten-cent-per-pound tax on margarine colored to resemble butter, thereby virtually destroying commerce in colored margarine by means of a tax clearly penalizing a particular type of trade.[20] The facts of the Oleomargarine Tax Act Case, *McCray* v. *United States,* cannot be meaningfully distinguished from those of the Child Labor Tax Case.

Nevertheless, the Court strongly articulated its stance against congressional use of taxation to accomplish otherwise impermissible regulation in *Carter* v. *Carter Coal Co.* (1936). That case upheld a constitutional challenge to a federal statute that sought to enforce minimum prices, maximum hours, and minimum wages in the coal industry by imposing a fifteen-percent tax on the sale price of coal at the mine, a tax automatically reduced by ninety percent, to one and one-half percent, if the mine owner "voluntarily" complied with a detailed code of national rules. Perceiving the tax as a penalty assessed for regulatory purposes, the Court observed:

> It is very clear that the "excise tax" is not imposed for revenue but exacted as a penalty to compel compliance with the regulatory provisions of the act. The whole purpose of the exaction is to coerce what is called an agreement — which, of course, it is not, for it lacks the essential element of consent. One who does a thing in order to avoid a monetary penalty does not agree; he yields to compulsion precisely the same as though he did so to avoid a term in jail.[21]

The Court held that the legislation exceeded Congress' constitutional power under the Interstate Commerce Clause.

Congress tried a similar technique in enacting the Agricultural Adjustment Act, and its efforts encountered a like judicial response. The Agricultural Adjustment Act was designed to regulate agricultural production by reducing acreage in commodities in order to increase financial return to farmers. The statute empowered the Secretary of Agriculture to declare a national economic emergency, during which the Secretary would make payments to farmers who "voluntarily" agreed to reduce their acreage, payments consisting of money exacted through a processing tax on farmers who refused to comply with the federally mandated acreage reductions. Labeling this type of legislation "coercion by economic pressure," the Court concluded that the statute invaded the reserved rights of the states by attempting to regulate agricultural production, a power not delegated to the federal government by the Constitution. The Court critically appraised the statutory device as "[a]t best . . . a scheme for purchasing with federal funds submission to federal regulation of a subject reserved to the states," and observed:

> If the act before us is a proper exercise of the federal taxing power, evidently the regulation of all industry throughout the United States may be accomplished by similar exercises of the same power. It would be possible to exact money from one branch of an industry and pay it to another branch in every field of activity which lies within the province of the states. The mere threat of such a procedure might well induce the surrender of rights and the compliance with federal regulation as the price of continuance in business.[22]

The Court's most extreme premonitions of unlimited expansion of federal power over the economy were realized in 1937 and the years thereafter.

UNLIMITED FEDERAL POWER OVER THE DOMESTIC ECONOMY: THE POST-1937 CONSTITUTIONAL REVOLUTION

The Supreme Court's consistent opposition to unlimited expansion of federal power over the domestic economy caused Franklin Delano Roosevelt to regard the prevailing majority of the Court's personnel as conservative old men whose political hostility to the President and anachronistic views of the scope of the Constitution were clearly out of touch with the dominant mood of the country. Armed with an immense popular victory in the 1936 election and convinced that the existing judges' views could not be swayed, FDR proposed legislative changes to the basic composition of the Court, "court-packing" schemes that would enable him to appoint enough new judges to subdue the conservative majority and allow his own politically divined social theories to prevail. Even constitutional amendments were contemplated. FDR's legislative proposals withered in the Congress, but the conveniently switched votes of two justices (Chief Justice Hughes and Justice Roberts) accomplished the result Roosevelt so ardently sought. Roosevelt later secured the enduring ideological support of the Supreme Court when the retirement of Justice Van Devanter in 1937 and of Justice Sutherland in 1938 enabled him to appoint two additional justices to the Court.

Thus 1937 inaugurated the complete reversal of the Court's prior opinions defining the limits of federal power over the economy under the Interstate Commerce Clause. Doctrinal barriers to expansion of the federal government were, in a word, obliterated. A facade of precedent for this vast judicial expansion of federal power over the economy was created by isolating out of context the most abstract language from the earliest cases defining the interstate commerce power, imposing on those words an interpretation far broader than their authors conceived or endorsed, and ignoring or reversing all intervening pre-1937 judicial restraints on congressional attempts to legislate unlimited federal economic power.

A. Local Production and Labor Relations Deemed "Commerce"

The Supreme Court expeditiously eliminated its prior distinction between production (manufacture) and commerce while simultaneously empowering the national government to regulate the theretofore largely inviolable local employment relation. One of the first cases to erode these historically viable distinctions was *NLRB* v. *Jones & Laughlin Steel Corp.*, a 1937 decision in which the Supreme Court upheld the constitutionality of the 1935 National Labor Relations Act (NLRA). Through the NLRA the federal government assumed comprehensive powers to control labor relations, to supervise the collective-bargaining process, and to punish employers who committed certain legislatively proscribed "unfair labor practices" in all industries affecting interstate commerce. While straining to insist that to preserve a federal form of government some matters must be left to local control, the Court argued that the primary issue was not whether activities are "manufacture" or "commerce," or whether they are properly labeled intrastate or interstate, but whether they "have such a close and substantial relation to interstate commerce that their control is essential or appropriate to protect that commerce from burdens and obstructions . . . ."[23] The Court explicitly stated that "the fact that the employees here concerned were engaged in production is not determinative."[24] Even the employment relation, historically immune from most federal control under the Interstate Commerce Clause, was held subject to federal regulation according to this "substantial relation" test. Pre-1937 cases that explicitly held unconstitutional the national government's attempts to control employer-employee relations were tersely deemed "not controlling here."[25]

40

Ironically, the already familiar phrasing of the "close and substantial relation" test was adopted almost verbatim from the 1914 *Shreveport* case, a decision which dealt solely with federal authority to control intrastate railway rates allegedly discriminatory against interstate transportation of similar goods. Neither the opinion's factual context nor its language anywhere suggested that production, manufacture, and the employment relation were deemed part of "commerce"; the *Shreveport* case implicitly defined commerce to include only transportation and trade. But the familiar ring of the *Shreveport* language imbued the *Jones* Court's radical expansion of federal power over the economy with an aura of conservatism useful in quelling potential opposition.

As post-1937 decisions became history, they acquired a useful precedential value of their own, which significantly lessened the Court's burden in justifying subsequent decisions further increasing the power of the central government. Combining broad language quoted out of context from the early transportation and flow-of-commerce decisions with citations from the Court's own post-1937 opinions enabled the prevailing majority to characterize all the intervening cases that had restricted federal power as "aberrations," whose unexplained existence merited summary reversal rather than reasoned evaluation. The facade of abundant precedent and superficial conformity to tradition thus became ever easier to maintain.

NLRB v. *Jones & Laughlin Steel Corp.*, for example, was reinforced by *United States* v. *Darby. Darby* was a 1941 decision that upheld the constitutionality of the Fair Labor Standards Act, a statute that prohibited the interstate shipment of goods manufactured by employees who worked for less than federally prescribed minimum wages or more than governmentally decreed maximum hours. Although the legislation approved by *Darby* was fundamentally similar to that declared unconstitutional in *Carter* v. *Carter Coal Co.* (minimum wages, maximum hours, and minimum prices fixed for coal industry by federal agency pursuant to the 1935 Bituminous Coal Conservation Act) and *Hammer* v. *Dagenhart* (uniform national child-labor laws), the Court summarily dismissed *Carter* as limited in principle by decisions under the National Labor Relations Act and calmly overruled *Hammer* v. *Dagenhart* as "a departure from the principles which have prevailed in the interpretation of the Commerce Clause both before and since the decision . . . ."[26] Holding that the Interstate Commerce Clause empowered the national government to control intrastate manufacture and local labor conditions in industries whose products were ultimately *intended* to be transported in interstate commerce, the *Darby* Court explicitly reversed the generally accepted doctrine that the central

41

government could not constitutionally regulate intrastate production (manufacture) and the employment relation. A well-established barrier to unlimited federal power fell; thereafter the producer's intent to export his product *did* transform local manufacturing activities and labor relations into interstate commerce.

B. Redefinition of "Commerce" Extends Federal Control to Activities Indirectly Affecting Interstate Trade

While upholding the constitutionality of the National Labor Relations Act, the Court in *NLRB* v. *Jones & Laughlin Steel Corp.* adopted the language of the *Shreveport* case in concluding that intrastate activities could be regulated by the national government "if they have such a close and substantial relation to interstate commerce that their control is essential or appropriate to protect that commerce from burdens and obstructions . . . ."[27]

The Court's technique in *Jones* established a pattern for future decisions. In essence the Court cited early Supreme Court decisions that originally defined the extent of the federal interstate commerce power, neglecting to mention that those decisions dealt with federal versus state power to control the *transportation* of goods, the universally acknowledged definition of "commerce." The post-1937 cases, typified by *Jones*, lifted attractive language from early transportation and flow-of-commerce cases to the effect that intrastate commerce substantially or directly affecting interstate commerce could be regulated by the national government. But "commerce" in its original judicial context meant transportation. Except in antitrust litigation, subsequent pre-1937 cases directly faced with the question of whether the central government could regulate intrastate production and labor relations had concluded rather consistently that these activities did not themselves constitute commerce and hence could not be controlled by the federal government unless they had a substantial and direct impact on interstate transportation or trade of goods. Post-1937 decisions deftly excised both the original factual context of the transportation and flow-of-commerce line of cases and the subsequent judicial delineation of the scope of the term "commerce." By deeming every economic activity to be commerce, the post-1937 decisions neatly transformed the issue into the very different question of whether a particular economic transaction had a substantial impact on the national economy. The subjective quality of this evaluation is palpable. Predictably, the outcome in any case depended more upon the justices' personal assessment of the desirability of federal regulation of a particular economic sphere than upon objective limitations on federal power. As both judicial and lay sentiment increasingly favored centralized economic controls, the threshold for labeling an activity's impact upon the economy "substantial" decreased correspondingly.

Every detail of the model described above was manifested by the *NLRB* v. *Jones & Laughlin Steel Corp.* opinion. Reaching back to 1871 to find quotable language superficially supporting its position, the Court quoted from *The Daniel Ball* without mentioning that that case addressed the much narrower issue of whether a federal licensing act could constitutionally be applied to a steamboat operating on navigable waters solely within Michigan but carrying some cargo received from or destined for other states. This tenuous precedent was the basis for the following assertion:

> The congressional authority to protect interstate commerce from burdens and obstructions is *not limited to transactions which can be deemed to be an essential part of a "flow" of interstate or foreign commerce.* Burdens and obstructions may be due to injurious action springing from other sources. The fundamental principle is that the power to regulate commerce is the power to enact "all appropriate legislation" for "its protection and advancement" [citing *The Daniel Ball*].[28]

The Court then concluded that *intra*state commerce could be freely regulated by the central government so long as it bore a "close and substantial relation" to interstate commerce. The Court implicitly acknowledged the vast potential scope of this fluid standard by observing that the interstate commerce power "may not be extended so as to embrace effects upon interstate commerce so indirect and remote that to embrace them . . . would effectually obliterate the distinction between what is national and what is local and create a completely centralized government."[29] That this modest concession constituted but a perfunctory nod to judicial predecent became clear as the Court proceeded to declare rather summarily that it was "obvious" that the effect upon interstate commerce of unfair labor practices in any of the defendant's steel plants would be "immediate" and perhaps "catastrophic," not "indirect or remote."[30]

Despite the opinion's profuse lip service to the inviolability of some local transactions from centralized federal control, these comments eroded still another barrier to expansion of federal power by implying that sheer magnitude of an industry's impact upon the national economy justifies federal control, regardless of how local or intrastate the nature of the regulated action viewed separately. Casually noting the defendant's "far flung activities" (a vertically integrated company, the Jones & Laughlin Steel Corporation was the fourth largest producer of steel in the United States and shipped approximately seventy-five percent of its products out of Pennsylvania, the state where it was incorporated), the Court substituted the emotional thrust of a rhetorical question for reasoned justification of its conclusion by asking:

> When industries organize themselves on a national scale, making their relation to interstate commerce the dominant factor in their activities, how can it be maintained that their industrial labor relations constitute a forbidden field into which Congress may not enter when it is necessary to protect interstate commerce from the paralyzing consequences of industrial war?[31]

The core message implicitly conveyed by *Jones* is that any industry judicially deemed sufficiently large or "basic" that its disruption might have a sizable impact upon the U.S. economy may be regulated in every detail of its purely local, intrastate activities by the central government.

The increasing ease of reaching decisions favoring expansion of federal power over the economy is revealed by the progression of opinions following *NLRB* v. *Jones & Laughlin Steel Corp.* The net result achieved by 1942 and continuing to the present is the complete elimination of any economic sphere that cannot be controlled in every detail by the central government. The very concept of intrastate commerce immune from centralized national regulation has been eradicated from the American people's consciousness and extirpated from its law.

We begin rather dramatically with *U.S.* v. *Darby*, the 1941 decision that gave a constitutional stamp of approval to centralized national control over minimum wages and maximum hours under the Fair Labor Standards Act of 1938. Echoing the *Jones* opinion's articulation validating federal regulation of intrastate activities that have a "substantial effect" on interstate commerce, the *Darby* Court made a startling statement, which foreshadowed the full scope of the centralized power to be condoned in the ensuing years:

> Congress, following its own conception of public policy concerning the restrictions which may appropriately be imposed on interstate commerce, is free to exclude from the commerce articles whose use in the states for which they are destined it may conceive to be *injurious to the public health, morals or welfare,* even though the state has not sought to regulate their use.[32]

It is imperative at this point to reflect upon how closely this principle matches the economic premises of a fascist state: that is, private enterprise is allowed to prevail *unless* the central government decrees that the collective national interest (public morals or welfare) requires centralized control.

44

That the justices who endorsed the *Darby* opinion recognized its breadth is indicated by the majority's treatment of the Tenth Amendment, which explicitly reserves to the states all powers not expressly delegated to the national government. No longer do we find self-conscious deferences acknowledging that despite expansive interpretation of the interstate commerce power, *some* (unspecified) sphere of intrastate economic activity remains immune from federal control. In *Darby*, the Court calmly noted that its conclusion was "unaffected by the Tenth Amendment," disparaging that constitutional requirement of limited national governmental power as "but a truism that all is retained which has not been surrendered."[33] Presumably, if the Court overtly construed the Constitution as granting total, unlimited power to the central government, the *Darby* majority would find that result in perfect harmony with the strangely superfluous mandate of the Tenth Amendment.

The 1942 decision of *Wickard* v. *Filburn* culminated the logical progression given so much momentum by *Darby*. *Wickard* made explicit what *Darby* had left to the astute reader's imagination. *Wickard* upheld the constitutionality of the Agricultural Adjustment Act of 1938, which provided for national marketing quotas and national wheat acreage allotments to be distributed by the Secretary of Agriculture as wheat acreage allotments for individual farms. The Court upheld the Act's imposition of monetary penalties upon farmers who produced or marketed wheat in excess of their allotments or quotas, fines applied not only to so-called excess wheat intended for interstate commerce, but also to wheat consumed entirely on the premises. *Wickard* made it constitutional for the central government, under the guise of the interstate commerce power, both to tell a farmer how much grain he was allowed to produce and market, and to fine him for exceeding these limits, even if the extra grain was never intended for interstate commerce and in fact was consumed on the farmer's own land. The proffered rationale follows:

> The effect of the statute before us is to restrict the amount which may be produced for market and the extent as well to which one may forestall resort to the market by producing to meet his own needs. That appellee's own contribution to the demand for wheat may be trivial by itself is not enough to remove him from the scope of federal regulation where, as here, his contribution, taken together with that of many others similarly situated, is far from trivial. . . . It can hardly be denied that a factor of such volume and variability as home-consumed wheat would have a substantial influence on price and market conditions. . . . But if we assume that it is never marketed, it supplies a need of the man who grew it which would otherwise be reflected by

purchases in the open market. Home-grown wheat in this sense competes with wheat in commerce.[34]

Regardless of one's appraisal of the Court's artful reasoning, its rationale for centralized national control over small amounts of home-grown and home-consumed grain may be just as easily used to justify federal regulation of *any* intrastate economic activity, for every economic transaction, however local in nature, can be said to affect interstate commerce by *competing* with it. The Court virtually extirpated the Interstate Commerce Clause from the Constitution by eliminating all distinction between interstate and intrastate commerce and conferring upon the federal government the power to regulate whatever economic activity it chooses to control. By its 1942 decision in *Wickard* v. *Filburn*, the prevailing majority of Supreme Court justices thus explicitly enshrined the basic economic premise of fascism as the governing law of the United States. Reiterating the shopworn and objectively indefensible assertion that its radical expansion of federal power was but a return to the principles first enunciated in the 1824 *Gibbons* v. *Ogden* decision, the Court assured itself that the full import of its opinion would not be overlooked by concluding:

> But even if appellee's activity be *local and though it may not be regarded as commerce*, it may still, whatever its nature, be reached by Congress if it exerts a substantial economic effect on interstate commerce, and this *irrespective of whether such effect is what might at some earlier time have been defined as "direct" or "indirect."* [35]

The rest of the story unfolded through judicial decisions is not very dramatic, providing additional examples and occasionally supplying more of the traditional phraseology of fascism but not changing the principle of unlimited federal economic control so lucidly promulgated by *Wickard* v. *Filburn*. In *Heart of Atlanta Motel* v. *United States*, for example, the Supreme Court held that it was within the federal government's power under the Interstate Commerce Clause to apply the 1964 Civil Rights Act to a motel operator whose business was entirely *local*, reasoning that Negroes to whom the motel owner refused service *might* be out-of-state travelers. Although the 1964 Civil Rights Act prohibited only "places of public accommodation" whose operations "affect commerce" from discriminating on the basis of race or color, local (intrastate) businesses providing lodging to transient guests were statutorily decreed to affect commerce per se. That Congress could reach this far in controlling individual businessmen was clear after *Wickard*. Of particular interest, however, is the Court's more explicitly fascist terminology in describing the scope of the central government's power over the economy: "[T]he determinative test of the exercise of power by the Congress under the Commerce Clause is simply whether the activity sought to be regulated is 'commerce which concerns more States than one' and has a real and substantial relation to the *national interest*."[36]

In the companion case of *Katzenbach* v. *McClung*, the same Court upheld the constitutionality of another portion of the 1964 Civil Rights Act even though the statute *conclusively presumed* that a restaurant affects interstate commerce (and is therefore subject to federal regulation under the Act) if it serves interstate travelers or if a substantial portion of the food it serves has moved in interstate commerce. Serenely impervious to reality, the Court remarked:

> Congress prohibited discrimination only in those establishments having a close tie to interstate commerce, i.e., those . . . serving food that has come from out of the State. . . .
>
> *The absence of direct evidence connecting discriminatory restaurant service* [the regulated act] *with the flow of interstate food . . . is not,* given the evidence as to the effect of such practices on other aspects of commerce, *a crucial matter*.[37]

Finally, in 1968, the Supreme Court in *Maryland* v. *Wirtz* gave its constitutional blessing to certain changes legislated by Congress in 1961 to the 1938 Fair Labor Standards Act, originally validated by *United States* v. *Darby*. The changes extended federally imposed minimum wages and maximum hours to state-operated hospitals, institutions, and schools, while simultaneously broadening the Act's coverage to include all employees of any *enterprise* engaged in commerce or production of goods for commerce rather than (as previously) only the individual employees working in this capacity. By 1968 few would be shocked to discover that the Court found the "enterprise concept" as an exercise of the omnipresent federal commerce power to be justified by two theories—first, the "competition" theory that wages paid *all* employees of an enterprise producing for commerce affect that company's competitive position and thereby affect interstate commerce; and second, the "labor-dispute" theory that "substandard" wages or working conditions lead to labor strikes, which disrupt the flow of goods in interstate commerce. Overruling opposition to centralized national control of working conditions in state schools and hospitals, the Court observed:

> It is clear that labor conditions in schools and hospitals can affect commerce [for] . . . such institutions are major users of goods imported from other States. . . . If a State is engaging in economic activities that are validly regulated by the Federal Government when engaged in by

private persons, the State too may be forced to conform its activities to federal regulation.[38]

The Court's utter lack of regard for the Tenth Amendment's reservation of power to the states prompted Justice William O. Douglas to protest as follows in his dissenting opinion:

> If constitutional principles of federalism raise no limits to the commerce power where regulation of state activities are [sic] concerned, could Congress compel the States to build superhighways crisscrossing their territory in order to accommodate interstate vehicles, to provide inns and eating places for interstate travelers, to quadruple their police forces in order to prevent commerce-crippling riots, etc.? Could the Congress virtually draw up each State's budget to avoid "disruptive effect[s] . . . on commercial intercourse"?
> . . . If all this can be done, then the National Government could devour the essentials of state sovereignty, though that sovereignty is attested by the Tenth Amendment.[39]

C. What Can Be Regulated Can Be Prohibited

The post-1937 Supreme Court wasted little time dispensing with *Hammer* v. *Dagenhart's* fragile defense of the principle that the federal power to regulate interstate commerce did not embrace the right to prohibit that commerce except insofar as the use of interstate trade was essential to accomplish a "harmful" result. In its 1941 decision of *United States* v. *Darby,* the Court tersely stated that the power to regulate interstate commerce "extends not only to those regulations which aid, foster and protect the commerce, but embraces those which *prohibit* it. . . . Congress . . . is free to *exclude* from the commerce articles whose use in the states for which they are destined it may conceive to be injurious to the public health, morals or welfare. . . ."[40] Peppering its comments with citations to the 1903 Lottery Case as its primary authority, the Court surgically excised what it regarded as a fundamental aberration by overruling *Hammer* v. *Dagenhart.* Henceforth whatever economic transactions the Interstate Commerce Clause empowered the national government to regulate, Congress could, at its discretion, prohibit. Coupled with the post-1937 omnipotence of a Commerce Clause expansively interpreted to permit federal control of virtually all economic pursuits, the *Darby* Court's recognition of federal power to prohibit that which it can regulate conferred upon the central government unlimited authority to *ban* from commerce any economic endeavor, however local or intrastate its character.

D. Taxation Deemed A Permissible Regulatory Device

The 1937 decision of *Steward Machine Co.* v. *Davis* inaugurated judicial approval of the tax and credit device previously condemned as coercive whenever used to achieve national regulation of matters reserved to the states by the Tenth Amendment. This development was a predictable corollary of judicial elimination of the concept of a realm of intrastate commerce immune from national control under the Interstate Commerce Clause, for one cannot logically condemn the use of taxation to achieve impermissible regulation of matters reserved exclusively to state control once all economic endeavors are deemed permissible objects of centralized federal regulation.

In *Steward Machine Co.* v. *Davis*, the Supreme Court upheld the constitutionality of a tax imposed by the 1935 Social Security Act on employers of eight or more workers, a so-called excise tax which provided for up to a ninety-percent credit against the federal tax for unemployment fund contributions made by the taxpayer-employer pursuant to a federally approved state unemployment statute. If a state did not "voluntarily" adopt an unemployment compensation statute that conformed to the federal rules, the tax exacted from local employers would be irretrievably absorbed by the U.S. Treasury. Retaining in the Court's words "undiminished freedom to spend the money as it pleased," the national government had absolutely no statutory obligation to spend such money either on unemployment compensation or in the states whose residents paid the federal tax.[41]

Nevertheless, the Court declared this arrangement not coercive. Raising the emotional specter of acute national unemployment during the depression years between 1929 and 1936, the Court apparently sought to create a smokescreen of extreme national crisis to discourage objective scrutiny of its constitutional analysis. The Court stated that use of a federal tax to *tempt* a state to conform to federal regulations does not constitute coercion but merely reflects congressional motive, never a proper object of judicial examination. Closing its eyes to the reality of the financial cudgel thus wielded over the states, the Court further concluded that the tax was not coercive both (1) because the taxpayer was only required to fulfill "the mandate of the local legislature" (ignoring the fact that the local legislature's arm was twisted by the federal government's promise to extract tax dollars from uncooperative states), and (2) because the Social Security Act technically left the states free to choose whether they would *voluntarily* enact unemployment legislation. The Court's sole disclaimer was: "We do not say that a tax is valid, when imposed by act of Congress, if it is laid upon the condition that a state may escape its operation through the adoption of a statute unrelated in subject matter to activities fairly within the scope of national policy and power."[42] Since the new reading of the Constitution places all local economic activities "fairly within the scope of national policy and power" under the Interstate Commerce Clause, a federal tax and rebate scheme designed to control any aspect of local economic life presumably falls short of this superficial limitation on the central government's use of the tax and credit technique.

Thus the Interstate Commerce Clause has served as the constitutional foundation for the national government's assertion of the right to control the entire U.S. economy. The current breadth of the central government's power is not disputed, nor is the trail of judicial decisions that led to this point. But scholars who favor the accretion of federal power often construe early cases containing language susceptible of broad interpretation as sweeping mandates for an omnipotent central government, regarding all conflicting judicial opinions as misguided and archaic relics of eighteenth-century conservatism. Advocates of limited governmental power over the economy, in contrast, are inclined to characterize the expansion of federal power as the abandonment of all constitutional restraints on the centralization of economic controls.

The primary purpose of this chapter is to describe the process by which unlimited power to regulate economic activity (through either the profound foresight of the founding fathers or aberrant departure from their ideals, depending on one's bias) has been conferred upon the central government. The validity of the analysis here presented thus does not depend upon philosophic appraisal of the constitutional evolution outlined. Any moral or economic appraisal of either the result or the historical progression that accomplished it is really irrelevant at this point. The central thesis of this chapter is the undisputed and unchallengeable one that by 1975 the national government in the United States possessed the power to regulate every aspect of the national economy, however local a particular economic activity may appear, if it but chose to exercise that power. Private enterprise, uncontrolled market factors, and local rules now prevail only if the federal government decides that the national interest does not require overt national regulation. Thus private enterprise serves at the whim of an omnipotent central government. This is capitalistic collectivism; this is fascism in the economic realm.

II. THE PREEMPTION DOCTRINE

The preemption doctrine is another tool artfully employed by Congress and the courts to expand federal control over the economy. When coupled with the government's unlimited power to regulate the economy under the now omnipotent Interstate Commerce Clause, the preemption doctrine enables the central government to *preclude concomitant local control* over any aspect of local economic activity.

The preemption idea has its roots in the Supremacy Clause of the United States Constitution, which declares the Constitution and all United States laws and treaties paramount over contrary state laws.[43]

If an overt conflict between state and federal laws exists, the Constitution requires that the federal law prevail. However, the concept of preemption extends this strict Supremacy Clause rationale to justify exclusive federal control in situations where there is no tangible conflict between federal and state laws. A functional definition of preemption is: judicially prescribed, subjective criteria the satisfaction of which causes courts to declare that only the central government, not the states, can make laws governing the activity in question. The rules governing preemption are invented by courts, applied by courts, and changed by courts to suit prevailing social philosophies or the predispositions of judges.

Two preliminary, nonpreemption issues must first be distinguished: exclusive federal regulatory authority based on *constitutional* grounds, and contradictory state and federal legislation. If the Constitution itself is interpreted to grant the central government exclusive lawmaking authority over a subject, state laws on the subject are not tolerated even if the central government has enacted no pertinent legislation. Federal power may be deemed exclusive either because the Constitution explicitly prohibits concurrent state regulation (as it does by expressly making federal legislative control over the District of Columbia exclusive,[44] and by prohibiting states from entering treaties),[45] or because the nature of a particular power given Congress is fundamentally inconsistent with concurrent state power. The latter category comprises state rules deemed impermissible not because any explicit wording in the Constitution so requires, but because reasonable people of diverse philosophic convictions concede that concurrent state regulation would undermine the basic structure of a federal system of government, impairing the United States' ability to function as a single nation by curtailing governmental action in areas where federal authority is not contested. Examples of such inherently exclusive federal powers include Congress' authority to borrow money on the credit of the United States and to declare war. Where exclusive federal legislative authority is not asserted although the federal government has the constitutional power to legislate concerning a particular subject, the legal issue is whether state laws can coexist with the federal rules. A preemption question is again avoided if the federal rule and the state rule are clearly opposite and incompatible, as where federal law prohibits activity deemed legal by state law, for the Supremacy Clause requires the federal rule alone to prevail.

Such are the easy cases, usually resolved without invoking the preemption doctrine. Preemption must be addressed, however, where it is constitutionally possible for state and federal laws regulating a subject to coexist, and the central government has enacted legislation that it has the constitutional power to adopt. The courts must decide whether the federal legislation precludes all state efforts to regulate the subject, even complementary state laws designed to further the same goals pursued by the federal statute. The issue used to be resolved in terms of *congressional intention*: if the courts found that Congress intended the federal legislation to be the exclusive rules governing the activity, then even complementary state laws were not tolerated.[46] Congress could attempt to short-circuit judicial preemption inquiry by explicitly stating in the legislation its intent to preempt state regulation of the subject; but absent an overt statutory statement of congressional intent, judges had only their own convictions and the statute's often ambiguous or scanty legislative history to guide them. Thus the passive judicial stance suggested by analyzing preemption in terms of congressional intention was inherently fraudulent, for Congress often gave no hint of its intent concerning preemption, allowing judges surreptitiously to interject their views of what Congress' intent should have been in phraseology that obscured creative judicial manipulation of sparse legislative history. With or without a clear indication of Congress' intent regarding preemption, this analysis provided a facade which allowed judges to arrange evidence of ambivalent congressional intent in a manner permitting the prevailing judicial majority to reach a conclusion on preemption compatible with the judges' philosophic predilections.

Modern cases have tended to eliminate this facade, clearly exposing the active role of judges in resolving preemption questions. Current tests of preemption are palpably subjective. Judges now ask whether Congress has "occupied the field" by its legislation in the area to the exclusion of supplementary state laws. They ask whether the subject is one where "national uniformity" of regulation is required. They ascertain whether any "federal purpose" served by the legislation would be "frustrated" by complementary state regulation.[47] These lines of inquiry have led commentators to note that the real issues addressed in preemption cases are questions of federalism—that is, whether the balance of power between the central government and the states is best served by exclusive national regulation or complementary federal and state laws. What has not been emphasized is that these subjective tests of preemption permit judges to promote their personal views of the "proper" distribution of power between the central government and the states. Simultaneously, this approach advances the notion that an alleged need for uniform national regulation or the potential frustration of the central government's goals justifies unlimited abrogation of local authority and individual rights.

The subjective nature of preemption decisions purporting to achieve this elusive "balance" between federal and state power is evident in the array of arguments ritualistically offered to rationalize the decision reached. For example, in assessing the central government's interest in exclusive regulatory power, judges who favor big government have upheld federal preemption where conduct is even *arguably* subject to a federal statute evincing a national purpose requiring uniform regulation.[48] Although they have prohibited states from providing legal remedies to individuals even where the federal agency that arguably has jurisdiction over the activity has expressly declined to act, such judges are more inclined to uphold exclusive federal lawmaking authority if it can be said that federal remedies *are* available to the litigants. Conversely, judges who oppose preemption and desire to perpetuate the state and local governments' regulatory power assert a legitimate state interest in regulating the activity, stressing that the subject in question is deeply rooted in local feeling and historically an object of local responsibility (such as public health and safety regulations).[49] They claim that no infringement of national policy or purpose would result from simultaneous local regulation and are delighted if they can plausibly declare that absent state regulatory power the litigants are remediless. But the judicial opinions have the ritualistic quality of well-known formulas; depending on the result desired, judges crank in the familiar "values" that produce the answer sought. Whether one is pleased or displeased by the outcome of a particular case, the system itself is flawed by its failure to recognize any limit on the preemptive power of the national government except judges' subjective notions of its proper scope.

This broad and subjective power to preempt is a devastating means of centralizing control over the United States economy, particularly when coupled with the central government's unlimited constitutional power over local economic matters under the expanded reading of the Interstate Commerce Clause. Since the Commerce Clause is now interpreted to authorize federal control over all local economic activity, the preemption doctrine eliminates every vestige of local authority by allowing national controls to be made *exclusive*, effectively banning even complementary state regulation. A court only needs to declare that a "national purpose" would be "frustrated" to satisfy the magic verbal incantation that proves that federal preemption is imperative. The fascist terminology employed to justify national preemption is striking: terms such as "national uniformity" and "national purpose" connote an essentially fascist recognition of the supremacy of the central government whenever the governmental hierarchy proclaims that the national interest so requires. Citizens are urged to stand in awe when courts tell them that the "national interest" prohibits local control over any detail of their economic activity, humbly deferring to the economic wisdom of the central government of a country nominally dedicated to democracy and the free market.

3

Centralized Control over Money and Banking

In order to implement its self-proclaimed power to regulate the United States economy, the government quite naturally sought legal authority to manipulate the fundamental financial levers that control the country's economic life: its money supply and commercial banking system. The federal government wrested these coveted powers from the public by means of little-understood legislation such as the Federal Reserve Act, whose detailed and seemingly esoteric provisions frequently obscure from laymen's eyes the nature and consequences of the basic powers conferred on the government. Through such legislation, the government succeeded in centralizing control over America's money supply and banking system.

This chapter will not describe every detail of federal control over money and banking, striving instead to outline only the most significant of the powers and techniques that enable the government to regulate these vital underpinnings of the economy. After examining certain statutory reporting requirements and so-called emergency powers that authorize government officials to act as omnipotent overseers of commercial banking activity, the chapter will analyze the government's tools for manipulating the money supply, discussing the economic and political repercussions for the individual of this intricate web of federal monetary and financial powers.

I. ECONOMIC SURVEILLANCE: COMPULSORY REPORTING OF FINANCIAL TRANSACTIONS

The Currency and Foreign Transactions Reporting Act[1] gives the federal government nearly unlimited authority to monitor all financial transactions in the United States. Consistent with fascism's predisposition to oversee rather than actively operate the economy, the government's powers under this statute are discretionary, not mandatory. Nevertheless, it is difficult to identify any financial transaction, however small or private, which could legally escape a government decree mandating full reporting to federal authorities if inquisitive government officials but chose to implement their ample statutory power.

Congress' goal in enacting the Currency and Foreign Transactions Reporting Act, declared to be its sole purpose in creating that law, is to compel the filing of reports and records asserted to "have a *high degree of usefulness* in criminal, tax, or regulatory investigations or proceedings."[2] To appreciate the unlimited authoritarian government implied by acceptance of this rationale as a valid congressional purpose in adopting legislation, one need only imagine that phrase proffered as a justification for some other activity, such as unrestrained electronic surveillance or other infringements of civil liberties. The fruits of any such infringement are always deemed "useful" by unscrupulous political rulers.

Nevertheless, on this tenuous foundation the statute erects an immense structure of compulsory disclosure of private financial transactions. The law requires that

> Transactions involving any domestic financial institution shall be reported to the Secretary [of the Treasury] *at such time, in such manner, and in such detail as the Secretary may require* if they involve the payment, receipt, or transfer of United States currency, *or such other monetary instruments as the Secretary may specify, in such amounts, denominations, or both, or under such circumstances, as the Secretary shall by regulation prescribe.*[3]

Recurrent use of the nonspecific, chameleonic word *such* subtly empowers the Secretary of the Treasury to compel private financial institutions to report *any* information about *any* financial transaction that the government wishes to scrutinize. Unconstrained by objective limitations on his statutory authority, the Secretary at any time could choose, for example, to force target institutions to disclose all financial transactions involving five dollars or more. More flagrantly than do many equally elastic laws, the Currency and Foreign Transactions

Reporting Act makes the breadth of government scrutiny of private economic activity a function of federal officials' whims rather than of objective statutory rules.

The restriction of mandatory reporting to "financial institutions" by no means protects private individuals from economic surveillance by the government. Indeed, "financial institution" is defined to include not only commercial banks, private bankers, and savings banks, but also insurance companies, operators of credit-card systems, stockbrokers, pawnbrokers, travel agencies, jewelry dealers, and telegraph companies, to name but a few.[4] In a modern society in which most transactions are effectuated by check or credit card, the compulsory reporting authorized by the Currency and Foreign Transactions Reporting Act constitutes a magnificent artifice for monitoring in detail the activity of private citizens. One's financial transactions reflect and embody one's interests, beliefs, resources — one's entire being — and that potent political cudgel is the ultimate weapon handed to the government by legislation that some would excuse as an innocuous reporting law.

Financial transactions involving foreign countries and their currencies also are closely scrutinized by the government. When monetary instruments transported via a foreign country exceed $5,000 in value, the Currency and Foreign Transactions Reporting Act requires anyone (including a private individual) who knowingly receives or transports such monetary instruments to produce and submit whatever reports the Secretary of the Treasury requires.[5] Again, there are no objective constraints on the potential contents of the compulsory reports, which can be ordered to include *any* information "in such form and in such detail, as the Secretary may require."[6] If the mandatory reports are not submitted, the monetary instruments may be seized in transit and expropriated by the U.S. government.[7] Further, failure to submit the reports or falsification of the reports may incur a civil penalty equal to the total value of the monetary instruments involved.[8]

Regardless of the dollar value of a foreign transaction, even private citizens who enter into any transaction or relationship with a foreign financial institution can be compelled to reveal the identities and addresses of the real parties to the transaction, and to describe it fully to government officials, "including the amounts of money, credit, or other property involved."[9] Since the same sweeping definition of "financial institution" applies, the government, whenever it fancies the idea, can require the reporting of the minutest transaction with a foreign jeweler, travel agency, banker, or broker.

The Treasury Secretary also may compel U.S. businesses and their foreign subsidiaries to submit detailed information concerning any aspect of foreign currency transactions in which they participate.[10] The Secretary has only to decree the type of information and the manner of its submission that he desires, allowing any "reasonable exceptions" that suit his fancy. And if the President asserts that a "national emergency" exists, which continually has been the case even in peacetime, the government has unlimited power to investigate and regulate *all* transactions involving foreign currency or credit.[11]

To sustain a cozy, characteristically fascist interplay between the government and those of its regulated subjects sufficiently powerful to wield political influence with government officials, the Currency and Foreign Transactions Reporting Act is riddled with discretionary powers allowing exemptions to be granted at the whim of the Secretary of the Treasury or his delegates. Exemptions under any of the statute's provisions may be awarded "as he may deem appropriate" — that is, whenever he wishes.[12] The Secretary is empowered to remit any forfeiture or penalty imposed for failure to report exports or imports of monetary instruments "in his discretion . . . upon such terms and conditions as he deems *reasonable and just*" — in short, whenever he feels like it.[13]

Nonobjective law reigns supreme. The statute urges the Secretary to favor those who "*legitimately* engage in transactions with foreign financial agencies,"[14] to prescribe "reasonable" classifications of persons to be exempt from the foreign transaction reporting requirement, to exclude favored countries from that reporting requirement whenever the Secretary deems such reporting "unnecessary or undesirable," and to specify the type and magnitude of transactions subject to the foreign transaction reporting requirement — in essence, to act as he pleases in dispensing politically inspired exemptions to groups or countries that curry favor with the government.[15]

II. THE "NATIONAL-EMERGENCY" FRAUD: "EMERGENCY" POWERS OVER BANKING INSTITUTIONS

The government attains the pinnacle of its power to regulate banking in the United States whenever an "emergency" is said to exist. This emergency condition becomes legally effective on the mere proclamation of its alleged existence by the President; no objective constraints (such as existence of a declared war) are made prerequisite to its existence. The fact that America has, according to official presidential decrees, been in a continual state of "national emergency" since 1933 illustrates both the nonobjective laxity of the national-emergency concept and the extent to which it is used as a mere semantic springboard to supplement the government's control over the economy. Indeed, as late as 1974, a national emergency declared by President Roosevelt in 1933 still served as the ostensible pretext for comprehensive government control over foreign currency and credit transactions pursuant to the laws described in this section.[16] Similarly, a national emergency proclaimed in 1950 in response to the Korean War was reaffirmed in 1968, providing a pretense for enforcing even more stringent controls over international financial transactions under the same laws.[17] Although the national-emergency fraud entices the public to tolerate massive government powers, believing them to be effective only during declared wars or other objectively apparent catastrophes directly involving the United States, in reality a national emergency legally exists on the unchallengeable say-so of the President, and allegations of continual peacetime national emergencies have provided a pretext for ongoing authoritarian controls over transactions involving foreign currency and credit from 1933 to the present.

During any emergency period proclaimed by the President, the government may assume overtly totalitarian control over the entire Federal Reserve banking system, which comprises approximately seventy-eight percent of the total commercial bank assets of the United States:[18]

> [D]uring such emergency period as the President of the United States by proclamation may prescribe, *no member bank of the Federal reserve system shall transact any banking business except to such extent and subject to such regulations*, limitations, and restrictions *as may be prescribed by the Secretary of the Treasury*, with the approval of the President.[19]

Member banks thus may be paralyzed by government fiat, prevented from transacting any business except in accordance with the government's wishes. A similar national-emergency provision empowers the government to control all *international* financial transactions conducted via the banking system by U.S. businesses. During a national emergency declared by the President, any governmental officials designated by him are authorized to "investigate, regulate, or prohibit any transactions in foreign exchange, transfers of credit or payments between, by, through or to any banking institution, and the importing, exporting, hoarding, melting, or earmarking of gold or silver coin or bullion, currency or securities. . . ."[20]

This measure authorizes the government to order the total cessation of international trade, forcing the public to suffer the consequences of economic isolationism. The inevitable decline in employment and personal income caused by such policies, and the inexorable economic logic that explains this deterioration, are discussed at length in Chapter 9.

However, it is not the purpose of this chapter to explore the economic ramifications of the government's economic surveillance of financial institutions and emergency power to control the banking system. For the present, it is sufficient to note that these statutory powers expose the jugular vein of the American economy to the whims of government officials, making the government a shadowy partner whose tacit or overt acquiescence is necessary to validate most transactions involving "private" financial institutions. This fundamentally fascist pattern in which private businesses retain their nominal independence only by operating in conformity with the rules and wishes of omnipotent government overseers, repeated in virtually every economic sphere, is of particular importance here because (1) the money and banking system is at the heart of the economy, enabling government regulation to affect an unusually broad range of economic activity, and (2) much of the government's arbitrary power is concealed in elastic national-emergency language, which allows the government to expand its economic power at will.

III. INFLATION AS NATIONAL ECONOMIC POLICY

One supremely powerful economic tool, passionately coveted by those seeking centralized control over an economy, is the power to control the country's supply of money and credit. While maintaining a facade of decentralization, the U.S. government, through implementation of the Federal Reserve Act,[21] has achieved exactly such absolute power to control the money supply. For reasons to be explained in the ensuing pages, this power has enabled the government to reduce the value of people's money, profoundly affecting the public's financial well-being.

The deceptive aspect of America's monetary controls is the *indirect* method by which they function. It would be easy for people to grasp the economic implications if the law simply stated that the government could print more money whenever it felt like doing so. One could readily understand that an increase in paper currency not accompanied by an increase in production of goods and services would necessarily cause a decrease in the purchasing power of the dollar. It is not so easy for the economic layman to appreciate the ramifications of the subtly indirect techniques employed by America's central banking system, though its effects are nearly identical. While keeping economic analysis to an absolute minimum in the interest of clarity, this section will describe the actual mechanisms that enable the government to inflate the money supply, focusing on the consequences for individuals of this government activity.

Inflation is a *general* rise in prices.[22] No matter how much any *indi-*

vidual price rises, that increase does not suggest that inflation exists. It is utterly fallacious to point to an individual price rise as substantiating the assertion that inflation is occurring. Inflation is present only when prices rise *generally*, so that the same amount of money no longer enables a consumer to purchase a level of satisfaction comparable to that which the money would buy before the inflation. A key indicator of the existence of inflation is thus the *utility* of the dollar: if the same number of dollars can no longer procure satisfaction of the same number of an individual consumer's wants — that is, if the money no longer purchases the same level of utility for him — inflation exists.

This observation contains the seeds of the consequences of inflation. When consumers cannot or do not anticipate and protect themselves against the inflation — because they do not foresee its occurrence, or do not have sufficient resources to marshal them in a manner that will shield them against inflation's impact (such as persons on fixed subsistence-level incomes), or do not have the knowledge or the determination to assume a financial stance that will enable their assets to appreciate as rapidly as inflation — then the inflation simply reduces the degree of economic satisfaction that the consumer is able to achieve. Such unanticipated inflation decreases the level of utility that a consumer can purchase with his dollars, causing his standard of living to deteriorate.

If inflation thus forebodes a decline in most people's economic well-being, one would expect public outrage to be directed at the source and cause of inflation. This does not occur. Any outrage that is voiced is misdirected, aimed at individual price hikes, which are effects rather than causes of the general inflationary situation that is harming the protesting consumers. The ineffectuality of most protests against inflation is because most people do not understand its basic causes, largely because the parties responsible for inflation have a vested interest in obscuring their role in the process.

In truth, a general rise in the price level — that is, inflation — can only be caused by (1) a world-wide shortage of all commodities, which has never occurred, or (2) government-caused increases in the country's money supply, which occur regularly.[23] If inflation were due to world-wide shortages of everything, price inflation would result because consumers, though holding the same aggregate quantity of money, would be willing to pay higher prices to acquire the reduced quantity of goods available. The general price level would be "bid up" to reflect the scarcity of goods. While this phenomenon is interesting, it has not been the source of the rampant inflation that now plagues the United States.

The prime source of America's inflation has been government-stimulated increases in the money supply, which cause inflation by putting more money into circulation relative to the goods and services available for purchase. In this form of inflation, prices increase because consumers with more money at their disposal relative to the quantity of goods available are willing to pay more to acquire those goods. Like inflation caused by world-wide shortages, the resulting situation is that more dollars are available relative to the aggregate quantity of goods on the market. In the case of world-wide shortages, this situation is caused by a decrease in the quantity of goods available. In the case of government-sponsored inflation, the situation is caused by an increase in the money supply willfully achieved by government officials. In both cases, it is the ratio of goods to money that determines whether there will be an increase in the general level of prices, which is inflation.

The subtle way in which the government engineers inflation in the United States is extremely interesting. It is a study in indirection. Intent on avoiding the public criticism that would be forthcoming if it increased the general level of prices by openly printing more paper money at will to suit its economic purposes, the government has chosen to achieve the same result by less obvious means. Two approaches are used to conceal the source of U.S. inflation. First, instead of empowering a single, overtly monolithic central bank to dictate and implement monetary policies, the United States has opted for a monetary authority called the Federal Reserve system, whose decentralized facade and superficially "private" structure masks supremely centralized government control over the country's money supply. Second, the actual techniques used by the Federal Reserve system to increase the money supply are exquisitely indirect mechanisms that deviously decrease the real value of the dollar more effectively than any printing press in history.

The Federal Reserve system is composed of twelve Federal Reserve banks, geographically dispersed over twelve Federal Reserve districts, which encompass the United States.[24] While each retains independence in select financial matters, all are dominated by policy decisions of the presidentially appointed Board of Governors, whose seven members formulate policies that are the prime determinants of America's money supply.[25] Although commercial banks are not forced to join the Federal Reserve system and play by its rules, the Federal Reserve system encompasses roughly seventy-eight percent of the commercial bank assets in the United States and thus effectively dominates the American banking system.[26] Thus, despite certain restrictions and controls imposed on member banks, the Federal Reserve's attractive facilities (for example, the member bank's ability to borrow from its Federal Reserve bank) entice the lion's share of commercial bank assets under the Federal Reserve's umbrella.[27]

To understand how the Federal Reserve system controls the money supply, one must identify the essential characteristics of money. To constitute money, an asset must be readily acceptable as payment for most other commodities—that is, it must be relatively risk-free and highly marketable in exchange for other goods without additional costs being imposed because the user employs that form of payment. Emphasizing this costless transferability, which is usually referred to as liquidity, most economists define the money supply to consist of *coin, currency, and demand deposits.*[28] Although other monetary instruments have many of the attributes of these three, no others have the perfect liquidity of coin, currency, and demand deposits. The Federal Reserve increases the money supply primarily by augmenting demand deposits, which are overwhelmingly the largest single component of the money supply. As the term itself suggests, a demand deposit is an account with a bank that represents funds payable "on demand"—that is, funds which the bank cannot legally require advance notice of intention to withdraw.[29] Typical checking accounts, which represent either money relinquished by an individual to his bank or a loan made by a bank to an individual, are the most common constituent of demand deposits.

It is one thing to state that demand deposits are the principal component of the money supply. It is quite another to understand why this is so. Nevertheless, this understanding is crucial to grasping both why the money supply expands when demand deposits are increased and how the Federal Reserve achieves desired increases in demand deposits. *All money basically represents debt.*[30] Phrased somewhat differently, money is a liquid asset that represents a claim to assets held by another party. What we call paper currency consists of debt claims against (that is, claims to the assets of) Federal Reserve banks; as stated on all paper currency, the bills are "Federal Reserve Notes," the Federal Reserve's promises to pay (although these promises have a disturbingly hollow ring since the government's paper money is no longer redeemable in gold or any other inherently valuable commodity). Similarly, checking deposits (demand deposits) represent claims to assets held by commercial banks, payable on demand.

To pay for something, a person (or a bank) either issues a debt claim against himself or surrenders (transfers) a debt claim he holds against another to the person being paid. For example, if a buyer is an individual, the debt claim he issues against himself may be no more than a formalized IOU such as a note or contract to pay, while any cash payment he makes merely transfers currency consisting of debt claims against the Federal Reserve to the seller. The individual might also pay by check, thereby transferring to the seller a claim to assets held by the buyer's bank.

Correspondingly, if the hypothetical purchaser is a bank, it also issues debt claims against itself to pay for any assets it acquires, but in the bank's case, the debt claims consist of demand deposits. Thus if a bank buys real estate, it may pay the seller by opening a checking account in the seller's name and crediting that new account with the price the bank agrees to pay for the real estate. Similarly, if the bank agrees to loan money to a customer — which, from the bank's perspective, means to "purchase" an asset consisting of the customer's contractual obligation to repay the loaned money with interest at a future date — it often does so by opening a checking account in the borrower's name and crediting that account with the amount of the loan. In both cases, new demand deposits are born. The seller of real estate or the borrower of funds obtains spendable assets. The bank's creation of a demand deposit creates money because by obtaining the demand deposit, the recipient acquires a perfectly liquid asset that society in general accepts in payment for other goods and services. By creating demand deposits to pay for newly purchased assets, it is thus possible for banks to increase the total supply of money, producing out of thin air new money that inflates the money supply and ultimately decreases the purchasing power of the dollar (unless increases in total production of goods and services offset the increases in the money supply).[31] Although the mind initially balks at the notion that an inked notation in a banker's records can produce previously nonexistent money, that is exactly how most new money comes into existence.

With these concepts in mind, it is now possible to understand the techniques that the Federal Reserve system uses to inflate the money supply. This deceptively diffuse central banking system achieves monolithic decision-making in matters regarding the money supply by means of the Board of Governors and the Federal Open Market Committee (FOMC), which is composed of the entire seven-member Board of Governors plus five representatives of the individual Federal Reserve banks.[32] By voting in unison, the Board of Governors can totally control the decisions of the FOMC, which operates by majority rule. The Board of Governors and the FOMC have the power to dictate policies that determine the money supply to the twelve Federal Reserve banks, causing these banks to take actions that increase or decrease the money supply (almost always the former). Dominated by policies formulated by the Board of Governors and the FOMC, the Federal Reserve banks control the banking activities of all the commercial banks that choose to become members of the Federal Reserve system ("member banks"), directing a federal banking network that comprises roughly seventy-eight percent of all commercial bank assets in the United States.

The critical lever that makes possible the Federal Reserve's manipulation of the money supply is its legal power to fix reserve requirements ("legal reserves") for member banks. Legal reserves are the percentage of its total outstanding demand deposits and time deposits which each member bank is required by law to hold "in reserve" in the monetary forms specified by the Federal Reserve. Currently these legal reserves can consist solely of deposits that a member bank has at its Federal Reserve bank, plus any cash held in the member bank's own vault (cash in vault).[33] The requirement of reserves is an effective lever on the amount of money in circulation, for it empowers the banking system to create demand deposits equal to many times the funds held as required reserves — that is, to multiply the amount of money in existence. Indeed, notwithstanding federally perpetrated myths to the contrary, the driving purpose behind the reserve requirements is to enable the government to exert centralized control over the money supply, not to guarantee maintenance of sufficient funds to pay off depositors in the event of a run on the bank, a purpose for which existing reserve requirements would be wholly inadequate.

REQUIRED RESERVE PERCENTAGE

Reserve requirements underlie two primary techniques deftly employed by Federal Reserve authorities to increase the money supply. First, the Federal Reserve (through the Board of Governors) can change the numerical percentage of reserves that member banks are required to hold, within certain parameters fixed by law.[34] An example will show the effect of such changes. If member banks initially were required to hold an amount equal to twenty percent of the total value of all time and demand deposits as legal reserves, the banking system could loan funds — that is, create demand deposits — worth five times the amount of its reserves (deposits at the Federal Reserve plus cash in vault). If the Federal Reserve suddenly announced that it had changed the reserve requirement to only ten percent, the banking system then could magically create demand deposits worth ten times the amount of its legal reserves. The switch in the reserve requirement would empower the banking system to create demand deposits — which means to create money — equal to twice the value of funds issued before the change in reserve requirements. In this manner the government-decreed percentage of required reserves indirectly controls the volume of bank credit (that is, loans, which banks grant by creating demand deposits [money]). Although member banks are not legally compelled to loan the maximum amount of money permissible under existing reserve requirements, the lure of profits causes bankers to prefer loaning funds, thereby earning interest, to maintaining nonlucrative reserves, which generate no interest.[35]

It must be emphasized that it is the *banking system as a whole* that, because of the Federal Reserve's activities, generates the multiple expansion of the money supply described above. While no single bank can loan more than its capital plus deposits less required reserves, as each bank's new demand deposits work their way through the banking system, new money worth the maximum multiple permissible under the prevailing required reserve percentage may be generated (for example, five times the initial demand deposit if the required reserve percentage is twenty percent), assuming that there is no cash drain from the system and that banks create loans with all of their "excess" reserves. For a thorough discussion of the precise mechanism that enables this multiple expansion of bank deposits to occur, see the economics texts here cited.[36]

OPEN MARKET ACTIVITIES

But changing the required reserve percentage is not the government's principal device for manipulating the money supply. That technique, in fact, is used only infrequently and is widely regarded as a rather gross, nonspecific method of monetary adjustment. While compulsory reserves are the underlying instrument without which the government could not employ its chief monetary control mechanism, the government's primary method of altering the money supply is an insidiously subtle, indirect procedure that entails the purchase or sale of government securities (bonds) on the open market.[37] Such purchases and sales are guided, controlled, and performed under the centralized direction of the Federal Open Market Committee. The transactions actually are executed exclusively by the manager of the open market account, a vice president of the Federal Reserve Bank of New York who is accountable to the FOMC.[38] Without the FOMC's approval, granted only in accordance with its fluctuating, carefully orchestrated plans for the money supply, no Federal Reserve bank can purchase or sell government securities on the open market.[39]

To appreciate the calculated subtlety of the Federal Reserve's expansion of the money supply by open market purchases of government securities, one must remember that this artful procedure is purposefully substituted for a more direct method of accomplishing the same result: either (1) printing more money, or (2) arbitrarily dictating to member banks the volume of credit (loans) that they can issue in the form of cash or demand deposits. Instead of employing one of these more direct and visible techniques, the Federal Reserve prefers the obscurity provided by superficially innocuous purchases of government securities on the open market.

But how do the Federal Reserve's purchases of government bonds increase the money supply? It is the Federal Reserve's method of paying for the bonds that triggers an expansion of the money supply. When a Federal Reserve bank purchases government securities, say, from a member bank, it ultimately pays for them by *adding to the member bank's legal reserves* an amount equal to the price of the government bonds.[40] This addition to a member bank's reserves is merely a bookkeeping notation that allows the recipient to act as if it had new assets; it does not represent any preexisting physical form of money. From the perspective of the member bank selling the bonds, it suddenly finds itself with an expanded volume of reserves on deposit with the Federal Reserve. Following its business incentive for profit, the member bank normally will respond by expanding its demand deposits (interest-generating loans) to the maximum level legally permissible under existing reserve requirements. For a single bank, the volume of its new loans may equal up to the amount of its new reserves less the additional reserves required by law to support the new loans. As these new demand deposits, which represent additions to the total stock of money in circulation, work their way through the banking system, the result is that the money supply may be expanded by the bank's newly added reserves *multiplied* by the largest factor allowable under the required reserve percentage. Using the previous example, if the required reserve percentage were ten percent, then a million-dollar Federal Reserve purchase of government securities could expand the money supply by ten times one million, or ten million dollars. Thus it is clear why economists call legal reserves "high-powered money," for any expansion of reserves ultimately expands the money supply by many times the actual dollar increase in reserves.[41]

It is quite a clever procedure. By the simple expedient of purchasing government bonds worth a mere fraction of the desired increase in the money supply, an action which would not arouse the suspicion of inflation-wary citizens untrained in economics, the Federal Reserve can inflate the money supply at will, expanding it at a rate far in excess of the dollar value of the transaction involved. All the while most citizens have no idea that Federal Reserve purchases of government securities cause inflation of the money supply, much less that they do so at such an accelerated rate.

Even if the seller of government securities to the Federal Reserve is a private individual, the same inflationary sequence usually results from the Federal Reserve's purchase. The sequence is simply more direct when the Federal Reserve buys from a member bank. If the seller is an individual, another step is interjected into the procedure in the following manner. First, the Federal Reserve pays the individual with a check drawn on itself. The individual then will probably deposit that check in his own commercial bank. If that bank is a member bank in the Federal Reserve system, when it forwards the check to the Federal Reserve for payment, the Federal Reserve will satisfy its obligation to pay the check by adding to the legal reserves of the collecting bank the amount indicated on the face of the check.[42] Just as in the case of Federal Reserve purchases from member banks, this addition of new high-powered reserve money initiates a multiplier effect stimulating accelerated expansion of the money supply.

The inflationary potential of Federal Reserve purchases of government securities is totally unlimited, because there is not a finite, unalterable quantity of government bonds in existence. More bonds are issued by the Treasury Department whenever the government feels like expanding its debt and spending more money. Although the Federal Reserve does not itself issue the bonds, it is usually more than cooperative in facilitating the government's sale of its debt (by such machinations, for example, as buying up existing government bonds which resemble in maturity and interest rate the new bonds that Treasury officials currently are attempting to peddle, thereby artificially stimulating demand for the new issue of government bonds). Fearing precisely such sympathetic "cooperation" between the central banking authority and the executive and legislative branches of government, the Federal Reserve Act limits the amount of government securities that the Treasury Department can sell *directly* to the Federal Reserve system to $5 billion.[43] However, this superficial restraint is both ineffective and fraudulent, a red herring concocted for public consumption. The purported restriction is utterly emasculated by the fact that the Federal Reserve can purchase an *unlimited* amount of government bonds *indirectly*, by buying them from third parties such as commercial banks or individuals to whom the Treasury Department initially sold the bonds. It is in this manner that the government's deficit spending unerringly becomes inflationary, for regardless of the nature of the initial purchaser of government bonds, the law enables the government's debt to find its way into the central banking system where it counts as reserves, thereby serving as a springboard for multiple expansion of the money supply.

Historically and currently, the Federal Reserve has used massive purchases of government securities to "fine tune" the money supply, increasing money and credit to whatever level federal officials find pleasing while willfully disregarding the consequences of the inflation they create for the individuals whose real purchasing power they steadily erode.[44] And yet, ironically, the little-understood artifice of purchasing government securities protects the government's clever frontmen at the helm of the Federal Reserve system from the public censure that would greet a comparable resort to the printing press to inflate the money supply to satisfy politically spawned governmental goals. Thus as each inflationary binge surpasses the last, the public futilely decries individual price rises while overlooking the central governmental architect of the decreased purchasing power they deplore.

DISCOUNT RATES

A third way in which the Federal Reserve controls the money supply is through the interest rates charged by Federal Reserve banks on loans to member banks. In contrast to the centralized role played by the Board of Governors and Federal Open Market Committee in altering the percentage of legally required reserves and purchasing government securities, the twelve individual Federal Reserve banks act independently in fixing this interest rate, called the discount rate.[45] Nevertheless, always tending to move in tandem, the various discount rates have a significant impact on the money supply. Like the Federal Reserve's manipulation of the percentage of required reserves, however, its management of discount rates pales in comparison to its use of open market purchases of government securities as a means of controlling the money supply.

As with open market purchases and the required reserve percentage, it is the effects of the Federal Reserve's discount policies upon member banks' legal reserves that stimulate inflation of the money supply. Reenacting a now familiar sequence, whenever a Federal Reserve bank loans money to a member bank, it does so by adding the amount of the loan to the member bank's existing reserves at the Federal Reserve bank. This increase in reserves ultimately enables the banking system to create demand deposits worth many times the value of the loan, expanding the money supply correspondingly.

The discount rate is no more than interest charged on borrowed reserves. The lower the Federal Reserve's discount rates in relation (1) to the prevailing interest rates on other sources of borrowed funds available to member banks, and (2) to the interest rate that member banks can charge on funds they loan to their customers, the more likely are member banks to seek to borrow reserves from the Federal Reserve banks.[46] Thus *low* discount rates presage inflation. As soon as a Federal Reserve bank makes a pen-and-ink entry adding previously nonexistent funds to a member bank's reserves, the member bank is economically motivated to grant loans that, as the new funds work their way through the banking system, create previously nonexistent money (demand deposits) by the maximum multiple that the new borrowings at the Federal Reserve will support under existing reserve requirements.

Thus a nominally private banking system bows to the government's desire to control the money supply. Characteristic of any fascist economic venture, the government puts on a self-effacing show of standing in the background, merely waiting in the wings to guide monetary policy in harmony with whatever federal officials intuit to be the government's or the nation's best interest. But in a more heavy-handed fashion than that manifested in other areas of federal control over the United States economy, the government has already quietly played its trump card and seized centralized control over the entire money supply. Giving the reality of total monetary control the best procapitalist face-lifting possible, the central banking system takes refuge behind a facade of geographic decentralization that touts the theoretical autonomy of member banks, but the facade is irreparably breached by the undeniable omnipotence of the Board of Governors and the Federal Open Market Committee in formulating monetary policy. Only the unwitting public is victimized, perpetually subjected to government-engineered inflation, which silently erodes the real purchasing power of their dollars while hypocritical federal officials publicly deplore the predictable and consciously selected results of the monetary policies they have knowingly designed and implemented.

4

The American Cartels: Compulsory Government Licensing and Rate Making

Statutory law gives the federal government absolute power to confer upon government-approved licensees the exclusive right to produce certain fundamental goods and services in the United States and to establish government-enforced rates or prices for these products. The statutes uniformly grant each federal agency total discretion in its sphere to act in accord with its concept of the "public interest, convenience, and necessity," thereby substituting the centralized rulings of a bureaucratic elite for the diffuse economic determinations that occur in an unregulated market.

In an open market environment, both consumers and producers are free to maximize their well-being by seeking mutually advantageous exchanges of goods and services. The *individual* consumer or producer independently judges whether a transaction is in his self-interest, bearing the costs of errors and reaping the rewards of correct economic judgments. Both responsibility for economic decision-making and its inherent risks are borne by the individual. The producer seeks to increase his wealth by producing a product that consumers want at a price they are willing to pay. He maximizes his profit not by arbitrarily charging high prices but by lowering his price to the point where the additional demand for his product created by lowering its price no longer generates a net gain in wealth for the producer. Similarly, the consumer strives to maximize his economic well-being by seeking those exchanges which he believes most enhance his personal satisfaction, given the economic resources at his disposal. In seeking such advantageous exchanges, the consumer communicates his effective demand to the producer, demonstrating his individual desires by either purchasing or refusing to purchase a commodity at the price offered. Independent of any external group, the individual consumer influences production by his private economic activity. In an unconstrained market economy, the aggregate of the individual decisions of all consumers controls what is produced; the economic will of consumers is sovereign.

Prices are the information transmitters that tell producers whether the quantities of commodities they are producing at the prices offered conform to consumers' desires, given the alternative goods and services competing for consumers' dollars. They also serve to allocate the existing supply of a product among consumers and to channel resources into production desired by consumers. If consumer demand for a product declines, increased competition for customers will drive the price down, marginal producers with high costs will shut down, and economic resources will be diverted into more profitable endeavors, inadvertently restricting the supply of the less desired product in conformity with consumers' preferences. Conversely, when supply of a product is too small relative to consumers' demand for it, consumers will compete to acquire the product by bidding the price up. By their willingness to pay higher prices, consumers tell producers that they want more of the product. The high price brought by the scarce commodity lures profit-seeking producers and investors into increasing the supply of the product, eventually tending to lower its price. Thus sale of scarce commodities to the highest bidder generally stimulates increased supply of such products and lower price levels.

If all producers of a commodity could establish and enforce an agreement to restrict entry into the industry by new producers or to charge prices uniformly above the market price for their product, producers could avoid the dictates of the market and thereby undermine consumer sovereignty. But in an unregulated market, the success of such collusion is likely to be transitory. Unless the colluders have some legal means of *enforcing* their agreement, all the profit incentives of the open market encourage its failure.[1] The individual producer is seldom motivated to restrict his production in order to charge a higher price, because consumer demand is not a fixed entity. It varies inversely with price: the lower the price, the greater the number of consumers willing and able to purchase a desired commodity. Any individual producer can increase his profits by lowering his price enough to increase his sales volume, up to the point where the cost of producing the additional unit (marginal cost) equals the revenue obtained by selling that unit (marginal revenue).[2]

Without an enforcement mechanism, it is both difficult and expensive for colluding producers to discover any breach of the agreement, and it will always pay any individual producer to cheat on the agreement. By slightly underpricing the other colluders, a producer who cheats on the agreement can vastly increase his sales and profits, assuming that an unsatisfied demand for the product exists and that no acceptable substitutes for the product are available. Moreover, high profits generated by collusion attract new investment capital and producers in the same manner as high profits caused by scarcity, for potential investors are extremely sensitive to opportunities to lure customers away from colluding producers by offering lower prices.

Thus the central problem for would-be colluders is to secure enforcement of their agreements. Government intervention provides that means of enforcement, enabling producers to police collusive agreements successfully.[3] Such intervention may take many forms, but this chapter concentrates on compulsory government licensing of business and government control of rates and prices within specific industries.

The open market's inducements toward lower prices and increased supplies of goods desired by consumers are contingent upon (1) free entry into the market by new producers, and (2) producers' freedom to adjust their prices and production level independently, in response to their private assessment of supply and demand.[4] Compulsory licensing and rate setting by government agencies destroy these inducements to increase supply and lower prices. Requiring a license as a prerequisite of engaging in certain businesses legally empowers the government to restrict entry into the industry, to make it *illegal* to produce specified goods or services without such a license. This restriction creates a government-sponsored cartel, a legal monopoly or oligopoly in which government-approved sellers are protected from potential competition, enabling them to raise their rates above normal market levels without fear of new entrants into the industry who might have the audacity to underprice them. If the government also possesses statutory authority to fix prices and establish rate levels for the industry, then another major problem is solved for producers who desire to avoid the market forces that tend to lower prices. Government price fixing relieves collusively minded producers of much of the burden of policing price fixing agreements, for laws that make it a *crime* to charge any price other than the government-approved rate form a substantial deterrent to producers who desire to lower their prices. Producers who would violate an industrywide collusive price fixing agreement in the absence of legal sanctions might be much more reluctant to subject themselves to criminal penalties for underpricing a government-enforced rate level.

The significance of compulsory licensing and price fixing for the producer is that he acquires from the government some measure of monopoly power: that is, he is the beneficiary of nonmarket (political) restriction of production, and his economic reward is a "monopoly rent" in the form of the higher prices he can charge because of the artificial limitation on the supply of his product.[5]

The significance of compulsory government licensing and price fixing for the consumer is that the individual cannot influence production and prices by his purchases as readily as he can in an open market environment. The consumer is forced to pay the monopoly rent of which the government-approved producers are the lucky recipients. This monopoly rent exacted from the consumer includes not only the increased cost and contrived scarcity of the product, but also the opportunity cost to the consumer implicit in having either to forgo other purchases that he would have made in the absence of the government-sponsored price increase, or to settle for a lower cost but less satisfactory alternative product.

The significance of government licensing and price fixing for consumers and producers alike is that arbitrary economic judgments of licensing and rate-fixing commissions replace the impersonal results of open market economic decision-making. When economic decisions worth millions of dollars are removed from the unregulated market and placed in the hands of a few politically appointed government bureaucrats, *political* decision-making controls the outcome. Only well-funded organized pressure groups are able to influence economic decisions. Diffuse economic interests, particularly the interests of unorganized individuals, have little impact on the government's decision. This fact is inherent in withdrawing economic decisions from the market; it does not assume any malevolence or corruption on the part of government officials. Regardless of how pure and beneficent the motives of government bureaucrats, there is no mechanism other than the market for enabling all consumers by their independent economic decisions to express, communicate, and influence the course of the economy.

The pressure groups that emerge in response to a compulsory government licensing system tend to represent factions having a large economic interest in the result, and the stakes are highest for existing producers. The entire impetus of government licensing and rate fixing — indeed, of political control over economic decisions in general — is to encourage the beneficiaries of government regulation to spend any amount up to the monopoly rents they anticipate in order to secure the coveted government license and thwart potential competitors. Such a system is ripe for corruption; it makes corruption in economic decision-making possible, no matter how noble the government officials in control. In an unregulated market, producers' primary avenue to economic reward is to satisfy consumers. Where government licensing and price fixing are compelled by law, producers are forced to seek economic advantages from a political elite, and the very existence of government-sponsored cartels permits economic decisions to be made in disregard of the aggregate will of individual consumers. Competition is transferred from the objective economic realm of satisfying customers and thereby attracting their voluntary purchases to the political realm of superiority in whatever attributes the political elite indicates are important in determining the lucky recipients of government-conferred monopoly power.

The statutory cartelization of the railroad industry, motor carriers, water carriers, freight forwarders, radio and television broadcasters, interstate water projects, electric utilities, and the natural-gas industry will be examined in the following pages.

I. GOVERNMENT REGULATION OF THE RAILROAD INDUSTRY

Part I of the Interstate Commerce Act creates the Interstate Commerce Commission (ICC) as a federal agency and asserts total governmental power over a railroad industry still nominally labeled "private." The most striking feature of the Interstate Commerce Act is the discretionary quality and the breadth of the powers conferred upon the ICC. The statute vests in the Commission absolute power to manipulate the railroad industry to achieve whatever the Commission asserts to be the "public interest, convenience, and necessity." As if flaunting the idea of a government of enumerated powers, the Interstate Commerce Act is literally riddled with references to the "national interest," "public convenience and necessity," and the ubiquitous "public interest." These vacuous phrases simply have no referents; they are empty labels that can readily be affixed to whatever transportation policies the government elects to pursue. In practice, vague terms like "public interest" are subjective, judgmental phrases that *connote* a favorable, emotionally satisfying evaluation of the thing referred to but that *denote* nothing.

The Interstate Commerce Act is a prototype of fascist economic control. It embodies essentially fascist economic principles not only by nominally preserving private enterprise to camouflage unlimited government authority over the regulated industries, but also by extensive reliance on compulsory licensing as the least offensive, most palatable method of establishing comprehensive government control over the economy. Citizens who wish to preserve the individual's right to use and dispose of his own property must overcome the semantic obstacle created by the fascist government's wholesale identification of the public interest with whatever economic policies it adopts. This linguistic trick neatly places omnipotent government economic controls on the side of the angels: to oppose federal economic regulation is by clever semantic manipulation made equivalent to opposing what is in the public's interest. Moreover, since the average citizen automatically interprets the public interest to consist of that which he as an individual subjectively perceives to be desirable economic and social ends, even communicating the fact that unlimited discretion is conferred upon the government is made extremely difficult. Many people with diverse economic goals incorrectly assume that federal power to act in the public interest is merely limited authority to pursue the concrete objectives that they as individuals deem to be laudable goals.

The Interstate Commerce Act gives the ICC unlimited power to restrict entry into the railroad industry. The statute makes it *illegal* for any railroad carrier to construct, acquire, or operate any line of railroad or extension thereof, "unless and until there shall first have been obtained from the Commission a *certificate* that the present or future *public convenience and necessity* require or will require the construction or operation, or construction and operation, of such additional or extended line of railroad."[6] A railroad line cannot even be abandoned without a certificate of public convenience and necessity, the granting of which is in the uncontrolled discretion of the ICC.[7] After explicitly giving the Commission unfettered power to issue or refuse to issue requested operating certificates, the statute emphasizes the ICC's total discretion by empowering it to "attach to the issuance of the certificate such terms and conditions as in its judgment the *public convenience and necessity* may require."[8] Furthermore, the Commission may on its own initiative *require* an unwilling railroad to extend its lines or to provide "safe and adequate" facilities if the Commission declares it to be "*reasonably required* in the interest of *public convenience and necessity.*"[9]

The ICC's power to structure the railroad industry is not limited to evaluating requests for certificates of public convenience and necessity and requiring extension of existing lines. In provisions that apply to carriers by water and motor vehicles as well as railroads, the statute explicitly *relieves regulated carriers from the operation of the antitrust laws,*[10] giving the ICC mandatory and exclusive power to review every proposed merger or consolidation of carriers as well as every agreement between carriers to pool or divide traffic, service, or earnings.[11]

One searches in vain for concrete standards controlling the ICC's omnipotent authority to judge proposed mergers. In phraseology that mocks objective limits constraining delegated governmental powers, the ICC is instructed to approve pooling or division agreements whenever it finds such agreements "will be in the interest of better service to the public or of economy in operation, and will not unduly restrain competition," and to prescribe rules and regulations governing the pooling agreements that are "just and reasonable."[12] Echoing this amorphous language, the statute exhorts the ICC to approve those proposed mergers it finds to be "consistent with the public interest" under terms and conditions that are "just and reasonable."[13] Egregiously insulting the reader's intelligence, the statute announces that "a public hearing shall be held in all cases where carriers by railroad are involved," then promptly destroys this guarantee by adding "unless the Commission determines that a public hearing is not necessary in the public interest."[14] Who is kidding whom? Stripped of legal jargon, the statute says that the ICC can approve or disapprove all proposed consolidations and pooling agreements between carriers using any criteria it chooses to reach whatever result pleases the eleven politically appointed ICC commissioners.

The statute also empowers the ICC to approve, free of antitrust review, agreements between carriers concerning rates, fares, classifications of property, allowances, and other matters.[15] If the carriers are of different classes (that is, railroads, motor vehicles, water carriers, and freight forwarders), the ICC cannot approve of the agreement unless it pertains only to transportation under joint rates or over through routes,[16] the formation of which is independently controlled by the Commission under other sections of the statute.[17] In superficial tribute to competition, the statute does purport to forbid approval of agreements between carriers to determine matters by any process of *joint consideration* that limits the parties' "free and unrestrained right to take independent action."[18] Nevertheless, this section's ineffectiveness can be measured by its failure to prevent regulated railroads and other types of carriers from using, with tacit ICC approval, industrywide "rate bureaus" as a clearinghouse for any rate proposals submitted to the ICC, thereby obliterating any remnant of competition that might have remained within the government-sponsored cartels.[19]

The ICC's consummate power to structure the railroad industry also includes the Commission's statutory authority to control the issuance of securities by railroads and the modification of the railroads' financial structure.[20] It is illegal for a regulated railroad corporation to issue stocks or bonds or to assume any other indebtedness (even if such indebtedness is permitted by the railroad's corporate charter) unless the ICC first finds issuance of the securities to be "compatible with the public interest" and "reasonably necessary and appropriate" to achieve a lawful purpose.[21]

The ICC's powers to establish the railroads' *rates* are equally comprehensive. The Commission need only decide that a railroad rate, fare, or practice is "unjust or unreasonable or unjustly discriminatory or unduly preferential or prejudicial" to acquire the right to prescribe and enforce "just and reasonable" rates and practices. Regulated railroads are compelled to file with the Commission *schedules* showing all rates, fares, and transportation charges.[22] Where a railroad operates a portion of a "through route" established in conjunction with another railroad, the ICC has the authority to prescribe joint rates whenever "necessary or desirable in the public interest" and to order a "just, reasonable, and equitable" division of such joint rates.[23] Moreover, resolving all doubts against the railroads and in favor of the Commission, the statute explicitly states that whenever a railroad carrier proposes to alter any fare, any charge for its services, any classification, regulation, or practice whatsoever, "the burden of proof shall be upon the carrier to show that the proposed changed rate, fare, charge, classification, rule, regulation, or practice is just and reasonable. . . ."[24]

Augmenting the ICC's plenary powers to dictate who may participate in the railroad industry and what may be charged for railroad services, Part I of the Interstate Commerce Act gives the ICC many supplementary powers. For example, the ICC is empowered to "establish reasonable rules, regulations, and practices" governing the supply, movement, and distribution of all vehicles used by regulated railroads to transport property.[25] The ICC may control the details of every contract for the use of any type of freight car, including the precise compensation to be paid.[26] The ICC's nebulous statutory guidelines instruct it to "provide *just and reasonable* compensation to freight car owners, contribute to *sound* car service practices (including *efficient* utilization and distribution of cars), and encourage the acquisition and maintenance of a car supply *adequate* to meet the needs of commerce and the national defense."[27] The Commission may exempt carriers from payment of certain compensation when it deems such exemption to be in the "national interest."[28]

The ICC also possesses statutory authority to reroute railroad traffic as it pleases whenever it declares that a regulated railroad carrier has failed "properly to serve the public," whereupon the Commission can dictate that "just and reasonable" routing and handling of railroad traffic which it thinks will promote "the interest of the public and the commerce of the people."[29] If the Commission finds it to be "in the public interest" and "practicable," it can order a railroad to permit other railroad carriers to use its terminal facilities upon the terms and for the compensation the ICC asserts to be "just and reasonable."[30]

The Commission achieves the apex of its power whenever it declares that an "emergency requiring immediate action" exists.[31] According to the statute, such an "emergency" might consist of shortage of equipment or congestion of traffic, hardly the type of disaster that would seem to merit total governmental usurpation of the private railroad industry. Nevertheless, the Commission need only unilaterally declare an emergency to exist, and it acquires the statutory power:

> (a) to suspend the operation of any or all rules, regulations, or practices then established . . . (b) to make such *just and reasonable* directions with respect to car service *without regard to the ownership as between carriers* of locomotives, cars, and other vehicles . . . as in its opinion will best promote the service *in the interest of the public and the commerce of the people* . . . (c) to require such joint or common use of terminals . . . as in its opinion will best meet the emergency and serve the public interest . . . and (d) to give directions for preference or priority in transportation, embargoes, or movement of traffic under permits . . . .[32]

The talismanic quality of a claimed emergency also empowers the ICC to "establish temporarily such through routes as in its opinion are necessary or desirable in the public interest."[33]

In spite of the seemingly all-encompassing powers explicitly conferred upon the ICC, the legislators meticulously avoided inadvertently constraining the ICC. The Interstate Commerce Act's enumeration of the Commission's powers closes with a potent caveat, the cautious legislators' hedge against those who would circumscribe the permissible endeavors of the ICC: "The foregoing enumeration of powers shall not exclude any power which the Commission would otherwise have in the making of an order under the provisions of this chapter."[34]

The pawn in the cartelization authorized by Part I of the Interstate Commerce Act is the railroad industry. Although allowed to remain nominally private in the fascist hope that competition and the profit motive will somehow work within the constraints of a government-sponsored cartel, the railroads are transformed into noncompetitive minions of the government. Their statutory duties are just as nebulous as the corresponding powers of the ICC. Stripped of their right to use their property as they as private entrepreneurs see fit, the railroads are compelled to provide whatever transportation the government deems proper. Regulated railroads have a legal obligation "to provide and furnish transportation upon *reasonable* request therefor, and to establish *reasonable* through routes with other such carriers, and *just and reasonable* rates, fares, charges, and classifications . . . ."[35]

The railroads are repeatedly told to charge only "just and reasonable" fees for their services, for every "unjust and unreasonable" charge is henceforth "prohibited and declared to be unlawful."[36] Likewise, the railroads can only establish "just and reasonable" regulations, practices, and classifications of property for transportation, for "every unjust and unreasonable classification, regulation, and practice is prohibited and declared to be unlawful."[37] Reiterating the total subjugation of the railroad industry to the arbitrary will of government officials, the statute announces that it is the *duty* of every regulated railroad

> to furnish *safe and adequate* car service and to establish, observe, and enforce *just and reasonable* rules, regulations, and practices with respect to car service; and every unjust and unreasonable rule, regulation, and practice with respect to car service is prohibited and declared to be unlawful.[38]

Finally, railroads are soberly warned that it is unlawful either to bestow an "undue or unreasonable preference or advantage" upon any entity or to inflict upon any individual or group an "undue or unreasonable prejudice or disadvantage."[39]

It is difficult to impart the sense of disingenuous charade conveyed by the Interstate Commerce Act's profuse verbal deference to the purposely undefined "public interest" and ends deemed "just and reasonable." A reader can randomly select almost any one of the fifty pages that compose Part I of the Interstate Commerce Act and find from two to twenty-five pretentious references to empty abstractions disguising the assertion of unlimited governmental power. The only possible reason for the statute's effusive deference to the public interest is to mask a politically unpalatable statement explicitly giving the ICC absolute power to structure and manipulate the railroad industry in any way it sees fit. Since neither the legislators nor the ICC commissioners are fooled by this obfuscation, the masquerade is apparently for the sole benefit of citizens whose gullibility the legislators presuppose.

II. GOVERNMENT REGULATION OF MOTOR CARRIERS

Part II of the Interstate Commerce Act empowers the ICC to license and regulate much of this country's transportation by motor vehicles. Before examining the Commission's compulsory licensing and rate-making powers under the statute, it is necessary to describe the scope and structure of this portion of the Interstate Commerce Act.

The statute purports to regulate only motor carriers engaged in *inter*state transportation, allowing *intra*state transportation by motor carriers to be governed exclusively by state regulation.[40] Although Congress has the constitutional power under the 1914 *Shreveport* case to authorize federal regulation of wholly intrastate transportation simply because it competes with nationally regulated interstate transportation, Part II of the Interstate Commerce Act specifically denies the ICC this power with respect to motor carriers. In language with no counterpart in the statutory provisions governing the railroad industry, the motor-carriers legislation states that

> nothing in this chapter shall empower the Commission to prescribe, or in any manner regulate, the rate, fare, or charge for intrastate transportation, or for any service connected therewith, for the purpose of removing discrimination against interstate commerce or for any other purpose whatever.[41]

The sole infringement of this pristine conceptual separation of interstate and intrastate transportation involves motor carriers that, though lawfully operating only within a single state, nevertheless to some degree engage in interstate commerce by transporting persons or property to or through other states or nations. If the ICC finds that such interstate operations are "of such nature, character, or quantity as not substantially to affect or impair uniform regulation by the Commission of transportation by motor carriers engaged in interstate or foreign commerce," then the Commission may exempt the carriers from the regulatory aegis of the statute upon such "reasonable terms and conditions as the public interest may require."[42] Although this provision gives the ICC broad discretion to exempt motor carriers with substantial interstate operations from the coverage of the statute, it does not allow the Commission to regulate motor carriers whose operations are wholly intrastate in nature. Thus the scope of the statute authorizing regulation of motor carriers is not as broad as the *constitutional* reach of federal power described in Chapter 2.

Moreover, certain categories of transportation by motor vehicle are explicitly exempt from regulation under Part II of the Interstate Commerce Act. For example, the statute excludes that motor vehicle transportation performed in terminal areas which is *incidental* to the primary operations of railroad carriers, water carriers, and freight forwarders subject to ICC regulation under other sections of the statute.[43] Such incidental motor vehicle operations are simply regulated by the ICC as part of the primary regulation of the railroads, water carriers, and freight forwarders. Also exempt from ICC regulation of motor vehicles are:

(1) *school buses*;

(2) *taxicabs*;

(3) motor vehicles used by *hotels* exclusively for the transportation of hotel patrons between hotels and local railroad or other common carrier stations;

(4) motor vehicles regulated by the Secretary of the Interior for use within *national parks and monuments*;

(5) motor vehicles operated by a *farmer* for transportation of agricultural products or transportation of supplies to his farm;

(6) motor vehicles used solely to transport *livestock, fish, and agricultural commodities*;

(7) motor vehicles used exclusively to deliver *newspapers*;

(8) motor vehicle transportation incidental to *aircraft* transportation;

(9) "*casual, occasional, or reciprocal*" interstate motor vehicle transportation provided for compensation by a person "not engaged in transportation by motor vehicle as a regular occupation or business."[44]

As to motor vehicles that are subject to regulation under Part II of the Interstate Commerce Act, the statute creates a three-tier structure of categories which control the degree of regulation authorized. Subject to most intensive federal regulation are "common carriers by motor vehicle," which are defined as those who hold themselves out to the general public to engage in interstate transportation of persons or property by motor vehicle for compensation.[45] "Contract carriers by motor vehicle" are somewhat less strictly regulated. Not holding themselves out as carriers to the general public, contract carriers provide interstate transportation under continuing contracts with a limited number of persons to furnish transportation services either (1) by assigning motor vehicles to the exclusive use of each customer, or (2) by designing the transportation service to meet the "distinct need of each individual customer."[46] Least subject to ICC control are "private carriers by motor vehicle," which are those who, though not within the definitions of common carriers and contract carriers, engage in interstate transportation of property of which they are the owners, lessees, or bailees if the transportation is "for the purpose of sale, lease, rent, or bailment, or in furtherance of any commercial enterprise."[47]

A grasp of this terminology is crucial, for whether an interstate carrier by motor vehicle is labeled a common carrier, contract carrier, or private carrier controls the scope of the ICC's legal power over it. Both common carriers and contract carriers are compelled to obtain licenses from the ICC as a prerequisite of engaging in interstate transportation, and both must obtain the government's approval of their rates and fares. However, in regulating common carriers the ICC is empowered to formulate "reasonable requirements with respect to continuous and adequate service, transportation of baggage and express," powers withheld from the Commission in its regulation of contract carriers by motor vehicle.[48] Private carriers by motor vehicle are not subject to general regulation by the government. They are not licensed, nor are their rates fixed by the government. The government's sole statutory authority over private carriers is:

> To establish for private carriers of property by motor vehicle, if need therefor is found, reasonable requirements to promote safety of operation, and to that end prescribe qualifications and maximum hours of service of employees, and standards of equipment.[49]

COMPULSORY LICENSING

The ICC's power to license common carriers and contract carriers by motor vehicle is as absolute as its authority to license interstate railroads. Only private carriers by motor vehicle are not required to obtain government licenses as a prerequisite of engaging in interstate transportation for compensation.

It is illegal for a common carrier by motor vehicle to pursue its business without a "certificate of public convenience and necessity issued by the Commission authorizing such operations."[50] Once again, the ICC is given unlimited power to pick and choose among applicants vying for the government's gift of monopoly power, for the Commission is vaguely instructed to grant a license to any "qualified" applicant who is "fit, willing, and able properly to perform the service proposed," provided that the proposed transportation service is "required by the present or future public convenience and necessity."[51]

The power to license common carriers by motor vehicle also enables the Commission to determine the distribution of motor vehicle transportation service throughout the nation, for the operating certificate granted by the ICC must specify the routes, fixed termini, or territory within which the licensee is permitted to do business. The monopoly power of this government motor vehicle transportation cartel is termed a "privilege," and government officials are empowered by statute to attach to the exercise of this privilege "such *reasonable* terms, conditions, and limitations as the *public convenience and necessity* may from time to time require."[52] In other words, the eleven politically appointed commissioners are legally authorized to disregard all market considerations and confer monopoly power upon select applicants

82

for any reason they choose and upon any conditions they specify. The sole statutory limitation upon the Commission's unfettered discretion to condition the grant of common-carrier licenses is that the ICC cannot restrict the carrier's right to increase its equipment within the area for which the certificate is granted.[53]

The Commission has equally comprehensive power to license contract carriers by motor vehicle. It is illegal to engage in interstate commerce as a contract carrier without a license from the ICC, called a "permit" to distinguish it from the "certificate" of public convenience and necessity for which common carriers compete.[54] Reiterating the subjective criteria governing the granting of common-carrier certificates, the statute requires issuance of a contract-carrier permit "to any *qualified* applicant" who is "fit, willing, and able *properly* to perform" the proposed service, provided that the proposed service will be "consistent with the public interest."[55] The Commission is further instructed to attach to the permit whatever "reasonable terms, conditions, and limitations" it sees fit.[56] Omnipresent discretion to fashion a government-approved cartel thus permeates the federal licensing of contract carriers as it does the entire statutory scheme authorizing government control of the major transportation industries in the United States.

The ICC also has statutory authority to license "motor transportation brokers," defined as those who offer to procure for another, for compensation, motor vehicle transportation otherwise subject to ICC regulation under Part II of the Interstate Commerce Act.[57] It is illegal for such a broker to do business without a government license. Once again, the government's power and discretion are total, for the Commission is told to license only "qualified" applicants, able "properly" to perform services that are in harmony with the "public interest."[58] It is the essence of nonmarket decision-making, for the Commission's political decisions on economic matters have the force of law.

PRICE FIXING

The statute takes almost three pages of fine print in creating a smokescreen of legal jargon to obscure an assertion of unlimited government control over the prices charged by common carriers by motor vehicle, an assertion which could be conveyed concisely in a single sentence. Common carriers must establish only "*just and reasonable* rates, charges, and classifications, and *just and reasonable* regulations and practices relating thereto."[59] They are required by law to provide "*safe and adequate* service, equipment, and facilities."[60] Although the statutory language has a pleasantly reasonable sound, the mellifluous phrases mask unlimited government power to determine and enforce, free of the market and hence of the consumer, what it unilaterally conceives to be "reasonable." The essence of the Commission's statutory power is communicated clearly if not succinctly:

> Whenever . . . the Commission shall be of the opinion that any individual or joint rate, fare, or charge . . . or any classification, rule, regulation, or practice whatsoever . . . affecting such rate . . . is or will be *unjust or unreasonable, or unjustly discriminatory or unduly preferential or unduly prejudicial*, it shall determine and prescribe the lawful rate, fare, or charge . . . thereafter to be observed, or the lawful classification, rule, regulation, or practice thereafter to be made effective . . . .[61]

The burden of proof is on the common carrier to demonstrate to the government that any proposed change in rate or related business practice is "just and reasonable."[62] Giving lip service to the very economic and social considerations whose influence federal control necessarily reduces, the statute ironically instructs the ICC, in exercising its plenary power to fix "just and reasonable" rates, to give "due consideration"

> to the need, in the public interest, of adequate and efficient transportation service . . . at the lowest cost consistent with the furnishing of such service; and to the need of revenues sufficient to enable such carriers, under honest, economical, and efficient management, to provide such service.[63]

It is precisely to these considerations that the market automatically responds absent government control. It is precisely these complex factors that government officials can never assess because of the impossibility of obtaining objective data capable of measuring them once the market mechanism is suppressed.

Government regulation of the rates charged by contract carriers by motor vehicle is somewhat less stringent than its regulation of common carriers' rates. Although the purported "standards" are just as subjective, the government is only empowered to fix the minimum prices that contract carriers can charge for their services, not the actual rates. Nevertheless, contract carriers are required by statute to file their actual charges with the government, and it is illegal for a contract carrier to charge a rate different from the actual rate so filed with the ICC.[64] The familiar standard of reasonableness again dominates the statutory provisions: contract carriers must "establish and observe *reasonable* minimum rates . . . and . . . *reasonable* regulations

84

and practices to be applied in connection with said *reasonable* minimum rates, fares, and charges."[65] The Commission is authorized to "prescribe such *just and reasonable* minimum rate or charge, or such rule, regulation, or practice as in its judgment may be necessary or desirable in the public interest."[66] Finally, as if to dispel any lingering doubt about the breadth of the Commission's power over the contract-carrier industry, the statute explicitly empowers the ICC to *exempt* any contract carrier from the foregoing requirements if the Commission deems it "consistent with the public interest."[67]

SUPPLEMENTARY POWERS

In addition to its compulsory licensing and rate-fixing powers, the ICC has other statutory weapons in its regulatory arsenal. A provision disconcertingly labeled "classification of motor carriers" bestows on the ICC comprehensive power to establish and enforce virtually any rule it formulates controlling any category of carrier by motor vehicle so long as the Commission discreetly calls its command "just and reasonable." The provision states:

> The Commission may from time to time establish such just and reasonable classifications of brokers or of groups of carriers included in the term "common carrier by motor vehicle," or "contract carrier by motor vehicle," as the special nature of the services performed by such carriers or brokers shall require; and *such just and reasonable rules, regulations, and requirements . . . to be observed by the carriers or brokers so classified or grouped, as the Commission deems necessary or desirable in the public interest.*[68]

This provision constitutes such a sweeping grant of authority that the legislators who drafted the statute might have forgone their delineation of the ICC's specific powers without in any way diminishing the Commission's authority. The words of the statute are all-encompassing.

One final statutory power of the ICC merits mention. We have seen that the ICC possesses the power to act as a surrogate antitrust division in structuring regulated transportation industries by its exclusive review of mergers, consolidations, and other agreements.[69] This power is augmented as to motor vehicles by a provision that nominally precludes a licensed common carrier from also being licensed as a contract carrier (and vice versa) over the same route or within the same territory.[70] Again dissipating a seemingly viable restriction on the Commission's action, the statute declares that such dual operations are permissible if the Commission finds that the licensee can operate in both capacities "consistently with the public interest."[71] The ICC's exclusive power to manipulate the structure of the interstate motor vehicle transportation industry is complete.

III. GOVERNMENT REGULATION OF WATER CARRIERS

Part III of the Interstate Commerce Act establishes a statutory framework for government regulation of water carriers that is virtually identical to the centralized authority over motor vehicle carriers created by Part II of the Act. The scope and structure of Part III correspond to Part II, except for specific exemptions granted certain categories of water carriers. For example, water carriers that transport not more than three commodities in bulk are excluded from government regulation, as are contract carriers by water that are "not actually and substantially competitive" with transportation by common carriers by water, rail, or motor vehicle.[72] These differences are not significant in principle, however. They merely reflect the political impact of special-interest groups whose influence prevailed when the legislation was drafted, in no way controverting the government's unchallenged power to include the exempted interests within the regulatory scheme if it elected to do so.

Substantively, the water-carrier legislation follows the pattern established in the motor-carrier statute. It is as if the legislation were produced by a computer programmed to substitute the word *water* for *motor vehicle* while generating an otherwise identical statute. In a sweeping provision identical to that contained in the Interstate Commerce Act's regulation of motor carriers, the ICC is authorized to

> establish from time to time such *just and reasonable* classifications of groups of carriers included in the terms "common carrier by water," or "contract carrier by water," as the special nature of the services performed by such carriers shall require; and such *just and reasonable* rules, regulations, and requirements consistent with the provisions of this chapter to be observed by the carriers so classified or grouped, as the Commission, after hearing, finds *necessary or desirable in the public interest.*[73]

Although this provision seems to encompass everything that follows, the statute nevertheless proceeds to enumerate the Commission's specific powers to control licensing and determine the rates and related practices of water carriers.

The distinction between common carriers and contract carriers established in the statute regulating motor vehicles is maintained in the legislation governing water carriers, the determining factor again being whether the carrier holds itself out to the general public as a transporter of persons or property in interstate commerce for compensation (common carrier), or whether it provides such transportation only under individual contracts (contract carrier).[74] Brokers of water-carrier services (that is, those who, for compensation, furnish water vessels to persons not otherwise subject to government regulation for the transportation of the recipient's own property) are also deemed contract carriers subject to government regulation, but the ICC is empowered to exempt any such broker from government control at will.[75] Although both common carriers and contract carriers by water must be licensed by the government, government regulation of common carriers' rates is more stringent than its control of contract carriers' rates.

COMPULSORY LICENSING

No common carrier by water can do business without a "certificate of public convenience and necessity" issued by the ICC.[76] The vacuous, subjective standards that the Commission is admonished to apply embody government discretion just as unlimited as federal power over motor carriers and railroads. In statutory language identical to preceding motor-carrier provisions, the Act instructs the Commission to certify any "qualified" applicant able "properly" to perform proposed water transportation service "required by the present or future public convenience and necessity."[77] The government is empowered to specify the routes over which the common carrier may operate, and, as one may by now legitimately expect, the government can attach to the "privilege" of doing business, so graciously granted to a common carrier, "such *reasonable* terms, conditions, and limitations as the *public convenience and necessity* may from time to time require."[78]

Contract carriers by water likewise can legally do business only at the pleasure of the government. Again, the Commission possesses unconstrained power to select only those applicants it deems "properly" able to perform the intended transportation.[79] It must license only those contract carriers whose operation will be "consistent with the public interest," conditioning its permission upon any terms it deems "reasonable."[80]

RATE FIXING

Under the government's careful scrutiny, common carriers by water are admonished to establish only "just and reasonable" rates, fares, charges, classifications, and regulations and practices relating thereto.[81] That is, common carriers by water can charge only those rates and can observe only those business practices that the government declares to be "just and reasonable." Any charge or related business practice that contravenes the government's wishes is branded illegal. Common carriers must file their rates with the ICC, which is empowered to reject any charge it labels "unreasonable."[82] If the government disapproves of a common carrier's rates or related business practices, it can prescribe and order the carrier to comply with whatever practices it thinks "just":

> Whenever . . . the Commission shall be of the opinion that any . . . rate, fare, or charge demanded, charged, or collected by any common carrier . . . by water . . . or any regulation, practice, or classification . . . relating to such transportation, is or will be *unjust or unreasonable, or unjustly discriminatory, or unduly preferential or prejudicial*, . . . it may determine and prescribe the lawful rate, fare, or charge . . . thereafter to be observed, or the lawful regulation, practice, or classification thereafter to be made effective.[83]

The rules governing contract carriers by water embody comparably vague terminology as a mask for unmitigated arbitrariness, but they only authorize the Commission to fix minimum prices, not actual rates. Thus contract carriers have a legal duty to establish, observe, and file with the ICC "reasonable" minimum rates and practices relating to such minimum charges.[84] If the Commission doesn't like the contract carrier's minimum rates or related practices, it may dictate those "just and reasonable" minimum rates or practices which it asserts are "necessary or desirable in the public interest."[85] The Commission also has the statutory power arbitrarily to exempt any contract carrier from the Interstate Commerce Act's rate-making provisions if it deems it "consistent with the public interest," a form of relief not available to common carriers by water.[86]

IV. GOVERNMENT REGULATION OF FREIGHT FORWARDERS

A freight forwarder is a person or corporation that, though not a carrier subject to ICC regulation, holds itself out to the general public as an interstate transporter of property for compensation. Although this function resembles that of a broker of motor-vehicle or water-carrier services in that both may utilize regulated carriers, a freight forwarder differs from a broker in that the freight forwarder assumes legal responsibility for the transportation of the property, whereas the broker merely acts as a middleman, procuring transportation by another who possesses legal responsibility but never himself becoming legally responsible for the transportation.[87] Further, the freight forwarder provides for the consolidation of shipments and for break-bulk and distribution operations for consolidated shipments at their destination.[88]

Extensive government regulation of freight forwarders is authorized by Part IV of the Interstate Commerce Act. The broad scope of the statute parallels government authority over the railroad industry, exceeding federal control over carriers by motor vehicle and by water. Under the 1914 *Shreveport* case, the government can regulate intrastate railroads simply because they compete with nationally regulated interstate railroads. While Part I of the Interstate Commerce Act does not modify this constitutional power of the government, its exercise is explicitly denied the ICC in its regulation of motor carriers and water carriers. In the case of freight forwarders, however, the statute specifically confers upon the Commission authority to exercise federal control over intrastate operations deemed to "discriminate" against interstate transportation:

> Whenever . . . the Commission . . . finds that any such rate, charge, classification, regulation, or practice [authorized by a state regulatory body] causes any undue or unreasonable advantage, preference, or prejudice as between persons or localities in intrastate commerce on the one hand and interstate commerce on the other hand, or any undue, unreasonable, or unjust discrimination against interstate commerce, which is forbidden and declared to be unlawful, it shall prescribe the rate or charge . . . thereafter to be charged, and the classification, regulation, or practice thereafter to be observed, in such manner as, in its judgment, will remove such advantage, preference, prejudice, or discrimination . . . the law of any State or the decision or order of any State authority to the contrary notwithstanding.[89]

COMPULSORY LICENSING

Further extending the government-sponsored cartelization of American transportation, the statute gives the ICC comprehensive and standardless power to restrict entry into the freight-forwarding business.[90] In the now familiar subjective incantation legalizing arbitrary government power to dictate who is allowed to engage in interstate transportation, the statute exhorts the Commission to issue a government permit to any "qualified" applicant able "properly" to perform freight-forwarding services deemed compatible with the "national interest."[91] The permit system authorizes detailed government control over the structure and distribution of American freight-forwarding operations, for each permit must specify the kinds of property that the freight forwarder is authorized to transport as well as the territory within which he can operate.[92] In superfluous language augmenting unlimited discretion to regulate freight forwarders, the Commission is empowered to attach to each permit "such reasonable terms, conditions, and limitations" as it deems consistent with its plenary powers under the Interstate Commerce Act.[93] Moreover, in a provision that corresponds to ICC authority over railroads but has no parallel in the legislation governing motor carriers and water carriers, the statute specifies that a freight forwarder that is controlled by or operating under common control with a common carrier by railroad, motor vehicle, or water cannot even *abandon* its operations without a certificate from the government officially declaring such abandonment "consistent with the public interest."[94]

RATE FIXING

The government's statutory authority to control freight forwarders' rates and charges in total disregard of the market is absolute. Freight forwarders must charge only "just and reasonable" prices for their services, which means any rate structure satisfactory to the eleven ICC commissioners, regardless of their reasons or the nature of the forces influencing them.[95] With due deference to linguistic symmetry, the statute also requires freight forwarders to establish only "just and reasonable" classifications and practices related to their operations.[96] Like other regulated transportation industries, freight forwarders must file documents showing their rates and related business regulations and practices with the Commission. If the government is displeased with a freight forwarder's rates or practices, it need only label them "unjust or unreasonable or unjustly discriminatory, or unduly preferential or prejudicial" to acquire the statutory power to dictate the government-approved rate or business practice that the freight forwarder must thereafter observe.[97]

SUPPLEMENTARY POWERS

In addition to its comprehensive powers to determine who is allowed by the government to engage in freight forwarding and what they may charge for their services, the government also controls with whom freight forwarders can do business. The statute prohibits freight forwarders from utilizing the services of any carriers except (generally) common carriers by railroad, motor vehicle, or water regulated by the ICC, certain carriers specifically exempt from ICC regulation, and air carriers subject to regulation by the Civil Aeronautics Board.[98] That is, freight forwarders can deal only with those most stringently regulated by the government and those whom the government has chosen not to regulate. The statute prevents freight forwarders from employing, for example, regulated contract carriers, even though their services might be more advantageous to the freight forwarder and ultimately to the consumer. This provision gives the ICC extremely tight control over freight forwarders, for the Commission is empowered to fix the actual rates charged by common carriers, whereas it can only enforce minimum rates for contract carriers.

Moreover, supplementing the Interstate Commerce Act's general provisions governing intercarrier agreements,[99] the statute gives the ICC unlimited authority to control contracts between freight forwarders and common carriers by motor vehicle. Any such contract must be submitted to the government for its approval.[100] Government approval may be granted or withheld at the whim of the Commission in response to political considerations, for the subjective criteria governing the lawfulness of contracts between freight forwarders and common carriers by motor vehicle require only that the contracts "establish *just, reasonable, and equitable* terms, conditions, and compensation which shall not unduly prefer or prejudice any of such participants or any other freight forwarder. . . ."[101] If the Commission is unhappy with a contract as submitted, it has full authority to rewrite it as it pleases.[102]

V. GOVERNMENT CONTROL OVER BROAD-CASTING

The United States government, not the listener or viewer, controls who may engage in broadcasting and what they may broadcast. Government regulation of broadcasting is a particularly important example of federal usurpation of economic decision-making, for it entails not only nonmarket manipulation of citizens' economic well-being but also political control over the ideas to which people are exposed.

The government's statutory power over broadcasters is as absolute as its control over interstate transportation. The governing statute, the Federal Communications Act of 1934, makes it illegal to construct or operate a braodcasting station without a government license.[103] The Federal Communications Act does not cautiously or warily create a narrowly defined federal regulatory power. Using the familiar guise of subjective standards to conceal omnipotent government authority over every aspect of the broadcasting industry, the statute empowers the Federal Communications Commission (FCC) to distribute government broadcasting licenses in accordance with its estimate of the "public interest, convenience, and necessity." These ubiquitous but meaningless terms permeate the Federal Communications Act, obscuring the government's claim of limitless authority over American broadcasting. Given power over broadcasting with only administrative precedent and subjective definitions of the public interest to guide them, the commissioners possess a blank check payable to whatever interests sway them. This assertion of the public interest as a goal independent of individuals' separate determinations of their own self-interest makes the public's interest whatever the seven commissioners by majority vote say it is. Mellifluous phrases avowing dedication to the public interest conceal the rejection of any attempt to let the public freely express its will.

The Federal Communications Act requires all aspiring broadcasters to obtain a government license. In vacuous words, which artfully imply a nonexistent restriction on government power, the statute instructs the FCC to grant a station license to any applicant "if public convenience, interest, or necessity will be served thereby."[104] Broadcasting licenses cannot be granted for more than three years, and after the expiration of any license, the FCC may renew the broadcaster's license "if the Commission finds that public interest, convenience, and necessity would be served thereby."[105] In addition, the FCC is vaguely instructed to strive "to provide a fair, efficient, and equitable distribution of radio service" among different states and communities.[106] A subsequent section of the Federal Communications Act, deceptively labeled "Considerations in Granting Application," lures the reader into an unwarranted expectation of specific standards governing the compulsory licensing of broadcasters. However, merely reiterating the preceding statutory formula, the Act again exhorts the Commission to consider "whether the public interest, convenience, and necessity will be served by the granting of such application," and to award the license if "public interest, convenience, and necessity would be served by the granting thereof."[107]

The extent of the government's legal power to probe the prospective broadcaster's background and broadcasting plans seems infinite. The FCC may require any information it desires on applications for broadcasting licenses, including not only concrete, objective data specifying the location of the station and the intended broadcasting hours, but also information concerning "the citizenship, *character*, and financial, technical, and *other qualifications* of the applicant to operate the station; . . . the *purposes* for which the station is to be used; and *such other information as it may require.*"[108] The burden of proof in all license-application proceedings is upon the applicant.[109] Making the prospective broadcaster bear the burden of proof in these circumstances is analogous to presuming a person guilty unless he proves his innocence, for in both cases the individual is powerless to satisfy unknown, shifting, fluid standards imposed by a body wielding vast legal power over him.

A dearth of objective standards is the hallmark of FCC action in all spheres. New stations cannot be constructed or licensed to operate unless the builder first obtains a construction permit from the FCC.[110] The government is authorized to make the same searching inquiries into the applicant's character and the purpose for which the station will be used as it does in evaluating station license applications.[111] Any station whose construction has been authorized by the government must be granted an operating license *unless* some "cause or circumstance arising or first coming to the knowledge of the Commission since the granting of the permit would, in the judgment of the Commission, make the operation of such station *against the public interest*."[112] The FCC also has the absolute power to waive the requirement of a construction permit whenever it wants to—more subtly phrased, whenever "it finds that the public interest, convenience, or necessity would be served thereby."[113] Moreover, the government can modify an existing construction permit or station license in any manner and for any reason it wants to—more graciously put, "if in the judgment of the Commission such action will promote the public interest, convenience, and necessity."[114] Further, the government has total power either to sanction or to prevent voluntary transfers of construction permits and station licenses whenever it pleases—that is, "upon finding by the Commission that the public interest, convenience, and necessity will be served thereby."[115] All agreements between competing applicants for a construction permit likewise must be evaluated by the government, which is empowered to approve such agreements whenever it feels like doing so, whatever its motives—in legal phraseology, the FCC "shall approve the agreement only if it determines that the agreement is consistent with the public interest, convenience, or necessity."[116] And finally, although the statute generally requires radio stations to broadcast announcements that reveal the source of any money or valuable consideration paid for broadcasting a program, the government can waive this requirement whenever it wants to—in statutory circumlocution, the Commission "may waive the requirement of an announcement . . . in any case . . . with respect to which it determines that the public interest, convenience, or necessity does not require the broadcasting of such announcement."[117]

The FCC's comprehensive power to regulate broadcasters is in fundamental opposition both to First Amendment rights and to the Federal Communications Act's explicit prohibition of censorship by the Commission.[118] Because of the enormous difficulty of proving unconstitutional grounds for FCC action in the face of the fluid public interest standard, the FCC's license-renewal power obviates the need for the agency to apply constitutional standards of what is protected free speech under the First Amendment. In practice, the sole restraint on FCC regulatory action that circumscribes the vague public interest, convenience, or necessity standard is the rule that administrative agencies may not act arbitrarily or capriciously.[119] Thus two separate norms governing freedom of expression have evolved, one applicable to the broadcast word and one applicable to all other forms of communication.[120] Overt and covert government restraints on broadcasting are tolerated that would never pass constitutional muster in any other context.[121]

Although the statute purports to shun government censorship, its authorization of wide-open inquiry into the character and plans of the aspiring broadcaster makes possible extensive government control of program content. An appreciation of the scope of the government's power to control programming can best be obtained by examining some specific examples of program-content control by the FCC. The relatively overt controls are exemplified by the FCC regulations that require licensed television stations to maintain program logs that record all programs and commercial matter transmitted, categorizing each program as an agricultural, entertainment, news, public-affairs, religious, instructional, sports, editorial, or educational institution broadcast.[122] Programs must be classified further as local, network, or recorded, and all public-service announcements must be identified.[123] Since these logs must be made available on request by the FCC[124] and must be submitted in part to the FCC with the broadcaster's application for license renewal, the ominous threat of denial of license renewal for failure to broadcast sufficient programs in any of these categories is evident.

It is a further indication of the FCC's enormous power to control programming that the type of information concerning program content now required of broadcast applicants is not codified by statute or agency regulations. The FCC's regulations simply state that the applicant must provide all information requested on the required forms to procure or renew a license;[125] the requisite form numbers are listed in subsequent sections of the regulations with no detailed explanation of their contents.[126] Since the forms are distributed exclusively by the FCC, one can only discover the extent of the Commission's probing into the nature of an applicant's proposed programming by contacting the FCC and requesting copies of the forms by number. At the very least, this practice constitutes a compromise of the principle of government by published rule rather than administrative fiat, for this procedure enables the FCC to change its operating rules without altering its published regulations. In addition to requiring specification of the steps the applicant has taken to ascertain community programming needs, the form now requires the license applicant to specify programs that are typical of those he intends to broadcast in the future, describe a typical week of proposed programming, and provide a detailed description of actual programming presented during a "composite week" selected by the FCC, categorizing programs as to type and source and indicating the number of public-service advertisements broadcast.[127]

Moreover, the FCC has explicitly claimed the authority to control programming and to regulate program content. Although the early judicial decisions based the FCC's legal authority on the need to prevent technical interference due to the scarcity of the radio spectrum resource, a dramatic shift was not long in coming. By 1943 the Supreme Court in *NBC* v. *United States* was able to state with equanimity:

> The Act itself establishes that the Commission's powers are *not limited to the engineering and technical aspects* of regulation of radio communication. Yet we are asked to regard the Commission as a kind of traffic officer, policing the wave lengths to prevent stations from interfering with each other. *But the Act does not restrict the Commission merely to supervision of the traffic. It puts upon the Commission the burden of determining the composition of that traffic.*[128]

The Court explicitly approved the 1934 Federal Communications Act's public-interest standard, and it held that FCC evaluation of station performance as well as potential technical interference was essential because of the necessity of choosing between competing applicants with equivalent technical and financial qualifications.[129] First Amendment objections were dismissed in a terse concluding paragraph, which used the scarcity rationale to refute the constitutional challenge to the FCC's broadcasting regulations.[130]

The Supreme Court's endorsement of program regulation presaged the tenor of future judicial determinations of the permissible scope of program-content control by the FCC. Most significant in this regard has been the evolution of the "fairness" doctrine. The fairness doctrine as currently codified states that free reply time must be granted to allow response to programs that deal with controversial issues of public importance.[131] Proof of inability to pay for the reply time is not a prerequisite of this gratuity, even if sponsors paid for the initial "controversial" broadcast. The courts have sustained the FCC's amorphous fairness doctrine in spite of the inherent ambiguity of its controversiality and public-issue requirements,[132] but the judiciary has found no logical terminus for these concepts. Controversiality, for example, has been defined so broadly that it is meaningless. Controversiality is now synonymous with "disputed in fact," for even a United Givers'-type charity appeal has been held to be a controversial issue of public importance, which confers the right to free reply time upon challengers who wish to advocate their preference for donations to individual charities.[133] Thus by FCC edict and judicial decision the broadcaster has become the pawn of irate minorities, who may impose their opinions on passive viewers free of charge. Ultimately, however, the public is forced to pay for these messages through increased prices for advertised goods, effectively subsidizing this allegedly free communication.

Until 1969, the fairness doctrine was construed to create only a *right of access* to the media, a right to transmit messages in response to programs voluntarily originated by a station. In *Red Lion Broadcasting Co.* v. *United States*, the Supreme Court foreshadowed what could become the wave of the future in broadcasting regulation, a First Amendment *right of listeners to hear*. What is most remarkable about this democratic-sounding right is the parties who will exercise it: the station operators and the FCC. More conspicuously absent than ever from this formula is the viewer whose right is being asserted. The right-to-hear rationale imposes an affirmative duty upon the media to seek out and present all viewpoints on all public issues. This duty is independent of any controversial presentation by a station; each station must structure its programming to reflect what it thinks the FCC thinks the public needs to know about everything.

The right-to-hear rationale has not yet been unequivocally embraced, but judicial impetus suggests its eventual adoption. In *Red Lion*, while paying verbal respect to the now-tattered First Amendment rights of broadcasters and invoking a proper amount of scarcity magic, the Supreme Court stated:

> There is nothing in the First Amendment which prevents the Government from requiring a licensee . . . to conduct himself as a proxy or fiduciary with obligations to present those views and voices which are representative of his community. . . . It is the right of the viewers and listeners, not the right of the broadcasters, which is paramount . . . .It is the right of the public to receive suitable access to social, political, esthetic, moral and other ideas and experiences which is crucial here.[134]

The terminology is blurred, but the message is clear. The FCC and the courts seem ready to implement the newly discovered right of viewers to obtain information by coercing broadcasters to present all sides of whatever the government labels public issues. Implicit in all the doctrinal discussion, two factors remain constant: increasing assumption of power over broadcasting by the government in the name of the public, and lack of discussion of any alternatives which would enable people to express their will directly.

Thus the government through statutory power over broadcasting has usurped control of another economic sphere. Although the case of broadcasting is basically no different from other areas of federal economic decision-making, its profound consequences are more readily apparent because communication is the product involved. Not only does federal control prevent the individual from influencing through his private economic decisions the nature of television and radio programs produced, but it also severely encroaches upon the individual's personal liberties — the rights of both broadcasters and viewers to communicate and to hear what they please, unrestrained by prior government censorship. In broadcasting as in all industries, government control of economic decision-making inherently politicizes the decisions that are made. Regardless of the motives of the bureaucratic elite empowered to resolve economic matters, it makes decisions in response to pressures by organized groups or government officials' personal ideologies, rather than according to the impersonal market process in which the individual influences the economic outcome by his purchases. Only the individual suffers, rendered powerless by law to vote with his dollars for the broadcasting products he prefers. Government usurpation of economic decision-making power necessarily implies the *economic disenfranchisement of the individual.*

A measure of government officials' desire to preserve this economic subservience of the individual is the FCC's continued opposition to pay television, a mechanism which would have allowed individual consumers to influence television programming. After thirteen years of consideration, the FCC, in response to great pressures by broadcasters, theater owners, and other organized groups with vested economic interests in preserving the monopoly power conferred upon them by governmental control of broadcasting, decided that pay television could only exist as a *beneficial supplement* to advertiser-supported television.[135] That is, the FCC declared it illegal for a free market to control the supply of television programs except in types of programming that were undesirable to producers of advertiser-supported television. While giving lip service to the concept of pay television, the FCC made it economically infeasible to market pay television, once again using the "public interest" to protect the monopoly power of organized groups at the individual consumer's expense.

The government also, through Congress and the courts, has consistently refused to recognize property rights in the airwaves as a viable alternative to massive government regulation. The federal legislature and the judiciary have so acted despite realistic proposals suggesting precise legal and technical mechanisms that would make property rights in the airwaves workable in practice as well as philosophically and economically desirable.[136] Congress and the courts continue to place great emphasis on the alleged *scarcity* of the airwaves as the justification for plenary federal control, ignoring the fact that it is chiefly the FCC, not any physical or technological barrier, that currently restricts the number of American broadcasters. Furthermore, the already ample supply of airwaves soon may be greatly multiplied as a result of recent scientific discoveries concerning the speed of light, as well as technological advances in cable broadcasting. Even more significantly, those who cry "scarcity" choose to ignore the fact that the scarcity rationale would justify totalitarian control over virtually every aspect of our economic life. Land, too, is scarce, yet property rights and the price mechanism allow equitable distribution of that resource.

Thus the thrust of government regulation of broadcasting is to maintain tight, centralized control over that area of economic decision-making, while relegating the individual to a subservient, impotent role. The economic decisions of a politically vulnerable elite once again replace the independent and voluntary actions of uncoerced individuals.

VI. GOVERNMENT REGULATION OF POWER GENERATION

Government control over the electric power generated in the United States is concentrated in the hands of the Federal Power Commission (FPC). This agency regulates three aspects of power generation: it controls water projects on interstate waterways, regulates electric utilities, and exercises comprehensive control over the natural-gas industry. With the ubiquitous public interest as its standard and guide, the FPC possesses wide-ranging discretionary authority over this branch of United States industry.

WATER PROJECTS
A. Compulsory Licensing

The five commissioners appointed by the President to serve on the FPC have the statutory power to dictate which water projects may be constructed on American waterways. A license from the FPC is a mandatory prerequisite to the construction of any "improvement" (consisting of dams, water conduits, reservoirs, powerhouses, transmission lines, and similar developments) upon *navigable* waters over which the federal government claims power under the Interstate Commerce Clause. Since the courts have construed the Interstate Commerce Clause and the concept of navigability to encompass respectively purely local commerce and mere tributaries of waters that could be made navigable only with major man-made alterations, the FPC has constitutional and statutory power over virtually any water project regarding which it chooses to exercise its licensing authority. The governing statute, the Federal Power Act, gives the FPC power to license any water project designed to improve navigation or to utilize hydroelectric power that the Commission labels "necessary or convenient."[137] It is illegal for any person to construct or operate any project on navigable waters for the purpose of developing electric power without a license from the FPC.[138] No consensual private agreement to transfer a license or the right to operate or maintain a water project is effective without the approval of the Commission, which can withhold its permission for any reason or no reason.[139] If the FPC favors a water project, whatever its reasons, it is authorized to enter into the record a "finding" that the project is "desirable and justified in the public interest for the purpose of improving or developing a waterway or waterways for the use or benefit of interstate or foreign commerce."[140] The FPC may impose any conditions it fancies upon the grant of a water-project license.[141]

It is difficult to convey the standardless breadth of the governmental powers implicit in the Federal Power Act without tedious repetition of the vague language that permeates the statute. Superseding and encompassing its licensing power are the FPC's plenary powers to investigate any intended development of electric power upon waterways or land over which the government has power under the Interstate Commerce Clause, and "to issue such order as it may find appropriate, expedient, and in the public interest to conserve and utilize the navigation and water-power resources of the region."[142] It is difficult to identify any power withheld from the Commission under this provision, which, read literally, essentially makes the rest of the statute superfluous.

The rules governing the Commission's power to pick and choose among water projects entail unlimited power to select any pattern of development it likes, regardless of the economic desires of the people affected. The FPC is ordered to give preference to states and municipalities, but only if their plans are as "well adapted" as any other applicant's "to conserve and utilize in the public interest the water resources of the region."[143] Among nongovernmental applicants, the Commission is ordered to grant a government license to the applicant whose plans "are best adapted to develop, conserve, and utilize in the public interest the water resources of the region."[144] Obviously, if the FPC prefers a particular applicant for reasons other than the objective merits of his proposal, the Commission *will* find the proposed water project "in the public interest." The pleasant words of the statute do not bridle omnipotent bureaucratic power.

Economic omnipotence is evident again in a subsequent section in which the FPC is instructed to adopt the water project "*best adapted* to a comprehensive plan for improving or developing a waterway ... for the use or benefit of interstate or foreign commerce, for the improvement and utilization of water-power development, and for other *beneficial public uses . . . .*"[145] As all the statutory ends sought sound desirable while the proper means to achieve those ends are matters of judgment subject to profound disagreement among individuals, the statute merely puts a superficial gloss of restraint on the reality of unlimited government power.

B. Rate Fixing

Although control of rates charged by licensees who provide electric power for use by the general public is left primarily to state agencies, the Federal Power Act authorizes the Commission to regulate the rates and services offered by its water-project licensees if a state fails to do so.[146] Moreover, since licensees are only required to comply with "reasonable" state regulations, the FPC impliedly retains the authority to declare disfavored state regulations to be "unreasonable" and hence unworthy of compliance by water-project licensees.[147] The statute further commands that when any power generated by a water-project licensee enters interstate commerce, "the rates charged and the service rendered by any such licensee . . . shall be *reasonable, nondiscriminatory, and just* to the customer and all unreasonable [*sic*] discriminatory and unjust rates or services are prohibited and declared to be unlawful."[148] Since by current standards interstate commerce can mean purely local commerce, the FPC has the power to second-guess the business judgment of most water-project licensees who are engaged in producing or distributing power and to compel business practices that conform to its notion of the "just" and "reasonable." Once again, entrepreneurs are forced to satisfy unpredictable demands of five politically appointed commissioners rather than impersonal market forces.

The FPC has other statutory levers on the financial structure of water-project licensees. In each case, vague statutory language gives the government the economic trump card whenever it chooses to play it. First, after a license has run twenty years of a possible fifty-year duration, the FPC can require the licensee to make payments of amounts specified by the Commission into "amortization reserves."[149] These payments must be made out of "surplus" earnings in excess of a "reasonable" rate of return, with the application of these amorphous terms left to the Commission's unilateral discretion.[150]

Further, omniscient government bureaucrats are empowered to assess annual charges upon licensees both to defray the expenses of the FPC's operation and to expropriate whatever the Commission chooses to denominate as "excessive profits."[151] Limited exceptions are provided for nonprofit state or municipal licensees. Clearly, "excess" profit is any income the five commissioners by majority vote decide to label excess—which means, any business income that the commissioners, for whatever reasons, do not want a licensee to keep. To authorize five bureaucrats to expropriate excess profits on behalf of the government in no way restrains abuses perpetrated by either business or government. It merely gives the government absolute power to take away from certain businessmen any portion of their earnings that the government wants to extract.

Finally, the FPC is empowered to declare unilaterally that one licensee has somehow benefited from the construction work of another licensee. Whenever the Commission deigns to make such a finding, it is authorized to compel the recipient to pay the owner of the improvement any annual amount that "the Commission may deem equitable."[152] That this constitutes a blank check on the resources of water-project licensees is particularly clear when one considers the fact that the government itself may be the owner of the alleged "improvement," and at a minimum will always have a vested political as well as financial stake in the constructor's success due to its prior approval of the new project and its hopes of extracting future "excess profits" from its new licensee.

C. Supplementary Powers

The FPC's most massive supplementary powers are those it can exercise upon the expiration of a license. If it gives the licensee at least two years' notice prior to expiration of the license, the government can take over and thereafter operate the water project when the license expires.[153] The statute's sole requirement is that the government pay the ejected owner the "fair value" of its "net investment" plus "reasonable" damages—which means, any amount the Commission feels like paying its ex-licensee.[154] Thus owners of water projects constantly endure the economic insecurity of possible government expropriation when their licenses expire. This threat alone is sufficient to distort radically the economic decisions of water-project owners, forcing them to cater to political appointees rather than customers to secure an economically viable enterprise. In addition, if the government (with or without objective economic justification) decides upon expiration of a license that a water project previously utilized to generate power should no longer be used for power generation, it may arbitrarily turn over the owner's property to another licensee for nonpower use.[155] In this case, the new licensee incurs the statutory obligation to pay the expelled licensee the "fair value" of its "net investment" plus "reasonable" damages, as ordained by the Commission, merely substituting a new licensee for the government as the direct and primary beneficiary of the government expropriation authorized by the statute.[156]

Another flagrant example of the government's monopoly of the use of force is the Federal Power Act's provision dealing with eminent domain. Extraordinarily effective when employed by the government alone to acquire by coercion property for anything labeled a desirable public use, the power of eminent domain is also conferred upon private licensees of the Commission by the Federal Power Act. The statute ornately frames its formula for coercion:

> When any licensee *cannot acquire by contract or pledges* an unimproved dam site or *the right to use or damage the lands or property of others* necessary to the construction, maintenance, or operation of any dam, reservoir, diversion structure, or the works appurtenant or accessory thereto, in conjunction with an improvement which in the judgment of the commission is *desirable and justified in the public interest* for the purpose of improving or developing a waterway . . . for the use or benefit of interstate or foreign commerce, *it may acquire the same by the exercise of the right of eminent domain* . . . .[157]

Public desires as expressed by individual consumers are disregarded and suppressed in this blanket substitution of government-backed force for voluntary economic agreement. If people won't trade with the FPC's licensee on terms agreeable to the licensee, the licensee can simply exercise its government-ordained coercive powers to take by force whatever it wants at whatever price it reckons "just" compensation.

ELECTRIC UTILITY COMPANIES
A. Government Control of Industry Structure
Although electric utility companies are not licensed by the FPC as are hydroelectric power projects, the government nevertheless possesses a virtual stranglehold on the structure of the industry. The Federal Power Act gives the FPC comprehensive power to regulate the interstate transmission and sale of electric power in order to satiate the fickle appetites of that shapeless creature labeled public interest. The word magic begins with a ritualistic incantation that the public has an "interest" in the interstate transmission and sale of electric power and that, therefore, centralized federal regulation by government bureaucrats is somehow essential. The statute intones as follows:

> It is declared that the business of transmitting and selling electric energy for ultimate distribution to the public is *affected with a public interest*, and that Federal regulation of matters relating to generation

. . . and of . . . the transmission of electric energy in interstate commerce and the sale of such energy at wholesale in interstate commerce is *necessary in the public interest* . . . .[158]

"Intrastate" distribution of electric power is nominally relegated to state control.

Denied overt licensing authority, the FPC has other equally effective levers on the economic viability of interstate electric-power distribution companies. For example, public utilities cannot sell, lease, or otherwise voluntarily dispose of their own facilities without the Commission's authorization and approval.[159] Nor can a public utility merge or consolidate with another utility, or even acquire the securities of another public utility, without prior approval by the government.

Probing for statutory standards to circumscribe these vast claims of government power, one finds the Commission solemnly instructed to bestow its approval only if the proposed transaction is "consistent with the public interest,"[160] and explicitly empowered to dispense its favors "upon such terms and conditions as it finds *necessary or appropriate* to secure the maintenance of *adequate* service and the coordination in the *public interest* of facilities subject to the jurisdiction of the Commission."[161] Thus, while claiming absolute governmental authority to divine and enforce the "public interest," Congress also tersely asserts the right to replace the public's (that is, the aggregate of all individual consumers') economic judgments with the notions of five government officials concerning what constitutes "adequate" service. This arrogant subjugation of the public through self-proclaimed governmental power to dictate the nature of "adequate" service and to compel public utilities to provide any type of service that satisfies the transitory wishes of current FPC officials is reiterated in a subsequent section of the statute: "Whenever the Commission . . . shall find that any interstate service of any public utility is *inadequate or insufficient*, the Commission shall determine the *proper, adequate, or sufficient* service to be furnished, and shall fix the same by its order, rule, or regulation . . . ."[162]

Supplementing the foregoing economic cudgels, the Federal Power Act makes it illegal for a public utility to assume any debt (by issuing securities or otherwise) without the Commission's approval, effectively preventing public utilities from acquiring capital for expansion or improvement of their facilities or services without the government's approval.[163] Again, the Federal Power Act gives the Commission a free hand to act without statutory restraint on its omnipotent bureaucratic muscle, for the FPC is vaguely exhorted to approve only those financial transactions "compatible with the *public interest*, . . . *necessary or appropriate* for or consistent with the *proper* performance by the applicant of service as a public utility and . . . reasonably necessary or appropriate [to attain a lawful purpose]."[164]

The FPC has extensive power over the physical as well as the financial shape of the public utility industry. The Commission has statutory authority to compel separate public utilities to establish physical connections between their respective transmission facilities whenever it "finds such action necessary or appropriate in the public interest."[165] It also can impose the terms and conditions of such forced exchanges, apportioning the cost or ordering compensation or reimbursement as it sees fit.[166] Further, if the Commission declares that an "emergency" exists, it is empowered to dictate temporary connections between public utilities and to require any generation, delivery, or transmission of electricity that it conceives will "best meet the emergency and serve the public interest."[167]

Although the alleged existence of emergency conditions imbues the FPC with sweeping powers to compel different electric utility companies to deal with each other on any terms declared by the Commission to be "just and reasonable," the Commission is loosely authorized to declare an emergency whenever it finds "a sudden increase in the demand for electric energy, or a shortage of electric energy or of facilities for the generation or transmission of electric energy, or of fuel or water for generating facilities, *or other [unspecified] causes* . . . ."[168] Merely representing normal market fluctuations, such conditions usually can be identified only through economic judgments whose inherent subjectivity would permit the Commission to declare an emergency no matter how normal the objective economic situation.

B. Rate Fixing

The government has absolute power to dictate the rates charged by public utilities that transmit or sell electricity in interstate commerce. The familiar pattern of nebulous, all-encompassing government price-setting guidelines is repeated. Public utilities are somberly admonished to charge only "just and reasonable" rates, for any "rate or charge which is not just and reasonable is hereby declared to be unlawful."[169] If the Commission alleges that a rate or related business practice is "unjust, unreasonable, unduly discriminatory or preferential," it has unrestrained statutory power to decree and compel adherence to whatever it labels the "just and reasonable rate, charge, classification, rule, regulation, practice, or contract to be thereafter observed and in force . . . ."[170] Since there is no objective measure of what constitutes a "just" or "reasonable" rate apart from individual purchasers' willingness to pay a specified price, the government can declare any given rate to be either just and reasonable or unjust and unreasonable. Thus this statutory provision again gives unfettered reign to the whims of five government officials, whether one approves or disapproves of their specific decision in any particular instance.

Regulated utilities are further ordered not to grant any "undue" preference or advantage to anybody or to maintain "unreasonable" differences in rates, with the "undue" and "unreasonable" to be decreed on a case-by-case basis by omnipotent government officials.[171] Public utilities must file with the Commission documents showing all their rates and charges and regulations pertaining thereto.[172] Public utilities bear the burden of proving to the government that any proposed rate increase is somehow justified.[173]

NATURAL GAS
A. Compulsory Licensing

In its statutory authority to control the production and interstate distribution of natural gas, the FPC achieves the apex of regulatory powers. The Natural Gas Act echoes the familiar formula for government usurpation of an economic activity. The docile citizen is first informed that his government has decreed that "the business of transporting and selling natural gas for ultimate distribution to the public is affected with a public interest," rendering massive government control of the industry "necessary in the public interest."[174] To appreciate the full significance of this formula as a rationale for a total government takeover of the economy, one need only imagine the word *shoes* or *toothpaste* substituted for *natural gas* in the above quotation.

No natural-gas company can sell or distribute natural gas in interstate or foreign commerce unless it has official authorization from the government in the form of a "certificate of public convenience and necessity" issued by the FPC.[175] No one can construct or expand facilities for interstate sale or distribution of natural gas without a certificate of public convenience and necessity.[176] No one can purchase or operate any facilities for interstate sale or distribution of natural gas without the coveted certificate of public convenience and necessity.[177] No natural-gas company can even abandon its facilities without the government's permission.[178] Nor can a natural-gas business discontinue or alter any existing service it provides without the FPC's official decree that "the available supply of natural gas is depleted to the extent that the continuance of service is unwarranted, or that the present or future public convenience or necessity permit such abandonment."[179]

The Commission can attach any terms or conditions it wishes to a license, being required by statute only to designate its edicts "reasonable terms and conditions" dictated by the "public convenience and necessity."[180] Thus absolute government discretion reigns. The dictates of the FPC are *a priori* "in the public interest," and persons in the business of marketing natural gas are simply subject to the Commission's decrees. The commissioners *create* the public interest; no such entity exists in reality apart from the aggregate effective demand of individual citizens and consumers, which demand is precisely what this and similar legislation is designed to suppress.

The government's power to choose among license applicants is unlimited. The lucky winners in the natural-gas monopoly sweepstakes are to be "qualified" applicants, "able and willing *properly* to perform" service that "is or will be required by the present or future public convenience and necessity."[181] In other words, the Commission can bestow its favors upon any applicant it prefers regardless of the influences that stimulate its preference.

B. Rate Fixing

The Natural Gas Act, like the statutes previously discussed, attempts to convince a passive citizenry that all things "just and reasonable" flow from the government. No economic decision is deemed just or reasonable unless the government says it is, manifesting its will through the supposedly omniscient judgment of five politically appointed bureaucrats. The economic decrees of five government officials replace the diffuse opinions of individual consumers of natural gas concerning price, service, and most business practices.

Feigning to create standards governing the FPC's price-fixing authority, the statute pretentiously declares:

> Whenever the Commission . . . shall find that any rate, charge, or classification . . . or that any rule, regulation, practice, or contract affecting such rate, charge, or classification is *unjust, unreasonable, unduly discriminatory, or preferential*, the Commission shall determine the *just and reasonable* rate, charge, classification, rule, regulation, practice, or contract to be thereafter observed and in force, and shall fix the same by order.[182]

In other words, any natural-gas rate or business practice that the commissioners can be persuaded by any pressure group to approve is ipso facto deemed "just and reasonable." Falsely suggesting that the statute provides some way for persons who operate natural-gas businesses to predict the government's economic decrees, the statute vaguely admonishes natural-gas companies to charge rates and to establish related rules and regulations that are "just and reasonable."[183] Documents showing all rates and related business practices and contracts must be filed with the FPC.[184] Natural-gas companies are forbidden from granting "undue" preferences or advantages to their customers and from maintaining "unreasonable" differences in rates, service, facilities, or any other matter between different localities or different types of service.[185] The natural-gas company bears the conceptually impossible burden of proving that a proposed rate increase is somehow "just and reasonable."[186] Stripped of legalistic pleasantries, these provisions empower the government to dictate the rates and practices of those engaged in the natural-gas business on a case-by-case basis in response to any nonmarket considerations that sway the five FPC commissioners.

C. Supplementary Powers

Augmenting the FPC's licensing and rate-fixing powers is the agency's comprehensive authority to control the physical facilities of natural-gas companies. The government can compel extension or "improvement" of physical facilities, require physical connection of transportation facilities owned by different natural-gas distributors, and force licensees to sell natural gas to local distributors.[187] The public interest again thinly veils unlimited governmental power:

> Whenever the Commission . . . finds such action *necessary or desirable in the public interest*, it may by order direct a natural gas company to extend or improve its transportation facilities, to establish physical connection of its transportation facilities with the facilities of, and sell natural gas to, any person or municipality engaged . . . in the local distribution of natural or artificial gas to the public . . . .[188]

The government also has absolute statutory power to control imports and exports of natural gas. No one can export natural gas to or import it from a foreign country without explicit permission from the FPC. The Commission is instructed to allow the proposed transaction unless it is "not . . . consistent with the public interest," and is empowered to impose any terms or conditions on the transaction that the FPC discreetly terms "necessary or appropriate."[189]

Finally, the companies that are recipients of government-created monopoly power to distribute natural gas also acquire the legal right to exercise the government's power of eminent domain. That is, if others will not voluntarily sell to the natural-gas licensee the property it wants at the price it wants to pay, the natural-gas company can simply take it by force. More ostentatiously phrased:

> When any holder of a certificate of public convenience and necessity cannot acquire by contract, or is unable to agree with the owner of

property to the compensation to be paid for, the necessary right-of-way to construct, operate, and maintain a pipe line . . . for the transportation of natural gas, and the necessary land or other property . . . for the location of stations or equipment necessary to the proper operation of such pipe line or pipe lines, it may acquire the same by the exercise of the right of eminent domain . . . .[190]

Indeed, the government through its statutory powers over the economy has a plethora of blessings to bestow on aspiring monopolists.

VII. GOVERNMENT REGULATION OF AIR CARRIERS

Government regulation of air carriers is more pervasive than its regulation of almost any other industry. Not only are air carriers subject to compulsory licensing and rate fixing at the hands of the Civil Aeronautics Board (CAB); they are also subject to extensive certification by the Federal Aviation Administration (FAA) for the avowed purpose of guaranteeing safety in air travel. The statutory standards that guide the CAB in its economic regulation and the FAA in its safety regulation of air carriers are sufficiently vague to permit the government to work its will upon the aviation industry free of the chafe of tangible legal restraints.

COMPULSORY LICENSING

Nobody in the United States can provide interstate transportation by aircraft for compensation without the approval of the government, acting through the CAB. CAB officials are empowered to issue a "certificate of public convenience and necessity" if they desire to permit an individual or group to engage in the aviation business.[191] The government license must specify both the terminal and the intermediate points between which the licensee is authorized to operate, giving the government full power to control the availability and geographical distribution of aviation services throughout the United States.[192] Vague statutory language gives the CAB a free hand to pick and choose among applicants for the mandatory government licenses, for the CAB need only label its licensee fit, willing, and able "properly" to perform transportation "required by the public convenience and necessity" to justify its award of monopoly power.[193] Such sweet-sounding words obscure the government's declaration that a few appointed government officials, not the public, will hereafter decree what is best for the people and have the legal power to compel the public to accept the government's determinations.

One is hard pressed to oppose this elitist approach to economics, for in doing so one is semantically cornered into opposing what is in the "public's interest" and favoring "unfit" air carriers. This clever linguistic technique permeates the legislation that establishes the CAB's and the FAA's powers. For example, the section that empowers the government to coerce airlines to do anything the government desires in order to secure the requisite license discreetly authorizes CAB officials to attach to the "privilege" of engaging in the designated air transportation "such *reasonable* terms, conditions, and limitations as the *public interest* may require."[194] The CAB can modify or suspend any license provided it terms such action prompted by "the public convenience and necessity."[195] No CAB licensee can voluntarily transfer its license without the CAB's accolade officially labeling the transaction in the "public interest."[196] Even abandonment of a route is prohibited unless the CAB first concludes that it is "in the public interest."[197] Inevitably, the public interest is whatever the CAB officials declare it to be, and the individuals who compose the public are legally prevented from expressing their own will in the matter.

The CAB's broad economic control over the routes, services, and structure of the airline industry is augmented by the FAA's regulation of air carriers for safety purposes. "Safety" joins "public interest" as the elastic verbal justification of federal control. The Administrator of the FAA may assign the use of navigable airspace in any manner "he may deem necessary in order to insure safety of aircraft and the efficient utilization of such airspace."[198] Chafing under the slightest hint of restraint upon federal powers, the legislators supplemented the FAA's safety mandate by giving the Administrator unlimited authority to change or revoke his orders and to grant exemptions whenever compatible with the Administrator's notions of what is "in the public interest."[199]

Broad statutory authority to certify aircraft personnel implements these general powers. Each pilot, mechanic, and crew member who helps to navigate aircraft while under way must hold an *airman certificate* from the FAA, as must aircraft dispatchers, air-traffic control-tower operators, and persons in charge of inspecting, maintaining, overhauling, and repairing aircraft.[200] The statutory standards are "proper qualifications" and physical ability to perform the job. The airman certificate may be granted upon any conditions that the FAA says are "necessary to assure safety in air commerce."[201]

The aircraft itself must hold myriad FAA certificates to operate with the legal sanction of the government. The first hurdle for aircraft is the *type certificate.* Not only aircraft, but also aircraft engines, propellers, and any other equipment designated by the FAA that is capable of being used in the operation of aircraft in flight (including parachutes and communications equipment) must obtain type certificates from the FAA.[202] After requiring the applicant to make any tests the FAA "deems reasonably necessary in the interest of safety," the FAA must issue the essential type certificate only if it deems the design, construction, and performance of the equipment "proper . . . for safe operation."[203] Substituting the "interest of safety" for the ubiquitous "public interest" as the password authorizing expansive federal economic regulation, the FAA legislation empowers that agency to attach any conditions to its many certificates which it asserts are "required in the interest of safety."[204] After securing type certificates, the aircraft equipment still cannot be manufactured unless it is favored with a *production certificate* from the FAA.[205] An individual aircraft cannot legally be flown for compensation unless its registered owner obtains an FAA *airworthiness certificate,* which may authorize operation of the aircraft for a limited time period and specify the type of service permitted as well as any other restraints on the aircraft's use that the FAA tags "required in the interest of safety."[206] In addition to the CAB certificate of public convenience and necessity and the foregoing FAA certificates, any person who desires to engage in interstate air transportation as a business pursuit, for compensation, must obtain from the FAA an *air-carrier operating certificate,* which brands the air carrier's service a "safe operation."[207] Like the CAB certificate of public convenience and necessity, the air-carrier operating certificate specifies the precise routes over which the licensee is authorized to operate.[208] The FAA can compel compliance with any limitations on the air-carrier operating certificate that it labels "reasonably necessary to assure safety in air transportation."[209]

Aircraft owners and manufacturers are not the only parties who must run the gamut of government licensing power. Airports must also obtain *airport operating certificates* from the FAA, attesting to the government's declaration that the airport is a "safe operation," "properly and adequately equipped," and in compliance with the FAA's safety standards.[210] Any "air agency" whose regulation is deemed "necessary in the interest of the public" is subject to rating and certification by the FAA, including civilian flying schools, aircraft repair schools, and aircraft repair or maintenance shops.[211] The FAA is also empowered to inspect, rate, and certify all civil air-navigation facilities, appraising their "suitability."[212] Air-navigation facilities include such navigation aids as landing areas, lights, weather information dissemination equipment, communications equipment, and any similar mechanisms for guiding or controlling aircraft flight, takeoff, or landing.[213] The final key to federal control over the physical structure of the airline industry is a provision that prohibits using federal funds outside of the government's aviation program for the creation, maintenance, or operation of landing areas or air-navigation facilities without a written recommendation and certification by the FAA that the project is "reasonably necessary for use in air commerce or in the interests of national defense."[214]

RATE FIXING

All interstate and overseas air carriers are subject to the unlimited rate-fixing powers of the government. The statute contains no standards to guide government bureaucrats in fixing the charges that air carriers can legally establish for their services. The government can manipulate air transportation rates in any manner it deems expedient, so long as it plays by the rules and labels its decrees "just and reasonable." Air carriers are solemnly told that they have a legal duty to establish only just and reasonable rates, fares, rules, and practices.[215] Air carriers must file with the CAB notice of all rates charged plus any information about business practices or services whose disclosure is required by CAB regulations.[216] They cannot charge a rate or provide a service different from the rates and services approved by the government.[217]

If the CAB doesn't like the rates or fares established by an air carrier, it is empowered to reject the charges deemed offensive, suspend their operation, and substitute any rate the Board says is just and reasonable.[218] In the words of the statute:

> Whenever . . . the Board shall be of the opinion that any . . . rate, fare, or charge demanded, charged, collected or received by any air carrier for interstate . . . air transportation, or any classification, rule, regulation, or practice affecting such rate, fare, or charge, or the value of the service thereunder, is or will be *unjust or unreasonable, or unjustly discriminatory, or unduly preferential, or unduly prejudicial,* the Board shall determine and prescribe the lawful rate, fare, or charge . . . thereafter to be demanded, charged, collected, or received, or the lawful classification, rule, regulation, or practice thereafter to be made effective. . . .[219]

Invoking the supple "public convenience and necessity" as its guide, the statute also empowers the CAB to compel establishment of through air transportation service, to specify "just and reasonable" rates for such joint services, and to enforce its conception of a "just, reasonable, and equitable" division of such joint rates.[220] Nominally private air carriers are also subject to government compulsion to carry the mail, for any licensed air carrier can be ordered by the Postmaster

General to carry mail on its authorized routes and even to increase its flights to accommodate the Postmaster General's demands. An air carrier can complain to the CAB, but the CAB has similarly unlimited power to enforce, modify, or suspend the Postmaster General's orders according to the CAB's appraisal of the "public convenience and necessity."[221] The Board also is empowered to fix and enforce "fair and reasonable" rates for transportation of mail, again subjugating the economic judgment of air carriers.[222]

SUPPLEMENTARY POWERS

Augmenting the CAB's licensing and rate-fixing powers, the statute broadly empowers the Board to require any report of an air carrier that it desires, and to compel "specific answers to all questions upon which the Board may deem information necessary."[223] The government can also require an air carrier to file an exact copy of all its contractual agreements and business understandings with the CAB.[224] The CAB must order air carriers to maintain the records and to follow the accounting procedures that satisfy the government's desires.[225] All mergers between air carriers, and all acquisitions by an air carrier of either another air carrier *or* the properties of a person engaged in any aspect of aeronautics *other than as an air carrier,* are illegal without prior CAB approval.[226]

An accurate summation of the scope of federal economic power over aviation (as well as the other economic endeavors examined in this chapter) is contained in a provision that sets forth certain principles which Congress ordered the CAB to regard as being in the public interest.[227] One of the principles designated to be in accord with the "public convenience and necessity" is:

> *Competition to the extent necessary* to assure the sound development of an air-transportation system properly adapted to the needs of the foreign and domestic commerce of the United States, or the Postal Service, and of the national defense.[228]

A more succinct expression of the guiding economic principle of fascism would be hard to formulate. By permitting competition — that is, capitalism — only to the extent the government believes it useful in accomplishing the government's goals, the government's statutory power over aviation joins federal control over railroads, motor carriers, water carriers, freight forwarders, communications, interstate water projects, electric utilities, and the natural-gas industry in implementing the most fundamental fascist economic doctrine.

5

Government Control over Product Quality

Although the federal government has not deigned to impose standards for every consumer product, it has acquired the power to select at will the consumer products forced to comply with government product-"quality" guidelines. The familiar fascist economic technique repeated in this sphere of economic controls is to arrogate to the government absolute power to intervene in "private" economic decision-making only when it suits the government's purposes. Businesses remain free to produce whatever they like—unless the government tells them otherwise.

Product-quality standards are ideally compatible with the fundamental premises of a fascist economy. Absolute power to fix standards of product quality implies total governmental authority to create rules that circumscribe "private" economic activity, to dictate the framework within which nominally independent businesses must operate. The government thereby claims all residual economic authority, tolerating private economic decision-making only insofar as it serves the government's political and social goals.

Acquisition of power to fix standards of product quality constitutes a uniquely tantalizing and vulnerable target for aspiring fascists. As a tactical matter, it is difficult to oppose government quality standards.

113

A multitude of words with positive, salutary connotations are adopted as exclusive proprietary terminology by the product-quality legislation. One cannot even describe the phenomenon without seeming to endorse it. To name the subject — product-*quality* laws — is to convey the impression that these laws in fact achieve their purported goal. In reality, these laws simply authorize the government to dictate the kinds of products that businesses can manufacture and distribute. They no more guarantee that the result of the web of government edicts will *enhance* product quality than touting the Federal Communications Commission as the incarnation of the "public interest" guarantees the beneficence of that agency's decrees. Further tightening the semantic noose around the necks of those who would challenge the propriety of government product controls, the government righteously claims to desire only to act in the "public interest" to preserve "public health and safety." Proponents of government quality controls equate any opposition to their schemes with preference for inferior products and with hostility to public health and safety, creating a nearly insurmountable semantic barrier that blocks any attempt to dissuade the public from accepting government quality standards.

But proponents of product-quality laws do more than expropriate the vocabulary of goodness and rectitude. They also use intensely emotional terminology, permeated with negative connotations, to beguile the public into uncritical aversion to and revulsion for the alleged evils the legislation is supposed to alleviate. It is really a very neat trick, one which can successfully sway even the most perceptive critic. The heart of the trick is the subtle substitution of subjective language for objective language, performed in a way that makes the reader *think* that objective terms have been used. Thus throughout the product-quality legislation, the statutes authorize the government to prohibit the distribution of products that are "adulterated" or contain any "filthy," "putrid," "decomposed," or "deleterious" substance. These inflammatory terms are never objectively defined in the statutes, and their dictionary definitions offer no objective standards by which challenged products might be evaluated. Nevertheless, a reader is lured into instantaneous agreement with the statutes, for each reader automatically supplies his personal idea of the concrete, objective characteristics that would prompt him to designate a substance "filthy" or "putrid," instinctively condemning such substances as abhorrent without realizing that the terms themselves embody no objective criteria that might serve as a standard of product quality.

The negative overtones of the language enable the government to avoid objective definition completely. The words themselves are subjective, connoting indignation and repugnance but denoting neither objective health hazards nor physical conditions, such as bacteria levels, which might threaten public health. This fundamental subjectivity bestows incredible power on the government, enabling government officials to create and change on whim rules controlling what products businesses may market, and to apply statutory penalties for political purposes totally unrelated to protection of public health and safety. Ironically, a well-meaning public endorses laws that it believes outlaw only products that pose objective threats to health and safety, while government officials cynically reap the power that the subjective language sows.

Despite the seemingly antisocial overtones implicit in challenging government manipulation of product quality, it is necessary to appraise the economic consequences of such controls. Absorbed by fear that without federal legislation they will encounter products that threaten their health and safety, people seldom perceive the economic costs imposed upon them by government quality standards.

Most tangibly, government quality controls raise the cost of the products affected.[1] These increased costs are paid by the consumer in the form of higher prices. All people would prefer to have only the highest-quality, safest, most durable, and most sanitary and risk-free products that business has the technological capacity to manufacture, if such products could be acquired at the same price as lower-quality goods. But since increased price usually accompanies enhanced quality, people form personal judgments concerning the relative value to them of price versus quality with respect to any given product, a judgment which varies with their appraisal of the product's risk, the purpose for which they desire the product, and the financial resources at their disposal. Although some consumers might prefer to pay a higher price to receive a more durable or sanitary product, other consumers would prefer to acquire a lower-quality product at the lower price for which it could be sold.

A monolithic federal standard of quality makes it legally impossible for consumers to choose a cheaper product whose quality is less than that mandated by the government. In effect, the government forcibly prevents the individual consumer from making an independent assessment of the relative value to him of quality versus price. The government imposes its view of the "proper" quality of products, and the consumer must pay for that level of quality or do without the product entirely. By replacing the independent judgments of individual consumers, federal product-quality standards deprive citizens of economic freedom to choose different levels of quality and voluntarily to assume varying levels of risk in order to obtain a lower price.

Federal standards also may discourage production of commodities that surpass the quality level enforced by government rule, to the detriment of consumers who might prefer to pay more for a higher-quality product. Further, government standards may serve as a barrier to technological innovation, effectively stagnating technology at existing levels of development. New producers may be thwarted (1) by overt federal rules that prohibit the use of cost-reducing production methods and/or forbid the marketing of safe, wholesome, or functional new products whose only vice is competition with the economic interests of established, politically influential industries; or (2) by the substantial administrative costs entailed in dealing effectively with the government's massive bureaucratic infrastructure.

The only plausible justification for government control of product quality is the difficulty and cost involved for both individuals and businesses in ascertaining through market forces mutually desirable trade-offs between price level and acceptable risk for any given commodity. These information costs, which constitute one aspect of what economists call transaction costs (the cost of making markets function effectively),[2] are said to be reduced by the government's creation of product-quality standards. They are indeed reduced, but they are reduced by refusing to recognize the existence of differing individual economic valuations. Thus the cost of discovering price/quality trade-offs satisfactory to all the individuals who compose the consuming public is "reduced" by the government's decision to abandon—more accurately, to prohibit—all attempts to find out the varying price/quality ratios that free individuals would prefer. Carried to its logical extreme, this reasoning would suggest that it would be economically "cheaper" and therefore preferable to impose a totally planned economy, for government decrees establishing the type and quantity of production would eliminate "needless" transaction costs entailed in a "disorderly" capitalist economy whereby desired production is ascertained by the "inefficient" accommodation of supply to demand. The flaw in both assertions is that this method of eliminating transaction costs also eliminates the individual's freedom to stimulate the type of production he personally prefers by independent decisions to purchase or not to purchase available merchandise. In essence, the costs of making the market function are allegedly reduced by preventing the market from functioning. To reduce transaction costs by this method is to impose the government's will in economic matters upon an economically disenfranchised public.

There are other detrimental ramifications of government controls over product quality. Even assuming a benevolent, conscientious bureaucracy formulating the product standards, absent the suppressed market mechanism of demand and supply, there is no way for the most diligent army of government officials to determine how much quality control, inspection, or labeling the public desires. The bureaucracy inevitably will fail to gratify the public's desires, for no *single* level of product quality could ever satisfy all of the diverse individuals who make up the public. Further, the existence of government standards for product quality tends to prevent development of a private market for consumer information regarding the aspects of product quality regulated by the government. This phenomenon creates spiraling dependence upon the government, facilitating ever broader economic controls by fostering public belief that economic uncertainties can be resolved only by government action.

Government formulation of product-quality standards enables political decision-making, characteristically responsive to well-organized pressure groups, to supplant the market's responsiveness to the economic influence of unorganized individuals. The political responsiveness of government agencies entrusted to formulate and implement product-quality standards is assured by the vague, all-encompassing statutory standards promulgated as guidelines for government officials' decisions (such as the diffuse "interest in public health and safety"), as well as by most agencies' unlimited authority to exempt favored businesses from economic regulations. Inherently vulnerable to corruption, this ornate system of government power to control the types and quality of products available to American consumers invites both random enforcement of agency regulations and use of the system to protect vested economic or political interests under the forgiving guise of the "public health and safety" maxim.

The government directly and indirectly manipulates the quality of products available to consumers by (1) overt regulations that delineate the minimum specifications necessary for government officials to allow a product to be marketed, (2) government inspection of certain products, and (3) requirements for government-approved labeling of specific types of products.

I. OVERT PRODUCT-QUALITY STANDARDS
THE CONSUMER PRODUCT SAFETY ACT

The most far-reaching legislation empowering the government to establish and enforce standards of product quality is the Consumer Product Safety Act.[2] This Act creates the Consumer Product Safety Commission and authorizes it to create "consumer product safety standards" for all products produced or distributed:

(i) for sale to a consumer for use in or around a permanent or temporary household or residence, a school, in recreation, or otherwise, or

(ii) *for the personal use, consumption, or enjoyment of a consumer* in or around a permanent or temporary household or residence, a school, in recreation, or otherwise . . . .[4]

Certain products comprehensively regulated by the government under other statutes, such as motor vehicles and tobacco products, are explicitly excluded from the Commission's authority.[5]

The heart of the Consumer Product Safety Act empowers the Commission to formulate consumer product-safety standards that consist of:

(1) Requirements as to *performance, composition, contents, design, construction, finish, or packaging* of a consumer product [and/or]
(2) Requirements that a consumer product be marked with or accompanied by clear and adequate *warnings or instructions*, or requirements respecting the form of warnings or instructions.[6]

Although the statute requires the Commission's standards to be "*reasonably* necessary to prevent or reduce an *unreasonable* risk of injury,"[7] that purported restraint on the agency's authority does little to curtail its blanket powers to decree the types of products that may be manufactured and made available to American consumers. The Commission's powers can be expanded infinitely merely by liberal definition of "unreasonable." It is likewise small comfort to note that the Commission is not supposed to promulgate a consumer product-safety rule unless that rule "is in the *public interest*."[8] If the Commission wants to enact a rule, one can rest assured that the Commission will label it "in the public interest."

Making it clear that the Commission's powers are not to be used solely to restrict products already proved to threaten consumers' safety, the statute allows the Commission to require prior clearance of any new consumer product before it can lawfully be marketed. The manufacturer may be required to "furnish notice and a description of such a [new consumer] product to the Commission before its distribution in commerce."[9] Giving the Consumer Product Safety Commission a stranglehold on development of new products, the Act defines a "new" consumer product as one that "incorporates a *design, material, or form of energy exchange* which (1) has not previously been used substantially in consumer products and (2) as to which there exists a lack of information adequate to determine the safety of such product in use by consumers."[10] Had this standard prevailed throughout United States history, all the beneficial consumer commodities that have immeasurably raised the average American's standard of living would have been subject to the prior scrutiny and the unlimited veto power of a govern-

118

ment agency more likely to respond to political pressure groups than to abstract concern about a nebulous public's safety.

If the Commission makes the subjective decision that a product poses an "unreasonable risk of injury" that cannot be corrected by a consumer product-safety standard, the Commission may totally prohibit the manufacture and sale of the product by the simple expedient of labeling it a "banned hazardous product."[11] Any commodity deemed an "imminently hazardous consumer product," as well as every banned hazardous product and any product that does not conform to an applicable consumer product-safety rule, is subject to condemnation and seizure through court action.[12]

Manufacturers, distributors, and retailers are required to notify the Commission whenever any product handled by them either creates a "substantial risk of injury to the public" or fails to conform to an applicable consumer product-safety standard.[13] Further, in a provision characteristic of all the legislation establishing government control over economic matters, every person who is a manufacturer, labeler, or distributor of a consumer product is compelled to "establish and maintain such records, make such reports, and provide such information as the Commission may, by rule, reasonably require."[14]

Any violation of the Consumer Product Safety Act may incur both civil and criminal penalties. Up to $500,000 in fines may be imposed as a civil penalty for a related series of violations, while the maximum criminal penalties consist of $50,000 and a one-year imprisonment.[15]

States and local governments are stripped of power to modify the monolithic federal standards which can be imposed upon any consumer product. The Act explicitly declares that whenever a federal consumer product safety rule is in effect,

> no State or political subdivision of a State shall have any authority either to establish or to continue in effect any provision of a safety standard or regulation which prescribes any requirements as to the performance, composition, contents, design, finish, construction, packaging, or labeling of such product which are designed to deal with the same risk of injury associated with such consumer product, *unless such requirements are identical to the requirements of the Federal standard.*[16]

Even if a state wishes to impose a *higher* standard, the Commission has unlimited power to decide whether or not to allow the proposed state or local standard, for the Commission can prohibit even a higher standard if it finds it either "unduly burden[s] interstate commerce" or is not required by "compelling local conditions."[17]

The range of products that may be regulated by the government under the Consumer Product Safety Act is incredibly broad. In recognition of this fact, the statute transfers to the Consumer Product Safety Commission the government's previously established powers to regulate flammable fabrics and hazardous substances under the Flammable Fabrics Act[18] and the Federal Hazardous Substances Act,[19] for there is no logical reason to isolate these particular functions from the ubiquitous reach of the Commission.[20] An unparalleled grant of standard-setting power, the Consumer Product Safety Act empowers the government to decree and enforce official government quality standards for products ranging from toilet bowl brushes to musical instruments.

THE FEDERAL FOOD, DRUG AND COSMETIC ACT

Equally comprehensive powers to set government standards for food, drugs, and cosmetics are established by the Federal Food, Drug and Cosmetic Act.[21] Although the law's paternalistic language stresses altruistic concern for the health and welfare of a naive public unable to respond intelligently to the unregulated marketplace, the Act is permeated with elastic terms and exemption powers that easily stretch to encompass any result desired by government officials administering the statute.

The regulation of food provides one enlightening insight into the political and economic motivations prompting product-quality legislation, usually masqueraded as selfless concern about the public's health and welfare. The mask is discarded in a statutory provision that regulates intrastate as well as interstate sale of colored oleomargarine. Congress announces that

> the sale, or the serving in public eating places, of colored oleomargarine or colored margarine without clear identification as such . . . *depresses the market* in interstate commerce for butter and for oleomargarine or margarine clearly identified and neither adulterated nor misbranded, and constitutes a *burden on interstate commerce* in such articles. Such burden exists, irrespective of whether such oleomargarine or margarine originates from an interstate source or from the State in which it is sold.[22]

With those epithets on the record, Congress felt free to use the government's coercive powers liberally. Even if the colored margarine involved is unquestionably wholesome and neither adulterated nor misbranded, Congress made it unlawful to sell any colored oleomargarine or margarine unless:

(1) such oleomargarine or margarine is *packaged*,

(2) the net weight of the contents of any package sold in a retail establishment is *one pound or less,*

(3) there appears on the label of the package (A) the word "oleomargarine" or "margarine" in type or lettering at least as large as any other type or lettering on such label, and (B) a full and accurate statement of all the ingredients . . ., and

(4) each part of the contents of the package is contained in a wrapper which bears the word "oleomargarine" or "margarine" in type or lettering not smaller than 20-point type.[23]

Since these restrictions are not contingent upon attributing any unwholesome quality to the margarine, one gets the uneasy feeling that a powerful butter lobby eager to outlaw potential competition feared that margarine could be manufactured and sold more cheaply unpackaged or in retail quantities exceeding one pound.

That impression is reinforced beyond a reasonable doubt by the provision governing the sales of oleomargarine in public eating places. The law imposes artificial restraints, unrelated to any concern about public health, that render the use of margarine in public restaurants both unattractive and prohibitively expensive:

No person shall possess in a form ready for serving colored oleomargarine or colored margarine at a public eating place *unless a notice that oleomargarine or margarine is served is displayed prominently and conspicuously* in such place and in such manner as to render it likely to be read and understood by the ordinary individual being served in such eating place *or is printed or is otherwise set forth on the menu in type or lettering not smaller than that normally used to designate the serving of other food items.* No person shall serve colored oleomargarine or colored margarine at a public eating place, whether or not any charge is made therefor, unless (1) *each separate serving bears or is accompanied by labeling identifying it as oleomargarine or margarine,* or (2) *each separate serving thereof is triangular in shape.*[24]

The facade is dropped, and one is given a rare, unshielded glimpse of a powerful industry using laws promulgated under the guise of public health and safety in order to eliminate by coercive means competition that otherwise might supply the public with cheaper and perhaps preferable products.

Parenthetically, the milk industry was also successful in passing similar legislation to outlaw the manufacture and sale of what it disparagingly refers to as "filled milk." Filled milk is defined as "any *milk, cream, or skimmed milk,* whether or not condensed, evaporated, concentrated, powdered, dried, or desiccated, *to which has been added*

. . . any fat or oil other than milk fat, so that the resulting product is in imitation or semblance of milk, cream, or skimmed milk . . . ."[25] The statute exempts from its edicts certain preparations "not readily mistaken *in taste* for milk or cream or for evaporated, condensed, or powdered milk."[26] Since the law condemns similarity in taste without (1) proving that filled milk is any more detrimental to public health than unfilled milk, or (2) suggesting appropriate labeling to remedy any possible fraud upon the public, it is quite clear that the law is designed to protect milk producers' vested economic interests rather than the public. The imperious and unsupported decree that filled milk "is an *adulterated* article of food, *injurious to the public health,* and its sale constitutes a *fraud* upon the public"[27] is but the legally sanctioned vituperation of producers using the government's coercive powers to forbid competition that otherwise might greatly benefit the public in terms of both lower prices and greater variety of available products.

Although the general pattern of regulation of product quality under the Federal Food, Drug and Cosmetic Act is more subtle than the approach used to control oleomargarine and filled milk, it permits the same type of government protection of vested economic interests under the aegis of public health and safety. The terms of art used throughout the statute are "adulterated" and "misbranded." The application of these magic epithets signals government wrath, social condemnation, and outright prohibition of manufacture and sale of the product so labeled. Although the definition of these terms varies depending upon whether the product is a food, drug, or cosmetic, the instructive feature of this legislative technique is the importance the government attaches to labels. Intended to popularize and justify the government restraints authorized by the statute, the labels invite automatic public censure of the condemned business practices while avoiding public scrutiny of the precise business activities that are outlawed. It simply would not do merely to specify the actions to be penalized by the government and then to declare those actions unlawful. Politicians deem the statute infinitely more salable if its phraseology permits them to tell their constituents that the legislation only bans "adulterated" and "misbranded" products.

In its regulation of food products, the Federal Food, Drug and Cosmetic Act empowers the Secretary of Health, Education and Welfare to create for any food a "reasonable" definition and standard of identity, a "reasonable" standard of quality, and "reasonable" standards of fill for its containers.[28] Although in the single paragraph that so empowers the Secretary we are twice told that he is to act only "for the purpose of promoting honesty and fair dealing in the interest of consumers,"[29] it is quite clear that the statute permits the Secretary to

122

establish any food-quality standards he wishes so long as he discreetly labels them "reasonable" and "in the interest of consumers."

But this latitude is too obvious. Employing the familiar linguistic technique in a bid to win popular approval of government control over the types of food products sold in America, the statute next declares that whenever the Secretary has promulgated a quality standard for a food product, that food will be deemed a "misbranded" and therefore prohibited product unless the food either conforms to the prescribed quality standard or bears a label that states that it "falls below" the standard.[30] Since the Secretary's powers are so broad that his rulings have no necessary relationship to objective health hazards posed by food products, this procedure provides an umbrella that shelters restrictions directly analogous to the stifling of oleomargarine sales described above. Further, even if one found that a particular regulation in fact identified an objectively inferior product, the ominous, subjective labeling required by the government might dissuade consumers from buying the product even though if presented with a truthful statement of the product's quality, absent the negative overtones of the government's labeling, consumers might decide that objective deficiencies in product quality were more than offset by the product's lower price. Since food products traditionally are sold at very low profit margins, loss of sales caused by such a stigma probably sounds the death knell for nonconforming products. Thus, although the law does not permit an absolute ban of products that do not satisfy the Secretary's product-quality standards, the regulations allow the government to influence significantly the foods that consumers "choose" in the marketplace, to that extent substituting the government's will in food product quality for the uncoerced choices of free individuals.

Food products are also prohibited if they are "adulterated." The most plausible statutory restraint is that which outlaws foods containing any "poisonous or deleterious substances [other than one added to the food] which may render it injurious to health."[31] However, the food *may* be manufactured and sold if the Secretary decides that "the quantity of such substance in such food does not *ordinarily* render it injurious to health."[32] One need not even observe the lack of definition of the crucial term "deleterious" in order to recognize the breadth of the power conferred upon the Secretary. Since the same objective condition could be characterized as conforming to either provision of the statutory test, the Secretary has virtually unlimited discretion to reach any result he subjectively favors in any particular instance.

Further, the Secretary has unlimited power to establish "tolerances" for added poisonous or deleterious substances. The statute empowers him to declare such an added substance "safe" simply by ruling that the poison is "*required* in the production [of the product] . . . or *cannot be avoided* by good manufacturing practice."[33] Similarly broad government discretion to establish tolerances prevails regarding added pesticide chemicals on raw agricultural commodities, food additives, and new animal drugs. In each case, the government has virtually unlimited authority (1) to exempt the poisonous or deleterious substance from government control,[34] (2) to specify a "tolerance" level for permissible use of the poison,[35] or (3) to ban the substance entirely by declaring it "unsafe."[36] Although the statute repeatedly informs the citizen that his government benefactors must act only for the purpose of "protecting public health,"[37] the nebulous quality of this guideline makes it clear that such soothing words are intended as salve for the wounds of the victims and the consciences of government officials rather than as a viable restraint on government power.

The pinnacle of the Secretary's power to prohibit foods he labels adulterated is reached in provisions that designate "adulterated" food to be that which "consists in whole or in part of any *filthy, putrid, or decomposed substance,* or . . . is otherwise *unfit for food*; or . . . has been prepared, packed, or held under *insanitary* conditions whereby it *may* have become contaminated with filth, or whereby it *may* have been rendered injurious to health . . . ."[38] The subjective quality of this language is palpable. By dissociating the statute's inflammatory words of condemnation from any required proof of an objective threat to public health, this subjectivity has enabled the government to promulgate purely political rulings such as that banning the sale of "cheap, high-protein, biologically sterile food made in powdered form, because . . . [government] employees say it is a filthy food — being made from *whole* fish."[39] Indeed, any food product, however wholesome, is vulnerable to censure under the imprecise, elastic terms of this provision if its producers dare to offend either the Secretary or their economic competitors who wield political influence with the government.

The government has comparably broad power to control the manufacture and sale of drugs. A typical provision requires all drug producers to register annually with the government and subjects registered firms to periodic inspections by the government.[40] However, predictably politicizing the registration procedure, the statute empowers the Secretary of Health, Education and Welfare to exempt favored classes of persons from this requirement at will, simply by asserting that their registration is "not necessary for the protection of the public health."[41]

Paralleling his broad authority to regulate food quality, the Secretary is empowered to forbid commerce in drugs that are identified as "adulterated" or "misbranded." The subjective "tests" of adulteration

124

echo those applicable to food products. A drug may be prohibited if it "consists in whole or in part of any filthy, putrid, or decomposed substance," or if it has been "held under insanitary conditions whereby it may have been contaminated with filth, or whereby it may have been rendered injurious to health."[42] Devoid of objective criteria with which to identify products that threaten public health, labels like "filthy" and "decomposed" enable the government to appear virtuous in reviling any product it dislikes, even if motivated by political goals unrelated to any altruistic concern about public safety. A drug also may be banned if

> the methods used in, or the facilities and controls used for, its manufacture, processing, packing, or holding do not conform to or are not operated or administered in conformity with *current good manufacturing practice* to assure that such drug meets the requirements of this chapter as to safety and has the identity and strength, and meets the quality and purity characteristics, which it purports or is represented to possess . . . .[43]

Since the Secretary alone has the ultimate power to define "current good manufacturing practice," he has absolute veto power over the manufacture and sale of all drugs subject to his edicts.

Further, the statute requires the safety and effectiveness of all "new drugs" to be attested to by the government before they can be marketed,[44] empowering the government to quash development and distribution of any drug, however medically beneficial, whether the government's opposition is motivated by honest bureaucratic timidity or desire for political reprisal. A "new drug" denotes any drug either not generally recognized as safe and effective by scientific experts or not proved by extensive usage to be safe and effective.[45] Although the definition itself is elastic enough to confer ample discretion upon the Secretary, the statute also explicitly empowers the Secretary to exempt new drugs from all government review whenever the avowed purpose of the proposed use is investigational, designed to obtain data on the drug's safety and effectiveness.[46] Indicating the extent to which this legislation belies its avowed intent to protect the public, the law expressly informs such investigational researchers that they may use the untested new drugs on human beings *without their consent* whenever "they deem it not feasible or, in their professional judgment, contrary to the best interests of such human beings" to obtain their consent.[47]

New drugs can be denied approval by the government and consequently banned from interstate commerce upon the subjective judgment of the Secretary that the manufacturer of the drug has not proved it to be safe and effective. Despite the superficial reasonableness of the vague statutory "tests" of a proposed new drug's merits, the government's unavoidably subjective decision to reject a drug under any of these tests can as easily rest on political as on scientific or medical considerations. For example, the government can disapprove of a new drug if the reports the manufacturer submits "do not include *adequate* tests by all methods *reasonably* applicable to show whether or not such drug is safe for use," or if test results submitted "do not show that such drug is safe for use" under the prescribed conditions.[48] The Secretary of Health, Education and Welfare can also reject a new-drug application if he asserts that the methods, facilities, or controls used in the manufacture and processing of the drug are "*inadequate* to preserve its identity, strength, quality, and purity."[49] The government can even prohibit a new drug simply by contending that there is "*insufficient information* to determine whether such drug is safe for use" or that "there is a *lack of substantial evidence* that the drug will have the effect it purports or is represented to have."[50] Almost identical government controls over the manufacture and marketing of drugs created for use in animals other than man or for use in animal feed ("new animal drugs") are established by the Federal Food, Drug and Cosmetic Act.[51] At best, the Secretary's decision substitutes the government's social and medical judgment for the consumer's right to weigh quality, risk, and price, and to choose freely the product that best reflects his economic values. At worst, the Secretary's decision may usurp the economic freedom of consumers and manufacturers alike, and stifle technological innovation merely to perpetuate a system of political favoritism that uses government licensing to protect vested economic interests from viable competition.

The government also is specifically required by statute to certify drugs containing insulin and all antibiotic drugs.[52] Any such drug not certified by the government is deemed "misbranded" and hence forbidden in interstate commerce.[53] However, the Secretary has unlimited power to exempt any antibiotic drugs he feels like exempting merely by declaring their certification "not necessary to insure safety and efficacy of use."[54]

Cosmetics are also targets of government quality standards so nebulous as to give government officials virtually unconstrained power to prohibit any cosmetic, whether the underlying offense stimulating the restriction is the chemical composition of the product or the political transgressions of its manufacturers. A cosmetic may be outlawed as "adulterated":

> (a) If it bears or contains any poisonous or deleterious substance which *may* render it injurious to users. . . .

(b) If it consists in whole or in part of any *filthy, putrid, or decomposed substance.*

(c) If it has been . . . held under insanitary conditions whereby it *may* have become contaminated with filth, or whereby it *may* have been rendered injurious to health.[55]

Again, while the suggestive terms used in the statute to revile banned substances provoke automatic aversion, their application is not contingent upon proof of an objective threat to public health or safety. However, unlike new drugs, cosmetics are not required by statute to be approved or certified by the government before they can be sold in interstate commerce.

One final statutory weapon is issued to the Secretary of Health, Education and Welfare by the Federal Food, Drug and Cosmetic Act to complete the government's arsenal in its battle against foods, drugs, and cosmetics that do not satisfy the government's notion of proper product quality. That weapon is publicity. It may indeed be the most potent tool available to the government in working its will upon producers of foods, drugs, and cosmetics, for adverse publicity, whether or not justified, is the kiss of death to manufacturers whose economic livelihood depends upon consumers' confidence. The government is empowered to disseminate information about foods, drugs, and cosmetics "in situations involving, in the opinion of the Secretary, imminent danger to health or gross deception of the consumer."[56] The very threat of such adverse publicity is probably sufficient in most cases to "persuade" regulated producers to comply with the government's wishes, regardless of the ultimate merits or judicial enforceability of the government's demands.

THE FEDERAL ENVIRONMENTAL PESTICIDE CONTROL ACT

The government also has comprehensive power to set standards for all pesticides under the Federal Environmental Pesticide Control Act of 1972, enacted to replace the Federal Insecticide, Fungicide, and Rodenticide Act.[57] Unlimited government discretion again is the hallmark of the federal legislation, concealed this time in avowed statutory concern about adverse effects on the environment. Under the statute, all pesticides must be registered with and approved by the government, and it is unlawful to distribute unregistered pesticides.[58] However, the government can refuse to register any pesticide that it claims will have "unreasonable adverse effects on the environment."[59] Since it is neither intuitively obvious nor objectively demonstrable what constitutes "unreasonable" environmental harm, this superficially appealing slogan authorizes government officials, whether moti-

127

vated by political pressure, hope of economic gain, or personal social philosophy, to impose their views of acceptable environmental consequences by prohibiting the distribution of disfavored pesticides.

If the Administrator of the Environmental Protection Agency decides that the pesticide "will not generally cause unreasonable effects on the environment," he is instructed to classify the pesticide for *general* use.[60] If the Administrator declares additional restrictions necessary to prevent unreasonable adverse environmental effects, he may classify the pesticide for *restricted* use only, requiring its application only under the direct supervision of a federally certified applicator and imposing any other regulatory restrictions he deems useful.[61] Should there be insufficient information about the pesticide to warrant federal approval of its registration, the government may grant an *experimental-use permit* and fix a temporary tolerance level for the pesticide's residue to govern its use while data on possible harmful effects of the substance are being accumulated.[62]

Somewhat ironically, not even registration and official government approval of a pesticide insulates its producers and distributors from the ultimate penalty to which a pesticide product is legally vulnerable, seizure by the government. The government may confiscate a pesticide produced, distributed, and used in accordance with the government's directions pursuant to approved registration of the product simply by asserting that it "nevertheless causes unreasonable adverse effects on the environment."[63]

Producers of pesticides must also register their business establishments with the government, and they are required by law to submit detailed annual reports to the government regarding the types and amounts of pesticides manufactured by such businesses.[64] Further, the law authorizes the Administrator of the Environmental Protection Agency to require such producers to maintain whatever additional records "he determines are necessary," categorically excluding only financial data, pricing data, and personnel data from government scrutiny.[65]

To guarantee that even the most inattentive of readers could not overlook the unfettered discretionary powers accorded the government by the Federal Environmental Pesticide Control Act, the law culminates by stating that the government can exempt any pesticide it wishes to exempt on the mere assertion that the pesticide is "of a character which is unnecessary to be subject to this subchapter in order to carry out the purposes of this subchapter."[66] Complementing the unlimited discretion accorded government officials to decree on a case-by-case basis what constitutes an "unreasonable" adverse environmental effect, this provision embodies the quintessence of absolute government power to control an economic endeavor by bureaucratic fiat. Even the civil and criminal penalties established by the statute are not to be imposed by any fixed objective standard. Instead, the fluid public interest, as divined by omnipotent government bureaucrats, is to be the test: "Nothing in this subchapter shall be construed as requiring the Administrator to institute proceedings for prosecution of *minor* violations of this subchapter whenever he believes that the *public interest* will be adequately served by a suitable written notice of warning."[67]

While pesticide manufacturers thus are compelled to solicit the government approval on which their economic survival now depends, public acceptance of the federal regulatory scheme is cultivated through careful co-optation of disparate interests whose "advice," as voiced by "qualified persons," the Administrator is encouraged "at his discretion" to solicit.[68] Finally, capturing in microcosm the essence of federal control over pesticide production, this still nominally private business activity is by law made the object of a comprehensive "national monitoring plan."[69]

AGRICULTURAL PRODUCT GRADING STANDARDS

Another group of statutes gives the government extensive authority to create standards for agricultural products. However, unlike federal power to establish standards for consumer products, foods, drugs, cosmetics, and pesticides, the government's power to devise standards for agricultural products does not include the power to prevent nonconforming products from entering interstate commerce by seizure, condemnation, or like means. Instead, the government's power to set standards for agricultural products entails only the power to require the commodity to be classified or graded in conformity with criteria and grade designations specified by the government. In this sense, government agricultural product-quality "standards" are more akin to labeling requirements than to product-quality requirements. Nevertheless, mandatory government agricultural product classification standards may effectively restrict use of commodities that do not please government officials either (1) by applying subjective labels whose emotional connotations discourage use of disfavored quality levels and encourage use of favored grades while obscuring the objective criteria on which the labels are based, or (2) by excluding "inferior" quality levels from the range encompassed by the compulsory government grading scale. Since the personal preferences of government officials cannot consistently coincide with the desires of consumers in an unregulated market, any influence thus achieved by government classification of agricultural products merely substitutes the government's will for the free choices of purchasers.

The United States government acquired power to devise and enforce quality standards for classifying cotton and grain (corn, wheat, rye, oats, barley, flaxseed, grain sorghum, soybeans, and other grains used for human food and animal feed) through the United States Cotton Standards Act and the United States Grain Standards Act. It is generally unlawful to designate cotton or grain for which the Secretary of Agriculture has formulated standards by any classification other than the official government grades, although private cotton sales by *sample* are not prohibited.[70] The Secretary of Agriculture is empowered to conduct official inspections in order to classify cotton and grain, either upon request or, in the case of cotton being shipped in interstate commerce, upon the government's unilateral decision to inspect the commodity.[71] To complete federal control over the inspection process, the government is authorized to license official cotton classifiers and samplers as well as grain inspectors.[72]

Both statutes overtly recognize that the systems they create invite corruption. Each statute makes it illegal to falsify official inspection reports or to attempt improperly to influence government officials authorized to inspect the regulated commodities.[73] The United States Grain Standards Act even acknowledges that conflicts of interest may exist, explicitly prohibiting government inspection officials from either holding a financial interest in or accepting gratuities from a business firm engaged in merchandising grain.[74] However, this self-negating provision simultaneously authorizes the Secretary of Agriculture to determine exactly how much conflict of interest will be approved by the government, for the statute empowers the Secretary to "provide such other exceptions to the restrictions of this section as he determines are consistent with the purposes of this chapter."[75] Further, giving the Secretary of Agriculture absolute discretion to decide whether or not to enforce the law, the statute encourages political favoritism by declaring that the Secretary can issue written warnings in lieu of instituting criminal proceedings for known violations of the law whenever he asserts such action to be in the "public interest."[76]

To deal with agricultural products other than cotton and grain, the United States Warehouse Act contains a categorical grant of power to the government to create standards for *all* agricultural products "by which their quality or value may be judged or determined."[77] The Warehouse Act guarantees the enforceability of such product-quality standards by establishing highly detailed controls over the marketing of agricultural commodities. It makes a government license mandatory for any "warehouseman" who engages in storage of agricultural products, empowering the government to inspect such warehouses at will and to dictate the characteristics of a warehouse "*suitable* for the *proper* storage of any agricultural product."[78] Even a licensed warehouseman remains fully at the mercy of government officials, for the Secretary of Agriculture is authorized to prescribe the duties of warehousemen,[79] to revoke a license if the warehouseman charges for his services any fee that the government deems "unreasonable or exorbitant,"[80] to compel a warehouseman to maintain records and submit reports "in such form and at such times as he [the Secretary of Agriculture] may require,"[81] and to prevent a warehouseman from selecting the customers with whom he chooses to do business.[82] A provision euphemistically captioned "Discrimination by warehouseman prohibited" compels every warehouseman to accept all agricultural products of the type he normally stores "without making any discrimination between persons desiring to avail themselves of warehouse facilities."[83] In the familiar fascist economic pattern, such businesses retain nominal private ownership, but all vital control rests in the hands of the government.

The Warehouse Act also authorizes the government to classify, grade, and weigh all agricultural products. Not allowing the slightest lever of economic control to evade the government's grasp, the legislation establishes federal power to license persons authorized to perform official classification and grading of agricultural products.[84] Official inspection and grading of all fungible agricultural products is mandated by the statute, and the government is empowered to examine at will agricultural products stored in licensed warehouses.[85]

The power to compel official government grading of fungible agricultural products is augmented by broader but less enforceable authority to establish both quality standards and grading systems for all agricultural products under the Agricultural Marketing Act of 1946. This statute empowers the government "to develop and improve standards of quality, condition, quantity, grade, and packaging, and recommend and demonstrate such standards in order to encourage uniformity and consistency in commercial practices."[86] The products subject to this provision include not only those conventionally regarded as agricultural, but also horticultural, viticultural, and dairy products, livestock, poultry, bees, forest products, fish and shellfish, as well as all products derived from these commodities, including manufactured and processed products.[87] To implement the government's power to create such quality standards, the Agricultural Marketing Act authorizes the Secretary of Agriculture to "inspect, certify, and identify the class, quality, quantity, and condition" of the foregoing products.[88] However, unlike the mandatory inspection and classification of fungible agricultural products compelled by the United States Warehouse Act, this more general power to inspect all agricultural commodities depends

131

upon the consent of the person in legal possession of the product, for the Agricultural Marketing Act expressly states that no one can be required to use the government's inspection or certification services.[89]

Nevertheless, even nonmandatory quality standards may have a profound influence on consumers' purchases and consequently on the economic fortunes of industries subject to the standards. First, "voluntary" standards tend to become compulsory in practice, for if some firms accede to government grading standards or inspection, competition will force other firms to capitulate to the standards also. Submission by some producers thus encourages submission by an entire industry because trusting consumers cannot help but be swayed by subjective statements that certain products have been highly rated by the government, regardless of the merits of the objective criteria that formed the basis for the rating.

Another aspect of the problem is that government quality standards or grading schemes usually employ subjective terminology, evaluating products in terms which express government officials' judgment about the desirability of a product, without any indication of the objective basis for that appraisal. A classic example is beef, which traditionally has been judged by the government according to fat content. The more fat marbled in red meat, the higher the government's rating. However, instead of informing the consumer about objective differences among beef that the government has inspected and rated, government-approved labeling merely tells the consumer that the beef is "choice," "prime," or only "good." A purchaser with the economic resources to afford any cut he preferred would tend to select "choice" over "good" cuts on the assumption that the meat was somehow better, inadvertently rewarding producers of grain-fed beef and discouraging production of grass-fed beef. However, if informed that the "choice" cut was just fattier, that same consumer, perhaps concerned about his longevity and cholesterol (triglyceride) level, might prefer meat judged inferior according to the government's unspoken criteria. To the extent that consumers' purchases are thus swayed by nonobjective government ratings, even "voluntary" product standards enable government officials effectively to impose their personal preferences upon unwitting purchasers.

II. INSPECTION LAWS

The quality-control laws designed to function primarily as inspection laws — the Poultry Products Inspection Act, the Federal Meat Inspection Act, and the Egg Products Inspection Act — are almost identical in the phraseology as well as the substance of many of their provisions. Therefore, these three statutes will be discussed in unison, with digressions into individual statutes provided to illustrate unique features.

Similar to federal regulations that permit only the manufacture of products that conform to specifications deemed "proper" by government officials—thereby precluding consumers from voluntarily choosing the level of quality and price they prefer—federal inspection laws compel consumers to pay for the level of *sanitation* that appeals to the social or esthetic sensibilities of lawmakers and government bureaucrats. For example, if the government orders meat processors to acquire elaborate modern equipment in the name of sanitation, the cost of that equipment will be reflected in the price of meat products, and no competitor is permitted to offer the consumer cheaper meat produced with less expensive machinery. The same analysis applies to any cost that producers are forced to assume by federal law.

The authors of the inspection legislation explicitly acknowledge that the laws are designed to prevent competition from less expensive products—that is, to forbid consumers access to cheaper goods. The laws' drafters preface each statute with a lengthy recitation of almost identical "congressional findings" designed to dissipate opposition by assuring citizens that an omniscient government knows what is best for them, and that the rules which follow, however harsh, are "essential, in the public interest," to protect the "health and welfare of consumers" and to ensure that poultry products, meat and meat-food products, and eggs and egg products "are wholesome, otherwise not adulterated, and properly labeled and packaged."[90] Unconcerned that these prefatory remarks become somewhat hackneyed upon the third recitation of the legislative formula, each statute proceeds to state:

> Unwholesome, adulterated, or misbranded [poultry products] [meat or meat-food products] [egg products] . . . *destroy markets* for wholesome, not adulterated, and properly labeled and packaged [poultry products] [meat and meat-food products] [eggs and egg products]. . . .[91]

This is an open admission that, given freedom of choice, consumers might not value the product attributes the government says they should, and might choose less expensive products than bureaucrats deem good for them. Further recognizing that the fundamental issue is freedom to weigh price against quality, the Federal Meat Inspection Act and the Egg Products Inspection Act add that the "unwholesome" products, alleged to exist absent government regulation, "can be sold at *lower prices* and *compete unfairly*" with the "wholesome" products which the government will henceforth require citizens to purchase.[92] There follows an explicit assertion that *all* meat, egg, and poultry products, including products produced and consumed entirely within a single state, somehow "substantially affect" interstate commerce and therefore will be subjected to the ubiquitous decrees of the federal government.[93] Behind the flowery, politically expedient phrases, the fundamental message of the thrice repeated "congressional findings" is that the government will henceforth determine the inspection, sanitation, and equipment it deems "appropriate" and "proper" for egg, meat, and poultry product producers, while taxpayers and consumers of those products are forced to finance the venture.

The inspection requirements vary somewhat among the three statutes. The Egg Products Inspection Act requires the Secretary of Agriculture to conduct "continuous inspection" of the processing of egg products, plus any other inspections of the operations of a broad category of persons labeled "egg handlers" as the Secretary "deems appropriate."[94] Under provisions of the Federal Meat Inspection Act, the Secretary of Agriculture must inspect cattle, sheep, swine, and other animals both before and after their slaughter, in addition to examining all meat-food products prepared by meat-producing businesses.[95] The Poultry Products Inspection Act requires postmortem inspection of every bird slaughtered, but gives the Secretary of Agriculture total discretion to conduct antemortem examinations only "where and to the extent considered by him necessary."[96]

In conducting these inspections, the statutory purpose assigned to the Secretary of Agriculture is to prohibit the manufacture and distribution of "adulterated" or "misbranded" products. Although it sounds appealing to oppose the sale of "adulterated" goods, each of the three statutes makes the definition of "adulterated" totally dependent upon the potentially arbitrary edicts of the government. In language almost identical to the Federal Food, Drug and Cosmetic Act, each inspection act defines "adulterated" as meaning any product that "consists in whole or in part of any *filthy, putrid, or decomposed* substance or is for any other reason *unsound, unhealthful, unwholesome,* or otherwise *unfit* for human food."[97] Since all the crucial terms in this statement are subjective in nature and remain undefined by the statutes, this "definition" of adulteration is little more than a series of vituperative epithets that empower the Secretary of Agriculture to ban at will any meat, egg, or poultry product not suiting the government's fancy.

Wholesale discretionary power again is vested in the government by a provision allowing the Secretary of Agriculture to outlaw any meat, egg, or poultry product that "has been . . . held under insanitary conditions whereby it may have become contaminated with filth, or whereby it may have been rendered injurious to health."[98] Products may also be forbidden if they contain any substance the Secretary of Agriculture chooses to call "poisonous or deleterious," although the government can promote the distribution of such products simply by alleging that the quantity of the poison involved "does not ordinarily render it [the product] injurious to health."[93]

To implement its inspection power, the government has secured a tight grip on the day-to-day business operations of egg, poultry, and meat producers. Poultry- and meat-product processors and distributors must register their businesses with the government.[100] Manufacturers and distributors of egg, poultry, and meat products must produce for government scrutiny whatever business records the government orders them to maintain.[101] The government has statutory authority forcibly to prevent these businesses from receiving *any* material the government chooses to blockade, for the inspection statutes empower the Secretary of Agriculture to "limit the entry into any establishment at which inspection under this subchapter is maintained" not only of egg, meat, and poultry products, but also of "other materials . . . under such conditions as he may prescribe."[102]

The government is also authorized to compel the regulated businesses to adopt any sanitary procedures and to purchase any equipment the government sees fit to require.[103] The most explicit statutory provision, repeated almost verbatim in the Poultry Products Inspection Act and the Federal Meat Inspection Act, declares: "Each official plant shall be operated in accordance with *such sanitary practices* and shall have *such premises, facilities and equipment* as are required by regulations promulgated by the Secretary . . . ."[104] In that terse sentence, the government claims unlimited power to coerce target businesses to purchase — and to compel consumers of egg, poultry, and meat products to pay for — whatever equipment or procedures appeal to government bureaucrats who have neither the incentive nor the training to devise optimum economic solutions to technical business problems.

As if to convince even the most devout advocates of government inspection laws that these statutes primarily seek government control over the regulated industries rather than public health and safety, the inspection legislation contains numerous exemption provisions that make it clear that its avowed concern about health and safety is only incidental. For example, the Poultry Products Inspection Act gives the Secretary of Agriculture unlimited authority to exempt from the law's provisions any small enterprise conducting intrastate operations that involve not more than 20,000 chickens or 5,000 turkeys.[105] Similarly, the sale of eggs by a producer with an annual egg production from a flock of no more than 3,000 hens may be exempted from government regulation under the Egg Products Inspection Act.[106] If public health and safety were the government's prime concern, and if lawmakers actually believed that the regulations created by the statutes were vital to preserve the public's physical welfare, there would be no logical reason to exclude such enterprises from federal control. Further illustrating the fact that economic control rather than public safety is the government's aim, the inspection laws all state that the Secretary of Agriculture need not prosecute known violations of the law if he does not feel like doing so. By the simple expedient of declaring the violation "minor" and asserting his action to be in the "public interest," the Secretary can avoid prosecuting favored businesses that wield political influence with the government.[107]

One final observation is necessary. Throughout the inspection statutes are scattered seemingly incongruous provisions empowering the government to restrict consumers' access to products that, although less expensive to purchase, in no way threaten public health. For example, the Egg Products Inspection Act allows the government to prevent producers from selling and consumers from buying *dirty* eggs in excess of the "tolerance" for dirty eggs established by the government, although it is hard to imagine a public health rationale for limiting the sale of unbroken eggs with dirt on their shells.[108] Similarly, the government can require meat products derived from horses to be prepared at business establishments that are physically separate from places where cattle, sheep, swine, and goats are processed.[109] While protection of the public from the spread of trichina might suggest the segregation of pork-processing operations from other meat production, this precaution is not required, and the statute advances no rationale for isolating horse-meat processing. The desire of beef, lamb, and pork producers to curtail competition from horse meat seems a more plausible explanation for the restriction than concern about public health.

If legislators thus openly enact legal rules whose predominant purpose is to protect established industries from the competition of producers who might otherwise supply the public with cheaper and equally wholesome products, one can only surmise the extent of political protection of vested economic interests that is veiled by the discretionary powers conferred on government officials by the noble-sounding phraseology of more discreet statutory provisions.

III. COMPULSORY LABELING

Many people initially would endorse the proposition that it is desirable for the government to compel businesses to label their products so as to avoid false and misleading representations to consumers. The proposition sounds reasonable because it condemns the root concept of fraud, and people rightly abhor nominally "voluntary" economic transactions that are in fact coercively induced by a seller's fraudulent claims.

However, serious problems flow from giving the government unlimited power to create and enforce labeling standards in the manner of existing United States laws. Instead of protecting consumers, the laws may serve primarily to protect industries that are encouraged by flexible statutes to direct their efforts toward befriending government officials rather than satisfying consumers' preferences. The major problems implicit in such legislation are: (1) government preference in matters of labeling replaces consumer influence on such business decisions, causing businesses to look to the government rather than to the market to determine appropriate labeling for their products; (2) government approval of labeling instills in the public an automatic sense of security, which may or may not be warranted depending on the basis for the government's decisions; and (3) vague statutory terminology coupled with broad powers to exempt favored firms invites use of labeling laws to harass politically uncooperative businesses, while rewarding with more lenient treatment firms that prudently nurture the government's political goals.

The primary statute that deals exclusively with consumer product labeling is the Fair Packaging and Labeling Act.[110] After prescribing certain relatively objective labeling requirements such as mandatory specification of net quantity of contents,[111] the statute sets forth discretionary and highly subjective decision-making powers of the government as to product labeling. Most significantly, the government is empowered to exempt a consumer commodity from the objective requirements of the law whenever the government has "good and sufficient reasons" for thinking that "full compliance with all the requirements otherwise applicable . . . is *impracticable* or is *not necessary* for the adequate protection of consumers."[112] Such is the sweet plum that can be served to politically attentive enterprises. However, the government also is given a powerful lever to bring recalcitrant firms into line, for the statute authorizes the government to impose certain additional packaging and labeling requirements whenever it declares such requirements "necessary to prevent the deception of consumers or to facilitate value comparisons."[113]

As the Fair Packaging and Labeling Act implicitly recognizes, these discretionary powers are vital to the government in maintaining that facade of harmony so crucial to any fascist scheme of private "ownership" of property coupled with collective control. After enumerating the government's discretionary powers over the regulated businesses, the law immediately suggests that product manufacturers, at the "request" of the government, develop "*voluntary* product standards" that will avoid any unpleasant overtones of coercion.[114] Further, in the familiar pattern of fascist co-optation of potentially dissident interests, the statute urges "adequate" representation of manufacturer, packer, distributor, and consumer interests in the development of these "voluntary" weight, measure, and quality standards.[115] And if businessmen fail to heed the government's request for "voluntary" action either by not developing standards or not abiding by them, the Secretary of Commerce is authorized to recommend to Congress appropriate legislation to deal with the intractable industry.[116]

Although food (except meat and poultry), cosmetics, and most drugs are subject to the Fair Packaging and Labeling Act, the labeling of these products also is regulated by the Federal Food, Drug and Cosmetic Act. The broad mandate of the Food, Drug and Cosmetic Act empowers the government to forbid the distribution of any product deemed "misbranded" because its labeling is said to be "false or misleading in any particular,"[117] an unavoidably subjective determination which gives the government comfortable flexibility to promote selective enforcement of the law. Similarly, a food, drug, or cosmetic may be deemed "misbranded" if the government asserts that its container is "so made, formed, or filled as to be misleading."[118] The government also may outlaw a product unless its labeling is located and expressed "with such conspicuousness . . . and in such terms as to render it likely to be read and understood by the ordinary individual under customary conditions of purchase and use."[119] Underscoring the discretionary nature of the government's power, most of the other specific labeling requirements – including the requirements (1) that foods not subject to federal standards of identity bear the usual or common name of the product's ingredients; (2) that food products containing artificial flavoring, artificial coloring, or chemical preservatives reveal that fact; and (3) that drugs bear the established names and quantities of certain active ingredients—may be *waived* by the government on the Secretary's mere assertion that an exemption is necessary because "compliance . . . is impracticable."[120] Comparably broad governmental powers to dictate mandatory labeling requirements for pesticides, poultry products, meat products, and egg products are established by the Federal Environmental Pesticide Control Act,[121] the Poultry Products Inspection Act,[122] the Federal Meat Inspection Act,[123] and the Egg Products Inspection Act.[124]

All these laws – product-quality laws, inspection laws, and labeling statutes alike – embody the fundamental premise of a fascist economic system, capitalistic collectivism, which exacts government control as the price for retention of "private" property. As these laws illustrate, that system is predominantly collectivist, cultivating capitalism only to the extent deemed necessary to carry out the government's social and economic policies. Underlying America's myriad product-quality laws, the tripartite theme of fascist economics reverberates unchallenged, asserting (1) government power to dictate the framework within which businesses are permitted to operate; (2) government power to substitute its preferences in matters of product quality for voluntary choices of individuals; and (3) government power to compel consumers and taxpayers to pay for the product-quality level imposed by government officials. The common denominator implicit in the legislation is unconstrained government power to limit economic freedom.

6

Stretching the President's Economic Power

This chapter deals with those direct powers over the *domestic* economy held exclusively and explicitly by the President, omitting any reference to the President's immense power to influence decision-making
by the other government entities whose broad authority is described
elsewhere in this book. Thus the President's ability to force the regulatory agencies to do his bidding is not examined here (see Chapters 4 and
5), nor is his power to control imports and exports (see Chapter 9).
Rather, this chapter analyzes the economic powers wielded by the
President in issuing executive orders and implementing the Economic
Stabilization Act of 1970.

Liberal use of executive orders has vastly increased the scope of
presidential power over the domestic economy. Although chief executives once acted unilaterally in using executive orders to stretch the
bounds of their powers, Congress is now an active accomplice in expanding the President's power to rule the American economy by executive decree. Gradual expansion of the scope of these decrees coupled
with steady attrition of viable judicial and congressional resistance to
aggrandizement of the presidency culminated in Congress' explicit imposition of one-man economic rule through the Economic Stabilization
Act of 1970, which gave the President unlimited power to issue execu-

tive orders to control all wages and prices in the United States. The engrossing story of how the United States moved from presidential use of executive orders as an instrument for resolving only minor administrative matters to congressional and presidential cooperation in making executive orders a vehicle of total presidential control over the domestic economy absorbs our attention in this chapter. Now, whenever an aggressive President and an acquiescent or actively cooperative legislature join forces, the President may override the uncoerced market choices of individuals and dictate wages and prices that suit the government's fancy. As in any fascist state, wages and prices are determined by market forces only until a disgruntled government chooses to establish them by fiat.

I. EXECUTIVE ORDERS

An executive order is simply a written command issued by the President directing a subordinate government official to take specified actions or implement designated policies. Although the Constitution does not mention executive orders, the courts have attributed to them the force of public law. Nevertheless, it was not until the 1935 enactment of the Federal Register Act that formal publication of executive orders in the Federal Register was made prerequisite to their legal effectiveness.[1]

PRESIDENTIAL LEGISLATION THROUGH EXECUTIVE ORDERS: THE HISTORICAL EVOLUTION

Although the courts originally approved of executive orders merely as vital *administrative* tools of the executive branch, modern use of executive orders to accomplish purely *legislative* goals of the President has immeasurably magnified their power and significance.[2] Executive orders were originally issued for such relatively innocuous and uncontroversial purposes as withdrawal of public lands to establish military and Indian reservations, construction of lighthouses, and management of public mineral reserves.[3] The gradual transformation of executive orders from routine administrative tools to predominantly legislative instruments was initiated by President Lincoln (who used executive orders and presidential proclamations to suspend the writ of habeas corpus during the Civil War[4] and to free the slaves) and furthered by Theodore Roosevelt's extensive withdrawal of public lands for national park purposes.

Use of executive orders to manipulate the nation's economy was inaugurated during World War I by presidential creation of such agencies as the War Trade Board, the Grain Corporation, and the Food Administration. Franklin D. Roosevelt enhanced this trend by his unprecedented peacetime use of executive orders to enact economic measures during the depression. (FDR still holds the record for executive orders issued during a single year: 654 in 1933, a time when executive orders were not even required to be published.)[5] Although President Truman was rebuffed by the Supreme Court in his attempt to seize the nation's steel mills via executive order,[6] his frustrated attempt to some degree augmented the scope of the executive order, for despite its use of strong language restricting executive power in overturning Truman's order, the Court relied heavily on the fact that such governmental seizure had been explicitly rejected by Congress.[7]

Use of executive orders for essentially legislative purposes culminated in several presidential civil rights orders issued with only the most tenuous statutory authority. The early executive orders required inclusion of a nondiscrimination clause in government defense contracts,[8] a requirement later extended to cover *all* government contracts as well as nongovernment contracts involving federal financial assistance.[9] Subsequent executive orders required government officials to *enforce* the boilerplate guarantee of nondiscrimination routinely included in government contracts.[10] Finally, President Kennedy used an executive order to compel the federal bureaucracy to prevent discrimination on the basis of race, color, creed, or national origin in any sale, lease, or rental of residential property wholly or partially financed by loans made or guaranteed by the federal government, on penalty of cancellation of the contract involved or withdrawal of future federal financial support, or both.[11] Such "presidential legislation" is far removed from the routine administrative functions originally served by the executive order.

SOURCES OF LEGAL AUTHORITY TO ISSUE EXECUTIVE ORDERS

Most of the executive orders mentioned above lacked a substantial statutory basis. Unable to claim that Congress had sanctioned executive action for the purposes served by the executive order, these Presidents had to rely upon their constitutional power as Chief Executive, for the only two sources of authority for executive orders are *statutory* authority delegated to the President by Congress, and *constitutional* authority granted by Article II of the U.S. Constitution. The President possesses his greatest power to issue executive orders when he acts pursuant to statutory authorization, for he then can invoke all his constitutional authority as well as the statutory delegation as justification.[12] Such executive orders in fact are almost never challenged, for the chances of convincing a court to overturn an executive order authorized by statute are minuscule.

Constitutional power constitutes a more nebulous basis for executive orders. If the executive order implements a specific power conferred on the President by the Constitution, such as his power as Commander in Chief of the armed forces, presidential power to issue executive orders is broadly construed by the courts and therefore seldom contested. Thus, where the President can plausibly declare that his order emanates from his constitutional power as Commander in Chief or from his power in the realm of international relations, the courts have recognized truly plenary authority to issue orders, however tenuously the executive orders are connected to the constitutionally granted power.[13]

Historically, the constitutional dispute has centered on the assertion of presidential authority to issue executive orders based upon a generalized executive power independent of the specific functions assigned to the President by the Constitution. The problem has arisen because of imprecision in drafting the Constitution, which vests the "executive power" of the United States in the President[14] and then assigns specific functions to the President without explaining whether the "executive power" was intended to comprise more than the specific functions subsequently enumerated. Despite this constitutional ambiguity, the clear tenor of judicial decisions has been to approve the exercise of some generalized executive authority beyond the limited presidential tasks specified by the Constitution. For example, the Supreme Court has validated unrestrained use of executive orders to remove subordinate government officials from federal agencies where Congress has not enumerated statutory grounds for their removal,[15] and also has established the constitutionality of presidential appointment of marshals to protect federal judges via executive order,[16] although neither of these functions can be implied from the specific presidential powers granted by the Constitution. Nevertheless, courts have not adopted the extreme position explicitly recognizing "inherent" or "aggregate" presidential powers advocated by those who desire to rule or be ruled by divine inspiration unchecked by constitutional limits. In the rare case where Congress fears that the courts might hold the President to have exceeded the bounds of his generalized executive authority, Congress has the power to ratify a questionable executive order, causing it to possess the same legal status as if it had been authorized by statute when issued.

THEORIES OF THE SCOPE OF PRESIDENTIAL POWER TO ISSUE EXECUTIVE ORDERS

Presidents have advanced three theories of the proper scope of their power to formulate executive orders: the constitutional theory, the stewardship theory, and the prerogative theory.[17] These theories are really presidential counterparts to the constitutional debate over specific versus generalized executive powers.

The constitutional theory holds that the President can issue executive orders only to implement the express powers granted to him by the Constitution and such implied powers as can clearly be derived therefrom. The stewardship theory maintains that the President, as supervisor of the nation, is constitutionally empowered to issue executive orders whenever he perceives a national need urgently requiring such action, unless his action is specifically forbidden by the Constitution or statutes of the United States. The prerogative theory asserts that the President embodies the nation's welfare and has the prerogative to act via executive order to secure the public good whenever he deems it to be in the national interest, *even if Congress has passed legislation that conflicts with the executive order.*

The constitutional theory envisions narrowly circumscribed executive powers characteristic of a limited government possessing only specifically delegated powers. A governmental model reflecting the stewardship theory resembles a constitutional monarchy, a chief executive whose otherwise unlimited powers are constrained only by explicit constitutional and statutory prohibitions. The prerogative theory is the philosophy of the dictator-king, the omnipotent ruler unrestrained by written law, responsive only to his own omniscient wisdom in creating a suitable society for subjects whose capacity for self-determination he disdains.

While the courts have not embraced the prerogative theory, they have emphatically rejected the constitutional theory by approving the use of executive orders for purposes that cannot be derived from specific constitutional grants of presidential authority. Judicial opinion seems to favor the stewardship theory, for the only limit on the scope of the executive order consistently recognized is contrary congressional legislation. Even Truman's attempted seizure of the steel mills, an executive order which could only be justified by asserting presidential "prerogative" to act in the national interest, was condemned by the courts as much because Congress had considered and rejected that means of dealing with economic crises when it enacted the Taft-Hartley Act as because it exceeded the constitutional bounds of executive power. One may validly question whether such an executive order would have been held to exceed presidential power had Congress *not* expressed a contrary view on the subject.

LEGAL BIAS FAVORING EXECUTIVE ORDERS

Absent conflict with an act or policy of Congress, courts are predisposed to validate presidential legislation via executive order. The courts have created a legal presumption that the President acts lawfully in promulgating executive orders,[18] thereby placing the burden of proof upon the party who challenges the constitutionality of the executive order. Further, executive orders are practically unassailable if based upon either statutory authority or a specific constitutional power of the President. In these situations, the President is invulnerable and can exercise virtually unrestrained "prerogative" power over the nation. For example, because of the specific constitutional grant of power, the courts allow the President unlimited authority as Commander in Chief, a power so broad as to encompass and validate Franklin D. Roosevelt's executive orders compelling the confinement of Japanese Americans in "relocation" camps during World War II.[19] Moreover, although constitutional authority to control foreign relations is shared by Congress and the President, the courts have accorded the President plenary power to conduct foreign relations.[20]

The vast significance of statutory delegation of power to the Chief Executive becomes clear when one recalls the unlimited reach of Congress' power over local economic activity discussed in Chapter 2's analysis of the Interstate Commerce Clause. Since the courts have given Congress absolute power to regulate wholly intrastate economic activity, Congress can delegate this comprehensive power to the President and thereby confer upon a single man the power to use executive orders to dictate economic policies and regulations designed to control every detail of what is still anachronistically referred to as a free market economy. Such an unlimited delegation of total economic power is exactly what Congress accomplished by the Economic Stabilization Act of 1970, which will be discussed in detail in the next section.

A final doctrinal coup for those who favor expansion of one-man rule in America has been the recurrent judicial thesis that long-standing presidential action coupled with congressional acquiescence creates a valid presidential power. Thus if the President, without statutory or specific constitutional authority, issues executive orders regulating novel areas never deemed subject to presidential decree, and Congress neglects to take action over a period of time challenging or altering such executive edicts, the courts are apt to conclude that Congress has "acquiesced" in ceding additional power to the President. In *United States* v. *Midwest Oil Co.*, for example, the Supreme Court in 1915 invoked this rationale in upholding presidential power to use executive orders to withdraw federal lands whose sale had been authorized by act of Congress. The Court stated that prior judicial decisions "clearly indicate that the *long-continued practice, known to and acquiesced in by Congress*, would raise a presumption that the withdrawals had been made in pursuance of its consent or of a recognized administrative power of the Executive in the management of public lands."[21]

In 1971, a federal Court of Appeals considering the validity of the "Philadelphia Plan" (which established target percentages of minority employees in six skilled crafts for Philadelphia area contractors on projects receiving any federal financial support) used similar reasoning in upholding the executive order pursuant to which the Secretary of Labor issued the Philadelphia Plan.[22] The executive order required "affirmative action" to eliminate discrimination in employment due to race, color, religion, sex, or national origin by construction contractors on projects receiving any federal funds.[23] Relying heavily on its version of the congressional acquiescence theory, the court stated:

> If no congressional enactments prohibit what has been done, the Executive action is valid. Particularly is this so when Congress, aware of Presidential action with respect to federally assisted construction projects since June of 1963, has continued to make appropriations for such projects. We conclude, therefore, that unless the Philadelphia Plan is prohibited by some other congressional enactment, its inclusion as a pre-condition for federal assistance was within the implied authority of the President and his designees.[24]

This rationale effectively shifts the burden of restraining executive excesses from the courts to the Congress, giving constitutional sanction to whatever power an aggressive President can wrest from an inattentive or disunited legislature.

The courts have not imbued the presidency with a royal prerogative; they have not approved of "inherent" or "aggregate" executive powers. They have had no need to do so. The scope of presidential control via executive orders has been radically expanded without recourse to such doctrines. The combination of myriad innocuous-sounding judicial presumptions—that the President acts lawfully, that congressional acquiescence validates the exercise of presidential power, that a presidential claim that an executive order emanates from specific constitutional or statutory authority is valid—and a vast increase in delegable congressional powers adds up to a profound judicial reluctance to interfere with presidential power to use executive orders for the President's own social and legislative purposes.

With little fear of judicial opposition, an aggressive President who wishes to rule by executive decree can effectively do so through executive orders; his only viable adversary is a united Congress that actively opposes him by passing legislation specifically prohibiting the presidential policies effected through executive orders. Absent such con-

146

gressional opposition, the Chief Executive can occupy a power vacuum created by a passive judiciary, which normally is provoked by only the most extreme presidential usurpation of legislative authority. And if Congress *shares* the President's goals and actively desires that he use executive orders to implement the full range of power it is constitutionally capable of conferring upon him, virtually limitless power can be exercised by the Chief Executive. We now turn to an example of just such a cooperative venture by Congress and the President, a venture which effectively established one-man rule over the entire domestic economy of the United States.

II. THE ECONOMIC STABILIZATION ACT OF 1970

Traditionally, the United States has vehemently rejected centralized governmental (political) control over ordinary market transactions. Except in wartime, prices charged for commodities and salaries paid employees have been established by market forces, reflecting supply of and demand for goods and services. Regardless of the rhetoric employed to obfuscate the issue, this basic principle of American economic life has been abandoned.

One of the major statutes that explicitly asserted the government's legal right to control the economy was the Economic Stabilization Act of 1970.[25] From 1970 until 1974, this law gave the federal government unlimited authority to fix all wages and prices in the United States. Although Congress allowed the statute to expire in April 1974, the Economic Stabilization Act merits extensive consideration, for the Act was abolished not on philosophical or constitutional grounds as an unwarranted governmental intrusion into the realm of private economic activity, but for the pragmatic reason that most congressmen believed the law ineffective in practice.

As the law approached its expiration date, myriad schemes were proposed to retain federal economic control in some more limited way for the avowed purpose of curtailing inflation. Many sought continuation of overt wage-price controls over the petroleum and health-care industries, desiring to maintain "standby" federal power to reimpose wage-price controls on any other industry whose wage-price structure subsequently was labeled "inflationary" by political appointees. Congress, the executive branch, and the country were not averse to the continuation of economic controls on the scale authorized by the Economic Stabilization Act, if only the controls would *work*. In this atmosphere, the Economic Stabilization Act lapsed into legal oblivion. In its place, a Council on Wage and Price Stability was established, with broad authority to monitor and cajole labor and industry but without power to force compliance with its wage and price "recommendations."[26] Nevertheless, in response to the public's increasing perception of inflation's inequities, influential congressmen continue to propose reimposition of wage-price controls.

The Economic Stabilization Act of 1970 accustomed the country to unlimited federal control over the most minute details of economic activity, and future adoption of similar statutes can be expected whenever economic discontent makes renewed controls politically acceptable. The Economic Stabilization Act deserves serious study both as a likely pattern for future economic controls and as a model of fascism's rejection of private economic decision-making whenever it is deemed politically expedient and economically desirable in the "national interest."

ECONOMIC CONSEQUENCES OF WAGE-PRICE CONTROLS[27]

Whenever it suppresses wage and price increases stimulated by market conditions, the government destroys the crucial incentive for production. That incentive is profit. To everyone's benefit, people produce things in a free market because they forecast a public demand for the commodity to be produced, anticipating a profit if they produce goods that satisfy that latent consumer desire. Absent government controls, the more intense the unsatisfied consumer demand, the higher the profit a prospective producer can anticipate and, consequently, the greater the potential financial rewards silently coaxing him to produce that which consumers would like to purchase. In a free market, high profits attract additional investment and consequently stimulate more production of the commodity, thus increasing the supply and ultimately reducing the product's price.

When the government intervenes by telling producers that they cannot charge more than a certain price, the incentive to anticipate and satisfy consumers' economic desires is stifled, the magnitude of the inhibitory effect fluctuating with the severity of the government-imposed restrictions. Existing producers will not expand their production, nor will new producers invest their time and capital if the government makes it unprofitable or excessively risky to do so. Thus if prices are throttled, shortages will usually occur. The government simply prevents consumers from signaling their desires to producers by means of the prices they are willing to pay. Businesses become unprofitable. Products become "scarce." Regardless of their affluence, consumers can no longer purchase the products they desire. By indirect action, the government effectively forces citizens to do without products that the market normally would supply.

148

Ironically, it is not only actual price restrictions that curtail production. The mere threat of government price controls is often sufficient to repress production. Prospective producers may be unwilling to assume the risks inherent in a new business venture if the government has asserted unlimited power to intervene at will and control the prices that determine the profitability of the business. When success depends on the whims of politically oriented government bureaucrats rather than on entrepreneurial ability to forecast and satisfy consumer demand, many potential producers will seek other, more predictable economic endeavors.

Government price controls cause shortages for other reasons as well. First, if domestic prices are suppressed while prices offered by foreign countries for U.S. goods are free to reflect market demand, American firms will simply choose to export their products to other countries where they can make a greater profit, magnifying domestic shortages. It is utterly inhumane to suggest restricting exports as a solution to this aspect of the shortage problem caused by price controls, for by implicitly embracing a policy of autarky (national economic self-sufficiency), such a "cure" portends a disastrous plummeting of both America's and the world's standard of living (see Chapter 9).

Further, at any artificially low price dictated by the government, there will be more demand for a product than would exist in a free market. Even if the bureaucracy avoided inconsistency and favoritism in its rulings and uniformly held prices to the exact level existing on the first day of the controls, some of the government-enforced prices would become artificially low relative to demand as soon as consumers' economic preferences and priorities shifted. If a product's price is held below the level that accurately reflects demand, more people will be willing to purchase the product than would desire to purchase it at the price that would prevail without government suppression of the price mechanism. Shortages once again emerge.

Simultaneously, the government's inflationary monetary policies actively increase consumer demand relative to supply, thereby intensifying shortages of goods and services. It must be remembered that the initial provocation for wage-price controls is inflation, the increase in the general level of prices caused primarily by the government's willful expansion of the money supply, especially credit in the form of demand deposits (see Chapter 3). The throttling of wages and prices is designed to conceal the fact that the government's bloating of the money supply is driving prices up and making each dollar worth less as ever more dollars exist relative to the quantity of goods available for purchase.

The catch is that even with wage-price controls, the government continues to inflate the money supply. Because of the actions of the Federal Reserve system, people are able to acquire more and more money in the form of bank loans, credit which did not previously exist (see Chapter 3). Possessing more money, people are eager to spend it, and their demand for products increases accordingly. But prices are simultaneously suppressed by government fiat. People can no longer acquire the goods they want simply by offering to pay the producers more, thereby demonstrating their need and desire for the product in an objective way. Similarly, the seller cannot determine objectively who wants the product most among his overabundant prospective customers. Nor can he increase his production, for if he produces more his costs usually will increase, and the government will not allow him to increase his price to reflect his increased costs.

Therefore—given (1) the same amount of goods to sell, (2) more customers (demand) than salable products (supply) at the existing price level, and (3) government-coerced inability to raise the price in order to select one's customers by the objective criterion of willingness to pay—the merchant must select his customers according to criteria other than the price they are willing to pay. The rationing function of prices is destroyed. This means that the government forces a seller to give rein to personal, subjective, arbitrary judgments in deciding to whom he wishes to sell his product. No longer encouraged by a free market to overlook customers' personal characteristics so long as they are willing to pay the price he asks for his product, a producer now may select his customers on the basis of their power, prestige, race, religion, physical attractiveness, or any other whim or idiosyncrasy dear to the merchant's heart. When the government prevents goods from being allocated to customers by the impartial price mechanism, it is this type of nonmarket, subjective rationing (which economists call nonprice discrimination) that follows in the wake of wage-price controls, originally touted as heralding the economic salvation of the masses.

Government price controls thus create shortages both by discouraging and diverting supply, and by artificially stimulating demand. But the economic consequences of price controls do not consist solely of shortages and the concomitant nonprice (yet still private) allocation of the now diminished supply of goods. It is a two-step process. When the inevitable shortages emerge, public dismay at the seemingly inexplicable dearth of goods usually becomes channeled into cries for government rationing of the "scarce" commodities. To the great delight of those seeking a totally controlled economy, the public clamors for a government takeover of the "allocation" or distribution of the dwindling output of the country's suppressed productive capacity. By some elusive "logic," this proposal prescribes more government control as the panacea for economic maladies caused by partial government economic control. If allowed to run its full course, the price control — shortage — rationing sequence can only lead to fewer goods distributed by government officials according to subjective criteria rather than by the impartial allocation of an unregulated market.

The function of prices (including wages, the price of labor) and profits as transmitters of market information and as crucial incentives for production have been known for decades. The hypocrisy of those economists and politicians frequently in the vanguard of those advocating wage-price controls is clearly evident, for it is only the general public, either untrained in economics or without access to reliable information, that is surprised by the consequences of such controls.

THE STATUTE

The Economic Stabilization Act of 1970 explicitly gave the government the power to control every aspect of what was originally a market economy. The Act conferred upon the President authority to:

> (1) stabilize prices, rents, wages, and salaries at levels not less than those prevailing on May 25, 1970, except that prices may be stabilized at levels below those prevailing on such date if it is necessary to eliminate windfall profits or if it is otherwise necessary to carry out the purposes of this title; and
>
> (2) stabilize interest rates and corporate dividends and similar transfers at levels consistent with orderly economic growth.[28]

The President was authorized to delegate his authority under the Economic Stabilization Act to such officers, departments, or agencies of the United States, as well as boards, commissions, or similar entities representing economic interests or the general public, as the President "deems appropriate."[29] The President possessed unlimited power to remove the officials he selected at his discretion, for the Economic Stabilization Act neither guaranteed his appointees any fixed term of office nor required that they be removed only for specified causes. The Act revealed no congressional effort to insulate the ultimate decision-makers from political influence; indeed, the legislation suggests that it was Congress' intent to guarantee political control over the decision-makers. Echoing the economic principles of previous fascist systems, the Economic Stabilization Act soberly identified *increased national productivity* as its aim and *labor-management "cooperation"* as the appropriate means to that end.[30]

One searches in vain for limits to the governmental power asserted in this Act. Of three possible statutory sources of restriction on this federal power—the overt *purposes* of the statute, *standards* imposed on the President by the Act, and *specific limitations* mandated by the statute itself—none effectively curtailed the massive federal powers established.

INDISCRIMINATE PURPOSES OF THE ECONOMIC STABLILIZATION ACT

The law contained congressional findings that sweeping presidential powers enabling "prompt judgments and actions by the executive branch of the Government" were necessary for the avowed purposes of (1) stabilizing the economy, (2) reducing inflation, (3) minimizing unemployment, (4) improving the nation's competitive position in world trade, and (5) protecting the purchasing power of the dollar.[31] Since the Act as originally passed contained no such statement of the controlling purposes of the legislation, one might expect that the above enumeration of purposes, contained in amendments to the Economic Stabilization Act, might constrain its application. That expectation is unjustified. The statute's stated purposes were no more than window dressing designed to create an illusion of limited executive authority. *Any* executive decree pertaining to the nation's economy falls within the supposedly restricted purposes of the statute, for the law's purposes are internally inconsistent and embrace diametrically opposite economic policies. Reducing inflation and minimizing unemployment constitute such inconsistent goals, for example; for any governmental action like deficit spending, which minimizes unemployment, is indisputably inflationary, while any federal refusal to increase the money supply will create unemployment so long as federal legislation prevents wage rates from fluctuating with market conditions. (That the government had no intention of repealing federal legislation preventing downward flexibility of wage rates is amply demonstrated by the explicit exemption of increased minimum wages under the Fair Labor Standards Act from the regulatory authority created by the Economic Stabilization Act.)[32]

Further, improving the nation's competitive position in world trade requires United States goods to be cheap relative to the goods of other countries, implying a United States dollar value that is low compared with the currencies of other nations. On the other hand, protecting the purchasing power of the dollar internationally demands high valuation of U.S. currency. Protecting the purchasing power of the dollar in the domestic economy is also inconsistent with inflationary policies justifiable under the statute's avowed purpose of minimizing unemployment. These internal inconsistencies are equivalent to saying that the President can issue decrees to further theism and to promote atheism, for the conflicting policies encompass the entire sphere of possible executive actions. As if to underscore the unlimited nature of the economic authority conferred, Congress stated that the Act's overriding purpose was "to stabilize the economy," a chameleonic policy whose vagueness comfortably embraced any economic purpose a political leader might choose to pursue.

SUPERFICIAL "STANDARDS" IMPOSED ON THE CHIEF EXECUTIVE BY THE ECONOMIC STABILIZATION ACT

Similarly, the "standards" imposed on the President by the Economic Stabilization Act in no way restrained executive action. The President repeatedly was directed to act in a manner consistent with "orderly economic growth."[33] A "standard" merits that label only insofar as it provides a guide for action, which means only to the extent that it functions to exclude certain actions from a range of possible activities. The term "orderly economic growth" does not qualify as a standard by this definition. While subtly suggesting the propriety of nonmarket control of economic policy, the concept of orderly economic growth is otherwise philosophically and politically neutral; that is, the phrase is broad enough to encompass opposite economic theories and philosophic tenets. Since fundamentally opposite economic convictions could justifiably be implemented under the aegis of orderly economic growth, it is clear that the phrase merely provides a pleasantly restrictive sound to what in reality constitutes a blank check authorizing unlimited federal economic power.

Moreover, although he could promulgate any regulations he "deem[ed] appropriate" to implement his authority under the Economic Stabilization Act, the President was directed to give *reasons* for the orders and regulations he issued.[34] While requiring reasons for executive decrees imbued the statute with an aura of conservatism, it did not limit presidential action; for by failing to identify permissible and impermissible reasons for executive orders, Congress stripped this superficial restriction of all substance.

The illusion of a circumscribed delegation of economic authority was further enhanced by the statute's enumeration of rules governing the President's formulation of standards to guide federal determination of wages and prices. The President was told that his edicts must be "generally fair and equitable," while providing for "such general exceptions and variations as are necessary to foster orderly economic growth and to prevent gross inequities, hardships, serious market disruptions . . . and windfall profits."[35] Presidential wage-price guidelines also had to "take into account changes in productivity and the cost of living, as well as such other factors consistent with the purposes of this title as are appropriate."[36] These rules, like the "orderly economic growth" slogan, did not exclude any executive action. The statute's mellifluous phrases did no more than somberly instruct the Chief Executive to do "whatever is right," leaving the propriety of presidential action to be determined by executive whim rather than objective constraints established by Congress.

The fluid subjectivity of terms like "gross inequities," "hardships," and "fair and equitable" is palpable, permitting a President to carry out his authority in any manner he deems appropriate and, cloaked in rectitude for the public's benefit, to label any wage-price guideline he promulgates as a fair and equitable implementation of the all-encompassing purposes of the legislation. The pretentious standards supposedly governing executive wage-price guidelines merely sugarcoated, for the public, the assertion of unlimited federal power over wages, prices, rents, corporate dividends, and interest rates. And it is abundantly clear that the public was the primary target of this felicitous language, for neither Congress nor the Chief Executive seemed to entertain any serious doubts about the unrestricted breadth of the claimed federal economic power. Congress did not even think it necessary to include any language purporting to restrain the President's authority in the originally enacted version of the Economic Stabilization Act. The flowery phraseology was apparently an afterthought, very likely designed more to placate public opinion and to dispel fears of constitutional challenges to a flagrantly unlimited delegation of legislative power, than effectively to restrict the range of executive action authorized.

THE FACADE OF STATUTORY LIMITS ON FEDERAL POWER ESTABLISHED BY THE ECONOMIC STABILIZATION ACT

Specific statutory limitations on the extent of the power conferred by the Economic Stabilization Act were as transparent as the statute's purposes and standards. The Act's few overt limits were replete with exceptions, which rendered them meaningless. For example, the statute said that the Chief Executive could not fix wages and prices at levels below those prevailing on May 25, 1970. However, this seemingly viable restraint was quickly followed by an omnipotent exception: prices and wages could be set below May 25, 1970, levels "if it is necessary to eliminate windfall profits or if it is otherwise necessary to carry out the purposes of this title."[37] Since without objective standards, what constitutes "windfall profits" is clearly judgmental, and since the legislation's much celebrated purposes encompass all conceivable economic goals, the purported protection of the May 25, 1970, minimum-price levels vanishes, consumed by its omnivorous exception. The May 25, 1970, rule, stripped of bureaucratic jargon, stated that the executive branch could set wage-price levels below those prevailing on May 25, 1970, whenever it elected to do so, for *any* economic reason.

Similarly, the Economic Stabilization Act explicitly required payment of wage increases secured by employment contracts executed prior to August 15, 1971, thereby purporting to recognize August 15, 1971, as a base date establishing a minimum-wage level for workers protected by employment contracts. Once again exceptions evaporated the superficial limitation on federal power. The President was given authority to ignore such wage guarantees whenever he unilaterally decreed the contractually protected salary levels to be "unreasonably inconsistent" with the wage-price guidelines he had issued.[38] Unlimited federal discretion again prevailed.

The Economic Stabilization Act contained one other internal limitation, an automatic expiration date, but for several years it too proved an insubstantial barrier to the economic authority conferred by the statute. The Act originally was to expire on March 31, 1971, but at the President's request this date was postponed first to April 30, 1973, and then to April 1974.[39] A concrete expiration date tended to palliate the vast powers delegated by the Economic Stabilization Act in the public's eyes, while providing no firm limit to federal authority. Recognizing the open-endedness of the claimed federal economic authority, spokesmen for the executive branch repeatedly stressed that while wage-price controls were to end in April 1974, the executive branch intended to continue economic controls in some form. Nevertheless, despite proposals by the executive branch to retain governmental authority to monitor industry and resume direct control over any private economic activity deemed inflationary, the Economic Stabilization Act expired in April 1974.

The long-term effect of the Economic Stabilization Act was to accustom a docile public to the massive economic controls permitted by the Act, minimizing future opposition by shifting the inertia of historical precedent in favor of such control. Proposals for reimposition of economic controls reveal that although it has temporarily become chic to characterize wage-price regulations as a failure, this judgment is strictly a pragmatic one: it recognizes the ineffectuality of specific rules while not questioning the federal government's self-proclaimed right to establish any rules it deems desirable to manipulate the American economy. Most critics of the wage-price controls, which are fascist in principle, do not challenge the propriety of the federal government's intervention in all aspects of the economy; they merely demand that the federally established rules *work*.

Miscellaneous other features of the Economic Stabilization Act merely emphasized the magnitude of the federal power established. For example, presidential delegates implementing the legislation were given authority to subpoena witnesses and relevant records.[40] The statute authorized the granting of "such exemptions . . . for small business enterprises as may be feasible without impeding the accomplishment of the purposes of this title,"[41] giving rein to the executive branch to grant or withhold exceptions sought by small businesses on subjective grounds and thereby inviting political decision-making.

The funding provision of the statute was particularly open-ended, for instead of following the usual pattern of authorizing a maximum dollar amount that could be appropriated by the legislature, Congress authorized the appropriation to the President of "such sums as may be necessary to carry out the provisions of this title."[42] Further, any funds appropriated were "to remain available until expended" rather than reverting to Congress if not expended within the fiscal year.[43]

The administrative procedure established by the Economic Stabilization Act is noteworthy only because it favored the federal government's actions implementing the statute over complaints by individuals or business enterprises protesting such rulings even more than do conventional procedural rules governing federal agencies. The statute explicitly stated that many significant procedural protections contained in the federal Administrative Procedure Act were not to be applied to the economic stabilization program.[44] For example, the Economic Stabilization Act did not require an agency acting under its authority to hold hearings to review its denial of a person's request for exemption from, or interpretation, modification, or rescission of the agency's regulations and orders.[45] Instead, the agency was required to hold a hearing only "where deemed advisable" in its unilateral discretion.[46]

These provisions empowered an agency administering the Economic Stabilization Act to deny aggrieved persons agency hearings whenever it pleased and to deny many procedural protections to those whom the agency benevolently granted an administrative hearing. Although some procedural protections are guaranteed by the Constitution, abstract constitutional protections are neither as substantial nor as tangible as the federal Administrative Procedure Act's concrete provisions requiring the administrative employee who hears the evidence to decide the case, prohibiting an administrator who investigates or prosecutes a case from participating in its decision, proscribing the administrative decision-maker from consulting with people on a disputed issue without notice and opportunity for all parties to participate, requiring the agency's decision to be made with reasonable speed, and compelling a complete record of the agency's decisions, to name but a few.[47]

Further, the Administrative Procedure Act's provision placing the burden of proof on the proponent of an agency's rule or order was significantly omitted. Although people were assured the right to submit *written* data to the agency, the few Administrative Procedure Act provisions that the Economic Stabilization Act did selectively adopt permitted the agency to avoid giving general notice of any proposed rule making "when the agency for good cause finds . . . that notice and public procedure thereon are impracticable, unnecessary, or contrary to the public interest."[48] The Economic Stabilization Act required formal public hearings to be conducted by the President or his delegates in formulating wage-price rulings only "[t]o the maximum extent possible,"[49] thus making the openness of federal economic decision-making contingent upon administrative benevolence rather than guaranteed by law.

The judicial review permitted by the Economic Stabilization Act was similarly weighted in favor of the federal government. The statute provided that U.S. district courts would have exclusive original jurisdiction to review cases or controversies arising under the Act; appeals were channeled through a "Temporary Emergency Court of Appeals" whose decisions could be appealed to the U.S. Supreme Court. Questions concerning the constitutionality of the Act or administrative orders thereunder were required to be sent directly to the Temporary Emergency Court of Appeals rather than decided initially by the district court, thereby centralizing the judicial decision-making process.[50]

The Economic Stabilization Act incorporated the normal rule of administrative law that an agency's ruling may be overturned if a final (unappealable) judgment holds it to be arbitrary, capricious, or an abuse of discretion, and based on findings not supported by substantial evidence, a rule strongly biased in favor of federal agencies.[51] The Act compounded this bias by providing that a district court or Temporary Emergency Court of Appeals could not enjoin or set aside an entire regulation issued by an agency exercising authority granted by the statute; although it could *declare* an agency's order to be invalid, such a court could only prohibit the application of the agency's order to the specific party seeking judicial relief.[52] The United States Supreme Court explicitly retained the ultimate power to declare the Economic Stabilization Act or its implementing regulations unconstitutional.

Having examined the broad statutory powers over wages, prices, rents, interest rates, and corporate dividends established by the Economic Stabilization Act, we will now analyze the executive order through which President Nixon implemented his authority under the Act.

THE EXECUTIVE ORDER

Through a series of executive orders, President Nixon created a vast administrative structure to effect the economic controls authorized by the Economic Stabilization Act. Since the last executive order superseded the preceding ones, this study will focus upon the final executive order.[53]

The administrative structure created by the President is as follows: The supreme body to which the Chief Executive delegated all of the powers and duties conferred upon him by the Economic Stabilization Act was the Cost of Living Council (CLC), composed primarily of cabinet-level officials such as the secretaries of Commerce, Labor, and Agriculture. Charged with implementing the national economic goals adopted by the Cost of Living Council were the Pay Board and the Price Commission, whose mission, within the framework of economic goals formulated by the Council, was to "take such steps as may be necessary, and authorized by or pursuant to this Order, to stabilize prices, rents, wages, and salaries."[54] Recognizing the lack of statutory restraint on his removal power, the President decreed that members of the Pay Board and Price Commission would serve "at the pleasure of the President."[55] The Pay Board was directed to "perform such functions with respect to the stabilization of wages and salaries as the Council delegates to the Board . . . including the development and establishment of criteria and standards for the stabilization of wages and salaries,"[56] while its counterpart, the Price Commission, had parallel authority to stabilize prices and rents.[57] The President also established a Committee on Interest and Dividends, a Committee on the Health Services Industry, a Committee on State and Local Government Cooperation, a Rent Advisory Board, and a Construction Industry Stabilization Committee.

The executive order illuminates even more fully than did the statute some of the distinctively fascist elements implicit in the Economic Stabilization Act. First is the direct involvement of the federal government in the daily operation of business enterprises. The executive order supplemented the general authority to control wages, prices, rents, interest rates, and corporate dividends by asserting the right of the central government to require businesses to maintain *economic records* for perusal by government officials and the public. The executive order stated:

Each person engaged in the business of selling or providing commodities or services shall maintain available for public inspection a record of the highest prices or rents charged for such or similar commodities or services during the 30-day period ending August 14, 1971 [the final base period for the wage-price controls].[58]

Stating the claimed power more fully at a subsequent point, the President declared:

The Council may require the maintenance of appropriate records or other evidence which are necessary in carrying out the provisions of this Order, and may require any person to maintain and produce for examination such records or other evidence, in such form as it shall require, concerning prices, rents, wages, and salaries and all related matters.[59]

Second, true to fascist economic tenets, the executive order exhorted business and the public to comply *voluntarily* with the government's economic desires, preferring voluntary conformity with whatever the central government decreed to be in the national interest to coerced compliance with government edicts. Although the Economic Stabilization Act gave the government ample power to force citizens to charge only the prices permitted by the government and to pay only the salaries that pleased the government, the executive order admonished the Cost of Living Council to "inform the public, agriculture, industry, and labor concerning the need for controlling inflation and [to] encourage and promote voluntary action to that end."[60] Lip service to voluntariness was offered again as the President instructed the Committee on Interest and Dividends to "formulate and execute a program for obtaining voluntary restraints on interest rates and dividends."[61] To cement the principle of unlimited governmental control over business while attempting in fascist mode to retain the pragmatic benefits of a market economy, the executive order preferred a facade of voluntariness to overt coercion.

Finally, the President's order made it abundantly clear that the lifeblood of a governmentally controlled wage-price system is political influence, which necessarily caters to large, organized groups. In developing policies to maintain the stability of wages and prices, the CLC was directed to "consult with representatives of agriculture, industry, labor, State and local governments, consumers and the public."[62] It does not require great political insight to perceive that the wishes of highly organized, amply financed segments of agriculture, labor, and industry would receive official governmental attention more frequently than would the views of a diffuse public and of individual farmers, laborers, and businessmen whose opinions were not voiced by well-funded lobbyists. The CLC twice was granted the explicit authority to make exceptions to its regulations whenever it chose.[63] The President himself specifically exempted raw agricultural products from the price controls until after the first sale of such commodities,[64] thereby responding in a limited way to the reality of market considerations (as any good fascist must) while ironically underscoring the political (that is, nonmarket) nature of the decision-making involved. Fascism's primary concern is production, and if a dedicated fascist sees that substituting government edicts for market decisions will, as in the case of price controls on raw agricultural produce, drastically curtail production, he must refrain from overt governmental manipulation of that aspect of the economy.

The Economic Stabilization Act thus simultaneously constituted the most massive legislative assertion of federal control over the economy ever enacted during peacetime in the United States and embodied a distinctively fascist commitment to unlimited governmental authority to control wages and prices. The uniquely fascist aspect of the legislation was that it recognized the government's right to usurp the functions of the free market whenever governmental authorities declared such control necessary to serve their economic goals of the moment. Ironically, although the Act has officially expired, it remains victorious in principle, for its massive regulation of the economy accustomed the public to the propriety of unprecedented governmental economic controls. The Economic Stabilization Act, though discarded as ineffective in practice, has not been repudiated in principle, confirming fascism's use of capitalism's market economics as a practical tool in limited spheres where deemed consonant with the government's omnipotent interests. The Act's shadow still lingers over U.S. political and economic life, to be given substance whenever Congress deems it politically expedient.

7

Government Dominion over Labor

The principles embraced by American laws governing private labor/management relations strikingly parallel those adopted by the fascist regimes in Italy and Germany. Since the legal mechanisms historically used by Italian and German rulers to control labor and management have been lavishly documented elsewhere,[1] this chapter is devoted to an analysis of United States laws that embody the principles that enabled previous fascist governments to manipulate labor and management in order to achieve the state's political and economic goals.

Eight major laws created between 1935 and the present establish the framework through which the U.S. government regulates labor/management relations.[2] Each of these will be discussed in turn. The eight statutes are:

1. the Employment Act of 1946
2. the National Commission on Productivity and Work Quality law
3. the Occupational Safety and Health Act of 1970
4. the Fair Labor Standards Act of 1938
5. the National Labor Relations Act
6. the Labor-Management Reporting and Disclosure Act of 1959 (discussed in the section that describes the National Labor Relations Act)

7. the Federal Mediation and Conciliation Service law
8. the Comprehensive Employment and Training Act of 1973

Before analyzing these laws individually, it is important to isolate and synthesize the fascist themes that recur throughout the legislation.

As have previous fascist regimes, the United States government has installed itself as supreme overseer of labor and management under the guise of the "national interest," which, not surprisingly, always coincides with the vacillating economic and political judgments of those currently wielding governmental power. The U.S. government is unabashedly at the helm in guiding labor relations, as it is in most other economic matters.

Labor and management now are regarded legally as powerful special-interest groups, entitled to "equal" status in the government's eyes. But since equality of management and labor in a fascist economy merely means equal opportunity to persuade government officials of the desirability of adopting positions favorable to labor or management, U.S. legislators have been content to pay meticulous attention to securing numerically equal representation of labor and management on myriad government-sponsored committees empowered to "advise" federal officials. While labor and management are equally encouraged to advise the government, the government asserts the power to act as ultimate decision-maker.

To achieve control over labor, fascist states typically centralize the representation and organization of labor. Monolithic legal representation of American labor is attained by empowering a government agency, the National Labor Relations Board, to designate a single union as the sole bargaining agent for governmentally defined groups of employees. As in previous fascist states, the central government now dominates virtually every aspect of resolution of "private" labor disputes.

Not enthusiastic over anything that detracts from public subservience to that which political leaders decree to be the national interest, fascist rulers in America, as elsewhere, deplore tangible evidence of industrial strife such as strikes and lockouts, expressing hostility toward any overt manifestation of conflict between management and labor. Labor and management are urged to "cooperate" with each other through "voluntary" interaction, even though "voluntary cooperation" in carrying out the government's wishes is compelled by law.

Mimicking previous fascist economies, the United States government also arrogates to itself the power to determine the working conditions that are "proper" for labor. Although the government-decreed standards may vary, depending upon what is politically expedient and economically feasible at any given moment, the government is broadly empowered to force individuals to accept whatever working conditions the government declares to be desirable.

Like fascist economies before it, the American government is becoming increasingly active in monitoring and assessing the supply of and demand for labor. Already heavily involved in channeling economic activity by subsidizing employment in favored endeavors, the government's next logical step could be allocation of the labor supply to suit the government's economic priorities, a step which previous fascist regimes have not hesitated to take.

We will now consider the specific laws that enshrine these principles as hallowed tenets of American labor law.

I. EMPLOYMENT ACT OF 1946

In the Employment Act of 1946,[3] the federal government, on a *policy* level, first assumed "responsibility" for directing the national economy, quietly embracing the most fundamental economic tenet of fascism. In that still operative statute, the government announced its intention to channel all its resources into "creating and maintaining . . . conditions under which there will be afforded useful employment opportunities . . . for all those able, willing, and seeking to work, and to promote *maximum employment, production, and purchasing power.*"[4] Ever responsive to powerful special-interest groups, the fascist economic approach is further manifested in the 1946 Act's declaration that the government must seek "the assistance and cooperation of industry, agriculture, labor, and State and local governments" in working its will upon the economy.[5]

Of course, superficial homage is paid to free enterprise. The government avows its intent to usurp power as ultimate controller of the economy "in a manner calculated to foster and promote free competitive enterprise and the general welfare."[6] Similarly, the Council of Economic Advisers, established by the statute to advise the President in wielding his mighty economic power, is instructed to recommend "national economic policies to foster and promote free competitive enterprise."[7] It is never mentioned that the very notion of "national economic policies" contradicts the free-enterprise concept so conscientiously lauded.

II. NATIONAL COMMISSION ON PRODUCTIVITY AND WORK QUALITY

A logical yet astounding outgrowth of the policies succinctly adopted by the Employment Act of 1946 is the law that established the National Commission on Productivity,[8] whose title and function were expanded when it was transformed into the "National Commission on Productivity and Work Quality."[9] This legislation explicitly embraces as the national policy of the United States many of the fascist economic principles more subtly interwoven throughout other labor laws.

First, the government asserts the right to formulate and implement "national economic policy,"[10] a concept which authorizes the government to direct the entire economy to achieve any objectives that federal officials choose to impose upon the public.

But this legislation sanctions much more detailed intervention into market operations than the formulation of national economic policy might suggest. As the Commission's title indicates, it is a mechanism through which the government asserts the power to oversee both economic productivity and work quality. Explicitly intervening in the production process, the government claims the right to direct the economy "to promote *efficient production, marketing, distribution, and use* of goods and services in the *private sector*, and to *improve the morale* of the American worker."[11] Free enterprise, now labeled the "private sector," is relegated to the status of just another special-interest group.

Displaying an inordinate concern about the mental state of U.S. citizens, the government claims the right to specify economic policy on a national level that will decree measures allegedly aimed at increasing economic productivity and the "*motivation* of the American worker."[12] Additional legislation approved on June 8, 1974, makes even more explicit the government's far-reaching desire to control economic matters traditionally resolved by private individuals. The new law authorizes government efforts aimed at "facilitating a *more satisfying* work experience for American workers" and "providing goods and services at *low cost* to American consumers."[13]

It must be a great comfort to the American worker to know that omniscient federal officials in Washington, D.C., are busy divining national policy on the basis of subjective revelations as to what constitutes a "satisfying work experience." Similarly profound government intervention into private economic decision-making is implied by the government's desire to lower the cost of goods and services. If market forces are prevented from determining the price structure which most accurately reflects consumers' preferences, the government is to that extent asserting the power to dictate which goods will be supplied at "low cost." This fact is implicitly acknowledged as the statute instructs the National Commission on Productivity and Work Quality to concentrate on lowering the cost of goods and services "generally considered to fulfill the *most basic needs* of Americans,"[14] which products, of course, will be identified by an elite corps of government bureaucrats empowered to second-guess consumers' wishes as expressed in the market.

164

Partisans who would use government power either to suppress or to promote labor or management exclusively will find no solace in this legislation. The National Commission on Productivity and Work Quality is empowered to probe the output and productivity of labor *and* management. The law avows not only the government's power to scrutinize "underutilization and obsolescence of production facilities,"[15] but also its concern about "increasing output per man-hour"[16] and reducing absenteeism.[17] Similarly, the Commission is authorized to promote "sound wage and price policies in the national interest"[18] and to seek "more effective use of labor and management personnel in the interest of increased productivity."[19]

The legislation dutifully reflects fascist deference to free enterprise. Credulous readers are informed of the government's allegedly passive role as promoter of "increased productivity through free competitive enterprise."[20]

But the novel feature of the legislation is the means by which heightened productivity and work quality are to be attained. They are to be achieved through none other than government-elicited *voluntary cooperation* between management and labor.[21] While announcing its desire for a "climate of cooperation and understanding between labor, management, and the public,"[22] the government further concludes, on the basis of alleged "mutual interest" of labor and management in increasing productivity and restraining inflation, that "machinery should be provided for translating this mutuality of interest into voluntary action."[23]

In predictable fascist phraseology, the statute declares that this blissful "climate of cooperation" must occur "within a framework of peaceful labor-management relations."[24] But the catch appears in the following phrase. The law glibly expresses the government's policy of seeking "free and responsible collective bargaining,"[25] an obvious contradiction in terms. Labor/management negotiations that are "free" are not "responsible" to any other entity. In this context, "responsible" implies "responsible *to*." Making it clear that "responsible" labor/management bargaining is that which conforms to the government's mutable economic policies, the statute empowers the National Commission on Productivity and Work Quality to "review collective bargaining agreements already in effect or those being negotiated to ascertain their effects on productivity; and . . . to make recommendations with respect to the agreements made or about to be made in specific industries."[26] Mussolini couldn't have said it better.

The remarkable culmination of this legislation is a uniquely fascist mechanism designed to implement the foregoing policies. The primary function assigned to the National Commission on Productivity and Work Quality is to "encourage and assist in the organization and work of labor-management committees which may also include public members, on a plant, community, regional, and industry basis . . . designed to facilitate labor-management cooperation to increase productivity or to help improve the morale and quality of work of the American worker."[27] Such committees are vividly reminiscent of fascist Italy's "corporative" hierarchy of government-controlled organizations, which were supposed to integrate the disparate interests of labor and management, as well as the government-dominated "Labor Front," which served a similar function in Nazi Germany. Although this emerging structure does not yet embody the same level of political control over management and labor as ultimately prevailed under the fascist regimes in Italy and Germany, the difference is one of degree, not of kind. A familiarly fascist tripartite structure composed of government officials overseeing the interaction of labor and management is well established by existing American law.

III. OCCUPATIONAL SAFETY AND HEALTH ACT OF 1970

With the Occupational Safety and Health Act of 1970,[28] we move from sweeping policy pronouncements into the realm of specific government programs undertaken to implement the vast economic powers enunciated in the Employment Act of 1946 and the legislation establishing the National Commission on Productivity and Work Quality. The Occupational Safety and Health Act gives the federal government statutory power to force workers and businessmen alike to conform to any rules that the government claims are "reasonably necessary or appropriate to provide safe or healthful employment and places of employment."[29] The Act empowers the Secretary of Labor to promulgate *mandatory* health and safety standards, creating an Occupational Safety and Health Review Commission to enforce the standards.[30]

Familiar fascist economic jargon permeates the statute, but one provision captures the essence of the entire law. That section is aptly captioned "Duties of employers and employees."[31] It makes both employers and employees subservient to the government's wishes in matters even tangentially related to occupational safety and health. Individuals retain their economic freedom only so long as they do not contravene the applicable government decrees. Under the Occupational Safety and Health Act, individuals have legal duties, not just to refrain from harming each other, but also to comply with prevailing government edicts. It is the employer's "duty" to

furnish to each of his employees employment and a place of employment which are free from recognized hazards that are causing or are likely to cause death or serious physical harm to his employees; . . . [and to] comply with occupational safety and health standards promulgated under this chapter [the Occupational Safety and Health Act].[32]

Employees have a corresponding duty to "comply with occupational safety and health standards and all rules, regulations, and orders issued pursuant to this chapter."[33] Employees and employers, transformed from independent individuals into what the statute refers to as "human resources" to be "preserved" by a ubiquitous government,[34] are said to have "separate but dependent responsibilities" in achieving working conditions deemed proper by the government.[35]

The states are also subservient to the national government in implementing rules pertaining to occupational safety and health. However, in an oft repeated statutory pattern designed to preserve a facade of state autonomy, the states are authorized "to assume responsibility for development and enforcement therein of occupational safety and health standards" on the condition that each state submit a *plan* that the government approves.[36] Not relinquishing any federal power in these matters, the statute makes it a prerequisite of government approval of a state plan that it be "at least as effective in providing safe and healthful employment and places of employment as the standards promulgated under . . . this title."[37] The government also has absolute power to reject a state plan if it asserts that the state's proposed standards are not "required by compelling local conditions" or that they "unduly burden interstate commerce."[38]

Since virtually any aspect of business operation could be asserted to be tangentially related to safety and health, the Occupational Safety and Health Act of 1970 confers enormous powers on the government to regulate private economic endeavors. As if to emphasize the unconstrained nature of these powers, the statute gives the Secretary of Labor unlimited authority to grant "variances" exempting individuals from an occupational safety and health standard,[39] assuring that the government is not even bound by its own prior edicts. The Occupational Safety and Health Act also empowers government officials to enter and inspect any place of employment and all associated equipment in any fashion deemed "reasonable" by the government. In the words of the law, such investigations may be conducted at "reasonable times, and within reasonable limits and in a reasonable manner."[40] In addition, employers are compelled to maintain any records relevant to occupational safety and health that the Secretary of Labor or the Secretary of Health, Education and Welfare orders them to maintain.[41]

It comes as no surprise that the statute encourages *cooperation* and *equality* between management and labor in achieving government-sanctioned objectives. The Occupational Safety and Health Act urges "joint labor-management efforts to reduce injuries and disease arising out of employment."[42] Representatives of management, labor, and the public are required on a National Advisory Committee on Occupational Safety and Health, which is authorized to make recommendations to the government.[43] A further attempt is made to mitigate conflict between management and labor by amalgamating on optional advisory committees "an equal number of persons qualified by experience and affiliation to present the viewpoint of the employers involved, and of persons similarly qualified to present the viewpoint of the workers involved."[44] The Occupational Safety and Health Act thus typifies fascist economic legislation by rendering labor, management, and the public equally subservient to the government's fickle policies.

IV. FAIR LABOR STANDARDS ACT OF 1938

While empowering the government to dictate minimum wages and overtime wage rates, the Fair Labor Standards Act of 1938[45] joins other legislation in proclaiming the government's role as economic overseer of businessmen and workers. In its initial declaration of congressional findings and policy, the law echoes many recurrent themes of fascist labor policy. The legislation opens by presuming the government's right to determine and enforce labor conditions deemed conducive to maintaining a federally formulated "minimum standard of living necessary for health, efficiency, and general well-being of workers."[46] In fluent fascist phraseology, the statute proceeds to express hostility toward labor disputes (which allegedly burden and obstruct commerce), and seeks to remedy labor conditions that impede what government officials envision to be the "orderly and fair marketing of goods in commerce."[47] Further asserting the government's unlimited power to monitor businesses, the law requires each regulated employer to preserve whatever "records of the persons employed by him and of the wages, hours, and other conditions and practices of employment maintained by him" federal officials order him to create for government perusal.[48]

MINIMUM WAGES

Although the Fair Labor Standards Act requires employers to pay specified overtime wage rates for work performed in excess of the "maximum hours" established by the Act,[49] its best-known provision is that which imposes minimum-wage levels on most employers and employees.[50] The statute's pages of fine print set forth in magnificently convoluted legal phraseology different wage schedules for different groups of workers (for example, agricultural versus nonagricultural employees) and different geographic areas (such as Puerto Rico and the Virgin Islands).

The most interesting aspect of the law is that it purports to be a measure that benefits disadvantaged workers. In fact, its economic effect is quite the contrary. While minimum wages compelled by law may increase the pay of the workers who retain their jobs, their primary effect is to reduce total employment.[51] If the minimum-wage rate is above the level that the market would establish, employers will simply demand fewer employees at the legally imposed wage rate.[52] The supply of labor offered at the above-market wage level will exceed employers' demand for it, causing some workers who would otherwise find employment to be without jobs.

Ironically, it is the workers least able to adjust who are most severely hurt by minimum-wage laws. "Marginal" workers, deemed least productive by employers because of inadequate training or physical or mental handicaps, are prevented by law from bargaining for lower wages to compensate for their lower productivity. They are the first to lose their jobs when minimum wages are established. If prospective employees exceed the number of jobs available, as they will when above-market minimum-wage levels are enforced, employers will select and retain only those workers whose anticipated or actual productivity is highest.

The Fair Labor Standards Act itself recognizes that unemployment is the natural economic consequence of its minimum-wage provisions. In a section that explicitly acknowledges that the least-productive employees are most vulnerable to the unemployment caused by minimum-wage laws, the statute provides, "in order to prevent curtailment of opportunities for employment,"[53] for special exemptions for learners, apprentices, students, and handicapped individuals "whose earning or productive capacity is impaired by age or physical or mental deficiency or injury,"[54] enabling them to be paid lower wages than the minimum-wage rate. Not only do these exemptible categories fail to encompass the entire range of marginally productive employees, but also the granting of such exemptions is in the unchecked discretion of government officials. The sheer administrative costs of dealing with the bureaucracy further discourage businesses from seeking the exemptions that would enable them to offer employment to less productive employees.

EQUAL PAY FOR EQUAL WORK

The same ironic twist is implicit in the portion of the Fair Labor Standards Act sometimes referred to as the Equal Pay Act of 1963.[55] In a measure that superficially appears to protect women from unjust discrimination in the job market, the law requires employers regulated by the Fair Labor Standards Act to provide men and women with equal pay for equal work, compelling employers to raise the wages paid females to the level paid males for the same work.[56] The provision states:

> No employer having employees subject to any provisions of this section shall discriminate . . . between employees on the basis of sex by paying wages to employees . . . at a rate less than the rate at which he pays wages to employees of the opposite sex in such establishment for equal work on jobs the performance of which requires equal skill, effort, and responsibility, and which are performed under similar working conditions, . . . *Provided*, That an employer who is paying a wage rate differential in violation of this subsection shall not, in order to comply with the provisions of this subsection, reduce the wage rate of any employee.[57]

The irony is that this provision has the economic effect of reducing the employment of women.[58] The reason is simple. If an employer is forced by law to pay the same wage to male and female employees, and that level must be the higher wage previously paid male workers, the employer who subjectively prefers male employees is given legal incentives to hire males instead of females whenever he can. Without the federal law, even avowed male chauvinists, as employers, may have economic incentives to hire women. Women can overcome employers' sexual prejudices by offering to work at a slightly lower wage than men, thereby compensating the employer for their subjective "defect" in the employer's eyes.

The freedom to bargain for a lower salary to offset subjective "inferiority" perceived by employers, called an "equalizing" wage differential,[59] is an absolute economic necessity for less-preferred minorities. One need only imagine passage of legislation requiring employers to provide equal pay for equal work performed by attractive airline ticket agents and by unattractive ones. Forced to pay all employees the higher rate formerly reserved for physically attractive counter personnel, an economically rational employer would select handsome/beautiful workers every time. Similarly, if a racially prejudiced, chauvinistic employer has to choose between a white male and a black female whose objective credentials are identical, he will select the white male every time so long as the black woman is legally prohibited from bargaining for a slightly lower wage to compensate for her "aesthetic" or subjective "inferiority" in the employer's eyes. It is only the ability to bargain for a lower rate of pay to offset characteristics that are unappealing to prospective employers that enables people with less-preferred attributes to secure and retain employment.

It is a measure of widespread public economic naivety and inculcated acceptance of government control that, to cure the problems just described, people propose quotas, dictating by government fiat the types of employees employers must hire, rather than repeal of the equal-pay-for-equal-work legislation responsible for restricting the job opportunities of disfavored minorities. The difficulty of challenging the equal-pay-for-equal-work slogan is intensified because its advocates comprise both those who honestly but incorrectly embrace it as a means of protecting disadvantaged minorities, and those economically astute competitors of the minority employees (such as white males) who righteously tout equal pay for equal work as a subtle means of excluding minorities from the job market.

V. NATIONAL LABOR RELATIONS ACT

The National Labor Relations Act[60] establishes the actual mechanisms through which the government controls private labor/management relations in the United States. That statute created the National Labor Relations Board (NLRB) as a government agency and empowered it to supervise collective bargaining. While many fascist economic themes are reiterated in the legislation, its predominant fascist motif exalts the government as ultimate decision-maker in labor disputes and collective bargaining.

The elastic standard that guides the use of these mighty powers is that old fascist favorite, the "public interest," which empowers the government to do exactly as it pleases in matters to which this "standard" applies. The statute transforms employers and labor alike into subservient vassals of the state, legally forbidden "to engage in any acts or practices which jeopardize the public health, safety, or interest."[61] When the statute's introductory passages conclude with the announcement that its policy and purpose are "to define and proscribe practices on the part of labor and management which . . . are inimical to the general welfare and to protect the rights of the public in connection with labor disputes,"[62] the legislative intent to give the government the total discretion characteristic of a fascist economy to guide and control "private" labor relations stands out in bold relief.

While throughout the National Labor Relations Act the government often postures as neutral toward collective bargaining — weighing equally the twin goals of "encouraging the practice and procedure of collective bargaining" and "protecting the exercise by workers of full freedom of association"[63] — the primary thrust of the law is to promote collective bargaining at the expense of individual workers' freedom of association. The National Labor Relations Act requires that only *one union* represent any given group of employees.[64] That union, after winning a majority in an election supervised and approved of by the

NLRB, is certified by the government as the *sole legal bargaining agent* for the employees it represents,[65] enabling the union to enjoy an absolute monopoly over the employer's labor supply. To enforce the monopoly power thus conferred on the union, the law compels both the employer and the certified union to negotiate or "bargain collectively" with each other,[66] an obligation which requires the parties to "confer in good faith" but which does not "compel either party to agree to a proposal or require the making of a concession."[67] The government determines what constitutes the proper grouping of employees for purposes of union representation, deciding such questions as whether a single union should represent an entire plant or whether certain specialized craft workers (such as electrical workers) should be separately represented.[68]

Once a union wins a majority of votes in a government-sanctioned election and obtains legal certification as exclusive bargaining agent for designated employees, it is by law the sole representative of *all* employees in the bargaining unit, even those who voted against the union.[69] Workers who voted against the union can be forced to join it, pay dues to it, and channel work-related grievances through its official machinery. Although it purports to guarantee employees the right to refrain from union activity,[70] the law authorizes the majority union to establish by contractual agreement with the employer a union shop, which means that new employees can be forced to join the union within thirty days of being hired, on penalty of losing their jobs.[71] A state can avoid the union-shop phenomenon only by passing a "right-to-work" law outlawing compulsory union membership.[72]

Although union-shop agreements are superficially "voluntary" contractual undertakings, it is the government-imposed exclusive bargaining-agent relationship that causes union-shop agreements to flourish. Once an employer is compelled by law to grant a union representing a majority of his employees a monopoly over his labor supply, it is of little consequence to him whether or not his employees are forced to join the union that will represent them anyway. Yet since a union shop remains crucial to union officials as a means of increasing the organization's credibility and financial resources by coercively bloating its nominal membership, union-shop agreements thrive as intense union pressure easily overcomes legally neutralized employer resistance. These two complementary devices—the legal power of the union to act as sole bargaining agent for designated employees, coupled with government-induced union-shop agreements—enable the union to exercise monopoly power over the supply of labor in unionized industries.

The National Labor Relations Act also empowers the NLRB "to prevent any person from engaging in any unfair labor practice,"[73] authorizing it to enforce its decisions with such penalties as orders compelling employers to reinstate discharged employees with back pay.[74] Although these "unfair labor practices" are ostensibly particularized in another section of the law, the specific unfair labor practices there enumerated are broad enough to give the NLRB nearly total control over the activities of employers and employees. For example, employers are forbidden "to dominate or interfere with the formation or administration of any labor organization."[75] Loose, accommodating phraseology again predominates as the statute declares it an unfair labor practice for employers to "interfere with, restrain, or coerce employees" in the exercise of such all-encompassing rights[76] as the rights "to self-organization, to form, join, or assist labor organizations, to bargain collectively through representatives of their own choosing, and *to engage in other concerted activities for the purpose of collective bargaining or other mutual aid or protection . . . .*"[77] Similarly, a labor union is guilty of an unfair labor practice if it *restrains* or *coerces* employees in the exercise of these rights.[78] Throughout the statutory delineation of unfair labor practices, broad, conclusory terminology empowers the NLRB to censure virtually any labor-related activity, carried out by either employers or labor unions, which it subjectively (or politically) finds distasteful or inconvenient.

In asserting the government's power to act as ultimate judge and arbiter of labor relations, the National Labor Relations Act strikes other chords hauntingly familiar to anyone who has studied fascist labor policies. The statute decries "inequality of bargaining power" between labor and management, seeking to achieve the government-orchestrated industrial harmony coveted by fascist states through "restoring equality of bargaining power between employers and employees."[79] Although the law professes the intent not to diminish the right to strike,[80] government hostility to strikes permeates the National Labor Relations Act. The law is replete with denunciations of strikes and all forms of "industrial strife." Congress asserts that "strikes and other forms of industrial strife or unrest" unavoidably burden and obstruct commerce, thereby damaging the public interest.[81] The Act prescribes government-supervised collective bargaining as a panacea by which "industrial strife . . . can be avoided or substantially minimized."[82] In lieu of the strikes and industrial unrest which it deprecates, the National Labor Relations Act encourages government-directed "friendly adjustment of industrial disputes,"[83] advocating "orderly and peaceful procedures" to settle labor controversies.[84] These diverse fascist refrains all support a single theme, consistently proclaiming the government's right to oversee and control all aspects of labor relations in economic endeavors arguably subject to the Act.

Another statute, the Labor-Management Reporting and Disclosure Act of 1959,[85] further tightens federal control over labor unions and employers by requiring them to file a multitude of reports with the government. Unions must file detailed reports with the Secretary of Labor describing virtually every aspect of their procedures, from selection of officers and shop stewards to issuance of work permits and authorization for bargaining demands, strikes, and disbursement of funds.[86] Unions must also make annual financial reports to the government.[87] Narrower reporting requirements apply to employers, who must only report to the government payments made to labor unions plus any expenditure or agreement the object of which is to influence employees in their labor-related organizational or collective-bargaining activities.[88]

Having traced in America's labor laws the typically fascist installation of the government as overseer of "private" labor relations as well as the fascist rallying cries that support this government power, a word must be said about the economic effects of labor unions per se, apart from the government's manipulation of them. Like the aims of minimum-wage laws and equal-pay-for-equal-work legislation, labor unions' appealing goals of raising workers' wages and improving working conditions often obscure their negative economic consequences.

Far from constituting the bulk of the labor force, only about one fourth of American workers are unionized.[89] By preventing nonunion workers from competing for certain jobs, unions may succeed in raising the wages of those union workers who are able to retain their jobs. However, although unions may raise some union members' wages above the level that would be established by the market,[90] they do so at a high price to nonunion workers, laid-off union members, and the rest of society.[91]

The ultimate consequence of above-market wages procured by a union's monopoly over the industry's labor supply is *decreased employment* of union workers.[92] At higher wage levels, employers demand less labor. Even industries with monopoly power will demand less labor at higher wage rates, just not as *much* less as firms in competitive markets.[93] Because the resulting unemployment swells the ranks of nonunionized workers competing for jobs, salaries of nonunionized workers tend to fall.[94] In addition, at above-market wage levels, marginal firms barely able to sustain themselves at the market rate of pay for labor will cease doing business, causing unemployment and reducing production in that industry. Those unionized firms that can survive must raise the price of their products to cover the higher union wages, which is accomplished by reducing their output (the supply of products they manufacture) to accommodate the decreased quantity demanded at the newly raised price level.[95]

As affected businesses curtail their economic activity, production shifts to fields where wages have not been forced above market levels, stimulating production of goods other than those which consumers most prefer. The consumer pays higher prices and encounters fewer and/or less-desired goods. Union members whose services cannot be supported at above-market union salary levels face unemployment and often must accept wages in nonunion jobs below those received before the union artificially increased union members' pay. These are the rather bleak economic facts that the seventy-five percent of the American public not participating in any benefits obtained by unions must consider before uncritically embracing government-nurtured labor unions as the salvation of the average worker.

But to alleviate the problems associated with labor unions, those who seek to maximize individual liberty should not be tempted to advocate curtailing the right of free individuals to form voluntary associations for collective bargaining. The crux of the problem is that unions presently exploit the coercive might of the State to acquire power over other individuals and to force the economic consequences of their activities onto others. It is the supportive legislation that has transformed labor unions from manifestations of individual workers' free choice into coercive creatures of government.

VI. FEDERAL MEDIATION AND CONCILIATION SERVICE

The fascist labor policies evident in the National Labor Relations Act are reinforced by other legislation that creates a tax-supported Federal Mediation and Conciliation Service.[96] Not content to dominate the certification of labor unions and the censure of employers and unions accused of unfair labor practices, the government by this statute acquired legal authority to intervene throughout the *arbitration* of labor disputes.

The statute opens with the usual fascist plaudits extolling "sound and stable industrial peace," the "general welfare," and "the best interests of employers and employees," all of which the law asserts can "most satisfactorily be secured by . . . conference and collective bargaining."[97] The law does not assess to whom this process is "most satisfactory," nor by what right the official government determination of what is "most satisfactory" is imposed on the people. Nevertheless, no sooner does the government declare that conference and collective

175

bargaining are in everybody's interest, than it compels people by law to act in the manner thus deemed "most satisfactory."

To facilitate conference and collective bargaining between employers and employees, the law establishes the Federal Mediation and Conciliation Service. Although employers and unions alike are coerced by law to use this service whenever the government asserts that a labor dispute threatens "a substantial interruption of commerce,"[98] the statute insists that the negotiations it compels be labeled "*voluntary* arbitration."[99] It is the avowed purpose of the Federal Mediation and Conciliation Service to make available government facilities "to induce the parties *voluntarily* to seek other means of settling the [labor] dispute *without resort to trike*, lock-out, or other coercion . . . ."[100] The dual fascist principles of government-ordered "voluntary" cooperation and conciliation in labor/management relations and government hostility to strikes and lockouts dominate this legislation.

The law accords due fascist deference to private arbitration, imposing government intervention only as a "last resort" in controversies that threaten a "substantial" interruption of commerce in the judgment of the bureaucracy.[101] Since the statute does not compel the disputants to accept the settlement favored by government officials,[102] the main function of the Federal Mediation and Conciliation Service is to cajole disputants and to postpone strikes and lockouts provoked by labor disputes. In the "normal" labor dispute, once the federal government's conciliation services have been used, the legal duties of labor and management are satisfied and there is no legal barrier to a strike or lockout.

However, if the President avers that an actual or threatened strike or lockout affecting a "substantial part" of an industry will "imperil the national health or safety,"[103] the law provides a legal procedure by which the President can obtain an injunction postponing the strike or lockout for sixty days, in addition to a final fifteen-day period in which the NLRB must conduct a secret ballot of the employees to ascertain whether they wish to accept the employer's final offer.[104] Nevertheless, if that offer is rejected and the "national emergency" sixty-day delay period has expired, the parties are not legally required to accept the settlement suggested by the government,[105] despite potentially enormous political pressure to do so.

Thus, although the apex of power over arbitration of labor disputes — the power to impose a settlement upon the disputants — has so far eluded the government, the Federal Mediation and Conciliation Service and the President's emergency powers make the government a compelling presence throughout the negotiation process.

VII. COMPREHENSIVE EMPLOYMENT AND TRAINING ACT OF 1973

The Comprehensive Employment and Training Act of 1973[106] consolidates and expands the fascist economic coalition of labor, management, and "public" interests already existing under the umbrella of government control. However, the statute also introduces a new and ominous element into this heretofore loose amalgamation of special interests vying for federal influence and public monies. The Comprehensive Employment and Training Act explicitly authorizes the government to monitor the "supply" of and "demand" for labor in the United States, empowering the government to act as omnipotent overseer of all jobs and the people who actually or potentially fill them. The foreboding implication of thus authorizing the government to monitor labor supply and demand is that the government may next claim power to *allocate* the "human resources" concerning which it is now so diligently collecting data, an act the government has previously accomplished only indirectly through selective use of financial incentives to favored individuals and industries.

In molding public opinion to support this law, Congress' first step was to unify and synthesize verbally all problems related to labor. Instead of discussing job-related problems of individuals, the legislation speaks of "the *Nation's* manpower problems," establishing "a comprehensive program of manpower research" in order to "assist the *Nation* in expanding work opportunities and assuring access to those opportunities for all who desire it."[107] By posing a "national" problem, the statute subtly corroborates its advocacy of a "national" solution.

Having thus centralized all manpower problems on a national scale, the Comprehensive Employment and Training Act of 1973 identifies an all-powerful federal government as the logical vehicle by which these alleged national problems are to be alleviated. The following broad investigatory powers compose an avowedly open-ended list of authorized government inquiries. The government, via the Secretary of Labor, is empowered to engage in any studies whose results "*may*" contribute to

(1) formulation of manpower policy;
(2) development or improvement of manpower programs;
(3) increased knowledge about labor market processes;
(4) reduction of unemployment and its relationships to price stability;
(5) promotion of more effective manpower development, training, and *utilization;*

177

(6) improved national, regional, and local means of measuring future labor demand and supply;

(7) enhancement of job opportunities;

(8) skill training to qualify employees for positions of greater skill, responsibility, and remuneration;

(9) meeting of manpower shortages;

(10) easing of the transition from school to work, from one job to another, and from work to retirement,

(11) opportunities and services for older persons who desire to enter or reenter the labor force, and for

(12) improvements of opportunities for employment and advancement through the reduction of discrimination and disadvantage arising from poverty, ignorance, or prejudice.[108]

This terse paragraph adopts as United States law the principle of unlimited government surveillance of the job market. Interestingly, this broad blueprint for government control over American labor is embedded deep within the Comprehensive Employment and Training Act, surrounded by other, less radical provisos. Yet even a few of these powers — for example, the authority to promote effective "manpower utilization," to measure future labor demand and supply, and to avoid manpower shortages — are sufficiently broad in principle to infuse a total government takeover of the distribution of American labor with an aura of legality, provided that such a takeover were politically feasible. These principles, in theory, would easily encompass a "workbook" type of permit system for labor such as that ultimately adopted in Nazi Germany, which allowed government officials to monitor and control every proposed job change, thereby directing workers into those jobs that politically controlled bureaucrats thought most conducive to the nation's well-being. If the U.S. government attempts to fulfill the role outlined in the statutory passage quoted above, the logical outgrowth of its efforts would be similarly comprehensive controls over American workers.

But the statute does not rest after embracing the abstract principle of government monitoring of labor supply and demand. The Comprehensive Employment and Training Act also creates some very concrete programs to implement the national policies it enunciates, programs through which government officials may procure precise statistical data concerning the labor force and job market. The government is authorized to "develop a comprehensive system of labor market information on a national, State, local, or other appropriate basis."[109] The government is further directed to "develop reliable methods . . . to produce more statistically accurate data on unemployment, underemployment and labor demand by State, local, and poverty areas."[110]

178

Threatening still more profound government intervention into people's economic lives, the statute even orders the government to "develop methods to establish and maintain more comprehensive household budget data at different levels of living, including a level of adequacy."[111]

But the final coup is the job bank. The law empowers the government to

> establish and carry out a nationwide computerized job bank and matching program . . . for the purpose of identifying sources of available persons and job vacancies, providing an expeditious means of matching the qualifications of unemployed, underemployed, and economically disadvantaged persons with employer requirements and job opportunities, and referring and placing such persons in jobs.[112]

Regardless of how appealing the notion of efficiently matching workers with jobs on a national scale, to give the government the power to conduct such a program is to authorize government officials to collect data on the most intimate details of individuals' economic lives. It is to empower the government to sift the lives of its citizens like so many grains of sand, using the information it culls in any manner thought politically expedient.

The expanded role envisioned for the government as overseer of labor supply and demand is supported by several statutory provisions that grant the government partial control over the actual distribution of American labor. Those provisions authorize the government to subsidize the employment of favored individuals while transferring the cost of those subsidies to the public. Although the Comprehensive Employment and Training Act is laced with subsidy provisions affecting virtually every program it authorizes, only those legalizing government payments to private employers to achieve the employment pattern sanctioned by government officials will be discussed.

The "manpower services" program, designed to sponsor employment-related training and to create jobs, authorizes "payments or other inducements to public or private employers to expand job opportunities," restricting subsidies to businesses organized for profit to "the difference between the costs of recruiting, training, and providing supportive services for low-income persons and those regularly employed."[113] No comparable upper limit restricts subsidies to private nonprofit corporations or to "public" endeavors.

Another statutory provision authorizes subsidies to private businesses to procure "public-service" employment in "areas of substantial unemployment" (that is, areas which have unemployment rates of at least 6.5 percent for three consecutive months).[114] But "public service" has a novel definition indeed. Public service, according to the statute, includes not only certain specifically enumerated fields such as transportation and health care, but also anything that can be labeled a field of "human betterment and community improvement,"[115] a description broad enough to encompass almost any conceivable economic endeavor. Rejecting the common understanding that public service comprises only projects that do not compete with private businesses, the law declares:

> "Public service" includes, but is not limited to, work in such fields as environmental quality, health care, education, public safety, crime prevention and control, prison rehabilitation, transportation, recreation, maintenance of parks, streets, and other public facilities, solid waste removal, pollution control, housing and neighborhood improvements, rural development, conservation, beautification, veterans outreach, and other fields of human betterment and community improvement.[116]

Recognizing that these public-service subsidies operate as economic incentives inducing private businesses to seek government-subsidized workers in lieu of nonsubsidized employees, the statute requires assurances from prospective recipients that

> no funds received . . . will be used to hire any person to fill a job opening created by the action of an employer in laying off or terminating the employment of any regular employee not supported under this subchapter in anticipation of filling the vacancy so created by hiring an employee to be supported under this subchapter. . . .[117]

The statute even acknowledges that these federal subsidies may jeopardize the promotional opportunities of nonsubsidized workers, requiring applicants to supply the government with "assurances that the jobs in each job category in no way infringe upon the promotional opportunities which would otherwise be available to persons currently employed in public service jobs not subsidized under this subchapter . . . ."[118] Nevertheless, armed with only the applicant's perfunctory assurances and the Secretary of Labor's unverifiable prediction that proposed federally subsidized jobs will not displace existing employment opportunities, the government can legally grant employment subsidies acknowledged to threaten serious disruption of the private economy.[119] With the public treasury at its disposal, the government unhesitatingly undertakes a subsidy program that subjugates the decisions of private individuals to the will of government officials concerning what economic activities should be performed and who should perform them. The cost of the program is borne by private individuals not only in the form of the taxation and inflation required to finance the subsidies, but also through the resultant less-preferred production pattern stimulated by the government's intervention in the job market.

The final provision for subsidizing private jobs appears in the portion of the Comprehensive Employment and Training Act that authorizes "research, training, and evaluation" programs.[120] Apparently seeking to deceive casual readers, the authors of the legislation first strongly state that "nothing in this subsection shall authorize the Secretary [of Labor] to carry out employment programs experimenting with subsidized wages in the private sector."[121] However, several columns of fine print later, the same statute openly authorizes the subsidized jobs it pretends to ban in the earlier provision. The statute declares:

> The Secretary [of Labor] is authorized to carry out a special program to demonstrate the efficacy of providing certificates or vouchers to economically disadvantaged, unemployed, and underemployed persons entitling private employers who provide employment, training, and services to each person volunteering to participate in such program to payment in amounts equal to the face value of the certificate for specified periods of time during which each such person may not be fully productive.[122]

If this stealthy turnabout was not designed to mislead either unwary legislators or the public, why was such a furtive reversal of policy used to establish this subsidy program? Whatever the reason, the authorized program of subsidized wages to private employers allows the government freely to alter and influence private employment decisions, shaping a still nominally "private" economy to fit into a governmentally constructed mold.

To convey the scope of government power here asserted, two other aspects of the statutory language require comment. First, the subsidization of private employment is *assumed* to be a commendable practice. Dropping any attempt to feign objectivity, the statute *requires* the subsidy program "to demonstrate the efficacy" of the government payments that it authorizes to private employers.[123] With its conclusion fixed at the outset, the government bureaucracy needs only to provide the "facts" to substantiate a thesis already written into law. Second, the potential recipients of government-subsidized employment form an almost infinitely elastic and nonexclusive category. To be eligible to benefit from the government's largesse, a person must be "economically disadvantaged," "unemployed," or "underemployed."[124] While "unemployed" and "underemployed" are precisely defined by the statute,[125] "economically disadvantaged" is nowhere defined. Without objective definition, this phrase enables government officials to use it as no more than a subjective affirmation of the desirability of subsidizing the individuals so labeled.

The Comprehensive Employment and Training Act is well equipped with other standard features of fascist economic apparatus. It creates a full complement of *planning councils* in which organized special interests meet under the government's supervision. One such council is authorized by the section of the Act that creates a national "comprehensive manpower services" program designed to develop and create jobs and training.[126] To procure public money from the federal government, a state or local government[127] must go through the usual charade of decentralized decision-making. It must appoint a "planning council" representing special interests including business, labor, community organizations, and agriculture.[128] In order to oversee all manpower services programs administered within its borders, a state seeking federal tax dollars must also create a "Manpower Services Council" that includes representatives of organized labor, business and industry, community-based organizations, and the general public.[129] Although these planning councils and Manpower Services Councils may submit their recommendations,[130] the federal government has ultimate control over all state or local efforts. The mechanism for federal control in this case is the "comprehensive manpower program," which each state or local government must submit to obtain national financial assistance.[131] If the federal government does not approve of the applicant's comprehensive manpower program, it simply does not fund it. Thus, in this as in other economic matters, the quest for federal tax dollars enables the national government to accomplish its objectives through local organizations as surely as it could by operating the programs directly.

The fascist economic policies so far discussed are reiterated in the section of the Comprehensive Employment and Training Act that creates the National Commission for Manpower Policy.[132] Petulantly complaining that its power over "manpower development" programs has heretofore been too diffuse for its tastes—"so diffused and fragmented . . . that it has been impossible to develop rational priorities"[133] — Congress envisions the National Commission for Manpower Policy as a means of altering what it views as a deplorable "lack of a coherent, flexible, national manpower policy" and of "solving economic and social problems which threaten fundamental national interests and objectives."[134] Among other things, it is the function of the National Commission for Manpower Policy to "identify the manpower goals and needs of the Nation."[135]

Through the National Commission for Manpower Policy, the federal government again is authorized to formulate national labor policies by controlling an elite covey of special-interest emissaries selected by government officials.[136] Reflecting the prevalent fascist economic environment, the law empowers a government-dominated amalgamation of special interests (labor, industry, commerce, education, and the public) to determine the policies, "priorities," and "needs" to which a servile citizenry must cater.[137] More clearly than ever, the fascist yearning for government power to impose upon the public its notion of what constitutes the "national interest" emerges into full view.

Thus, through a relatively small number of statutes, the U.S. government has claimed the right and mobilized the power to control what are still anachronistically called "private" labor relations. As on all fascist economic fronts, the government defers to private economic decision-making until its will is stymied by that entity known in fascist jargon as the "private sector." Although many of the principles typically adopted by fascist states in dealing with labor/management relations are enshrined in American law, the United States government does not yet totally dominate the day-to-day activities of labor and management, as did previous fascist economies. But whether political considerations prompt the government to exercise that total dominance or to grow ever more adept at manipulating labor relations by less overt means, the principle of unlimited government authority to supersede private economic choices related to labor is firmly established under existing law.

8

Federal Control over Agriculture

Although in theory private businessmen still own and operate American farms, the government has seized absolute control over United States agriculture. More than any other economic endeavor except perhaps the defense industry, agricultural production and distribution must conform to government specifications establishing the quantity and quality of output desired and the manner in which that output may be marketed. Both the style of government regulation of agriculture and its intensity follow the fascist pattern. Juxtaposed against a familiar backdrop of nominal private ownership coupled with ultimate government direction, American agriculture, like German agriculture under Hitler's "Food Estate" and Italian agriculture under Mussolini's "Battle of the Wheat" and "Bonifica Integral" (integral land reclamation) programs, has been singled out for stringent and pervasive government controls of a severity virtually unparalleled elsewhere in the fascist economy. Unwittingly emulating its fascist predecessors, the American government asserts that unmitigated abridgment of farmers' economic freedom is required in the "national interest," all the while lauding farmers' pastoral endeavors and the concept of private agricultural enterprise.

In order to appreciate the full significance of the statutes that confer these plenary powers upon the government, it is essential to understand the economic context and consequences of the United States government's manipulation of American agriculture. To this end, the economic characteristics of agriculture in a free economy, as well as the consequences of government attempts to obstruct the free operation of agricultural markets, will be discussed before describing the governing farm legislation.

I. GRADUAL EXODUS FROM AGRICULTURE: AN ECONOMIC IMPERATIVE IN A GROWING ECONOMY

It is one of the most indisputable principles of economics, supported by extensive scholarly research, that as people's incomes rise, their demand for food products rises less rapidly than their demand for nonfood products.[1] When people earn more money, they increase their spending for both farm and nonfarm products, but overall people spend a smaller percentage of their increased earnings on food than on non-agricultural products. Economists label this phenomenon "income inelasticity of demand" for agricultural products.[2]

The implication of this rather sterile-sounding principle is very poignant indeed. It means that, when economic growth causes an overall rise in people's incomes, a smaller percentage of the population needs to work in agriculture than previously in order to satisfy society's proportionately diminished desire for agricultural products relative to nonagricultural ones. If political intervention prevents the percentage of the labor force engaged in farm employment from declining, then *more* agricultural products will be supplied than consumers desire to purchase at the existing prices, and *fewer* nonfarm products will be supplied than people would like to purchase at their new income level. Absent the necessary shift to nonfarm employment, agricultural prices will fall as the market adjusts to the oversupply of farm products, and other prices will rise in response to increased consumer demand for nonfarm products.[3] Unless there is a gradual transition to nonfarm employment, farmers in a growing economy will earn ever lower incomes and consumers will encounter higher prices than they otherwise would for desired nonfarm products. To maintain the income distribution between farm and nonfarm workers that prevailed prior to a period of economic growth without reducing consumers' ability to purchase desired products, a steady shift of labor and capital from farming to nonagricultural endeavors is economically imperative.[4]

While these principles govern even when productivity levels remain static as between farm and nonfarm occupations, their effects are intensified when productivity in agriculture increases at a greater rate

185

than in nonfarm industries. For a variety of reasons (including highly intensive farming stimulated by government-imposed acreage restrictions and government-financed agricultural research), agricultural productivity has advanced at a rate far in excess of productivity gains in other industries.[5] Since heightened productivity enables more output to be generated with less labor, increased productivity alone constantly reduces the number of agricultural workers required to produce the food products that consumers desire. When coupled with agriculture's declining proportion of total production in a growing economy, agricultural productivity advances accelerate the rate at which the shift from farm to nonfarm employment must occur.

But however clear the necessity of a steady outflow of labor from farm to nonfarm employment appears to a student of economics, from the farmer's perspective the needed transition is neither obvious nor easy. For an individual farmer, the understandable tendency is to persevere in agriculture longer than objective economic considerations warrant, for financial as well as psychological ties to farming as a way of life are often difficult to sever. Further, not only is it extremely difficult for farmers to perceive and accept the economic inevitability of transition to nonagricultural endeavors, but also it is all too easy even for economically astute farmers to resist translating the abstract mandate of economic theory into a personal prescription for change.

II. FORCIBLE OBSTRUCTION OF TRANSITION TO NONAGRICULTURAL EMPLOYMENT

Feeling that economic reality was too harsh a mistress, farmers marshaled their considerable political influence to win government programs designed to block the needed transition to nonfarm employment. It was, after all, much more comfortable to perpetuate the status quo by government fiat than to change jobs just because consumers' economic needs had shifted. The farm legislation that emerged as a result of farmers' efforts is silent testimony to the political savvy of the agricultural lobby.

Through agricultural legislation, the government has attempted to prevent the necessary economic transition to nonfarm employment. The government programs explicitly aim to preserve the economic structure that existed in the dim, idyllic wonderland of 1909–14, when farmers experienced a rare period of prosperity that temporarily reprieved them from the trend away from agriculture. The unifying purpose of farm legislation is to perpetuate a rigid economic structure in which just as many farmers receive just as fat a slice of the nation's economic pie as they did in the 1909–14 period.

This approach is, of course, quite appealing if you happen to be a farmer. Similar legislation for members of their own profession undoubtedly would have been favored by blacksmiths, glassblowers, steamboat manufacturers, and other producers who saw their trades gradually squeezed out by technological advances in a growing economy.[6] Only historical accident makes the economic consequences of preserving these obsolete trades readily apparent while legislation compelling taxpayers to provide a "fair share" of the nation's economic wealth to farmers evokes spontaneous sympathy for the beleaguered farmer's plight. In both instances, however, the economic effect of using government power to perpetuate outmoded production is to raise the incomes of an elite group of beneficiaries (blacksmiths, farmers, etc.) at the expense of the vast majority of citizens forced to subsidize the obsolete activity. The economy is thereby throttled, tied to economically unjustified, inefficient production patterns that prevent the attainment of optimum economic growth.[7]

III. RATIONALIZATION OF GOVERNMENT ATTEMPTS TO RAISE FARMERS' INCOMES: OFFICIAL FANTASY AND ECONOMIC FACT

Realizing that recommending government-imposed stagnation of the economy for the benefit of the four percent of the labor force engaged in agricultural production[8] is not their most appealing argument, most lobbyists for government control over agriculture prefer to rationalize their case on altogether different grounds. Agriculture, they argue, is unique. After all, food is *basic* to our national economy and our physical well-being. Avoiding analysis of why food allegedly differs from clothing, energy, or therapeutic drugs in this regard, agricultural partisans subtly instill consumer fear that without government assistance essential food production might vanish from the economy. The economic fact never mentioned is that however great the shift to nonfarm employment required by economic growth, the ongoing demand for food would cause food production to continue to be profitable (and therefore abundant) when conducted by the smaller percentage of the population employed in agriculture after the transition.

Agriculture's truly unique characteristics pertain to the classic *instability* of agricultural markets.[9] First, agricultural fortunes depend on the vagaries of weather, insects, and disease. A widespread drought can nullify farmers' most diligent efforts, destroying their crops and their fortunes.

Second, consumers' demand for food remains relatively stable regardless of the supply of agricultural crops. Consumers' purchases may increase slightly when prices are low and decrease slightly when prices are high, but compared to demand in nonagricultural industries, demand for farm products is far less responsive to price changes.[10] This phenomenon, called "price inelasticity of demand," causes more pronounced price fluctuations for agricultural products than for nonfarm products. When supply is low (for example, because of drought), the fact that consumers' demand stays relatively constant causes much greater price increases than characterize other industries. Correspondingly, when supply is abundant, the low prices do not stimulate very much additional food consumption, causing prices to fall much more sharply than most nonagricultural prices would fall under similar circumstances.

Accentuating the problem of price fluctuations is the fact that economic incentives may encourage farmers to produce their maximum output regardless of market conditions. An individual farmer has a tremendous investment in capital goods—his land and equipment—the expense of which continues whether or not he restricts his planting. Since it may not cost much above fixed farm expenses to plant a full crop, farmers have substantial economic incentives not to limit their production in response to market conditions. As long as the farmer can sell his crop for more than the variable costs entailed in planting the seed and harvesting the crop, it pays him to plant, for the money he obtains makes some contribution, however minimal, towards the fixed costs of operating the farm.[11]

Compounding the tendency to supply more farm products than consumer demand warrants is the fact that the market structure for agriculture tends to be *perfectly competitive*, because without government intervention the ease of entry into farming prevents established producers from acquiring market power.[12] Perfect competition implies that no individual farmer can alter the price of the product by changing the amount he produces—he is a price-taker and can sell only at the existing market price.[13] This means that each farmer can sell any amount of output at the prevailing market price, which encourages him to produce his utmost even if the market price provides only a minimal contribution to fixed farm expenses. Nevertheless, although the market price is a fixed entity for the individual farmer, the aggregate of all individual farmers' decisions to produce maximum output intensifies problems of oversupply and may cause market prices to fall precipitously.

Advocates of government control over agriculture wax eloquent bewailing the economic problems described above. They seldom mention the free market's solution to such problems: the commodity futures trader. The commodity futures trader, in search of a profit, inadvertently provides a very beneficial social service.[14] Although he does not produce crops and has no intention of accepting delivery of any crop, he buys and sells pieces of paper that represent the right to future delivery of crops. The commodity futures trader acquires the acumen and foresight to anticipate that although a present glut on the market has depressed farm prices, future demand for a farm product ultimately will drive prices up. Therefore, he buys commodity futures at low prices and holds them in reserve for the future when increased prices will enable him to sell at a profit. His "social service" is that his very purchase tends to eliminate the prevailing oversupply, stabilize prices and curtail their further decline. In addition, his acquisitions have the salutary effect of withholding currently oversupplied agricultural produce until a future date when a more meager supply can beneficially be supplemented by the agricultural products the commodity trader will then sell. Correspondingly, when agricultural supplies are exceptionally small, the commodity futures trader sells produce, thereby increasing agricultural supply and stimulating price decreases at a time when supply is short and prices are high. Thus it is the seldom-mentioned commodity futures trader who, by acting in his own financial interest, tends to stabilize agricultural markets without the imposition of the rigid government controls so ardently coveted by agricultural lobbyists.

Ignoring the stabilizing role of the commodity futures trader, Congress enacted legislation that empowers the government to increase the price and limit the supply of agricultural products available to American consumers. Although the government never hesitates to claim that its altruistic purpose in adopting such measures is to benefit financially oppressed small farmers and domestic consumers, the actual results of federal agricultural programs are altogether inconsistent with the government's professed aims.

IV. ECONOMIC CONSEQUENCES OF GOVERNMENT AGRICULTURAL PROGRAMS

Despite the government's insistence that its goal is to protect consumers and small farming enterprises, federal programs aimed at raising farmers' incomes are economically detrimental to consumers and provide only meager benefits to marginal farmers, channeling the lion's share of public assistance to the largest farms, which need it least. In addition, the cost of public support of agriculture is much higher than necessary because of the *form* of farm subsidies used by the government.

The three primary forms of subsidy utilized under existing agricul-

189

tural legislation are price supports, restriction of supply, and direct payments, the last usually increasing with increased farm output. All three approaches seek to increase farmers' incomes by expropriating wealth from consumers and taxpayers and "redistributing" it to farmers.

Price supports are perhaps the most insidious form of agricultural subsidy. Agricultural price supports enable the government to increase the wealth of farmers by paying them a fixed price for their crops regardless of how much the market price falls below the support price. Whenever the government promises to pay farmers a support price for their crops that exceeds the market price, the price support causes farmers to produce too much of the product relative to consumers' demand for it.[15] Even if production levels were unchanged by price supports, consumers simply demand less of a product at higher price levels. Yet high price supports simultaneously encourage farmers to produce even more of the politically favored commodities.[16] This means that economic resources are lured by the government into inefficient production, which is not desired by consumers, thereby diminishing the productive resources available for endeavors preferred by the public.

As farmers respond to the government's bait and consumers curtail their consumption, an oversupply of the commodity favored by artificially high price supports emerges, a surplus which the government must discreetly dump apart from the normal channels of trade in order to maintain an above-market price structure in domestic markets. To rid itself of unsightly agricultural surpluses without allowing domestic prices to fall to market levels, the government usually dumps the "excess" produce either through international gifts and "sales" at below-market prices to foreign countries, or through domestic giveaway programs.[17] While domestic agricultural giveaway programs cause a redistribution of wealth within the United States, international dumping of agricultural surpluses has the even more profoundly disruptive consequence of undercutting foreign nations' agricultural industries and thereby provoking economic retaliation against the United States. Such government support of artificially high domestic prices is extremely damaging to the standard of living of citizens in all countries, as Chapter 9 demonstrates.

The economic burden of wealth transfer through government price supports falls on consumers and taxpayers. First, the cost of the government's purchases of farm products is borne directly by American citizens in the form either of taxation or of inflation, the government's only two means of financing such ventures. Second, consumers pay higher prices for farm products as a result of government price-support

190

activity, for by its purchases the government restricts the supply of agricultural products marketed domestically in order to sustain the artificially high agricultural price structure it favors. Whenever the market price dips below the support price, only the amount of the farm product that can be sold at the higher price set by the government is made commercially available to the public. The government buys the rest and disposes of it as it pleases. Third, nonfarm products may also become more expensive, for price supports encourage inefficient agricultural production and thus may divert economic resources from non-agricultural uses preferred by consumers. Finally, consumers encounter less than optimum quantities of agricultural as well as non-agricultural goods. Fewer *nonfarm* products are available because above-market price supports channel economic resources away from nonfarm endeavors and into less than optimum farming operations. Yet, ironically, despite government-induced overproduction of agricultural goods, the supply of *farm* products also is reduced because of the government's siphoning off a portion of farm output.

Because the surpluses caused by government price supports are an embarrassing reminder of the negative economic consequences of government intervention in agriculture, the government prefers to rely on what is euphemistically labeled "supply management" — bluntly stated, government restriction of farm output — to raise farmers' incomes.[18] The government employs a variety of techniques, discussed in the following section, to limit agricultural production, intending to raise agricultural prices by reducing the supply of farm products. Although this form of wealth transfer is somewhat less visible than price supports and hence preferred by farmers and legislators alike, its economic effects for consumers are similar. To the extent that the government is successful in restricting farm output, consumers are forced to pay higher prices for farm products. Some farmers are enriched and many consumers are impoverished, but through "supply management" the government avoids those nasty surpluses which remind voters of who is responsible for the high prices charged for food.

Ironically, it is exactly this desire to avoid visible wealth transfer that has caused American farmers and legislators to favor the most inefficient forms of farm subsidy throughout the history of U.S. agricultural programs. Government actions designed either to restrict farm output or to raise prices paid for farm products (such as price supports and payments linked to high farm output) are the *least* efficient methods of raising farmers' incomes.[19] These programs simply do not reach the struggling, impoverished, destitute small farmer in whose name most farm legislation is so nobly enacted.[20] Wealth transfer techniques such as price supports encourage farmers to persist in marginal farming operations, when economic reality and their ultimate financial self-interest necessitate a shift to nonfarm employment. Rather than assisting marginal farmers to transfer to more lucrative endeavors that conform to prevailing patterns of consumer demand, government intervention through price supports and through direct subsidy payments, which increase as farm output increases, tend to perpetuate economically inefficient agricultural production.

Moreover, most of the benefits of existing farm subsidy programs are paid to farmers in high income brackets, least in need of government assistance.[21] In fact, only about ten percent of the annual benefits of farm programs goes to the poorest twenty-nine percent of farmers.[22] Further, these meager government benefits represent only four percent of the income of operators of the smallest farms, whereas they represent twenty-five percent of the income of operators of the largest farm units.[23]

Besides being distributed primarily to wealthier farmers, existing subsidy programs funnel government assistance primarily to *landowners*, not to the sharecroppers or tenant farmers who often experience much more severe economic hardship than agricultural landowners. Further, because many subsidies are paid on farm *output*, subsidized gains in income a farmer receives are partially offset by corresponding increases in expenditures for farm inputs such as seed, fertilizer, feed, and fuel. And if the supply of an input necessary for farming is inelastic, price increases for that product may totally eliminate farmers' financial gains from the subsidies.[24]

Another flaw of the current subsidy structure is that it only benefits those who own a farm at the time when a new farm subsidy program benefiting that land is enacted. After the magic moment when the government subsidy is approved (for example, a quota permitting a landowner to produce a certain quantity of a particular crop such as tobacco on his land), the value of the government subsidy becomes incorporated or "capitalized" into the value of the land.[25] This means that any subsequent purchaser of the farm will pay the owner the amount the land is worth *with* the government subsidy. While the farmer who owned the land when the subsidy was created reaps a financial reward when he sells his land, all subsequent farmers who buy and sell that land acquire no benefit from the subsidy. They purchase the capitalized subsidy when they buy the land and sell it when they sell the land, receiving no net benefit as a result of the existence of the subsidy. And if a subsidy is withdrawn after a subsequent purchaser has paid its capitalized value in buying the land, he will actually lose that value when he later sells the land devoid of the subsidy right.[26]

Thus, despite politically motivated protestations to the contrary, the government's agricultural programs benefit neither the consumer nor the much extolled small farmer. Hurting low-income people most acutely, the government's actions force consumers to pay higher prices for agricultural commodities while necessitating inflation or higher taxes, or both, to finance the subsidies. Yet the subsidies for which consumers suffer chiefly benefit affluent, efficient farmers with the largest farms and the greatest agricultural output, not the superficially revered low-income operators of small farms. Furthermore, the government's determination to maintain above-market domestic agricultur l prices has required it to erect a massive wall of tariffs and quotas that prevent other countries from selling inexpensive agricultural goods to American consumers. Without this protectionist barrier to imported agricultural products, the entire government-sponsored structure of above-market domestic prices would collapse. These international repercussions of fascist economic intervention are explored fully in Chapter 9.

V. AGRICULTURAL LEGISLATION

Improbable as it seems when one contemplates the myriad programs and ubiquitous bureaucracy that it has spawned, the core legislation that authorizes government control over agriculture comprises a relatively small number of statutes. The vast bulk of agricultural legislation is contained in the following post-1932 federal statutes:

1. Agricultural Marketing Act of 1946
2. Agricultural Adjustment Act of 1933
3. Agricultural Adjustment Act of 1938
4. Agricultural Act of 1949
5. Federal Crop Insurance Act
6. Rural Environmental Conservation Program
7. Soil Conservation and Domestic Allotment Act
8. Agricultural Commodity Set-Aside legislation
9. Public Law 480

To the chagrin of politicians and farm lobbyists who would prefer that citizens regard agricultural legislation as an impenetrable bulwark without which the food supply would vanish and the economy would collapse, the agricultural laws are, in their fundamental principles, quite easy for the average person to comprehend. After setting forth the statutory jargon used to obscure the nature and consequences of government domination of agriculture, the rest of this chapter will describe these agricultural laws functionally, examining (1) government sponsorship of agricultural cartels, (2) government inducements stimulating agricultural production, (3) government efforts to curtail agricultural production, and (4) federal dumping of government-induced surpluses.

STATUTORY CODE WORDS: THE JARGON OF TOTAL GOVERNMENT TAKEOVER

Although one cannot expect those aspiring to total government control over a portion of the economy to issue forthright declarations of that intention, the phraseology of the agricultural statutes achieves new pinnacles in the well-practiced art of fascist euphemism. The Agricultural Marketing Act of 1946[27] captures the essence of this polished linguistic coverup. While self-consciously alluding to the glory of private enterprise, the Agricultural Marketing Act asserts government power to supervise virtually every aspect of the marketing and distribution of agricultural products.[28] Unconcealed yearning for a governmentally planned economy repeatedly emerges in statutory pleas for the more "orderly" marketing and "efficient" distribution of agricultural products to be engineered by government bureaucrats.[29] The government is empowered to develop "plans for *efficient* facilities and methods of operating such facilities for the *proper* assembly, processing, transportation, storage, distribution, and handling of agricultural products."[30] Immediately after declaring that "a sound, efficient, and *privately operated* system for distributing and marketing agricultural products is essential to a prosperous agriculture and is indispensable . . . to the welfare, prosperity, and health of the Nation,"[31] the Act directs the Secretary of Agriculture "to determine the best methods of processing, preparation for market, packaging, handling, transporting, storing, distributing, and marketing agricultural products."[32] A more concise expression of fascism's principal economic tenet would be difficult to formulate. Private entrepreneurs are envisioned as useful subordinates, entitled to economic freedom only if their activities conform to supposedly infallible economic judgments of government rulers who are pleased to decree the "best" way for people to conduct their "private" business.

The language becomes more entertaining as one progresses through the legislation. Instead of stating that the government will henceforth dictate to the people the quantity of agricultural products that should be marketed, the Agricultural Adjustment Act of 1938 proclaims that the government must strive to maintain "a *continuous and stable supply* of agricultural commodities from domestic production *adequate to meet consumer demand*"[33] and to avoid "abnormally excessive and abnormally deficient supplies."[34] The same implicit assertion of government power to dictate the "proper" supply of agricultural products reappears in statutory declarations that it is the government's role to prevent "burdensome surpluses and distressing shortages."[35] Similarly, instead of openly proclaiming government power to impose any prices for farm commodities that federal officials find appealing, the 1938 Act empowers the government to secure "prices *fair* to both producers and consumers,"[36] to mitigate "violent fluctuations in the price" of agricultural commodities,[37] and to prevent both "disastrously low prices" and "unreasonably high prices."[38] Again suffusing the politically unpalatable claim of government power to take over target agricultural markets with the glow of rectitude, the 1938 Act employs mellifluous language that proclaims the government's intent to avoid "*disorderly* marketing" of certain agricultural commodities,[39] "to promote, foster, and maintain an *orderly* flow" of agricultural supplies,[40] and to provide for "orderly marketing" of selected agricultural products.[41]

The same technique is used by the 1933 Agricultural Adjustment Act. Before launching its program for promoting government-sponsored cartels of agricultural producers, that statute repeatedly declares it to be congressional policy to secure "*orderly* marketing conditions" for farm commodities, expressing the lawmakers' longing for "an *orderly* flow of the supply [of any regulated agricultural commodity] to market throughout its normal marketing season to avoid unreasonable fluctuations in supplies and prices."[42] Throughout the agricultural legislation, the magic of words thus transforms the concepts of efficiency and orderliness into code words for that which conforms to the government's view of proper economic results. In the surrealist world of fascist euphemism, nothing could be more "disorderly" than an unregulated private market operating free of government "guidance."

The authoritarian implications of accepting these fascist economic principles are made explicit in legislation that established a temporary "National Commission on Food Marketing" empowered to "study and appraise the marketing structure of the food industry."[43] Dispensing with even superficial deference to private enterprise and completely negating any concept of economic freedom, the law authorized that Commission (two thirds of whose members were congressmen) to determine:

> The *kind of food industry* that would assure *efficiency* of production, assembly, processing, and distribution, provide *appropriate* services to consumers, and yet maintain *acceptable* competitive alternatives of procurement and sale in all segments of the industry from producer to consumer; . . . [as well as]
>
> The changes in statutes or public policy, the organization of farming and of food assembly, processing, and distribution, and the inter-

relationships between segments of the food industry which would be *appropriate* to achieve a *desired* distribution of power as well as *desired* levels of efficiency.[44]

When one asks "acceptable" to whom, "appropriate" according to whom, or "desired" by whom, the inescapable answer is an elite group of government officials now believed to possess constitutional power to prescribe economic activities "proper" for a subservient citizenry.

One other linguistic innovation of American fascism must be mentioned before proceeding: the notion of "cooperation" as defined by existing agricultural laws. "Cooperative principles and practices" denote federally supervised sharing of markets and market information within the shelter of government-sanctioned cartels.[45] "Cooperator" is the felicitous code word for an agricultural producer who "voluntarily" complies with government programs designed to restrict farm output in order to raise farmers' incomes by increasing the price consumers pay for agricultural products.[46] With this characteristically fascist terminology clearly defined, one is equipped to evaluate the specific agricultural programs implemented by the government.

GOVERNMENT SPONSORSHIP OF AGRICULTURAL CARTELS

To attain its goal of raising farmers' incomes, the government possesses virtually unlimited statutory power to sanction and promote agricultural cartels. Antitrust laws notwithstanding, agricultural producers are explicitly authorized to "act together in associations . . . in collectively processing, preparing for market, handling, and marketing" agricultural products.[47] These producers' associations, which are actually agricultural cartels, can engage in monopolistic practices without fear of reprimand so long as the Secretary of Agriculture approves of the results of their collusion. Only when the Secretary of Agriculture feels that "any such association monopolizes or restrains trade *to such an extent* that the price of any agricultural product is *unduly* enhanced" need he file a complaint against the association.[48] However, if an association's monopolistic practices raise agricultural prices to a level the Secretary personally favors, he is free to tolerate and encourage the association's activities.

Effectively guaranteeing agricultural producers exemption from antitrust scrutiny, the law authorizes them to collude in restricting supply, fixing prices, and dividing markets, all by the simple mechanism of government-approved sharing of economic information. In defiance of established principles of antitrust law, the statute empowers agricultural producers who are engaged "in *collectively* processing, preparing for market, handling, and marketing" agricultural products to "acquire, exchange, interpret, and disseminate past, present, and prospective crop, market, statistical, economic, and other similar information by direct exchange between such persons, and/or such associations or federations thereof, and/or by and through a common agent created or selected by them."[49]

Another major way the government supports agricultural cartels is by means of its "cooperative marketing" services. Through its cooperative marketing services, the government itself actively disseminates market information to enable agricultural cartels to limit supply, standardize marketing procedures, and centralize control over agricultural production. Without such government-sponsored "sharing" of market information, attempted agricultural cartels would disintegrate. For the benefit of the producers' associations (cartels), as well as individual producers, the government is authorized:

> To acquire from all available sources information concerning crop prospects, supply, demand, current receipts, exports, imports, and prices of the agricultural products handled or marketed by cooperative associations, and to employ qualified commodity marketing specialists to summarize and analyze this information and disseminate the same among cooperative associations and others ... [and]
> To promote the knowledge of *cooperative principles and practices* and to cooperate, in promoting such knowledge, with educational and marketing agencies, cooperative associations, and others.[50]

Other mechanisms by which the government facilitates the operation of agricultural cartels are established by the Agricultural Adjustment Act of 1933.[51] In hopes of raising farmers' incomes by increasing food prices, this Act empowers the government to promote both voluntary and compulsory measures to restrict the quantity of any agricultural commodity (or of any grade, size, or quality of an agricultural product) that can legally be marketed. Unlike restrictions on agricultural supplies discussed in subsequent portions of this chapter, these restraints limit the *marketing*, not the production, of agricultural products.

The "voluntary" marketing restrictions arranged between agricultural producers and the government are known as "marketing agreements." The 1933 Act authorizes the Secretary of Agriculture, on behalf of the government, to establish with producers, handlers, processors, or associations of producers of agricultural products, agreements that are designed to raise their incomes by such means as limiting the quantity of farm output allowed to be marketed.[52] The making of marketing agreements is explicitly declared by the statute to be exempt from the antitrust laws.[53] While the marketing-agreement device provides the government backing essential to effective enforcement of cartel decisions, it does not permit the government to impose the cartel's market-restricting decisions upon unwilling producers or handlers.

But legislators have not been content to let the government's vast powers to promote agricultural cartels remain noncoercive. Through the 1933 Act, marketing decisions approved by agricultural cartels also may be made legally enforceable. Even recalcitrant producers and handlers of agricultural products can be compelled to comply with government-approved marketing restrictions through mandatory government rulings called "marketing orders."[54] Marketing orders permit a cozy government/business agricultural alliance that utterly prevents the free market from operating. Through marketing orders, government bureaucrats and agricultural producers legally may combine to limit the quantity of agricultural products that can be sold and to decide who will be allowed to sell them, all for the sole purpose of enriching farmers. The 1933 Act states that marketing orders may contain provisions:

> (A) Limiting . . . the total quantity of any such [agricultural] commodity or product, or of any grade, size, or quality thereof . . . which may be marketed in or transported to any or all markets . . . during any specified period or periods by all handlers thereof.
> (B) Allotting . . . the amount of such commodity or product . . . which each handler may purchase from or handle on behalf of any and all producers thereof, during any specified period or periods . . . .
> (C) Allotting . . . the amount of any such commodity or product . . . which each handler may market in or transport to any or all markets . . . .
> (D) Determining, or providing methods for determining, the existence and extent of the surplus of any such commodity or product . . . and providing for the control and disposition of such surplus. . . .[55]

Even if a majority of the handlers of agricultural products in the area to which a prospective marketing order applies disapprove of the order, the government can force handlers and producers alike to accept the order if (1) the Secretary of Agriculture says that it is "the only practical means of advancing the interests of the producers," and (2) the order is favored by either two thirds of the producers of the commodity in the area concerned or the producers of two thirds of the volume of the commodity in that area.[56] Thus handlers of agricultural products can be forced to comply with a marketing order totally against their will.

Producers are similarly vulnerable to coercion at the hands of an influential elite, for the 1933 Agricultural Adjustment Act also provides that the government must regard the approval of a producers' association (cartel) as signifying the approval of all the producers who participate in the cartel.[57] This provision potentially enables a numerical minority to impose a marketing order on a majority of producers who oppose the order. A hypothetical example illustrates how this might occur. If two thirds of all producers of an agricultural commodity were members of cartels, with the remaining one third either not cartelized or composing a separate cartel, and the cartels were operated internally on the basis of majority rule, approval of a marketing order by barely more than half of the two-thirds majority necessary to adopt a marketing order could be sufficient to validate the order. Thus, where cartels prevail, roughly one third (numerically) of the producers could effectively empower the government to compel all the handlers and a dissident two thirds of the producers to comply with the government decrees.

It is even more possible for marketing orders to be imposed on an unwilling majority of producers if one considers obtaining approval of producers of two thirds of the *volume* of a commodity. A small fraction of the total number of producers in a given area may produce most of that area's agricultural output, enabling the few large producers to impose their economic will on a numerically superior group of smaller producers. In such circumstances, if the few large producers also happened to be joined in a cartel, the possibility of government-enforced market restrictions being imposed for the benefit of a minority of agricultural producers is further compounded.

Perceiving that no amount of market restriction could achieve its intended result without government power to police regulated businesses and penalize violators, the authors of the 1933 Agricultural Adjustment Act provided ample government enforcement powers to guarantee the effectiveness of agricultural cartels. First, daily fines may be imposed for violation of any marketing order.[58] Second, the government may require submission of any information the Secretary of Agriculture desires from persons subject to marketing agreements and from agricultural product handlers who are subject to marketing orders.[59] Finally, any person who violates an allotment fixed for him under the 1933 Act (such as a handler who is forbidden to market more than a specified quantity of an agricultural commodity by a marketing order) is legally compelled to *forfeit* the market value of agricultural products sold in excess of his allotment.[60]

Severe as these measures are, government sponsorship and enforcement of agricultural cartels constitute but a muted prelude to the government intervention in agricultural production authorized by other statutory provisions.

GOVERNMENT INDUCEMENTS STIMULATING AGRICULTURAL PRODUCTION

All of the government expenditures to stimulate agricultural production discussed in this section seek to achieve "parity" income for farmers. Although the notion of parity is often vaguely equated with fairness, justice, or equity for farmers, "parity" actually denotes the incomes and purchasing power of farmers relative to the rest of society during the idyllic 1909–14 period, when farmers enjoyed unprecedented prosperity.[61] The underlying idea is to compel the rest of society to bestow upon farmers the same purchasing power they possessed in that period. If by selling a bushel of wheat during 1909–14 the farmer received enough money to purchase a pair of shoes, those seeking parity contend that a present-day sale of a bushel of wheat should automatically *entitle* the farmer to income sufficient to purchase modern goods comparable in value to that pair of shoes in 1909–14.[62] Thus parity seeks to rigidify the earning power of farmers at 1909–14 levels, in total disregard of the subsequent economic growth that has reduced the amount of agricultural labor now necessary to produce the farm output that society voluntarily would choose to purchase.[63] The theory behind parity is that consumers and taxpayers must be *forced* to pay farmers the same amount that they would have had to pay for agricultural products if no technological advances or productivity gains had occurred since 1914.

The yearning for parity permeates agricultural legislation. It is the declared purpose of the 1933 Agricultural Adjustment Act "to establish and maintain such orderly marketing conditions for agricultural commodities . . . as will establish, as the prices to farmers, parity prices."[64] The Secretary of Agriculture, given legal power to make any payments he deems "fair and reasonable" to achieve parity, is authorized by the 1933 Act to dispense the following types of government subsidy payments to raise farm product prices to parity levels:

> (a) To remove from the normal channels of trade and commerce quantities of any basic agricultural commodity or product thereof;
> (b) To expand domestic or foreign markets for any basic agricultural commodity or product thereof; [and]
> (c) [To make payments in] . . . connection with the production of that part of any basic agricultural commodity which is required for domestic consumption.[65]

In addition to these parity payments, the 1933 Act appropriates thirty percent of the tariffs collected annually under customs laws for farm subsidies designed to "reestablish farmers' purchasing power by making payments in connection with the normal production of any agricultural commodity for domestic consumption."[66] Tariff revenue also may be used (1) to subsidize — in the statute's slanted phraseology, to "encourage" — the export of American agricultural products, and (2) for the ostensible purpose of promoting domestic agricultural consumption, a feat the statute asserts will somehow be accomplished by government purchases intended to *remove* farm products from normal channels of trade.[67]

Augmenting the parity subsidies authorized by the 1933 Act, the Agricultural Adjustment Act of 1938 gives the government broad power to make parity payments directly to producers for their "normal" output of specified farm commodities. The Secretary of Agriculture

> is authorized and directed to make payments to producers of corn, wheat, cotton, rice, or tobacco, on their normal production of such commodities in amounts which, together with the proceeds thereof, will provide a return to such producers which is as nearly equal to parity price as the funds . . . made available will permit.[68]

The farmer's gain is the taxpayer's and the consumer's loss, for the government's magnanimous generosity can be financed only by taxation or inflation, or both.

The most subtle form of government payment to induce agricultural production and achieve parity incomes for farmers is that authorized by the Agricultural Act of 1949.[69] This statute empowers the government to provide price supports for agricultural commodities, usually expressed as a percentage of "parity" prices. The Secretary of Agriculture generally wields wide discretionary power in fixing the price-support levels for such products.[70]

If the price supports consisted of overt government promises to purchase any amount of an agricultural product offered to it at the guaranteed price, one could criticize the program's economic consequences but could not accurately term it subtle or surreptitious. The actual technique employed to provide agricultural price support does merit such labels. Although the purpose and the effect of the price supports are to establish the government as the guaranteed purchaser of last resort at specified support levels, the machinations used to achieve that result are a masterpiece of dissimulation.

The primary conduit used to funnel price-support payments to agricultural producers is the "nonrecourse loan." This antiseptically labeled technique operates as follows. First the government (through the Commodity Credit Corporation) "loans" a farmer the amount of money his *anticipated* crop would be worth at the price-support levels then in effect. The Commodity Credit Corporation takes a "lien" on, or "security interest" in, the crop, which thus serves as "collateral" for the "loan." When the farmer harvests his crop, if the market price exceeds the support price and the crop yield is good, the farmer usually sells his crop at the prevailing market price, pays off the loan, and earns profits accordingly. If, however, either the market price dips below the support price or the crop fails, the farmer simply keeps the government loan money and lets the government (via the Commodity Credit Corporation) take possession of his crop. Thus this form of subsidy functions both as a price support and as a crop-yield guarantee, for the government loan is based on anticipated yield at the supported price and need not be repaid if actual yield falls below anticipated yield, even if the market price exceeds the support price.

In authorizing nonrecourse loans, the Agricultural Act of 1949 states explicitly: "No producer shall be personally liable for any deficiency arising from the sale of the collateral securing any loan made under authority of this Act unless such loan was obtained through fraudulent representations by the producer."[71] Although the facade of a loan makes the statute's significance difficult for the average citizen to comprehend, the farmers who cash in on its subsidies have no trouble decoding its dissembling terminology.

Another statute, the Federal Crop Insurance Act,[72] overtly authorizes crop-yield guarantees. Creating a government entity called the Federal Crop Insurance Corporation to implement the law's provisions, this statute generally empowers the government to insure up to seventy-five percent of the average yield of a farmer's land as measured by the farm's output during some period deemed "representative" by federal officials.[73]

All of these agricultural production subsidy programs seeking parity prices and parity income for farmers share the common deficiency of inducing high-cost, inefficient production. To remedy the "surplus" farm output its own production subsidies generate, the government pursues two counteractive policies: programs that encourage farmers *not* to produce, and programs that authorize the dumping in foreign as well as domestic markets of the government-induced surpluses.

GOVERNMENT EFFORTS TO CURTAIL AGRICULTURAL PRODUCTION

Wary of overproduction and visible surpluses stimulated by its price-support and other production subsidy programs, the government simultaneously strives to discourage farmers from producing. The theory underlying government efforts to curtail agricultural production is that if the supply of agricultural products can be reduced, farmers will receive higher prices from consumers for the governmentally limited agricultural supply, thereby increasing farmers' incomes without generating unsightly surpluses. The government's three primary techniques for preventing agricultural production are quotas, acreage allotments, and payments to farmers for not producing on their land, the last felicitously labeled "conservation" measures.

For certain basic agricultural crops—corn, wheat, cotton, rice, tobacco, and peanuts—the government uses quotas and/or acreage restrictions to limit farm output, as authorized by the Agricultural Adjustment Act of 1938.[74] Quotas are government decrees specifying the exact quantity of a controlled crop (measured in pounds or bushels) that the government allows each farmer, county, and state to produce. Through acreage allotments, in contrast, the government specifies the precise number of acres upon which each farmer, county, and state shall produce regulated crops, but does not restrict the quantity of output that may be produced from the allotted acreage.

Although government production limits do not become mandatory until approved by two thirds of the producers polled in a governmentally conducted "referendum," quotas and acreage allotments are extremely effective in restricting agricultural production even without general approval by producers. The key to their effectiveness is the government-financed bribe. To make the farm output-control system work without uniform endorsement by producers, legislators designed the government's efforts at reducing the agricultural supply to dovetail with federal production subsidy programs. If agricultural producers reject the government's supply reduction scheme, the government nevertheless has statutory authority to promulgate farm output guidelines to farmers, and government price supports and other production subsidies can be withheld from farmers who refuse to comply with the output restrictions favored by the government.

The Agricultural Act of 1949, for example, explicitly empowers the Secretary of Agriculture to make price-support-payment eligibility contingent upon compliance with government-formulated farm output limitations: "Compliance by the producer with acreage allotments, production goals and marketing practices (including marketing quotas when authorized by law), prescribed by the Secretary, may be required as a condition of eligibility for price support."[75] Reinforcing its threat of withholding production subsidies from farmers who disregard suggested acreage limits, the government further sweetens its supply-control proposals by promising farmers who "cooperate" additional payments for *not* producing on their land, subsidies discussed in some detail below.

Although independent farmers may theoretically remain free to implement private economic decisions, the size of the federal subsidies involved makes it virtually impossible for noncomplying producers to compete successfully with heavily subsidized farmers who bow to government-sanctioned output limits. Subsidy payments thus provide a coercive lever over farm output, predictably eliciting the desired "voluntary" enthusiasm for government agricultural output limits without the necessity of general producer approval of mandatory quotas or acreage allotments. Nevertheless, because the myth of farmers' freedom is useful to a fascist government, the twin charades of producer referendums and voluntary cooperation by regulated farmers remain standard features of the relevant legislation.

Government restriction of America's wheat supply typifies federal regulation of other commodities, utterly dispelling the persistent American myth that all one needs to start a successful farm is good land, equipment, and a willingness to work. Although some other products (such as tobacco) are subject to more stringent output regulation and some to less, such variations are more significant to farmers who must master statutory nuances to operate successfully within the system than to nonfarmers concerned about America's legislative approach to government manipulation of agricultural production.

After routine overtures intimating that government takeover of the wheat industry is necessary because "wheat is a basic source of food for the Nation,"[76] the Agricultural Adjustment Act of 1938 authorizes the Secretary of Agriculture to proclaim a national wheat-marketing quota, in bushels, whenever his omniscient perception of economic conditions indicates that wheat production otherwise would be "excessive."[77] Before this quota may be made mandatory, the Secretary of Agriculture must conduct a referendum in which farmers are polled by secret ballot. If more than one third of the farmers oppose the quota, the quota cannot be forcibly imposed on the farmers.[78] If two thirds of the farmers favor the scheme, however, it becomes mandatory, and a farmer who violates the terms of the quota must either relinquish his "extra" wheat to the government or be forced to pay massive fines on all wheat produced in excess of his assigned quota.[79]

Besides allowing forcible restriction of production, the quota referendum mechanism is weighted in favor of vested wheat-producing interests and the economic status quo. Only producers who already possess farm acreage allotments by virtue of their historical involvement in wheat production are permitted to vote in the referendum.[80] And if the proposed quota is expressed as a percentage of a preceding year's production, so much the better for declining producers whose financial viability is currently a product of government intervention rather than economic efficiency. The further back in time the quota's point of reference, the more the quota favors deteriorating areas of production.[81] Thus farm quotas based on eighty percent of 1970's crop will tend to overstate the market share of a declining producer or production area and understate the market share of developing new production areas. In this manner established wheat producers who believe their financial interests to be served by suppressing new competition can beckon the government to do their bidding in throttling economically efficient changes in the persons and areas engaged in wheat production.

But the government's power over wheat production does not depend exclusively on producers' approval of mandatory quotas. Providing an alternative means of accomplishing results identical to those sought by the quota system, the 1938 Act requires that each year, as part of its "normal" operation, the government must proclaim a national acreage allotment for wheat.[82] The national acreage allotment is defined as the number of acres whose cultivation would be required to produce the hypothetical wheat quota that would be proclaimed if the Secretary saw fit to proclaim such a quota.[83] To secure government power over the *distribution* of wheat production as well as the total acreage planted with wheat, the 1938 Act also provides for the "apportionment" of the national wheat acreage allotment among states, counties, and individual farms.[84] By this means the government of a nominally free economy is empowered to dictate to an individual farmer precisely how many acres he should plant with wheat seed.

The thrust of the legislation is to rigidify historical production patterns[85] and virtually eliminate entry of new producers into wheat production, thereby bestowing monopoly power upon existing wheat producers. Whether the apportionment in question pertains to a state, county, or single farm, the primary criterion for the current year's acreage limit is "the preceding year's allotment."[86] The economic death sentence for prospective new producers is this statutory declaration: "Not more than 3 per centum of the State allotment shall be apportioned to farms on which wheat has not been planted during any of the three marketing years immediately preceding the marketing year in which the allotment is made."[87] Another statutory allocation of acreage allotments excludes producers who had no allotment for the preceding crop from all but one percent of the state's acreage allotment,[88] giving the government total discretion to distribute even these allotments on political grounds through such amorphous or irrelevant distribution criteria as

> suitability of the land for production of wheat, the past experience of the farm operator in the production of wheat, the extent to which the farm operator is dependent on income from farming for his livelihood, the production of wheat on other farms owned, operated, or controlled

by the farm operator, and such other factors as the Secretary determines should be considered for the purpose of establishing fair and equitable farm allotments.[89]

One cannot even gain eligibility for an allotment by starting a new wheat farm without an allotment and planting wheat independently for three years. The statute explicitly outlaws such impertinence by hopeful new producers: "The planting on a form [sic] in the commercial wheat-producing area of wheat . . . for which no farm wheat acreage allotment was established shall not make the farm eligible for an allotment as an old farm. . . ."[90] Throughout, the Secretary of Agriculture retains broad discretionary authority to dispense politically motivated favors to friendly, cooperative regions and producers; he may adjust the historically based allotment "to the extent deemed necessary . . . to establish a fair and equitable apportionment base" or allotment.[91]

Besides the threat of withholding price supports, the Secretary of Agriculture has a multitude of financial and political levers to stimulate "voluntary" compliance with his wheat acreage allotments. One clever statutory provision appeals to the wheat producers' inclination not to burn bridges before crossing them, threatening that the current wheat acreage allotment of any producer who exceeded his previous year's allotment automatically will be reduced unless the farmer has surrendered his "excess" produce to the government.[92] Another provision limits government subsidy payments for producing wheat to projected yield from a farm's *allotted* acreage.[93] Further, providing a subtle form of subsidy insurance, the statute requires the government to loan "cooperative" wheat producers seventy-five percent of the anticipated value of the production payments to which they will be legally entitled, a "loan" which producers do not have to repay even if their actual production subsidy ultimately is less than the government funds already advanced to them.[94] Similarly, while the Secretary of Agriculture has the power to advance money to cooperative agricultural producers to enable them to pay insurance premiums assessed by the Federal Crop Insurance Corporation, such payments are denied to farmers who do not "voluntarily" agree to crop limitation programs formulated pursuant to the Soil Conservation and Domestic Allotment Act.[95]

The government also has broad authority to pay farmers for *not* producing wheat on their allotted acreage. One such program attempts to neutralize public aversion to the payments it authorizes by labeling land held fallow through government bribery "diverted acreage" devoted to "conservation" uses.[96] Under another program similar to this acreage diversion scheme, if the Secretary of Agriculture asserts that

206

"the total supply of wheat or other commodities will . . . likely be excessive"—that is, if he wants to raise producers' incomes further by withholding agricultural supplies from consumers—the Agricultural Adjustment Act of 1938 authorizes him to impose a "set-aside" for such agricultural commodities.[97] Finally, for wheat crops—as for rye, flax, barley, cotton, field corn, grain sorghums, hogs, cattle, rice, potatoes, tobacco, peanuts, sugar beets and sugarcane, and all milk products— the 1933 Agricultural Adjustment Act broadly empowers the Secretary of Agriculture to make whatever subsidy payments for not producing he deems "fair and reasonable."[98] The lucky "cooperators," financially bludgeoned into "voluntary" compliance with the government's wishes, thus may receive overlapping subsidy payments (1) for producing on their allotted wheat acreage, (2) for not producing on the "diverted acreage" which is part of the farm's allotted acreage, (3) for not producing on any land deemed "set-aside acreage," and (4) for not producing on any other acreage the Secretary of Agriculture wishes the farmer not to put to productive use.

But government authority to pay producers for not producing is far more extensive than even the foregoing provisions suggest. Waving the banner of "conservation," the Soil Conservation and Domestic Allotment Act[99] and the Rural Environmental Conservation Program[100] together give the government a blank check to pay any farmer for not producing any crop, provisions far more inclusive than the 1933 and 1938 Agricultural Adjustment Acts' power to restrict output of specific basic agricultural commodities.

The Soil Conservation and Domestic Allotment Act, the older of the two laws, was originally enacted in 1935. The emotional tone of the legislation is clear at the outset, for the law's opening provision deplores "wastage of soil and moisture resources on farm, grazing, and forest lands of the Nation, resulting from soil erosion" as "a menace to the national welfare."[101] To annihilate this "menace" once and for all, the statute authorizes the government to finance "soil conservation" measures on private land, compensating consenting landowners for nonproduction of anything that can be termed an "agricultural commodity."[102] The statutory definition of that phrase is all-encompassing, containing no enumeration of specific agricultural commodities to which the subsidies are limited.

Although the 1935 statute quietly acknowledges its goal to be parity purchasing power for farmers, that admission is carefully embellished with an impressive volume of rhetoric lauding such high-sounding purposes as "preservation and improvement of soil fertility," "economic use and conservation of land," and "diminution of exploitation and wasteful and unscientific use of national soil resources."[103] To implement these noble purposes – as well as the more mundane one of transferring wealth from taxpayers and consumers to farmers – the Secretary of Agriculture is empowered to pay agricultural producers whatever sums he deems "fair and reasonable" for keeping land out of productive use.[104]

The sole breach in the law's otherwise flawless concealment of the intended consequence of its purported "conservation" measures is a proclamation that those inevitable economic effects somehow must be prevented from occurring. The statute commands: "Such powers shall not be used to discourage the production of supplies of foods and fibers sufficient to maintain normal domestic human consumption. . . ."[105] Unfortunately for the public, such legislative wishes do not alter economic reality. Since "normal domestic human consumption" is an invention of bureaucratic minds and not a static, objectively ascertainable quantity, the quoted sentence merely reasserts the government's claim of power to fix the amount and therefore the price of agricultural products available for human consumption.

The Soil Conservation and Domestic Allotment Act is augmented by legislation that creates the Rural Environmental Conservation Program.[106] Adopting the legislative purposes enumerated in the Soil Conservation and Domestic Allotment Act – that is, parity in the guise of conservation – the Rural Environmental Conservation Program authorizes government contracts of three, five, ten, or twenty-five years with farmers, ranchers, and other landowners who agree not to produce commercial agricultural crops on some of their land.[107]

To obtain the subsidy, landowners must submit a "plan" that describes the cropping systems and land use to be employed on the land during the period covered by the contract. After preliminary tribute to certain pastoral delights deemed valid goals of the land-use plans (such as seeking "to conserve surface water and preserve and improve habitat for migratory waterfowl and other wildlife resources and improve subsurface moisture"), the statute reveals that these "conservation" plans may also consist of proposals for "the reduction of areas of new land coming into production" and "the enhancement of the natural beauty of the landscape."[108] Thus, behind its verbal artistry, the Rural Environmental Conservation Program authorizes government payments to farmers and other landowners to prevent land from being put to productive use. A masterpiece in pastoral imagery, the legislation appears designed to deter citizens from recognizing that it allows their tax dollars to be spent to keep land out of agricultural production, thereby inevitably increasing food prices and diminishing agricultural supply.

Significantly breaching its facade of single-minded devotion to nature, the Rural Environmental Conservation Program also explicitly authorizes "multiyear set-aside contracts" for certain agricultural commodities, agreements currently permitted to extend to the 1977 crop.[109] Under such contracts, producers participating in the government's quota/allotment programs for wheat, feed grains, or cotton may be awarded additional subsidies for taking agricultural land out of production and devoting it to vegetative ground cover.[110]

Such are the actual mechanisms of quotas, acreage allotments, and so-called conservation programs through which the government strives to increase farmers' wealth by diminishing agricultural production, knowing that farmers will receive higher prices if the government succeeds in reducing agricultural supply. Simultaneously, the government must cope with the "surpluses" or overproduction of agricultural commodities caused by its price supports and production subsidy programs. Legal authority for government dumping through noncommercial channels of this allegedly "excess" production is described in the following pages.

FEDERAL DUMPING OF GOVERNMENT-INDUCED SURPLUSES

To the extent that the government relies on production subsidies and above-market price supports to raise farmers' incomes, it encourages economically inefficient production and causes an oversupply of agricultural products relative to consumer demand for them. To government officials intent upon maintaining high agricultural prices, this agricultural abundance poses a real threat, for if such profuse production is allowed to expand the commercial supply, the prices of farm products will fall. In order to protect the above-market price structure created by its agricultural programs, the government must acquire this "excess" produce and somehow dispose of it without disrupting the high domestic food prices it has methodically engineered.

We have already seen that one important technique by which the government acquires agricultural products it believes to be excess — that is, farm products that cannot be sold without reducing agricultural prices below the level the government deems suitable — is the "nonrecourse loan," which is used to implement price supports. If the market price falls below the support price, the producer keeps the money "loaned" to him by the government, and the government (through the Commodity Credit Corporation) takes possession of his crop, the "collateral" for the loan. Supplementing this method of acquiring farm output, the Commodity Credit Corporation has additional acquisition authority under statutory provisions that permit the government to own up to $2,500,000,000 worth of agricultural products as a "commodity set-aside."[111]

To dispose of its inventories without lowering domestic food prices, the government is authorized by law to engage in political dumping of agricultural products apart from normal commercial channels. Such disposal operations may be performed in international as well as domestic settings. To dump its stocks of agricultural produce in foreign countries, safely isolated from protected American markets, the government's primary legal authority is a statute popularly known as Public Law 480.[112]

Public Law 480 authorizes the President to sell agricultural commodities to "friendly" foreign nations for dollars or foreign currencies.[113] The catch is that, historically, sham "sales" have served as a facade for agricultural giveaway programs. Using its authority to finance such transactions,[114] the Commodity Credit Corporation has "sold" its agricultural inventories for "soft," inconvertible foreign currencies worthless to the United States in acquiring imported products.[115] Gratuitous distribution of food is openly authorized, however, by another statutory provision, which allows government disposal of American agricultural supplies in any foreign nation, friendly or not, for the following all-inclusive purposes: "to meet famine or other urgent or extraordinary relief requirements, to combat malnutrition, especially in children; . . . and for needy persons and nonprofit school lunch and preschool feeding programs outside the United States."[116] "Friendly developing areas" also can be given American food products "to promote economic and community development."[117] Not only does this activity cost U.S. consumers money, but it does not even win foreign friends for America. Indeed, foreign countries are progressively alienated as U.S. international agricultural dumping programs both undercut foreign suppliers of agricultural products and encourage recipient nations to become dependent upon a politically inspired and therefore an inherently unstable source of food.

Public Law 480, like so much other American legislation, touches the familiar fascist bases while quietly conferring absolute power upon the government. The national interest and that stalwart fascist stalking-horse called private enterprise receive most careful attention. The President is admonished to "take appropriate steps to assure that *private trade channels* are used to the maximum extent practicable."[118] It is declared to be Congress' policy "to stimulate and maximize the sale of United States agricultural commodities for dollars through the *private trade* and to further the use of *private enterprise* to the maximum."[119] And, of course, the avowed purpose of the government's domestic as well as international dumping of agricultural products is "the attainment of the *humanitarian objectives* and the *national interest* of the United States."[120] The American government's *economic* objective of sheltering domestic agricultural producers from the world market is not given comparable publicity.

The government has legal authority to engage in domestic as well as international dumping of agricultural produce. Following his instincts concerning what is in the "public interest," the Secretary of Agriculture may, if he so desires, "donate food commodities acquired through price-support operations to Federal penal and correctional institutions" and certain state correctional facilities.[121] The President is empowered to give away the agricultural commodities that compose the commodity "set-aside" for such domestic projects as:

> Donations to school-lunch programs; . . . Donation, sale or other disposition for research, experimental, or educational purposes; . . . [and] Donation, sale, or other disposition for disaster relief purposes in the United States or to meet any national emergency declared by the President . . . .[122]

Similarly, if the Secretary of Agriculture feels that it is "in the public interest," the Commodity Credit Corporation may give away agricultural products acquired through its price-support operations "for use in relieving distress" in "an acute distress area" as well as "in connection with any major disaster."[123] Provided that the proposed action conforms to the Secretary of Agriculture's view of the "public interest," the Commodity Credit Corporation may also give away its agricultural stocks whenever necessary "to prevent the waste of commodities."[124] The allowable objects of these domestic dumping efforts include federal agencies, the Bureau of Indian Affairs, nonprofit school lunch programs, nonprofit summer camps for children, needy persons, and charitable institutions serving needy persons.[125]

Excepting only distress relief, set-aside reduction, and waste-prevention measures, the law requires the Commodity Credit Corporation to dispose of all its agricultural stocks in a manner that carefully protects agricultural support prices.[126] Pursuant to statutory instructions to "dispose of all stocks of agricultural commodities held by it,"[127] the Commodity Credit Corporation generally must not sell any agricultural produce *domestically* at less than five percent above the commodity's support price.[128] Following the predominant United States policy of using the government to support domestic prices and to undercut foreign competitors, the law predictably exempts sales for export from this requirement.[129]

After surveying the government's multifarious efforts to manipulate agricultural markets by sponsoring cartels, promoting production, curtailing production, and dumping government-induced surpluses apart from normal commercial channels, one needs to focus on the consistent themes that unite the many-faceted legislation. The government's myriad forms of intervention into agricultural markets achieve perfect unanimity in three omnipresent features. In legislative technique, the agricultural statutes consistently embody the fascist prototype of profuse deference to the private enterprise system, which is concomitantly harnessed to carry out the government's orders. In economic purpose, the laws unanimously seek to enrich farmers by maintaining more persons in lucrative farm employment than a growing United States economy needs to satisfy people's desire for food products. In economic consequence, the agricultural laws unite in callous disregard of the higher food prices, agricultural shortages, taxes, and inflation that nonfarmers must endure to pay for the government's compulsion to control agricultural production and to placate the agricultural lobby.

9

Fascist International Economic Policies: Import/Export Controls, Protectionism, and Autarky

Almost no other fascist economic doctrine portends more dire consequences for the individual consumer than fascist international economic policies. These policies would rapidly become politically untenable if voters understood their consequences. In international economic matters as in other areas, the fascist seeks government control over an economy nominally allowed to remain dedicated to capitalism, discreetly shrouding omnipotent government in a veil of private enterprise. In a three-pronged assault on the concept of economic freedom, however, fascism advocates (1) total governmental power to direct the international flow of goods and services through import tariffs, quotas, export controls, foreign exchange controls, and other restrictive mechanisms; (2) artificial government protection from international competition of industries that curry favor with the government; and (3) national economic self-sufficiency (autarky). The thrust of these tenets is to put private business at the mercy of government officials, to bestow unearned economic rewards upon favored special-interest groups, to suppress the price mechanism as the determinant of and means to the most efficient pattern of world production, and quietly to sacrifice mankind's standard of living on the altar of government control.

The American consumer has been sold a bill of goods by groups with vested interests in the foregoing policies. To avoid public scrutiny of the economic policies advocated, a successful campaign has been waged to convince the average noneconomist that basic economic principles are too complicated and esoteric for the layman to comprehend. In lieu of rational economic discourse, American citizens have been fed a steady diet of catch phrases that, though superficially appealing, may be exposed as fallacious by the most rudimentary economic analysis. That most citizens are fully capable of understanding the issues involved is a secret closely guarded by the government and those business interests that profit from the political control over the economy implicit in the existing protectionist posture of the United States in international economic relations.

In essence, the various international economic policies codified in United States law empower the government, in response to pressure groups or its own whim, to sever America's economic ties with the rest of the world by erecting artificial barriers to international trade. The purported justifications for this protectionist philosophy will be dealt with later. First, it is essential to perceive the value of unrestricted international trade to consumers in all nations.[1]

Unrestricted international trade enables a nation to specialize in producing those commodities that it can produce most efficiently relative to other nations. Just as specialization within the domestic economy enables production of a greater absolute quantity of goods and services than can be supplied if each economic unit (individual, family, or region) independently attempts to produce all of its own goods, so specialization among nations increases worldwide productivity and raises everyone's standard of living. Absent artificial barriers to trade, each nation tends to produce those commodities in which it has a comparative advantage *vis à vis* other nations.

Comparative advantage poses no threat to less efficient or less naturally endowed countries; it implies only that a nation will produce things that represent its *greatest* economic superiority relative to other nations. Comparative advantage means that although one nation may have an absolute advantage in the production of every commodity relative to another country, still it will produce only those items in which its productive advantage is greatest. The reason for this is easy to grasp if one hypothesizes the most highly skilled mathematician in the United States also being the nation's most efficient bookkeeper. Obviously, American bookkeepers would not believe their jobs to be threatened by such a situation. For the same reasons, less developed countries will not be overpowered by more productive economies so long as trade barriers do not prevent national specialization according to the principle of comparative advantage.

214

Although unrestricted international trade is thus necessary to maximize the standard of living of all nations, businessmen, politicians, and government officials constantly extol the virtues of domestic industry, deploring foreign imports as a threat to American business. One quick way to cut through the rhetorical fog that enshrouds impassioned appeals for tariffs and quotas to "protect" American industry is to analyze who gains and who loses under a system of governmental barriers to international trade.

The domestic consumer suffers, for tariffs and quotas increase the prices he must pay for imported goods and competitive domestic products. Not only do prices go up, but these artificially high prices also lead to increased production of the protected commodity, thereby channeling more U.S. resources into production which is both less efficient and less desired by American consumers.

Unprotected domestic producers are hurt, because consumers paying artificially high prices for goods sheltered from international competition have less money available to purchase other products.

The foreign exporter is hurt, for the artificial trade barrier deprives him of the right to offer his product to American consumers at the lower price or in the more abundant quantities that competitive considerations would allow.

American exporters also are harmed, because the decrease in U.S. imports causes contraction of the flow of U.S. currency abroad, ultimately curtailing foreign imports of goods exported by the United States. This decline in U.S. exports occurs because (1) a foreign country's *willingness* to import is linked to its own economic vitality, which necessarily is diminished by the reduction in U.S. imports; and (2) a foreign country's *ability* to import United States goods depends upon its acquisition of U.S. currency with which to pay for such imports, and its access to U.S. currency is prevented to the extent that the United States government erects barriers to exports from the foreign nation. U.S. consumers and foreign consumers alike indirectly suffer additional economic harm by partially losing the benefits obtained by international specialization according to the principle of comparative advantage. Succinctly stated, world productivity declines and everybody's standard of living deteriorates.

Tariffs and quotas on imported goods are simply a direct subsidy to domestic producers of the restricted commodity. Their effect is to shift production away from more efficient industries in which the United States holds a comparative advantage relative to other nations and into less efficient industries in which America does not have a comparative advantage. Only two groups gain from the use of tariffs and quotas to impede international trade. The government gains power over the economy, coupled with all the adulation such power can command. The protected industries, the other prime beneficiaries and supporters of the tariffs and quotas that shelter their inefficiencies against the competition of world trade, gain artificially bloated profits. Unconcerned that the American consumer pays for their luxury in the form of higher prices and a lower standard of living, the protected industries perceive only that tariffs give them monopoly profits on a silver platter. Freed of international competition that would directly benefit domestic consumers, and constrained only by diminished consumer demand at higher price levels, the protected industries can charge any amount up to the competitive world price plus the tariff, and consumers have no cheaper alternative. Tariffs and other trade barriers thus create a situation that is ripe for political corruption, because industries seeking protection from international trade can profitably spend any amount up to the financial reward to be gained through the trade barrier to sway politicians to support their position.

Although the victims of international trade barriers far outnumber the beneficiaries, the beneficiaries historically have prevailed. This has occurred for two reasons. First, although consumers and exporters have more to lose in absolute terms than the protected industries have to gain from trade barriers, the financial rewards available to protected industries are much more tangible, direct, and concentrated than the harm suffered by consumers. Dispersed among the entire population, the destructive consequences of trade barriers are by comparison diffuse, indirect, and somewhat difficult to conceptualize. Each isolated individual seems to have less to lose than a beneficiary stands to gain, although the aggregate losses of all consumers in fact outweigh the beneficiaries' gains. For a single beneficiary of the protectionist system, however, the stakes are very high indeed. The diffusion of the deleterious repercussions of trade barriers leads to the second reason for their ongoing victory: the victims of trade restrictions are less organized and therefore less effective in giving political expression to their economic interests than the well-organized lobbyists financed by industries seeking protection from competition by imports.

To make their pleas for import barriers politically palatable, industries coveting government protection dress their desire for subsidies in patriotic garb. Advocates of protectionist policies assiduously avoid rational discussion of the consequences of their schemes, content to coin appealing emotional phrases that politicians can effectively sell to their constituencies with frequent exposure on the news media. Repeatedly subjected to images of cheap foreign labor inundating American markets, citizens are encouraged to believe that import restrictions are necessary to protect American labor. People are not told, however, that wages are a function of the productivity of labor. American wages can be five times as high as foreign wages, and so long

216

as they reflect higher productivity per man-hour characteristic of capital intensive American industries, the highly paid American workers are probably more than five times as productive as their foreign competitors. Thus regardless of absolute wage levels, American industry can successfully market those products in which the United States has a comparative advantage, and workers need not fear foreign competitors as a threat to American wages. A corollary of the protect-American-labor slogan is the assertion that tariffs and quotas are necessary to increase employment in the United States. The fallacy of this rationale is that if America's productive resources are fully employed, any such increase would merely divert American labor and capital from more efficient industries and channel them into the relatively less productive industries sheltered from world competition by import restrictions.

The slogans are endless. Citizens are told that trade barriers are essential to protect "infant" industries until they become firmly enough established to compete on world markets. But Americans are discouraged from questioning either how the government can distinguish between industries that legitimately require protection during their initial existence and those that are merely inefficient, or how the public can identify the point at which an infant industry has attained a maturity warranting termination of its subsidy. Further, one is not encouraged to recall that, historically, immense capital investment requirements seldom have deterred new competitors from challenging established domestic industries.

National security is another potent appeal for trade barriers against importation of strategic materials. However, not only is national security an all-encompassing term that may be used to disguise bogus claims by inefficient industries for government protection, but also restrictions on the importation of scarce strategic natural resources cause the United States to consume its domestic supply of the resource more rapidly, leaving the country even more vulnerable in the event of military crisis. Further, the international economic interdependence created by eliminating trade barriers would enhance national security and reduce the threat of war by making the interdependent nations reluctant to fight because of the severe eonomic hardships that would ensue.

Undaunted, protectionists further exhort citizens to support trade barriers out of a superficial sense of fairness, to equalize the costs of production in different countries. But it is possible to increase world productivity by specialization among nations precisely because costs of production are different in different countries. To argue in favor of equalizing the costs of production in different nations is thus to denounce the very existence of world trade, which is to condemn mankind to the lowest conceivable standard of living and to advocate minimizing rather than maximizing the real income of the world. The concept of equalizing the costs of production worldwide is the antithesis of the principle of comparative advantage. Its advocacy entails implicit renunciation of all the increased world productivity that national specialization according to comparative cost advantages can bestow upon humanity.

Americans also are told of the alleged importance of keeping money within the domestic economy. But this enticing slogan, carried to its logical extreme, also totally denounces specialization and trade among nations. It also ignores the fact that wealth consists not of money but of the goods and services that money can buy. Just as one's personal income is worthless apart from the commodities it buys, so the income a nation derives from its exports is utterly without value apart from the foreign imports it purchases. Exports are merely a means to an end, and that end is purchasing power on the world market (that is, imports) and the increased standard of living which that purchasing power represents. (The economic rationale for this is discussed in the section of this chapter entitled "Promotion of Exports.") The ultimate irony is that the keep-money-within-the-domestic-economy rationale also implies the reduction of the ability of the United States to export, for if America restricts importation from foreign countries, those foreign nations are deprived of the U.S. currency which they must have to buy goods from the United States.

The last-ditch battle cry of protectionists is *retaliation*: if other nations penalize imports from the United States, the United States should penalize theirs. The fallacy concealed in this appeal to equity is that such retaliation by the United States only contracts world trade further, causing the real income and the standard of living of America and of the world to deteriorate even more. Nothing is usually gained by retaliatory trade restrictions except an endless cycle of increasing trade barriers as detrimental to the imposing nation as to its foreign victim.

Regardless of its fallacies, the catch-phrase justification of foreign trade restriction has dominated and guided America's international economic policies as reflected in national legislation. The pertinent statutes will be discussed in the next section. The logical culmination of dedication to restrictive international trade policies is a suicidal call for national self-sufficiency (autarky), a plea that the nation strive to produce all the material commodities that its citizens need and want without trade from the rest of the world. The cry for national self-sufficiency seems like an old refrain at its very inception, because advocacy of all lesser forms of international trade barriers rests upon essentially autarkic arguments for protecting inefficient domestic industries despite other nations' comparative cost advantages. Like tariffs and quotas, national self-sufficiency entails utter disregard for the price its victims must pay for their government's pursuit of national economic isolation: the decline in world productivity, reduction in real income, and deterioration in living standards inevitably caused by international trade barriers. The only difference is one of degree. Advocates of autarky magnify a thousandfold the themes used to rationalize tariffs and quotas, overtly embracing as an explicit national goal the economic isolationism only implicit in narrower restrictions on international trade.

While the propaganda used to popularize tariffs and quotas facilitates public acceptance of the desirability of national self-sufficiency, the international repercussions of inexorably intensified trade barriers make autarky increasingly necessary for the survival of a nation unrelentingly committed to restricting foreign trade. Nations victimized by tariffs and quotas tend to retaliate in kind, stimulating ever-spiraling trade barriers that eventually prevent the aggressor nation from acquiring the foreign currency it needs to purchase essential commodities on the world market. At this point, the aggressor must either relax its restrictions on imports from other countries, or seek to produce domestically the goods it formerly imported from abroad. Since no country has the natural resources to be totally self-sufficient without a precipitous collapse of its people's standard of living, the ominous long-range "solution" to its economic problems is to usurp the physical resources of other countries. Thus the prognosis for autarky is *war*. At the conclusion of this chapter, the current attempt to popularize the concept of national self-sufficiency in the United States will be discussed.

As an analysis of U.S. statutes will demonstrate, the United States has adopted a fundamentally fascist approach to America's economic relations with the rest of the world. Although the government soft-pedals its vast powers for public relations purposes, in America a person may import or export goods only if his activity conforms to the government's current economic plans for the nation. Government discretion and national planning have supplanted individual choice and private decision-making in international economic matters, and a well-manipulated citizenry is unwittingly paying the economic price for its government's stranglehold on America's productivity and standard of living.

I. GOVERNMENT CONTROL OVER IMPORTS: TARIFFS, QUOTAS, EXCLUSION, AND RETALIATION

The Tariff Act of 1930 as modified over the years is the basic statute governing importation of foreign goods into the United States.[2] A significant indication of current efforts to popularize the trade barriers it authorizes is the recent renaming of the U.S. Tariff Commission, the agency empowered by law to administer the Tariff Act. In a bowdlerization that strips the Commission's heretofore indelicate title of all protectionist overtones, the Trade Act of 1974 changes the name of the U.S. Tariff Commission to the International Trade Commission.[3] Through the Tariff Act, Congress, either independently or upon recommendation of the International Trade Commission, establishes detailed tariff schedules that specify the precise rate of duty the government imposes as a surcharge upon a foreign company desiring to export its products to the United States. These tariff schedules list products as either "dutiable" or "free," and dutiable goods are categorized and assessed specific charges as a prerequisite of importation. The rate schedules are statutory law. They may be changed at any time by Congress, and there is no constitutional limitation upon the tariff rates that Congress can apply to imported products. The consumer pays for these subsidies to United States producers in the form of higher prices for both foreign commodities subject to import tariffs and competitive domestically produced goods whose prices may be raised under the shelter of the tariff umbrella.

To supplement the tariff schedules, the statute gives extensive powers to the President and the International Trade Commission to use tariffs artificially to "equalize" the costs of producing American products and foreign imports, thereby explicitly rejecting the beneficial and humanitarian principle of comparative advantage. Equalization of production costs is an apt epitaph for a civilization doomed to an ever-deteriorating living standard by its own unwillingness to compete on the world market.

The statute empowers the International Trade Commission to investigate differences in costs of American and foreign products either upon its own initiative or when requested to do so by the President, Congress, or (if the Commission feels sympathetic) an "interested party" such as a domestic competitor of the importer. If the Commission discovers that existing statutory tariffs "do not equalize the differences in the costs of production of the domestic article and the like or similar foreign article," the Commission is instructed to report the increases or decreases in tariff rates "necessary to equalize such differences."[4] Generally, the Commission can recommend increases or decreases in tariff rates of up to fifty percent of the existing rate, although it cannot use this procedure to impose a tariff on a product that is not "dutiable" under existing tariff schedules.[5] The statutory objective is to make the selling price of the import the same as the selling price of similar domestically manufactured products, thus eliminating by government fiat any cost advantages possessed by the foreign producer that otherwise could be passed along to the consumer.[6] The President is compelled by law to approve and make effective any tariff changes recommended by the Commission if he finds them factually necessary to equalize costs of domestic and foreign producers, regardless of whether he regards such changes or their objective as desirable. Again, the consumer directly bears the burden of the tariffs through the higher domestic prices engineered by government restriction of international trade.

The Trade Act of 1974[7] gives the President more flexibility in altering tariff schedules to suit his personal fancy. This new law, widely but incorrectly touted as an uncompromising step toward free trade and the elimination of trade barriers, empowers the President to *raise* as well as to lower tariffs for a variety of purposes.

The Trade Act allows tariff hikes to be imposed (1) to implement trade agreements, (2) to reduce balance-of-payments deficits, and (3) to protect domestic industries "threatened" by import competition.

The trade agreements that form one basis for increased import barriers under the Act may be concluded by the President whenever he asserts that "existing . . . import restrictions of any foreign country or the United States are unduly burdening and restricting the foreign trade of the United States."[8] Contrary to popular impression, such presidentially negotiated trade agreements are not merely innocuous instruments for expanding trade among nations, but may in fact also be used to restrict trade. For example, the President may use trade agreements to *increase* tariffs to his liking through his statutory power to "proclaim such modification or continuance of any existing duty, such continuance of existing duty-free or excise treatment, or *such additional duties*, as he determines to be required or appropriate to carry out any such agreement."[9] Further, whenever the United States modifies its rights or obligations under a trade agreement, the President has broad power to increase trade barriers as he sees fit: "[T]he President is authorized *to proclaim increased duties or other import restrictions*, to the extent, at such times, and for such periods as he deems necessary or appropriate, in order to exercise the rights or fulfill the obligations of the United States."[10]

The President has similarly broad powers under the 1974 Trade Act to throttle imports in protectionist response to balance-of-payments deficits. Whenever he labels U.S. balance-of-payments deficits "large and serious," the President may impose both tariffs and quotas to restrict imports of foreign products.[11] These tariffs and quotas may only last 150 days unless this period is extended by Congress.[12] Although the law states that such trade barriers are to be applied in a "nondiscriminatory" fashion, the Trade Act simultaneously negates this appealing sentiment by adding that the President can direct the tariffs and quotas exclusively at nations with "large or persistent" balance-of-payments surpluses.[13] Authorizing U.S. trade barriers to be discriminatorily applied not only to Congress' current target, the Middle Eastern oil producers, but also to any prosperous foreign nation, the Act states:

> [I]f the President determines that the purposes of this section ["nondiscriminatory treatment"] will best be served by action against one or more countries having large or persistent balance-of-payments surpluses, he may *exempt* all other countries from such action.[14]

Underscoring the government's power to use discriminatory trade barriers as a political weapon, the law adds that the import restrictions should be "of broad and uniform application with respect to product coverage except where the President determines . . . that certain articles should not be subject to import restricting actions because of the needs of the United States economy."[15] And just as unspoken congressional protocol requires such discriminatory measures to be packaged in rhetoric that superficially denounces discrimination, so it would be an unthinkable breach of etiquette to authorize these protectionist trade restrictions without repudiating protectionism. Thus ritualistic lip service disavowing protectionism is predictably tucked into the interstices of the Act: "Neither the authorization of import restricting actions nor the determination of exceptions with respect to product coverage shall be made for the purpose of protecting individual domestic industries from import competition."[16]

Nevertheless, other statutory passages are not so discreet in concealing the purpose of import restrictions. The protectionist theme of the Trade Act becomes explicit in provisions that authorize tariffs for the express purpose of shielding American firms from actual or potential impairment of profitability due to competition from imported products.[17] The President is authorized to impose tariffs or quotas, or both, for a maximum of eight years[18] whenever the International Trade Commission determines that "an article is being imported into the United States in such increased quantities as to be a *substantial cause of serious injury, or the threat thereof, to the domestic industry* producing an article like or directly competitive with the imported article."[19] The mere threat of import competition, not necessarily the actuality, is sufficient pretext for import barriers under this provision.

The statute's explanation of "threat," "serious injury," and "substantial cause" destroys whatever superficial plausibility the quoted

222

rhetoric might otherwise muster, exposing Congress' single-minded determination to protect inefficient domestic industries from world competition at the public's expense. Contrary to the connotation of physical violence suggested by the words, the Act lists as indications of a "threat of serious injury" to domestic industry such normal symptoms of economically unjustified production as a decline in sales or a "downward trend in production, profits, wages, or employment."[20] Again naming normal precursors of desirable, market-stimulated shifts in the use of productive resources as signs of serious injury, the law states that "serious injury" is indicated by "a significant idling of productive facilities in the industry, the inability of a significant number of firms to operate at a reasonable level of profit, and significant unemployment or underemployment within the industry."[21] Then, in a yet more visible embrace of autarky's underlying premises, the law asserts that a mere decline in the percentage of American consumption of a product supplied by domestic industry, when accompanied by increased imports, is a factor suggesting "substantial cause" of injury to domestic firms.[22] Finally, as if to demonstrate beyond dispute the government's eagerness to intervene to protect American industry from world competition, the Act defines a "substantial cause" of such threatened "injury" as "a cause which is *not less* than any other cause."[23]

Thus the Trade Act of 1974, that supposed beacon of free trade, authorizes the government to raise tariff barriers and thereby force consumers to subsidize virtually any domestic industry potentially subject to foreign competition, even if the industry's economic troubles are chiefly due to its own inefficiency or to changes in consumer tastes. Since the Trade Act allows publicly financed protection of domestic firms even if increased import competition is *not* a result of lowered U.S. import barriers, the attempted justification of its tariffs as a short-term mechanism for "orderly adjustment" to newly relaxed trade barriers is totally implausible.[24]

Even where the Trade Act of 1974 empowers the President to lower import barriers, the Act's preoccupation with sheltering domestic firms from world competition consistently constrains his tariff-reduction authority. While the President has specific authority to enter into agreements (if Congress approves) to grant foreign countries the lower tariff rates associated with "most-favored-nation" status,[25] the statute echoes familiar protectionist sentiments by requiring most-favored-nation agreements to include "safeguards" (that is, provision for import restrictions) to avoid what is called "market disruption," defined as any rapid increase of imports that potentially might be a factor in reducing the prosperity of a domestic industry.[26] The pattern is repeated in provisions that empower the President, until 1984, to accord duty-free treatment to "eligible articles" from "beneficiary developing countries."[27] "Beneficiary developing countries" and "eligible articles" are quite simply defined as those nations and commodities upon which the President chooses to bestow his favors, with certain politically mandated exclusions codified into the law by Congress.[28] (For example, Canada, East Germany, and members of the Organization of Petroleum Exporting Countries cannot be named "beneficiary developing countries," nor can textiles, watches, and other "import-sensitive" items be declared "eligible articles.")[29] Here too the President must wield his discretionary power to lower tariffs with a protectionist eye cocked on "the anticipated impact of such action on United States producers of like or directly competitive products."[30]

Unwilling to rely on tariffs alone to achieve government-favored import configurations, Congress through the Trade Act of 1974 also instituted an interesting new technique to supplement the government's tariff authority. The euphemism coined to popularize this congressional innovation is "adjustment assistance."[31] Despite the pleasant ring that phrase leaves in the public's ear, adjustment assistance accomplishes the subsidization of inefficient domestic production as surely as does an import tariff. By providing *direct government payments* to firms, workers, and communities "threatened" by import competition, adjustment assistance simply subsidizes inefficient domestic industries with money expropriated from taxpayers rather than through artificially high prices generated by tariffs. Since the Act nowhere makes reductions in American tariffs a prerequisite of adjustment assistance, these payments cannot be viewed merely as compensation for losses resulting from good-faith reliance on government-imposed trade barriers.

In provisions currently scheduled to expire on September 30, 1982,[32] the 1974 Trade Act allows adjustment assistance to be paid to businesses, workers, and communities (regrouped by government officials into "trade-impacted areas")[33] whose economic position is impaired by import competition. Loans and grants to businesses and communities,[34] weekly paychecks to workers ("trade readjustment allowances") for up to seventy-eight weeks,[35] training,[36] job search,[37] and relocation[38] payments — all are there for the asking. Whether discussing workers, firms, or communities, the statute's explicit avowal of Congress' protectionist desire to force American taxpayers to pay for sheltering the American economy from world competition is the same. Businesses, employees, and certified communities in trade-impacted areas are eligible for government aid if the government determines:

(1) that a significant number or proportion of the workers in such

224

firm [or community] have become totally or partially separated, or are *threatened* to become totally or partially separated,

(2) that *sales or production*, or both, of such firm [or firms located in the trade impacted area] *have decreased absolutely*, and

(3) that increases of imports of articles like or directly competitive with articles produced by such firm [or firms] *contributed importantly* to such total or partial separation, *or threat thereof*, and to such decline in sales or production.[39]

Of these stated conditions, the single factor which is a fixed, tangible prerequisite of subsidy eligibility is an objective decline in sales or production. The two other conditions of eligibility are satisfied by the mere "threat" or possibility of their occurrence.

But the statute goes even further, unveiling the government's intent to control which waning businesses and communities shall remain artificially prosperous (at taxpayers' expense), whether or not their economic decline is due to increased import competition. Although the statute says that increased imports must have contributed importantly to the impending economic problems of the firm or community, "contributed importantly" is defined as "a cause which is important but not necessarily more important than any other cause."[40] To the consternation of concerned citizens, this facile statutory technique of capitalizing on misleading language and novel redefinition of commonly understood words is becoming a hallmark of Congress' accelerating drive to expand the government's power to control the economy. As a consequence of this provision, the Trade Act allows public subsidies to be paid to any declining firm or community (or the workers therein) even if the predominant cause of the recipient's trouble is not increased import competition but pure economic inefficiency. Since government officials determine which applications for public money are approved and may also participate in formulating and financing the proposals for adjustment assistance prepared by applicants,[41] there is little doubt that the proposals ultimately accepted will substantially embody the government's economic preferences.

The government's power to restrict imports does not rest on tariffs and adjustment assistance alone. The Tariff Act of 1930 also gives the International Trade Commission authority, subject to presidential veto, to *exclude* imports from entering the United States whenever the Commission asserts that their importation has

the *effect or tendency . . . to destroy or substantially injure an industry*, efficiently and economically operated, in the United States, or to prevent the establishment of such an industry, or to restrain or monopolize trade and commerce in the United States . . . .[42]

The Commission's power under this provision is totally discretionary, for the Act instructs the Commission to exclude such imports from entry into the United States "unless . . . it finds that such articles *should not* be excluded from entry."[43]

In a flagrant effort to make negative labels divert the public's attention from the nature of the behavior declared illegal, the statute alternately calls the detrimental impact of foreign competition "unfair methods of competition," "unfair practices in import trade," and "unfair acts."[44] Since the statute does not require malevolent intent on the part of the foreign competitor, merely condemning the *effect* or *tendency* to injure an American industry, the importer's allegedly unfair behavior can be merely the result of normal competition. That is, if one hypothesizes a foreign producer whose comparative cost advantages enable him significantly to underprice U.S. producers of the same commodity, this statute empowers the International Trade Commission to prohibit importation of the product and thus to force American consumers to pay the higher price demanded by the less efficient domestic producers.

The effect of such exclusion of imported products is to coerce unwitting consumers to pay a direct subsidy to the particular domestic industry sheltered by the import restriction. Unlike restrictive tariffs, which force consumers to subsidize domestic industries only up to the dollar amount of the tariff, the total exclusion of foreign competitors provides an open-ended subsidy to U.S. producers of the same commodity. No matter how much domestic producers charge, imports may still be forcibly prevented; there is no point, as there is with a tariff, at which it again may become economically feasible for the importer to compete with domestic producers. The emotionally charged window dressing denouncing foreign monopoly of U.S. markets aside, this statutory provision in essence authorizes the International Trade Commission and an acquiescent President to make autarky (economic self-sufficiency) a reality, to exclude from U.S. markets any foreign producer who has comparative cost advantages over domestic producers, and to force the public to endure the decline in real income and living standards that any effort to achieve autarky guarantees.

Another statute supplements governmental power to exclude imports by making it a *criminal* offense intentionally to import goods that "injure" U.S. industry in a manner that would justify exclusion of the products under the Tariff Act. The statute declares it illegal to import foreign goods "at a price substantially less than the actual market value or wholesale price of such articles . . . in the principal markets of the country of their production . . . ."[45] However, unlike the Tariff Act of 1930, this law explicitly declares these alleged "unfair methods of competition" to be unlawful only if performed "with the *intent* of destroying or injuring an industry in the United States, or of preventing the establishment of an industry in the United States, or of restraining or monopolizing any part of trade and commerce in such articles in the United States."[46] *Intentional* behavior is required to justify conviction under this law, which imposes criminal penalties including fines, imprisonment, and treble damages on behalf of "injured" domestic businesses.

Statutory law also makes *retaliation* one of the guiding principles governing the international economic relations of the United States. Ignoring the fact that retaliation for foreign trade barriers to U.S. goods harms the American public by further restricting international trade, the Tariff Act of 1930 proclaims the President's power, in the "public interest," to impose new or additional tariffs on imports whenever a foreign country

> (1) Imposes . . . any unreasonable charge, exaction, regulation, or limitation which is not equally enforced upon the like articles of every foreign country; or
> (2) Discriminates in fact against the commerce of the United States, directly or indirectly, by law or administrative practice . . . in such manner as to place the commerce of the United States at a disadvantage compared with the commerce of any foreign country.[47]

The Tariff Act thus hypocritically authorizes retaliation against other nations for establishing trade barriers fundamentally indistinguishable from the tariff wall the statute encourages the United States to erect in the name of "equalization of production costs." This retaliation may include not only new tariffs but also total exclusion of any or all imports from allegedly discriminatory nations if the President "deems it consistent with the interests of the United States."[48]

If the alleged foreign discrimination against U.S. commerce is found to benefit *other* countries, the President also is empowered to impose tariffs of up to fifty percent upon commodities produced by beneficiary industries of such third-party foreign nations.[49] Any article imported in violation of these retaliatory provisions of the Tariff Act may be seized and condemned by the U.S. government.[50]

The government also has statutory authority under the Tariff Act to retaliate against foreign countries' export subsidies by imposing additional import tariffs called "countervailing duties" on the importation of subsidized products into the United States. The Act requires supplementary import tariffs equivalent to the export subsidy to be assessed against such products before they can enter the United States. Blithely mandating a totally different response to other nations' export subsi-

227

dies than it would hope to encounter in response to America's massive export subsidy programs,[51] the law states:

> Whenever any country . . . shall pay or bestow, directly or indirectly, any bounty or grant upon the manufacture or production or export of any article or merchandise manufactured or produced in such country . . . then upon the importation of such article or merchandise into the United States, . . . there shall be levied and paid, . . . in addition to any duties otherwise imposed, a duty equal to the net amount of such bounty or grant . . . .[52]

The Trade Act of 1974, however, contains America's most sweeping and explicit embrace of retaliation as a cardinal principle of international economic relations. In a statutory provision that has no scheduled expiration date, the Trade Act empowers the government to use trade barriers as a retaliatory political weapon not only to eliminate foreign trade barriers but also to coerce foreign nations into handing over their economic output to the United States at a price the American government deems satisfactory. This unprecedented addition to American law, discussed further in section six ("Spiraling Protectionism") of this chapter, is the ultimate extension of the concept of economic retaliation.

The Trade Act first authorizes the President to retaliate against foreign countries for carrying out exactly the same policies that U.S. legislation applauds when implemented by the American government.[53] The President is empowered to impose whatever import restrictions he "deems appropriate"[54] if foreign nations dare to implement import barriers or export subsidies that the U.S. government doesn't like. The President may thus retaliate whenever another country:

> [1] maintains *unjustifiable or unreasonable tariff or import restrictions* which impair the value of trade commitments made to the United States or which burden, restrict, or discriminate against United States commerce, [or]
>
> [2] *provides subsidies* (or other incentives having the effect of subsidies) *on its exports* of one or more products to the United States or to other foreign markets *which have the effect of substantially reducing sales of the competitive United States product or products* . . . .[55]

In addition to this garden-variety mandate for international economic retaliation, the 1974 Trade Act also explicitly transforms trade barriers into an instrument for *political* retaliation. The Act empowers the President to "retaliate" with import restrictions in response to

228

foreign political actions that are unrelated to any import barriers or export subsidies maintained by the foreign countries, authorizing economic retaliation against any nation that "engages in *discriminatory or other acts or policies* which are *unjustifiable or unreasonable* and which burden or restrict United States commerce."[56] Thus Congress casts the U.S. government into the role of omnipotent judge of the political policies of foreign countries, forcing the public to pay, through higher prices, for government attempts to use import restrictions to coerce other nations into political subservience.

But the 1974 Trade Act seeks the *economic* as well as the political subservience of other nations. Openly revealing the government's desire to force other nations to trade with the United States on terms and at prices that please the U.S. government, the Act authorizes the President to impose import restrictions against any country that "imposes *unjustifiable or unreasonable restrictions on access* to supplies of food, raw materials, or manufactured or semi-manufactured products which burden or restrict United States commerce."[57] Subverting the very concept of voluntary economic relations among individuals and nations, Congress implicitly asserts it to be the *right* of the United States to compel other nations to turn over their economic resources to America at prices dictated by U.S. government officials. Such is the insidious reality cloaked in the notion of "access" to foreign resources.[58] In its incredible expansion of the U.S. government's power to use "retaliatory" import barriers to work its economic and political will on countries economically dependent on U.S. trade, the Trade Act addresses neither the moral issues at stake nor the logical inconsistency of refusing to recognize a corresponding foreign right of "access" to the economic output of the United States.

The governmental powers to retaliate for alleged foreign barriers to American goods established by the Trade Act and the Tariff Act are enhanced by other statutory provisions. Partially overlapping the previously described measures, one statute authorizes the President to retaliate against nations that prohibit imports from the United States by forbidding importation into America of similar articles or of other commodities if no "similar articles" conventionally are imported.[59]

Another statutory provision, misleadingly entitled "Retaliation against restriction of importations in time of war," contains broad language that extends far beyond military crises that actively concern the United States.[60] Contrary to its title's implication, the statute is not defensive in either a military or an economic sense. The economic retaliation it authorizes is not directed exclusively at belligerent nations actively engaged in war or toward military conflicts in which the United States takes an active role. Potentially among the broadest of

America's retaliatory trade laws, this provision authorizes the President, during the existence of any war in which the United States is *not* engaged, to prohibit or restrict importation of any or all goods from *any* country that the President has "reasonable ground to believe" prevents or restricts imports from the United States of goods "not injurious to health or morals."[61] This means that a minor military conflict between globally insignificant combatants in which the United States has no active role or interest can constitute the "justification" for America's erection of massive trade barriers against major economic powers. Since war is virtually always occurring somewhere in the world, the President continually possesses the power to restrict foreign imports under the terms of this statute. Apart from providing incentive for encouraging small wars, the statute gives the President arbitrary and unreviewable power to pick and choose the victims of American import restrictions. With the "public interest" as his statutory standard and guide, the President could respond differently to foreign nations that maintained identical postures toward U.S. imports by invoking either the malleable public-interest rationale or the other statutory escape hatch, the proviso that the U.S. product in question not be detrimental to health or morals. The maximum penalty for importing in violation of the President's decrees under this statute is $50,000 and two years' imprisonment.[62]

A recently enacted statute that radically expands government power to restrict foreign imports is the Consumer Product Safety Act. This Act, discussed in detail in Chapter 5, gives the Consumer Product Safety Commission vast power to promulgate and enforce government standards for "performance, composition, contents, design, construction, finish, or packaging of a consumer product," as well as mandatory product-labeling requirements.[63] The Commission also is empowered to outlaw entirely products felt to pose an "unreasonable risk of injury" by declaring them to be "banned hazardous products."[64] Although these government controls on domestic industry are said to be necessary to protect the consuming public from dangers it is unable to discover, the Commission's standards in fact extend to common products whose inherent hazards, if any, are well known. Thus when a government bureaucrat decides that roller skates or bicycles must meet government performance or construction standards, he may in fact merely raise the cost of the product while procuring no appreciable change desired by the product's consumers. When product risks are known, such a government decision effectively preempts the consumer's right to purchase and the manufacturer's right to produce articles with specifications other than those approved by the government.

Since the government's standards usually raise the ultimate price of the commodity, the government's consumer product standards often reduce the number of consumers able to afford the regulated product. To make certain that consumers cannot satisfy economic desires that contradict the government's product controls through nondomestic suppliers, the Consumer Product Safety Act makes government control absolute by *banning imports* of products that do not conform to its specifications and decrees.[65] The maximum civil penalty for importing in violation of the statute is $500,000 for a related series of violations.[66] Criminal penalties of up to $50,000 and one year's imprisonment also may be imposed.[67]

The economic repercussions of the import controls authorized by the Consumer Product Safety Act are colossal. Although restricting importation of consumer goods that do not satisfy government product regulations could be accomplished in part by use of the statutes previously discussed, the Consumer Product Safety Act augments government control of imports in several significant ways. First, the Act obviates the need for the government to claim either that U.S. production costs exceed foreign production costs or that domestic industry is threatened with substantial injury by foreign competition. The government need only establish that the Consumer Product Safety Commission has issued a rule requiring that only certain types of products can be marketed in the United States.

Second, since assertion of noncompetitive American production costs or harm to domestic industry as a result of foreign competition accentuates the costs imposed on American consumers by government production controls, the government's repressive economic tactics are made less obtrusive and superficially more palatable by the import restraint procedure established by the Consumer Product Safety Act. Conveniently cast by the Act's wording into the role of champion of consumers' health and safety rather than protectionist suppressor of international trade, the government is able to conceal more readily the reduced real income and deteriorating standard of living that result from government trade barriers, beguiling the consumer into thinking he is the beneficiary rather than the victim of such protectionist policies.

Third, the Consumer Product Safety Act effectively fine-tunes government control over the domestic economy, establishing far more detailed production controls than previously sanctioned in America and guaranteeing their enforcement by coercively isolating the United States from the foreign competition that could preserve some measure of consumer sovereignty.

Disregarding consumers' desires as well as the increased prices and reduced standard of living consumers are compelled to suffer, the import prohibitions codified in the Consumer Product Safety Act provide the legal mechanism for effective government suppression of both domestic and foreign competition. A government elite is thereby empowered to decide what products are "safe" enough for an economically disenfranchised public to purchase, and the economic costs of government bureaucrats' preferences are forcibly imposed upon U.S. consumers, businessmen, and throttled foreign exporters.

Agricultural goods are subject to import controls as stringent as the Consumer Product Safety Commission's controls over consumer products. In statutory language less subtle than the Consumer Product Safety Act, the federal government is empowered to impose tariffs, quotas, and outright prohibitions upon the importation of agricultural products into the United States. Pursuant to laws described in detail in Chapter 8, the Secretary of Agriculture administers programs under which the government subsidizes agricultural production, dictates the quantity and type of production in which producers of basic agricultural commodities are permitted to engage, and establishes government production quotas for states, counties, and individual farms. Reflecting the economic truth that the more extensive the government's interference with the domestic economy, the more pervasive must be its restriction of international trade in order to prevent foreign competition from replacing federally manipulated domestic competition, the agricultural import controls authorized by statute parallel in scope the vast network of domestic production controls. The Secretary of Agriculture is instructed to inform the President, who in turn is authorized to order an investigation by the International Trade Commission, whenever

> the Secretary of Agriculture has *reason to believe* that any article or articles are being or are *practically certain to be imported* into the United States under such conditions and in such quantities as to render or tend to render ineffective, or materially interfere with, any program or operation undertaken under [federal laws regulating agricultural production], . . . or to reduce substantially the amount of any product processed in the United States from any agricultural commodity or product thereof with respect to which any such program or operation is being undertaken. . . .[68]

If the President believes that the Commission's investigation substantiates the foregoing beliefs of the Secretary of Agriculture, or if (on recommendation of the Secretary) he unilaterally decides to take "emergency" action without awaiting the report of the Commission, he may impose tariffs of up to fifty percent or such "quantitative limitations" (that is, quotas) as he declares necessary to avoid interference with the government's control over domestic agriculture.[69] So flexible is the President's power to restrict imports of agricultural goods that he may identify targets of U.S. trade barriers "by physical qualities, value, use, or upon such other bases as he shall determine."[70] In perfect conformity with paradigmatic fascist international economic policies, this statute gives the government omnipotent control over the international flow of agricultural products into the United States.

Further extending governmental control over the supply of agricultural products available to domestic consumers, another statutory provision gives the President blanket authority, "whenever he determines the action appropriate," to seek agreements with foreign countries to limit foreign exports of agricultural or textile products to the United States.[71] He may issue any regulations he deems necessary to implement and enforce his agreements. Further, if the nations that are parties to the agreement can be characterized as "accounting for a significant part of world trade in the articles with respect to which the agreement was concluded," the President can also enforce the agreement by issuing regulations controlling imports from *countries not parties to the agreement*.[72]

The preceding provisions by no means exhaust the government's control over importation of agricultural articles. For example, government-established sugar quotas are made applicable to foreign imports as well as domestic production, precluding American consumers from acquiring sugar in excess of the government-controlled supply even if foreign producers are willing and able to supply it. Government control over the quantity and price of domestic sugar is assured by legislation that authorizes the Secretary of Agriculture to

> Forbid processors, persons engaged in handling of sugar, and others from importing sugar into continental United States for consumption . . . therein, and/or from . . . processing or marketing in, continental United States, and/or from processing in any area to which the provisions of this chapter with respect to sugar beets and sugarcane may be made applicable, for consumption in continental United States, sugar . . . from foreign countries . . . in excess of quotas fixed by the Secretary of Agriculture. . . .[73]

Foreign competition in other named agricultural commodities is limited by a statutory provision that forbids importation of sixteen specifically listed fruits, vegetables, and nuts unless the imports comply "with the grade, size, quality, and maturity" requirements imposed upon domestic producers by the Secretary of Agriculture.[74] Tea cannot be imported unless it satisfies the standards of "purity, quality, and fitness for consumption" established by the government.[75] The importation of rice also is restricted by law under the "rice certificate program," which requires foreign importers as well as domestic producers to obtain certificates from the Secretary of Agriculture as a prerequisite to importing, producing, or marketing rice, thereby enabling the Secretary of Agriculture to enforce government-established quotas limiting the total supply of rice permitted annually in American markets.[76]

Finally, the Natural Gas Act provides that natural gas cannot be imported from a foreign country without the express permission of the Federal Power Commission. The Commission can either prevent or restrict such importation, for it has unlimited statutory power to withhold its permission whenever it deems the proposed transaction "not . . . consistent with the public interest," and to impose upon the transaction "such terms and conditions as the Commission may find necessary or appropriate. . . ."[77]

Thus through a combination of statutes the federal government has claimed absolute power to control importation of foreign products into the United States. Using tariffs, quotas, direct government payments, and prohibition as its weapons, the government has acquired the statutory power to substitute at will its judgments for consumer preferences regarding the desirability of importing products from foreign nations. Stripped of ultimate economic power, the public pays for the government's import restrictions through higher prices for domestically produced substitutes for imported goods. Only domestic producers of restricted products benefit from the monopoly power conferred by such government import controls.

II. GOVERNMENT CONTROL OVER EXPORTS

The United States government has become imbued with a fascist predilection for asserting total *power* to control and direct American exports. The export legislation does not express a desire for the government actively to take over the function of exporting, however. Instead, as in other economic areas, the uniquely fascist approach is to rely on private enterprise to provide the economic engine whose force can be guided, channeled, and manipulated by the government whenever federal authorities choose to exercise their omnipresent statutory power to occupy the driver's seat. This fascist motif is summed up in a typical export statute endorsing the principle that "in authorizing exports, full utilization of *private competitive trade channels* shall be encouraged *insofar as practicable*. . . ."[78]

A correlative theme of American export legislation is a blind mercantilist passion for promoting exports for their own sake, devoid of the recognition that exports are valuable to the public only to the extent that they enable the country to acquire imports. Indeed, fascist economic policy consciously regards imports as a threat to preservation of domestic industry, which is valued above all else in the fascist state's self-destructive emotional and economic surge toward autarky. While the bulk of the official rhetoric is devoted to encouraging exportation, the government has maintained characteristic flexibility in these matters by acquiring the statutory capability both to restrict and to promote exports.

RESTRICTION OF EXPORTS

Unlike the diffuse and often circuitous statutes governing imports, the primary statute authorizing government control over exports is very direct and terse in empowering the President to limit U.S. exports in any way he pleases. The Export Administration Act of 1969 succinctly states that "the President may prohibit or curtail the exportation from the United States, its territories and possessions, of any articles, materials, or supplies, including technical data or any other information, except under such rules and regulations as he may prescribe."[79]

The President is given unlimited authority to require *export licenses* and to impose *export license fees* as prerequisites of any exportation from the United States.[80] The Export Administration Act overtly embraces export controls as a political weapon to coerce economically dependent countries to trade with the United States on its own terms:

> It is the policy of the United States to use export controls, including license fees, to secure the removal by foreign countries of restrictions on access to supplies where such restrictions have or may have a serious domestic inflationary impact, have caused or may cause a serious domestic shortage, or have been imposed for purposes of influencing the foreign policy of the United States.[81]

Reaffirming the government's intention to act as supreme economic overseer of all international trade, the statute further states Congress' intent to impose export controls "to the extent necessary to protect the domestic economy from the excessive drain of scarce materials and to reduce the serious inflationary impact of foreign demand."[82] It is indicative of Congress' increasing boldness in these matters that the 1974 amendments to the Export Administration Act deleted the word "abnormal," which previously modified "foreign demand" in the quoted language.[83]

The President is told to use his powers only in harmony with the congressional policies stated in the Act. But the fluid declaration of policy included in the statute announces Congress' policy "to encourage trade with all countries with which we have diplomatic or trading relations, *except those countries with which such trade has been deter-*

mined by the President to be against the national interest,"[84] thereby entrusting ultimate decisions to the President's unfettered discretion. The President elsewhere is empowered to deny any request for an export license if he claims that the export would be detrimental to national security, even if like goods nevertheless will be supplied on international markets by other friendly nations, although he must report to Congress the reasons for his decision.[85] The Chief Executive retains this power despite perfunctory admonition that he not use it unless he really has evidence that national security requires it.[86]

To implement the authority conveyed by the Act, the Export Administration Review Board was established by executive order within the Department of Commerce, replacing its less subtly named predecessor, the Export Control Review Board.[87] Both fines and imprisonment may be imposed for violation of any governmental license, regulation, or order issued pursuant to the Export Administration Act.[88]

Further restricting the public's freedom to export U.S. products, the Natural Gas Act makes it unlawful to export natural gas without the express approval of the Federal Power Commission (FPC). The Commission can withhold its approval for any reason whatsoever upon the mere assertion that the proposed export is "not . . . consistent with the public interest."[89] Further, the FPC can modify the private export agreement at will, for the Natural Gas Act empowers the Commission to impose whatever "terms and conditions" it fancies simply by labeling them "necessary or appropriate."[90]

Corporations that engage exclusively in export trade also are legally restricted by a statutory requirement that such corporations file written statements with the Federal Trade Commission. In addition to furnishing routine information, including the location of the business, names and addresses of officers and stockholders, and copies of the company's articles of incorporation and bylaws, such firms must submit to the Commission "such information as the Commission may require as to its organization [sic] business, conduct, practices, management, and relation to other associations, corporations, partnerships, and individuals."[91]

Thus the Export Administration Act of 1969 and complementary statutes give the central government unlimited power to prohibit or curtail exports from the United States. Such plenary power of a paternalistic government to oversee, direct, guide, and veto "private" economic decision-making is the stuff of which fascist economies are made.

PROMOTION OF EXPORTS

Another recurrent theme, as evident in U.S. international economic

236

policy as it has been in countries that advocated or practiced government protection of domestic industry from the mercantilist period to
the present, is overt government pressure to stimulate exports. The
superficial rationale usually given is that exports are necessary to
maintain a "favorable" balance of trade, a positive net balance of re-
ceipts of foreign currency (foreign exchange) over outflow of U.S. currency. The layman is encouraged to accept the desirability of a
"favorable" trade balance as an article of faith. We have seen that the
real reason a country must export is not to hoard foreign currency or
justify an accountant's statistical glee at the country's being financially solvent, but to enable a nation to purchase imports. That is, given
the fundamentally barterlike trade that occurs between nations, the
claims against another country's goods and services, which are represented by the foreign exchange that pays for U.S. exports, in turn
serve to finance the purchase of foreign goods (that is, imports). Without claims against other countries' goods and services, a nation cannot
buy anything on the international market.

But if imports are the goal, why does the United States (1) not
spread this knowledge widely, and (2) simultaneously restrict imports?
The multifaceted anwers dovetail. First, the principle that exports
(and a "favorable" balance of trade) are chiefly necessary to finance
imports is not actively communicated precisely because it would lead
people to question the desirability of restricting imports, restriction
which is fundamental to a fascist government's economic role as the
overseer, benefactor, and director of "private" business. Second, the
strong national government central to a fascist economy seeks to dispense the foreign exchange acquired through exports largely for its
own purposes, whether those purposes are military bases in foreign
nations, loans to less developed countries, or other international projects.[92] Since these governmental goals are rather abstract and intangible (and perhaps unappealing) to the public, the government has
ample incentive not to encourage public realization that such governmental drains on the balance of payments are at the expense of private
use of foreign exchange to import goods that would very tangibly improve the standard of living and increase the real income of U.S.
citizens.

Moreover, simultaneously seeking to restrict imports and to promote
exports is absolutely consistent with the economic role and motives of
a fascist government. Both techniques enable the government to exercise profound control over domestic production, preserving its position
as collectivist overseer of "private" enterprise. Like import restrictions, export "encouragement" in the form of subsidies enables the
fascist government to function internally as the benefactor of those

industries that curry favor with government officials within the political pressure-group environment of the fascist domestic economy. Both methods of government control also are perfectly congruent with the fascist economy's protectionist premise that its interests are in fundamental conflict with those of the rest of the world, and that it can advance its position relative to other nations by giving its industries an artificial, governmentally enforced edge in international markets, whether that edge takes the form of tariffs on foreign imports or subsidies to American exports.

Besides encouraging exports to maintain a "favorable" balance of trade, fascism encourages them for another reason. The more severe the trade barriers a fascist economy erects to shield domestic industries from international competition, the more likely is retaliation by foreign nations through restrictions against entry of U.S. goods. Hence the natural consequence of accelerating fascist economic policies is increasing difficulty for domestic industries attempting to export U.S. goods to foreign markets. A fascist government will therefore find it progressively more necessary actively to promote exports in hopes of maintaining a viable balance of trade in the protectionist international economic environment that it has fostered. When export promotion efforts fail, the international economic climate created by fascist trade policies makes autarky necessary for survival as well as theoretically appealing to a government committed to the economic philosophy of fascism.

Government promotion of exports through subsidies can restrict international productivity as profoundly as a system of import barriers. Government export subsidies tend to shift production away from those industries in which America has a comparative cost advantage relative to other nations, and into subsidized export industries in which the United States is relatively less efficient and productive. While subsidized export industries may prosper, their prosperity often is purchased at the expense of more productive nonsubsidized industries. The government export subsidy artificially makes it appear economically more attractive to businesses to export goods in which United States resources may be less than optimally employed. Fundamentally distorted by export subsidies, world prices are prevented from functioning as reliable indicators and determinants of the optimum allocation of the world's productive resources, causing global productivity and real income to decline.

Further, while export subsidies necessarily entail a sacrifice of both world productivity and individual freedom to trade, it is possible that such subsidies might not even achieve the improved balance of payments that is claimed to justify them. First, since foreign countries have limited foreign exchange, the subsidized exports could simply replace export activity that occurred without government intervention, altering the composition but not the total value of U.S. exports. Second, total U.S. exports could decline even if sales of the subsidized American export to a foreign nation replaced sales of a third country to the foreign purchaser, if the third country would have used the proceeds from its now defunct export activity to purchase other products from America.[93] Finally, foreign retaliation for government export subsidies that enable U.S. industries to usurp the markets of other nations' industries ultimately tends to contract the total volume of American exports, hurting rather than helping the United States balance of trade.

Many existing U.S. statutes explicitly state the government's active desire to promote exports. For example, the International Economic Policy Act of 1972 authorizes an executive Council on International Economic Policy to recommend programs with the objective of "increasing exports of goods and services."[94] The National Commission on Productivity and Work Quality is instructed by statute to seek "means to expand exports of the products of United States industry."[95] The Agricultural Adjustment Act of 1938 makes it the official *duty* of the Secretary of Agriculture "to increase in every practical way the flow of . . . [all farm] commodities and the products thereof into the markets of the world."[96] An Export Expansion Advisory Committee was established in 1968 by executive order to advise the Board of Directors of the Export-Import Bank, a government organization whose functions are discussed in section four of this chapter, regarding proper use of bank funds to finance export expansion.[97] Finally, in late 1973 the President created a "President's Export Council" to advise him on export expansion activities, which council he empowered to "identify . . . the need for industry to improve its export efforts" and to "encourage the business and industrial community to enter new foreign markets and to expand existing export programs."[98]

But the government's avowed dedication to expanding exports is not limited to verbal exhortations. The export of many commodities is made possible by federal subsidies authorized by statute. The vast array of government subsidies paid to American industries for domestic production of all sorts artificially lowers the apparent cost structure of those industries, making export of the subsidized products feasible even if America lacks a comparative advantage in the government-favored production. Subsidies explicitly aimed at increasing exports also abound. For example, export of agricultural products is artificially stimulated by government subsidies, in defiance of both international market prices and the most beneficial worldwide production pattern indicated by comparative cost advantages. The Secretary of Agriculture is empowered to

> encourage the exportation of agricultural commodities and products thereof by the payment of benefits in connection with the exportation thereof or of indemnities for losses incurred in connection with such exportation or by payments to producers in connection with the production of that part of any agricultural commodity required for domestic consumption . . . .[99]

The Secretary of Agriculture also can effectively subsidize exports of agricultural products by implementing his broad powers to provide *governmental financing* of international sales of agricultural commodities. The relevant statute grants virtually unlimited power to the Secretary to provide such financing, simultaneously expressing mock deference to the private trade to be manipulated by government financing:

> It is also the policy of the Congress to stimulate and maximize the sale of United States agricultural commodities for dollars through the private trade and *to further the use of private enterprise to the maximum*, thereby strengthening the development and expansion of foreign commercial markets for United States agricultural commodities. In furtherance of this policy, the Secretary of Agriculture is authorized . . . to enter into agreements with foreign and United States private trade for *financing the sale of agricultural commodities for export* over such periods of time and on such credit terms as the Secretary determines will accomplish the objectives of this section.[100]

The Secretary can use these financing powers to reinforce the government's export subsidization efforts either by providing credit at below-market interest rates or by supplying financing otherwise unavailable through private channels.

In addition, the Commodity Credit Corporation — a government-operated "corporation" that functions primarily to subsidize domestic agricultural production through loans, purchases, and price-support payments — is authorized by statute to use its general powers to loan and advance funds in order to "procure agricultural commodities for sale to . . . foreign governments, . . . [and to] export or cause to be exported, or aid in the development of foreign markets for, agricultural commodities."[101]

Tax subsidies (for example, tax credits or other waivers of tax liability) also enable U.S. firms to export American products without encountering the same cost structure as either foreign competitors or U.S. domestic industries.[102] Notoriously political in nature, tax subsidies

240

are as ephemeral as the fickle congressmen whose favors ardent lobbyists court.

Government subsidies to favored export industries also are authorized in principle by recurrent statutory admonition to various government agencies to keep American industry competitive on world markets. To maximize the economic well-being of the public, comparative cost structures should determine which U.S. industries can most beneficially export their wares. Since American industries that have a comparative cost advantage over other nations are *by definition* competitive on world markets, government efforts to "keep U.S. industry competitive" internationally can only mean government intervention to give an artificial, nonmarket edge to industries that do *not* have a comparative cost advantage over other nations, thereby distorting international prices and subverting the principle of comparative advantage to the detriment of world productivity and the public's standard of living.

Nevertheless, United States statutes are replete with government commitment to keeping American industry competitive in world markets. For example, implicitly undermining the principle of international economic specialization, the International Economic Policy Act of 1972 makes it the duty of the Council on International Economic Policy to recommend policies aimed at "strengthening the United States competitive position in world trade" and "preserving the diversified industrial base of the United States."[103] The Council is also required to submit to Congress an annual report that includes "recommendations for appropriate policies and programs in order to insure that American business is competitive in international commerce."[104] Similarly, the National Commission on Productivity is instructed "to promote policies designed to insure that United States products are competitive in domestic and world markets."[105]

Another statutory technique used to promote United States exports is to bestow an advantage other than a direct monetary subsidy upon U.S. exporters while penalizing foreign exporters trying to market their goods in the United States. As with monetary subsidies, the thrust of such a double standard is always to suppress the normal functioning of domestic and international prices as the determinant of optimum allocation of productive resources, thereby benefiting the protected domestic industries while lowering the average citizen's standard of living. One example of this protectionist technique is contained in the Consumer Product Safety Act. While the Act forbids importation of foreign goods not satisfying the government's performance, design, and construction rules, domestic industries have the government's permission to *export* products that do not meet the government's standards.[106] Again, while the government condemns both domestic monopoly and other nations' international cartels,[107] the law authorizes U.S. industries to form American cartels to operate exclusively on international markets, explicitly exempting export trade associations from U.S. antitrust legislation, provided only that the American cartels do not detrimentally affect domestic firms or prices.[108] Finally, the law may require a refund of any domestic "processing tax" payable under the statutes controlling agricultural production whenever a domestically produced commodity is intended for export to a foreign country, although foreign exporters desiring to market goods in the United States may be compelled to pay the tax.[109]

III. FOREIGN EXCHANGE CONTROLS

By controlling transactions involving foreign exchange (which includes foreign currency plus any other claim against foreign goods or services), a government can determine the persons allowed to trade as well as the commodities permitted to be bought and sold on the international market. The control of foreign exchange transactions, that other classic fascist tool for manipulation of "private" international economic dealings, has not eluded the United States government.

A long-standing provision of United States law authorizes the government to regulate or to prohibit foreign exchange transactions whenever the President claims, as Presidents are wont to do even in the most halcyon times, that a "national emergency" exists.[110] The relevant statute empowers the President to use mandatory government licenses for these restrictive purposes if he so desires. The mere cry of "national emergency" allows the President, "by means of instructions, licenses, or otherwise" to "investigate, regulate, or prohibit any transactions in foreign exchange."[111]

Making matters quite graphic even for those to whom "foreign exchange" seems somewhat of an unreal abstraction, the statute goes on to authorize overt government takeover of all private economic dealings with foreign producers under the alleged national-emergency conditions. The law's sweeping language allows the government to mandate any disposition of private property involved in international economic transactions that pleases federal officials, authorizing the President to

> investigate, regulate, direct and compel, nullify, void, prevent or prohibit, any acquisition, holding, withholding, use, transfer, withdrawal, transportation, importation or exportation of, or dealing in, or exercising any right, power, or privilege with respect to, or transactions involving, *any property in which any foreign country or national thereof has any interest* . . . .[112]

The law minces no words in empowering the government to confiscate and dispose of the private property involved, directing that "such interest or property shall be held, used, administered, liquidated, sold, or otherwise dealt with *in the interest of and for the benefit of the United States.*"[113]

Thus the few strokes of a presidential pen required to declare a fictitious "national emergency" provide sufficient legal pretext for the government to impose rigid foreign exchange controls and to seize at will property in which foreign producers or purchasers own an interest. Past Presidents have not hesitated to pen those crucial lines. As of September 1973, four separate proclamations of national emergency remained concurrently effective.[114] In 1934 Franklin D. Roosevelt issued an implementing executive order that, on the basis of its declaration that a national emergency continues to exist, to this day gives the Secretary of the Treasury total discretion to require private banks to solicit government licenses as a prerequisite of any foreign exchange transaction.[115] Providing the mechanism for totally throttling U.S. participation in world trade, the executive order states:

> Every transaction in foreign exchange, transfer of credit between any banking institution within the United States and any banking institution outside of the United States . . . and the export or withdrawal from the United States of any currency or silver coin which is legal tender in the United States, by any person within the United States, is hereby prohibited except under license therefor, issued pursuant to this Executive order. . . .[116]

Reserving the government discretion to intervene selectively in private economic transactions so characteristic of a fascist economy, the executive order provides elastic exceptions to its mandate:

> [E]xcept as provided under regulations prescribed by the Secretary of the Treasury, foreign exchange transactions and transfers of credit may be carried out without a license for (a) normal commercial or business requirements, [and] (b) reasonable traveling and other personal requirements. . . .[117]

Even broader foreign exchange controls were made applicable to transactions involving certain named countries by a subsequent executive order issued in 1940.[118] And still crying "national emergency" as recently as 1968, President Lyndon Johnson by executive order gave the Board of Governors of the Federal Reserve Board full discretionary power

> to investigate, regulate or prohibit any transaction by any bank or

243

other financial institution subject to the jurisdiction of the United States involving a direct or indirect transfer of capital to or within any foreign country or to any national thereof outside the United States....[119]

Thus, like previous fascist economies, the United States government has procured comprehensive power to manipulate private economic relations between American citizens and foreign producers through foreign exchange controls. The critical issue is not the extent to which these powers are implemented at any given time, but the fact that this reservoir of statutory power exists, waiting to be fully tapped by enthusiastic or desperate government officials bent on tightening their grasp on private economic transactions in the world market.

IV. GOVERNMENT FINANCING OF INTERNATIONAL TRADE: THE EXPORT-IMPORT BANK

Another major technique used by the government to manipulate international trade for its own ends is government financing of import and export transactions. The Export-Import Bank of the United States is the primary instrument used by the government for this purpose. In perfect accord with the economic tenets of fascism, the government steadfastly maintains that its actions in financing international trade are intended only to supplement, not to supplant, the functioning of the private market.[120] Nevertheless, federal power to dole out money and credit to finance export and import transactions that it favors enables the government both to control in large measure the availability of foreign products in the United States, and to subsidize the exporter and foreign purchaser of selected domestic products. Although more abstruse than import tariffs, quotas, and overt export subsidies, the economic effects of government financing of international trade are much the same as the consequences of the more direct forms of government regulation. The consumer again pays the bill for government distortion of unregulated prices as the determinant of comparative cost advantages among nations, enduring higher prices and encountering fewer desired products because of the government-induced distortion of consumer demand.

The Export-Import Bank (Ex-Im Bank) is a federal agency that performs most functions of a huge private bank, with the express statutory objective "to aid in financing and to facilitate exports and imports and the exchange of commodities between the United States . . . and any foreign country."[121] In pursuit of these goals, the Ex-Im Bank can borrow and lend money, guarantee payment of any evidence of indebtedness such as a check, note, or draft, and generally engage in a normal banking business.[122] Although the Ex-Im Bank nominally is prohibited from extending credit to or guaranteeing the credit of a Communist country, with the President's approval the Bank can extend credit for the purchase of U.S. products by *any* country, for the prohibitions do not apply in the case of any transaction which the President determines "would be in the *national interest*" if he reports that determination to Congress before the Bank takes final action on the matter.[123] The national-interest slogan permits the President to authorize U.S. government financing of trade with any foreign country whatever its consequences to the United States, absent open rebellion in Congress. In addition, the Ex-Im Bank explicitly is empowered to insure U.S. exporters against "*political and credit risks of loss* arising in connection with United States exports."[124] However, the Chief Executive is given ultimate veto power over all extension of credit and insurance in connection with the purchase of a product by a foreign country or its citizens, for the Bank is prohibited from extending such government credit or insurance "if the President determines that any such transaction would be contrary to the *national interest*."[125]

Like the export statutes discussed in section two of this chapter, the Export-Import Bank legislation voices dedication to expanding United States exports. The familiar strain echoes throughout the statute:

> It is the policy of the United States to foster expansion of exports of goods and related services, thereby contributing to the promotion and maintenance of high levels of employment and real income and to the increased development of the productive resources of the United States.[126]

And again:

> It is the policy of the Congress that the Export-Import Bank of the United States should facilitate through loans, guarantees, and insurance . . . those export transactions which . . . offer sufficient likelihood of repayment to justify the Bank's support in order to actively foster the foreign trade and long-term commercial interest of the United States.[127]

The proffered economic rationale for expanding exports is patently fallacious and misleading, interweaving appealing but inaccurate slogans to promote public acceptance of Congress' protectionist philosophy. Contrary to the statute's assertion, government-subsidized expansion of U.S. exports does not necessarily contribute to high levels of employment; its more predictable consequence is to shift the country's production from the industries in which it has a natural cost advantage relative to other nations, to those industries selectively subsidized by the government. National productivity may in fact decline as a result of such government intervention, although of course the people operating subsidized export enterprises prosper.

Further refuting the statute's claim, government-subsidized export expansion neither enhances the public's real income nor beneficially develops the productive resources of the country. The public's real income would be increased by allowing the economy to produce and export those goods in which it has a comparative cost advantage in relation to other nations. If the government alters this employment of the nation's productive resources by subsidizing exports and thereby tinkering with international prices, the consequent distortion of the optimum resource allocation represents a *decrease* in the public's real income and standard of living. Despite the lilting language favoring "increased development of the productive resources of the United States," it is detrimental to the country to expand industrial development in any field where the country does not have a comparative advantage relative to other nations as reflected by unregulated world prices for the product in question. To approve such phraseology, a Congress would have to be either economically naive or bent upon playing word games with the public regarding vital economic matters.

To grasp the magnitude of the Ex-Im Bank's activities, several facts must be understood. First, a recent amendment to the Ex-Im Bank legislation *exempts all of the Bank's expenditures from the United States budget.*[128] This means that net lending by the Bank accomplished by borrowing from the U.S. Treasury is simply not reported as part of the budget, obscuring the economic reality that such net lending is very much a part of the expenditures of the federal government and one source of government inflation of the country's money and credit.[129] At any one time, the Ex-Im Bank is authorized to have unpaid debts of up to *six billion dollars* owed to the U.S. Treasury.[130] Elaborate verbal artistry attempts to conceal the fact that regardless of which federal agency nominally "absorbs" losses incurred by the Ex-Im Bank, the American public ultimately pays the bill. Thus the statute requires the Ex-Im Bank to absorb the first $100,000,000 of its losses, after which the U.S. Treasury is required by law to bear the next $100,000,000 of Ex-Im Bank losses.[131] Subsequent losses are borne by the Bank. The limit on the Ex-Im Bank's total outstanding loans and insurance has been raised in recent years from $13.5 billion to $25 billion.[132] It is a huge operation, totally exempt from public scrutiny through normal budget review procedures.

246

In considering the effects of the Ex-Im Bank, one must evaluate two situations: that in which government financing provides funds not otherwise available from the private market, and that in which government financing merely replaces available private financing. If financing is totally unavailable on the private market, this implies that the buyer in one country and the seller in the other country simply prefer not to transact business at the undistorted world prices of the product and the credit necessary to purchase the product. If the prohibitive factor is the *price* of the commodity, to stimulate its export by below-market rates for government financing is fundamentally the same as any other type of export subsidy and has identical economic ramifications for the public. If the prohibitive factor is the high cost of *credit* because of risk of loss caused by political or economic instability in the borrowing nation, to provide government funds to finance the transaction is to transfer the incidence of that risk to U.S. taxpayers, sacrificing their economic welfare to the vagaries of the internal politics of foreign nations.

If government financing merely replaces financing available through the private market, several consequences may follow. If private credit were available but at a higher rate of interest than provided by the Ex-Im Bank, the analysis suggested in the preceding paragraph applies to the extent that the cost of private financing exceeds the government's subsidized rate. But even if private financing costs were the same as the Ex-Im Bank rate, government financing could be detrimental to the American economy. First, absent government financing, the foreign buyer might pay *cash* for the product, by giving the U.S. seller either dollars or claims against foreign currency. Either type of cash payment would help the economic position of the United States relative to other nations by (1) reducing foreign claims against U.S. goods and services (where cash payment is *dollars*), or (2) increasing U.S. claims against foreign goods and services (where cash payment is in the form of *claims against foreign currency*). Unlike a United States loan, which constitutes a drain on the American balance of payments, both forms of cash payment increase the ability of the United States to acquire imports, which acquisition is crucial to increasing the public's standard of living. Even if the foreign buyer could finance his purchase through a private U.S. bank loan at the same rate as that available through the Ex-Im Bank, the inflationary increase in the government's debt (money and credit) implicit in the financing of the Ex-Im Bank still harms the American public in a way that private financing normally would not.

There is one other vital economic consequence implicit in the Ex-Im Bank financing of international sales of U.S. goods. In any situation in which the government subsidizes the export by offering more favorable terms than would be available on the private market, it may contribute to the economic problems of the recipient (borrowing) nation. As with a private bank loan, eventually the borrowing country must pay back its Ex-Im Bank loan with interest, and if its investment of the loan proceeds has not created enough economic growth to stimulate sufficient exports to offset the interest payments due on the debt, the borrowing country's ability to import (and its economic well-being) will suffer a net loss. The likelihood of this eventuality is increased to the extent that the government, through the Ex-Im Bank, applies considerations other than economic growth potential in deciding whether or not to finance a proposed international transaction.

Finally, it is important to mention that although the Ex-Im Bank often is touted as a means of providing financing not available in the private capital market, there is no empirical evidence to substantiate any unwillingness by the private capital market to finance exports. The only available empirical data prove that in the case of nonmilitary aircraft, the private capital market readily provided financing of exports to the extent that Ex-Im Bank financing was reduced.[133]

V. MANIPULATING THE "PRIVATE SECTOR"

One distinctive aspect of fascist economics, as characteristic of its international trade policies as of its domestic economic approach, is its consistent effort to superimpose collective (government) decision-making upon a nominally capitalistic economic system. Private enterprise is relied upon to effectuate government policies, while government regulations and controls are imposed to the maximum extent possible without making the subservient private sector either unable or unwilling to function. As in its domestic economic role, the fascist state institutionalizes political decision-making in its regulation of international trade. The individual is without power to influence the government benevolence upon which his economic well-being depends; only large, amply financed organizations can win the government's coveted favors. One no longer speaks of an individual or a business; one speaks of "sectors," of groups, of organizations whose diverse interests must be reconciled and harmonized under the government's omnipotent guidance and control. Thus a facade of harmony between business and government and among pressure groups becomes crucial to the fascist state's efforts to make its economic victims feel that their interests are somehow integrated into a larger collective purpose, usually designated by an accommodatingly amorphous label such as the "national interest."

All of these themes are evident in the international trade legislation of the United States. The International Economic Policy Act of 1972, for example, is quite explicit in asserting that it is the proper role of the government to guide and direct United States international economic policy and to manipulate private business to achieve its ends.[134] The statute creates a Council on International Economic Policy, composed of various cabinet officers including the secretaries of State, Treasury, Defense, Agriculture, Commerce, Labor, and Transportation.[135] The purported goal of the organization is "interagency coordination in the development of a more rational and orderly international economic policy for the United States."[136] The oft repeated dedication to *rational, consistent, and orderly economic policy* euphemistically expresses thinly suppressed yearning for a monolithic, governmentally orchestrated economy, for private industry is consistently treated as a pawn whose movements are to be carefully "coordinated" and synchronized with the government's economic policies. Thus the Council is broadly empowered to examine "the economic activities of (A) the various agencies, departments, and instrumentalities of the Federal Government, (B) the several States, and (C) private industry"[137] in order to recommend to the President "domestic and foreign programs which will promote a *more consistent* international economic policy on the part of the United States and private industry."[138] Making the United States synonymous with the U.S. government, the statute relegates private business to the status of a tractable outsider, the proper object of governmental guidance.

The Export Administration Act of 1969 sugarcoats its assertion of total government power to control exports with solicitous pleas for "information and advice" from private industry.[139] Verbal deference is shown to private industry, but the statute makes it quite clear that the government possesses ultimate control in economic matters. Thus, carefully interweaving concerned recognition of all the private economic interests over whom government control is asserted in hopes of blunting opposition to such federal power, the statute intones:

> In authorizing exports, full utilization of *private competitive trade channels* shall be encouraged *insofar as practicable,* giving consideration to the interests of small business, merchant exporters as well as producers, and established and new exporters, and provision shall be made for *representative trade consultation* to that end.[140]

Similarly, legislation pertaining to the Commodity Credit Corporation, a government "corporation" authorized by statute to subsidize and promote exports of agricultural products, expresses verbal deference characteristic of a fascist economy for the private commerce that supplies its parasitic lifeblood:

249

Congress hereby reconfirms its long-standing policy of favoring the use by governmental agencies of the usual and customary channels . . . of trade and commerce, and directs the Secretary of Agriculture and the Commodity Credit Corporation *to the maximum extent practicable* . . . to encourage orderly marketing of farm commodities through *private competitive trade channels* . . . .[141]

The statutes are replete with attempts to quell potential opposition by incorporating subjugated interests into the system of government import and export controls. The Export Administration Act of 1969, for example, states Congress' policy to subject government-decreed export controls "to review by and consultation with [sic] representatives of appropriate United States Government agencies and *qualified experts* from *private industry*."[142] The statute also provides for committees composed of representatives of industry and government to be formed at the request of a "substantial segment of any industry" subject to export controls (or being considered for such controls for national security reasons), to "advise and assist" government officials.[143] To minimize overt friction between government and business, the Secretary of Commerce is instructed to keep the "*business sector* . . . fully apprised of changes in export control policy."[144] Further attempting to mitigate conflict by covering business/government relations with a veil of procedural harmony, the law states:

In order to enable United States exporters to *coordinate* their business activities with the export control policies of the United States Government, the . . . officials responsible for implementing the rules and regulations authorized under this Act . . . shall, if requested, and *insofar as it is consistent with the national security, the foreign policy of the United States, [and] the effective administration of this Act* . . .
    (1) inform each exporter of the considerations which may cause his export licence [sic] request to be denied or to be the subject of lengthy examination; . . .
    (2) . . . inform each exporter of the circumstances arising during the Government's consideration of his export license application which are cause for denial or further examination; [and]
    (3) give each exporter the opportunity to present evidence and information . . . .[145]

Similarly, the federally controlled Export-Import Bank is required by statute to seek the advice of an Advisory Committee "broadly representative of production, commerce, finance, agriculture and labor."[146] Conforming perfectly to the established pattern, the Trade Act of 1974 admonishes the President to "seek information and advice from *representative elements of the private sector* . . . before entering into a trade agreement."[147] Indeed, the fascist economic art of minimizing private opposition to government control by co-opting, synthesizing, and encompassing it has been honed to a fine edge. United States economic laws demonstrate the apex of what might aptly be labeled participatory fascism.

VI. SPIRALING PROTECTIONISM

Government efforts to interpose political buffers to prevent the United States economy from freely competing in world markets currently are being intensified. An unprecedented drive initiated by Congress in 1973 and 1974 to empower the government to monitor international trade, to intimidate other nations into providing the United States with "access" to their resources at prices that please government officials, and to popularize the concept of autarky forebode a spiraling economic protectionism that threatens both the economic liberty and material abundance that formerly characterized America.

MONITORING INTERNATIONAL TRADE

In 1973 and 1974 Congress passed legislation that authorizes the government to monitor *all* international trade participated in by U.S. citizens. (See section one of Chapter 10 for a discussion of new statutes enabling the government to monitor domestic economic activity.) Though the new provisions are scattered in different laws, they are cut of the same legislative cloth. In each case the government is envisioned as a superior, surrogate market whose economic judgments are assumed to override voluntary, private economic decision-making.

It is the Trade Act of 1974 that empowers the government to monitor all imports into the United States:

> The Secretary of Commerce and the Secretary of Labor shall establish and maintain a program to monitor imports of articles into the United States which will reflect changes in the volume of such imports, the relation of such imports to changes in domestic production, changes in employment within domestic industries producing articles like or directly competitive with such imports, and the extent to which such changes in production and employment are concentrated in specific geographic regions of the United States.[148]

The 1974 amendments to the Export Administration Act of 1969 establish corresponding government power to monitor exports. To "protect" the U.S. economy from the supposed evils of world trade (in the statute's heart-wrenching phraseology, the "excessive drain of scarce materials and . . . the serious inflationary impact of foreign demand"),[149] the Secretary of Commerce is instructed to monitor exports, and contracts for exports, of any article, material, or supply . . . when the volume of such exports in relation to domestic supply contributes, or may contribute, to an increase in domestic prices or a domestic shortage, and such price increase or shortage has, or may have, a serious adverse impact on the economy or any sector thereof.[150]

Further revealing the government's expanded role as monolithic overseer of world trade, the same statute identifies the tangible output desired from such export monitoring:

The results of such monitoring shall . . . be aggregated and included in weekly reports, setting forth, with respect to each article, material, or supply monitored, actual and anticipated exports, the destination by country, and the domestic and worldwide price, supply, and demand.[151]

To assure that these vast amounts of data are integrated and coordinated in a convenient format for the government officials who would substitute their personal judgments for the results of private, voluntary economic interaction, the 1974 Trade Act directs government development of "an enumeration of articles which would result in comparability of United States import, production, and export data."[152] To achieve this goal, the Trade Act modifies the Tariff Act to order preparation of

an enumeration of articles in such detail as . . . may be necessary, comprehending all merchandise imported into the United States and exported from the United States . . . . All import entries and export declarations shall include or have attached thereto an accurate statement specifying . . . the kinds and quantities of all merchandise imported and exported and the value of the total quantity of each kind of article.[153]

Its insatiable appetite for detailed information about private economic activity still unsatisfied, Congress established yet another monitoring program under the Trade Act of 1974. That program singles out trade between the United States and "nonmarket" economies for particular scrutiny by a new bureaucracy to be known as the "East-West Foreign Trade Board."[154] Assuming the United States to be a "market" economy with the untroubled abandon of those who have internalized fascism's economic outlook, Congress directs the International Trade Commission to

establish and maintain a program to monitor imports of articles into the United States from nonmarket economy countries and exports of articles from the United States to nonmarket economy countries. . . . [Summaries of data collected under the "East-West Trade Statistics Monitoring System"] shall include data on the effect of such imports, if any, on the production of like, or directly competitive, articles in the United States and on employment within the industry which produces like, or directly competitive, articles in the United States.[155]

Explicitly embracing the only conceivable purpose of such monitoring —to pass official government judgment on the propriety and permissibility of the monitored economic transactions — the Trade Act orders the East-West Foreign Trade Board to "insure" that any private economic transactions between U.S. citizens and nonmarket economies "will be in the *national interest*."[156] Private persons who export annually to a nonmarket economy more than five million dollars' worth of technology that government bureaucrats deem "vital to the national interest," must file a report with the East-West Foreign Trade Board "in such form and manner as the Board requires which describes the nature and terms of such export."[157]

Similarly, the Federal Energy Administration Act of 1974 gives the head of the newly created Federal Energy Administration (FEA) unprecedented powers to monitor exports of certain petroleum products. Although not yet empowered to prohibit such exports, the Administrator of the FEA is required to keep detailed records of every U.S. export transaction involving coal, crude oil, residual oil, and refined petroleum products.[158] For every such export, the Act authorizes the government to record the name of the exporter, the volume and type of product involved, the manner of shipment, the identification of the carrier or vessel in which the product is shipped, the product's destination, and the name of the purchaser. And in language that forebodes omnipotent federal authority to forbid private exports of energy-related products in the future, the Act also empowers omniscient government officials to record "a statement of the reasons justifying the export."[159]

So, too, every domestic producer who exports agricultural products must report all export transactions to the Secretary of Agriculture. Threatening recalcitrant exporters with maximum penalties of $25,000 and one year's imprisonment, the statute authorizing this government monitoring of agricultural exports states:

All exporters of wheat and wheat flour, feed grains, oil seeds, cotton and products thereof, and other commodities the Secretary may designate produced in the United States shall report to the Secretary of Agriculture, on a weekly basis, the following information regarding any contract for export sales entered into or subsequently modified in any manner during the reporting period:

> (a) type, class, and quantity of the commodity sought to be exported,
>
> (b) the marketing year of shipment,
>
> (c) destination, if known. . . .

All exporters of agricultural commodities produced in the United States shall upon request of the Secretary of Agriculture immediately report to the Secretary *any information with respect to export sales of agricultural commodities* and at such times as he may request.[160]

Finally, an obscure provision of the Trade Act of 1974 indicates the intensity of Congress' desire to establish the government as overseer of all economic interaction between the United States and the rest of the world. Simultaneously illustrating the fundamental economic antagonism that protectionists imagine to exist between nations and revealing the autarkic implications of protectionism's restriction of world trade, this incredible new statute advises private entrepreneurs that "before moving productive facilities from the United States to a foreign country, every firm should . . . provide notice of the move to the Secretary of Labor and the Secretary of Commerce . . . ."[161] Coupled with this new proviso, the recent surge of legislation authorizing federal monitoring of international trade leaves little room to doubt the government's power, legal authority, and aspiration to assume the international economic role of a fascist state.

TRADE BY INTIMIDATION: THE CONCEPT OF "FAIR AND EQUITABLE ACCESS" TO FOREIGN PRODUCTS AT "REASONABLE PRICES"

America's accelerating drive to politicize economic decision-making has resulted in yet another disturbing addition to statutory law: the desire for "fair and equitable access" to foreign products at "reasonable prices." In 1974 this principle was for the first time made the explicit objective of the import and export laws of the United States. The idea behind this pleasantly worded slogan is to employ restrictive trade barriers as a political weapon to coerce nations economically dependent on U.S. trade into surrendering their economic output to the United States at prices that appeal to the U.S. government.

One must pause to admire the finesse of the slogan's wording. Subtly subverting the concept of voluntary trade, the slogan speaks only of "access" to other countries' economic resources. For similar reasons, a thief or extortionist undoubtedly would prefer to describe his aim as "access" to his victim's resources. This "access" to what other nations produce must of course be "fair and equitable" — which means, on terms and conditions that the U.S. government likes. Similarly, for-

254

eign nations are supposed to hand over their economic output at "reasonable" prices, meaning prices favorable to the U.S. government, not prices the foreign country could obtain on the world market absent the American government's intervention. If evaluated only for its felicitous wording, the slogan cannot be faulted. Professional admen could not have done better.

But the slogan must also be evaluated as a significant step in the emergence of a fascist economy. Besides portraying the government in its classic fascist stance as overseer of a "private" economy, the fair-and-equitable-access concept effectively politicizes all of America's international economic dealings. By saying to nations more acutely dependent on U.S. trade than America is on theirs that America will use its economy as a political weapon, imposing trade barriers to sever trade with any nation that refuses to capitulate, the government passed another critical turning point in its commitment to fascist economic policies. With the fair-and-equitable-access slogan, America announced to the world, as any fascist economy must, that it will henceforth rely on threats and intimidation to secure the "trade" it desires, not voluntary exchange between uncoerced producers. Physical force, of course, is the ultimate stock-in-trade of nations that choose so to politicize their international economic relations. As the access slogan is bandied about and politicians discuss without apparent moral qualms the possibility of using military force to seize Arab oil resources if the selling price is not to America's liking, one is haunted by the memory of Germany's "trading" relationships with neighboring states vulnerable to Nazi military might.[162]

When Congress added the fair-and-equitable-access concept to American law, it was not a mere legislative slip of the tongue. In two different statutes Congress added more than five separate provisions inserting the access principle at critical junctures in the law. First, the Trade Act of 1974 makes "fair and equitable access" a guiding objective in the government's negotiation of trade agreements:

> A principal United States negotiating objective . . . shall be to enter into trade agreements with foreign countries . . . to assure the United States of *fair and equitable access at reasonable prices* to supplies of articles of commerce which are important to the economic requirements of the United States and for which the United States does not have, or cannot easily develop, the necessary domestic productive capacity to supply its own requirements.[163]

The Trade Act elsewhere empowers the President to impose import barriers against any country that "imposes *unjustifiable or unreasonable restrictions on access* to supplies of food, raw materials, or manu-

255

factured or semi-manufactured products which burden or restrict United States commerce."[164]

Similarly, the Export Administration Amendments of 1974 effectively interlaced the fair-and-reasonable-access terminology into the Export Administration Act of 1969. Carefully inserting a "congressional finding" to add credibility to its novel statutory amendments, Congress slipped in a prefatory paragraph asserting, "*Unreasonable restrictions on access to world supplies* can cause worldwide political and economic instability, interfere with free international trade [!], and retard the growth and development of nations."[165]

Congress also doctored up its policy pronouncements to fit its new conclusions, adding as official U.S. policy the quest for "international rules and institutions to assure *reasonable access to world supplies*."[166] Feeling a need for still further supportive rhetoric, Congress patched in another new U.S. policy:

> It is the policy of the United States to use export controls, including license fees, to secure the removal by foreign countries of restrictions on *access to supplies* where such restrictions have or may have a serious domestic inflationary impact, have caused or may cause a serious domestic shortage, or have been imposed for purposes of influencing the foreign policy of the United States.[167]

With these reinforcing policy statements carefully pieced into the Export Administration Act, the 1974 amendments proceeded to alter the basic grant of presidential export licensing power. With audacity politically tenable only because the average citizen cannot spend as much time and money deciphering the laws as Congress spends enciphering them, the legislature labeled it a mere "technical and conforming change" (that is, an insignificant alteration designed solely to make the amended statutory language internally consistent) when it rephrased the President's export licensing authority to incorporate the new government policy of seeking "fair and equitable access" to foreign resources:

> Nothing in this Act or the rules or regulations hereunder shall be construed to require authority or permission to export, except where required by the President to effect the policies set forth in section [2402, the policy pronouncement section that contains Congress' fair-and-equitable-access amendments] of this Act.[168]

Thus the statute's backhanded conferral of presidential authority now incorporates by reference the broad new government policies established by the fair-and-equitable-access language previously quoted.

It is cautiously indirect tactics like this that have enabled the government to politicize all U.S. international economic transactions without even a whimper from the public, which will ultimately suffer the detrimental economic and political consequences of future government use of intimidation to procure "fair and equitable access" to foreign resources.

To complement its new statutory powers to intervene as protectionist overseer of all economic transactions between U.S. citizens and foreign producers, the U.S. government is currently intensifying a public relations campaign to popularize autarky, the ultimate realization of fascist international economic policies.

AUTARKY

Explicit pursuit of national economic self-sufficiency (autarky) is both the logical culmination and the death rattle of the restrictive international trade policies of a fascist economic system. Despite its manifold trade barriers, America has not yet wholeheartedly embraced the concept of autarky. Nevertheless, there are disturbing indications that the United States government is beginning to promote autarky as a goal of national economic policy.

The United States government recently has behaved in a manner ideally suited to create mass emotional support for autarky. If one wished to convince the American public that national economic self-sufficiency is desirable, one would not introduce the theory in a dispassionate, scholarly context, inviting objective public scrutiny of its deleterious economic consequences. A crisis would be preferable, a situation that would induce emotional, range-of-the-moment judgments conceding the superficial necessity of national self-sufficiency. If national defense or military security could be invoked for good measure, so much the better. Moreover, the test case should involve a product both tangible and seemingly vital to the vast majority of the American people.

The Arab oil embargo of 1974 provided just such model circumstances for advocacy of autarky, and the federal government played it to the hilt. Barraged with government officials' threats of an impending dearth of petroleum products as a result of the Arabs' so-called blackmail of America for political purposes, the public was encouraged to feel outraged at the audacity of the embargo and to demand that the government "do something" to prevent similar crises in the future. In a double-barreled assault on public sentiment, the media were saturated with foreboding commentary on allegedly disastrous military consequences as well as personal hardships predicted to flow from the embargo.

After a full-scale media campaign to arouse public anger and frustration, the government offered its "solution" to the problem. That solution was patriotically christened by government admen as Project Independence. Project Independence is the government's program for national self-sufficiency in energy production.

Resting its case on the intuitive appeal of abundant energy resources to preserve military security and to supply the economic necessities of an industrialized society, the government is openly striving to achieve national self-sufficiency in energy production in the near future. With striking unanimity, government officials, politicians, and private economists alike consistently refrain from enlightening the public concerning the indisputable economic effects of implementing such policies. There has been no discussion of the impact of self-sufficiency as a government-imposed barrier to international trade, or of the potential economic costs of forcing America's productive resources to be employed in energy production. Neither government spokesmen nor private analysts have sought public consideration of (1) whether the pattern of energy production demanded by government bureaucrats necessarily will be that most desired by consumers; (2) whether consumers really desire to relinquish control over the pattern of United States energy use to omnipotent government officials; (3) whether satisfying the nation's "energy needs" as perceived by government officials most productively employs America's domestic industry, when the comparative cost structures of all potential energy-producing nations are evaluated; and (4) whether the worldwide political goals of the government that necessitate energy independence are significant enough to American citizens to stimulate their voluntary support for self-sufficiency in energy production, given the personal economic hardships involved. Further, although government-sponsored energy production implementing a policy of national self-sufficiency might provoke international economic retaliation and induce a decline in world productivity and America's standard of living, not one of these issues has been publicized. Not even the readily evident military problem posed by relying exclusively on domestic energy sources and thereby accelerating depletion of scarce strategic natural resources such as oil has been publicized extensively.

This peculiar throttling of objective analysis of the government's commitment to national self-sufficiency in energy production stimulates apprehension that the slogan "Project Independence" and the government-induced public fervor favoring that program might be but a preliminary campaign aimed at popularizing the general concept of autarky. That campaign has been successful indeed. By first raising the issue in the most appealing of contexts, the government proselytized the public to approve national self-sufficiency to a degree inconceivable under more dispassionate circumstances. Although public concern about the nation's economic well-being should be aroused by government advocacy of artificially induced national self-sufficiency in any economic field, Project Independence has achieved substantial public acceptance and benevolence regarding that notion.

If Project Independence is indeed but a trial balloon designed as a prelude to more encompassing future government programs for national self-sufficiency, the American public may witness the culmination of the ubiquitous government control over international trade that permeates U.S. statutes. As a defiant but suicidal rejection of international specialization according to comparative cost advantage, any such *generalized* attempt to implement the preachings of autarky would inevitably herald a precipitous collapse of world productivity and America's standard of living.

Thus a wide variety of statutes coalesce to confer upon the government vast discretionary powers characteristic of a fascist economic system to control the international flow of trade to and from the United States. Although the degree to which the government chooses to exercise this power will fluctuate, depending upon vagaries of the economy and the personalities that occupy high political office, the all-encompassing power of the government endures. As in any sphere of a fascist economy, private economic decisions regarding international trade are subordinated to the political might of the state, tolerated only if they conform to the government's protectionist plans for U.S. foreign trade relations. Regardless of transitory revisions to existing foreign trade legislation, it is highly unlikely that the fundamental assertion of total government control over international trade will be modified. One can expect details of the statutes to be altered as Congress and the President bicker over the spoils of federal power, but basic statutory premises regarding the unlimited scope of that power will endure.

10

America's Accelerating
Fascist Economy

A marked acceleration of America's fascist economic policies commenced during 1973 and 1974. As this chapter will show, the United States has witnessed the sudden emergence of a new breed of legislation that portends the complete substitution of the government's will for voluntary choices of citizens in all economic spheres. Most significantly, newly enacted legislation explicitly asserts the government's power to monitor the entire production process and to issue reports specifying the "proper" supply and price of *any* commodity. A surge in federal desire and authority to collect economic information from private businesses accompanies this increased power. Complementing vastly expanded federal economic surveillance, recent legislation reveals unprecedented government aggressiveness in seizing an active role in the actual management and operation of traditionally private industries. A zest for rationing the output of target industries consummates the U.S. government's newly swollen authority to formulate the economic ends toward which "private enterprise" is envisioned as the means.

A number of statutes coalesce to accomplish these results. Through the little publicized National Commission on Supplies and Shortages Act of 1974,[1] the government openly expresses its desire to establish

260

by government decree the appropriate type, quantity, and price of any and all products created by American businesses, totally usurping the function of consumers in a free market. Although this law does not yet permit the government to use coercion to implement these economic decrees, Congress of late has not hesitated to enact compulsory measures requiring an active government role in the management and operation of traditionally private industries whose performance it deems unsatisfactory. In this manner the government already has acquired unprecedented coercive power to participate in the management of a major portion of U.S. railroads and to control the operation of the entire energy industry. The railroad takeover was authorized by the recent Regional Rail Reorganization Act of 1973,[2] while expansion of government power over energy production was achieved primarily through the Federal Energy Administration Act of 1974[3] and the Federal Nonnuclear Energy Research and Development Act of 1974.[4] And where a particular economic endeavor has thus been singled out for coercive controls, Congress has shown a similar willingness to confer upon government officials the corollary power to *ration*, during peacetime, the product whose supply and price the government wishes to manipulate, as demonstrated by federal authority to "allocate" petroleum products created by the Emergency Petroleum Allocation Act of 1973.[5]

As the government asserts ever broader power to dictate the supply and price of goods produced and marketed in the United States, it must of necessity compel increasingly comprehensive disclosure of information about the economic activities of private businesses. Just as more rigidly controlled economies adjust their authoritarian economic decrees in response to information extracted from local industry managers,[6] so the American government, as it covets greater economic power, predictably solicits ever more voluminous data from the "private sector" it strives to dominate. Thus it is no surprise that recent statutes, like the National Commission on Supplies and Shortages Act and the Standard Reference Data Act,[7] propose government extraction of private business information on a scale broad enough to provide government economic proclamations with some link to reality, while fostering the eventual dependence of private businesses upon the government as a monopolistic repository of essential technical data.

With this brief introduction, let us turn to the statutes themselves, which so eloquently document the acceleration of America's fascist economic policies currently in progress. After describing these new laws, the book will conclude with an analysis of the economic and psychological forces that effectively blunt popular opposition to the government's increasingly overt seizure of power over "private" business activity.

I. GOVERNMENT AS MARKET SURROGATE: THE NATIONAL COMMISSION ON SUP-PLIES AND SHORTAGES ACT OF 1974[8]

This short, unnervingly comprehensive statute authorizes the government to monitor and report on the production, employment, and business practices of any American industry, whether the product involved is an agricultural commodity, a natural resource, or a manufactured product.[9] An independent federal agency called the National Commission on Supplies and Shortages is created to perform this function.[10]

Carefully phrased congressional findings provide a transparent pretext for this unparalleled assertion of government power to oversee the economy. Insinuations of economic crises predominate. Readers are informed:

> Shortages of resources and commodities are becoming increasingly frequent in the United States, and such shortages cause undue inconvenience and expense to consumers . . . [and]
>
> Existing institutions do not adequately identify and anticipate such shortages and do not adequately monitor, study, and analyze other market adversities involving specific industries and specific sectors of the economy.[11]

This deft use of the scare word "shortage" typifies the entire statute, generating an emotional impact repeatedly relied upon to discourage dispassionate analysis of the powers conferred upon the government. Although the term is never explicitly defined by the statute, adroit lawmakers implicitly develop a concept of shortage that is a highly novel addition to America's vocabulary.

The trick is that through all its innuendo about shortages, the law implies that it is referring to nonrenewable natural resources essential to human well-being for which no plausible potential substitutes could be developed. The law's wording consistently blurs any distinction between nonrenewable natural resources and products whose supply can be supplemented by the market-stimulated efforts of private producers, always implying that nonrenewable natural resources are the target of its concern. Yet when specifying the functions and powers of the National Commission on Supplies and Shortages, the lawmakers make quite explicit the fact that they have no intention of restricting the agency's activities to nonrenewable natural resources.

This approach provides a clever means of deceptively inducing public support for the Act. Many people unfamiliar with the rationing and incentive functions of free markets might believe it valid for the government to monitor supplies of certain natural resources in order to anticipate, and forewarn the public of, the unexpected but inevitable exhaustion of nonrenewable natural resources commonly thought to be in more abundant supply. But the same people properly might believe it an entirely different matter to empower government officials to monitor industries whose output is otherwise determined by market forces, controlled by the voluntary efforts and interaction of willing producers and consumers unconstrained by unavoidable physical scarcity. To propose government monitoring in the latter situation is to imply that government bureaucrats somehow possess knowledge and ability superior to uncoerced individuals to determine which products *should* be produced in greater quantities. The wish for centralized power to declare "shortages" under such conditions signifies an ill-concealed desire to substitute government decrees concerning price or output levels for those signaled by consumers' voluntary actions in a free market.

It is precisely this type of government authority that the National Commission on Supplies and Shortages Act of 1974 seeks.

Counting on scare tactics to disarm rational opposition and to convince the skeptical that nonrenewable natural resources are the exclusive object of the government's attention, the National Commission on Supplies and Shortages Act opens with these congressional "findings":

> (1) The United States is increasingly dependent on the importation from foreign nations of certain natural resources vital to commerce and the national defense.
>
> (2) Nations that export such resources can alone or in association with other nations arbitrarily raise the prices of such resources to levels which are unreasonable and disruptive of domestic and foreign economies.[12]

Then, in the passage previously quoted, the public is informed about the shortages that allegedly plague America, instructed that existing institutions do not adequately anticipate such shortages, and told that existing government data collection on these matters is too diffuse for current congressional tastes — "not systematically coordinated and disseminated," as the statute puts it.[13]

Such is the initial rhetoric of the statute. Upon rereading it, one becomes disturbingly aware that even in these opening passages the statute subtly shifts from voicing dismay at shortages of foreign-supplied natural resources to decrying shortages of "resources *and commodities*."[14] Indeed, the avowed purpose of creating the National Commission on Supplies and Shortages was "to facilitate more effective and informed responses to resource *and commodity* shortages and to report . . . on the existence or possibility of shortages with respect to essential resources *and commodities*."[15] Similarly, the statute augments its stated concern about anticipating shortages with wistful longing for government power to "monitor, study, and analyze *other market adversities* involving specific industries and specific sectors of the economy."[16] Thus at the outset the law clearly hints that the government's interests include not only nonrenewable natural resources but also all "commodities" that attract its attention, not only "shortages" but also any "other market adversities" it wants to scrutinize, and not only mere anticipation of shortages but also efforts to "monitor, study, and analyze" any economic phenomenon that displeases government officials.

The accuracy of these early hints is fully verified by the remainder of the statute. The Commission is authorized to investigate not only shortages of natural resources but also business practices and pricing policies pertaining to virtually any commodity, specifically including manufactured products.[17] Giving the Commission unlimited power to scrutinize private economic activity and to prepare government studies designed to second-guess consumers' and producers' voluntary economic choices, the statute empowers the Commission to issue reports on:

> (1) the existence or possibility of any long- or short-term shortages; *employment, price or business practices;* or market adversities affecting the supply of any natural resources, raw agriculture [*sic*] commodities, materials, *manufactured products* (including any possible impairment of productive capacity which may result from shortages in materials, resources, commodities, manufactured products, plant or equipment, or capital investment, and the causes of such shortages, practices, or adversities);
> (2) the adverse impact or possible adverse impact of such shortages, practices, or adversities upon consumers, in terms of price and lack of availability of desired goods. . . .[18]

Clearly implying that Congress ultimately aims to translate these reports into government action, the National Commission on Supplies and Shortages is also authorized to study:

> (3) the need for, and the assessment of, *alternative actions* necessary to increase the availability of the items referred to in paragraph (1) of this subsection [quoted above], to correct the adversity or practice affecting the availability of any such items, or otherwise to mitigate the adverse impact or possible adverse impact of shortages, practices, or adversities upon consumers referred to in paragraph (2) of this subsection. . . .[19]

264

Thus the government assumes the role, so far only through reports, of functioning as a surrogate market, interjecting its judgments concerning the type, quantity, and price of economic output most beneficial to the citizens whose voluntary choices federal officials would supersede.

A most interesting feature of the National Commission on Supplies and Shortages Act of 1974 is the technique used to secure its passage. Although it authorizes government perusal of private economic activity on a scale unparalleled in U.S. history, this law was quietly slipped through as part of the Defense Production Act Amendments of 1974,[20] which amended the Defense Production Act of 1950. It is particularly odd that such a radical alteration of the government's economic function was incorporated into a defense law, both because the subject matter of the two statutes is so incongruous, and because the supplies-and-shortages legislation originally passed by the Senate was in no way associated with the Defense-Act Amendments.[21] Yet even the published legislative history of the Defense Production Act Amendments offers no explanation for inclusion of the broad provisions of the Supplies and Shortages Act. Never so much as mentioning the Supplies and Shortages Act by name, the legislative history only marginally addresses the contents of that new law, limiting its brief commentary to discussion of shortages of defense-related "essential natural resources" such as oil.[22] Moreover, while Congress secured passage of the law in this inconspicuous manner, the one-year expiration date for the Commission's activities established by the Senate bill was deleted.[23] One can only speculate on the congressional motives behind this studied avoidance of public scrutiny. However illogical the approach, concerned citizens and prudent scholars hereafter are well advised to search the Defense Production Act of 1950 to discover the government's latest statutory authority to oversee the economy.

Perhaps the most ominous aspect of the National Commission on Supplies and Shortages Act is a provision that authorizes the Commission to report on "the advisability of establishing an independent agency to provide for a comprehensive data collection and storage system, to aid in examination and analysis of the supplies and shortages in the economy of the United States and in relation to the rest of the world."[24] Though it is difficult to convey the implications of this superficially innocuous data-bank proposal, it is precisely such a comprehensive economic data collection system that is the *sine qua non* of all advanced collectivist economies, be they fascist, socialist, or communist. Only by compelling detailed disclosure of people's economic activities can a collectivist system achieve the economic control it desires. It is so in the Soviet Union, it is so with the French system of "indicative" planning, and it is so in the emerging fascist economy of the United

States. Actual establishment of such a centralized economic data collection agency should serve as a bellwether heralding far broader government efforts to dictate the constraints within which the "private sector" is forced to operate than America has yet known.

The proposed data bank on commodity supplies would supplement already massive economic data collection authority possessed by the federal government. Virtually every law described throughout this book contains provisions empowering the government to compel businesses to disclose whatever "relevant" records and other data government officials seek to peruse. Although the government's push to acquire information about private business activity thus has been a historical process, that effort has been significantly accelerated in recent years. For example, in addition to the National Commission on Supplies and Shortages Act's proposed data collection scheme, the Standard Reference Data Act,[25] passed in 1968, authorizes the government to engage in unprecedented collection and dissemination of technical information about the physical composition of privately manufactured substances. The Secretary of Commerce is directed to "arrange for the collection, compilation, critical evaluation, publication, and dissemination of standard reference data."[26] In a definition as elusive as the phrase itself, "standard reference data" is said to mean "*quantitative information,* related to a measurable physical or chemical property of a substance or system of substances of known composition and structure, which is critically evaluated as to its reliability [by the Secretary of Commerce] . . . ."[27] While standard reference data clearly include the composition of manufactured products such as metals, plastics, and dyes, the statutory definition is seemingly broad enough also to encompass such things as the manner in which manufactured products are constructed. Detailed information about construction or assembly procedures would seem equally well described as "quantitative information, related to a measurable physical . . . property of a . . . system of substances of known composition or structure."[28] Regardless of the law's technical limits, however, the Standard Reference Data Act typifies the government's current efforts to consolidate its information-gathering powers.[29] Government attempts to stretch the bounds of the statute's authority await the future.

II. GOVERNMENT TAKEOVER OF ENERGY PRODUCTION AND DISTRIBUTION

While government-preferred output and price patterns identified under the National Commission on Supplies and Shortages Act of 1974 as yet remain devoid of direct coercive enforcement power, the government's now unlimited authority to control energy production and distribution is backed by a full arsenal of legal sanctions and financial inducements that guarantee implementation of the government's will. The three primary statutes that create this plenary authority are the Federal Energy Administration Act of 1974,[30] the Emergency Petroleum Allocation Act of 1973,[31] and the Federal Nonnuclear Energy Research and Development Act of 1974.[32]

Amidst typical fascist rhetoric lauding competition, free enterprise, and cooperation between large interest groups,[33] the Federal Energy Administration Act of 1974 gives the government sweeping powers to control the supply, price, distribution, and usage of energy. As in the National Commission on Supplies and Shortages Act, here too the battle cry used to justify burgeoning federal power is "scarcity," with Congress voicing its commitment to "positive and effective action to conserve scarce energy supplies."[34] Yet despite the colorful language, it is apparent that the cry of scarcity is a response more to politically contrived high prices and supply restrictions – largely provoked by United States intervention in foreign nations—than to absolute resource limitations.

Without addressing the source of the scarcity, Congress minces no words in stating its intent that government officials dictate to whom and at what price energy will be available – in Congress' more appealing phraseology, "to insure fair and efficient distribution of, and the maintenance of fair and reasonable consumer prices for, such [energy] supplies."[35] To ensure that these fine-sounding abstractions are translated into tangible government decrees, the Federal Energy Administration, created by the 1974 Act, is authorized to fix prices and wages in energy industries (performing functions previously assigned to the Cost of Living Council)[36] and to allocate petroleum products (assuming the former role of the Interior Department's Office of Petroleum Allocation).[37]

The predominant collectivist view of the economic task of energy production is everywhere apparent in the 1974 Federal Energy Administration Act. Monolithic government "solutions" to anything that can be designated an energy problem are the order of the day. The Federal Energy Administration is instructed to prepare and maintain a "*comprehensive plan* to alleviate the energy shortage,"[38] while advising the President and Congress on the formulation of a "*comprehensive national energy policy*."[39] In a linguistic maneuver that adeptly transfers energy production decisions from the economic to the political realm, Congress repeatedly proclaims the government's right "to assure that adequate provision is made to meet the energy needs of the Nation,"[40] clearly implying that the satisfaction of the central government rather than the satisfaction of consumers is the proper goal of energy producers. Making explicit the fact that the *"nation's* needs" are something very different from the wishes of the people who compose the nation, and that to exalt this collective need is often to subjugate the individuals who compose the collective, the Act further instructs the Federal Energy Administration to "assure that energy programs are designed and implemented in a fair and efficient manner so as to *minimize hardship and inequity while assuring that the priority needs of the Nation are met."*[41]

The Federal Energy Administration Act of 1974 provides valuable insight into the extent to which Congress envisions the government as superior to uncoerced market forces and the economic choices of free individuals. Insofar as such powers are assigned to the Federal Energy Administration by statute or by the President, the Act authorizes that agency to "assess the *adequacy of energy resources to meet demands,"* to "develop plans and programs for dealing with energy production *shortages,"* to "promote *stability in energy prices* to the consumer," and to "prevent *unreasonable profits* within the various segments of the energy industry."[42] True to the facile self-contradictions of fascist jargon, such government activity—which amounts to absolute government control over the supply and price of energy—is to be carried out in a manner that promotes "free enterprise" and "free and open competition."[43] In addition to its authority to use government decrees to manipulate the supply and fix the price of energy, the Federal Energy Administration is empowered, where so ordered by Congress or the President, to conduct programs to control the *"distribution, rationing, and allocation* of all forms of energy."[44] Finally, capping the government's unlimited power to control energy supply, price, and distribution, the Act empowers the Federal Energy Administration to develop *mandatory* energy conservation programs as it sees fit.[45]

But all this power would be unwieldy for government overseers directing America's energy production without corollary power to compel disclosure of private economic information. Thus, as night follows day, the statutory authority to extract such data accompanies federal power to dominate the industry. The Federal Energy Administration Act authorizes government perusal of the private records of energy consumers as well as of producers:

> All persons owning or operating facilities or business premises who are engaged in any phase of energy supply or major energy consumption *shall make available to the Administrator* [of the Federal Energy Administration] *such information* and periodic reports, records, documents, and other data, relating to the purposes of this Act, including full identification of all data and projections as to source, time, and methodology of development, *as the Administrator may prescribe* . . . .[46]

Such are the general powers over existing energy production technology that are vested by statute in the Federal Energy Administration. But the government's control over petroleum products is both more extensive and more concrete than the Federal Energy Administration Act suggests.

The Emergency Petroleum Allocation Act of 1973[47] is the vehicle Congress used to extend and particularize government power over petroleum-related industries. The emotional pitch of the introductory rhetoric is an apt indicator of the severity of the measures that follow. Before enunciating the government's new powers, Congress carefully denounces *shortages* of oil and petroleum products, bewails the "severe economic dislocations and hardships" allegedly caused by such shortages, and announces the existence of "a national energy crisis."[48] This fearful state of affairs prompts Congress to assert, totally without supporting evidence, that this "crisis" is a "threat" that "can be averted or minimized most efficiently and effectively through prompt action by the Executive branch of Government."[49]

Relying on the emotional fervor thus raised to eliminate opposition to its program, Congress proceeds to accord unconstrained power to the President to divvy up America's crude oil, residual fuel oil, and refined petroleum products. Also given power to fix the prices of these commodities, the President is required to "promulgate a regulation providing for the *mandatory allocation* of crude oil, residual fuel oil, and each refined petroleum product, in *amounts* specified in . . . and at *prices* specified in . . . such regulation."[50] The President not only is accorded power to dictate which users can acquire petroleum products, how much each may purchase, and the prices purchasers must pay; he also may forcibly prevent owners of domestically produced or refined crude oil, residual fuel oil, and refined petroleum products from exporting these products.[51] To supplement the President's discretionary authority in the exercise of these comprehensive powers, the Emergency Petroleum Allocation Act grants him broad authority to exempt products from his decrees.[52] Quick to implement the new executive-branch functions mandated by the Act, President Nixon, within a week of the statute's enactment, delegated his power under the Act to a new entity called the Federal Energy Office.[53]

Despite the pervasiveness of government power over energy supply, price, and distribution thus achieved by the Emergency Petroleum Allocation Act and the Federal Energy Administration Act, this power pales in comparison with the new federal controls authorized by the little publicized Federal Nonnuclear Energy Research and Development Act of 1974 (hereafter referred to as the Nonnuclear Energy Act).[54] This law establishes a rather ominous new technique for securing government control over an economic function traditionally performed by private businesses—a technique, however, which fully embodies the familiar economic premises of fascism. With this largely unnoticed statute, the federal government has seized political control over the development of nonnuclear energy technology, effectively preventing economic considerations from directing the optimal form of future energy production.

To implement its provisions, the Nonnuclear Energy Act uses a federal agency called the Energy Research and Development Administration (ERDA), recently created by the Energy Reorganization Act of 1974.[55] Although the Energy Research and Development Administration also manages nuclear energy research and development, a function performed for many years by the federal Atomic Energy Commission, it is its broadened power over developing nonnuclear energy industries that represents a significant expansion of government power and hence is the focal point of this discussion.

Groping for "findings" to justify its actions, Congress introduces the Nonnuclear Energy Act with standard denunciations of the "energy shortage" that allegedly prevails.[56] Embracing at the outset the fascist economic theme that permeates the Act, Congress states its desire, however massive the federal controls that follow, to take "full advantage . . . of the existing technical and managerial expertise in the various energy fields within Federal agencies and *particularly in the private sector.*"[57]

The primary function of the Energy Research and Development Administration under the Nonnuclear Energy Act is to "formulate and carry out a comprehensive Federal nonnuclear energy research, development, and demonstration program."[58] The Act empowers the government to design, construct, and even to operate energy production facilities in order "to demonstrate the technical and economic feasibility of utilizing various forms of nonnuclear energy."[59] All forms of nonnuclear energy (including coal, solar, and geothermal energy projects formerly promoted through other federal programs) are included within ERDA's jurisdiction.[60]

To implement this authority, the agency is given unrestricted power to subsidize energy research, development, and demonstration programs through grants, loans, contracts, and government purchases.[61] Loaded with tax- or inflation-generated dollars, the government has authority not only to finance the research and development it favors, but also to provide price supports for the output of pet demonstration projects whose "economic feasibility" the government is determined to prove.[62] Thus it is that federal money spent by government officials will henceforth determine the specific types of nonnuclear energy production to be developed, for private businesses will be both unwilling and financially unable to compete with massively subsidized government-sponsored projects. Because of the injection of unpredictable political risks into nonnuclear energy activities, even businesses formerly willing to assume normal economic risks of the private market will find it necessary to align themselves with government programs or cease operations in the energy field.

However extensive, the federal intervention under the Nonnuclear Energy Act so far described at least has the dubious virtue of being relatively overt. The quite unprecedented and much more disturbing form of federal intervention into the production of nonnuclear energy is a distinctively fascist economic creation that enables the government to maintain a facade of private enterprise while securing absolute power to control "private" business activity. The Act authorizes ERDA to create, upon obtaining the approval of Congress, "*joint Federal-industry* experimental, demonstration, or *commercial corporations*" to produce nonnuclear energy.[63] Each such joint government-industry corporation is to be controlled by a board of directors composed of political appointees selected by the President.[64]

The statute's efforts to perpetrate the illusion of preserving private enterprise do not end with the establishment of political control over these "mixed" government-industry corporations. The real coup, the provision that guarantees the ultimate elimination of all truly private nonnuclear energy production, is yet to come. The reader first is informed that the government's "participation" in any joint corporation must terminate within twelve years of the corporation's creation.[65] When government participation allegedly ceases, the corporation is officially dissolved, and the board of directors is required to dispose of the corporation's physical facilities in any manner it sees fit in an attempt to recoup the government's "investment" in the project.[66] Lulled by this explicit promise of federal withdrawal, the casual reader's attention is diverted from subsequent statutory provisions that transform this professed government withdrawal into exactly the opposite of what it purports to be.

Although the destruction of the joint government-industry corporation suggests a phasing out of government control accompanied by a corresponding shift to private production of nonnuclear energy, the procedure is but a carefully concocted charade. In fact, the dissolution signals a net gain in federal control over nonnuclear energy production. The crux of the government's retention of control is that when the joint corporation is terminated, the Energy Research and Development Administration *takes over ownership of all patent rights held by the joint corporation on the date of its dissolution.*[67] As a result of this patent seizure, any "private" business that subsequently desires to use

271

the technology is reduced to the status of a government licensee, utterly dependent on government patent licenses for its economic viability.

Not content with federal seizure of the fruits of joint government-industry corporations, Congress also authorized the government to take patent rights in every invention whose creation is in any way supported by federal funds. The Act's patent policy states:

> Whenever any invention is made or conceived in the course of or under any contract [defined by §9(m)(2) to include grants, agreements, understandings, "or other arrangement"] of the Administration [ERDA] . . . *title to such invention shall vest in the United States* . . . .[68]

Although the government has broad discretionary power to waive these patent rights,[69] it is unlikely that federal officials will eagerly relinquish the vast political control over energy production that the patent rights represent.

More significant than the government's power to waive patent rights is its power to license patent users. The Nonnuclear Energy Act gives the government full power to decide who will be allowed to use the patented technology and whether the patent licenses issued will be exclusive (granted to one licensee only), partially exclusive, or nonexclusive.[70] Such licenses may be restricted by any terms and conditions the government wishes to specify, and federal officials by statute retain the power to change their minds at a later date,[71] creating an effective political/economic lever over uncooperative licensees.

Thus, in combination with its subsidy provisions, the patent policy of the Federal Nonnuclear Energy Act of 1974 portends gradual but ultimately total government usurpation of the technology by which nonnuclear energy is produced. The Act's subsidy provisions enable the government to determine on political rather than economic grounds the types of technology developed, while the law's patent provisions give the government future political power to dictate both the persons allowed to produce nonnuclear energy, and the terms and conditions of its production. When the process here outlined fully evolves, it will constitute a fascist dream come true. The nonnuclear energy industries will remain privately operated, but the government will possess absolute power to manipulate and control the industries' activities. It is a tribute to the legislative finesse of modern advocates of fascist economics that the Nonnuclear Energy Act enables this total transformation to occur so discreetly that the average citizen is not even made aware of the process.

The Nonnuclear Energy Act includes one final provision, as if to dispel any lingering illusions concerning the government's willingness to eliminate private economic decision-making entirely if unable to bribe or otherwise manipulate producers into compliance with its wishes. That provision explicitly authorizes the government to *ration*, by presidential decree, any product or material allegedly "essential" to the production of nonnuclear energy. Using the predictable rhetoric of crisis while granting powers susceptible of implementation with or without a crisis, the statute provides:

> The President may, by rule or order, require the allocation of . . . supplies of materials and equipment if he finds that—
> (1) such supplies are *scarce, critical, and essential* to carry out the purposes of this Act; and
> (2) such supplies cannot reasonably be obtained without exercising the authority granted by this section.[72]

While it typifies the economics of fascism, this overt readiness actively to intervene in market operations when indirect attempts to manipulate the "private sector" fail represents a quantum jump in the level of economic activism the United States government is willing openly to acknowledge.

III. GOVERNMENT TAKEOVER OF NORTH-EAST AND MIDWEST RAILROADS

The energy-producing industries are not alone in having been earmarked for government takeover. In 1970 Congress, through the Rail Passenger Service Act, authorized the government takeover of America's passenger train service.[73] More recently, dissatisfied with increasing railroad bankruptcies and unwilling to relinquish the Interstate Commerce Commission regulatory power largely responsible for the railroads' problems,[74] Congress passed the Regional Rail Reorganization Act of 1973[75] to enable the federal government to dictate which railroads were to survive and to pump taxpayers' dollars into those railroads to make their survival possible. Through this statute, the core of another major American industry has fallen victim to the government's recent hair-trigger willingness to usurp the functions of the market.

Apart from providing federal financial support for railroad workers whose jobs are destroyed by the government's activities,[76] the Regional Rail Reorganization Act performs three basic functions: (1) it empowers the government to take over all bankrupt railroads in the Midwestern and the Northeastern United States, picking and choosing which railroads will be preserved and which scrapped;[77] (2) it establishes a government-controlled "corporation" called the Consolidated Rail

Corporation to operate the railroads selected for preservation;[78] and (3) it creates permanent conduits through which government tax- or inflation-generated money can be funneled into any bankrupt railroad in the Midwest or the Northeast that the government feels like preserving.[79]

Above and beyond these specific functions, the Act explicitly substitutes the judgments of federal officials for the judgments of the public expressed through private economic decision-making. Through the Regional Rail Reorganization Act, the government asserts the right and seizes the power to impose on an impotent citizenry that combination of rail services which government bureaucrats deem "adequate" to fulfill the public's "needs." Indeed, it is the stated purpose of the statute to identify "a rail service system in the midwest and northeast region which is adequate to meet the needs and service requirements of this region and of the national rail transportation system."[80]

Displaying a remarkably low estimate of the average citizen's mentality, Congress finds self-serving, undocumented assertions — that the railroad service it will force taxpayers to subsidize is "essential," that this railroad service is "threatened," and that both the "national interest" and the "public convenience and necessity" require government-sponsored maintenance of "adequate and efficient rail service"[81] — sufficient pretext to give it a blank check to "reorganize" the railroads as it pleases. Without pausing to prove or justify this heady rhetoric, Congress swiftly reaches its foregone conclusion: "These needs cannot be met without substantial action by the Federal Government."[82] If this highly transferable statutory formula is an acceptable justification for government takeover of an industry, any economic activity is vulnerable to similarly massive government control, provided only that the political climate is right. If the political climate would tolerate government takeover ("reorganization") of the clothing industry, for example, a statutory preamble modeled after the Regional Rail Reorganization Act would "justify" that move as well as it justifies government takeover of the Midwest and the Northeast railroads. It only remains for Congress to assert that it desires economic takeover ("substantial action by the Federal Government") and for the people to accept it.

The tool Congress created to make the initial determination of which bankrupt Midwest and Northeast railroads to preserve is a non-profit government corporation called the United States Railway Association.[83] The first task of the Railway Association was to prepare the "final system plan."[84] This plan constitutes the government's blueprint for restructuring the region's railroads. Its sole function is to order the disposition of bankrupt railroads in the region, identifying which railroads are to be subsidized, which sold to profitable railroads, and which used for other "public" purposes.[85] Any action in compliance with the final system plan is exempt from the antitrust laws.[86] Meticulously following the fascist pattern, the Act claims that this overt government economic intervention should strive for "the retention and promotion of *competition* in the provision of rail and other transportation services in the region."[87]

The other primary function of the U.S. Railway Association is to spend "government" money. The Act authorizes the Association to issue and maintain up to $1.5 billion in government debt outstanding at any one time.[88] Two thirds of this expenditure ($1 billion) may be channeled to the Consolidated Rail Corporation for the operation of bankrupt railroads, half of which ($500 million) is earmarked solely for railroad modernization and rehabilitation.[89] The Railway Association is empowered to make loans to any railroad that connects to a bankrupt railroad and allegedly needs money to avoid its own bankruptcy, as well as to the Consolidated Rail Corporation, state or local transportation authorities, and other railroads to assist in implementation of the "final system plan."[90] Exhibiting the exquisite subterfuge of much modern legislation, the statute specifically exempts the Association's expenditures from the government's published budget and hence from public scrutiny:

> The receipts and disbursements of the Association [except administrative expenses] . . . shall not be included in the totals of the budget of the United States Government, and shall be exempt from any annual expenditure and net lending (budget outlays) limitations imposed on a budget of the United States Government.[91]

This overt effort to conceal a major subsidy makes it increasingly difficult to sustain faith in the benevolent intent of supporters of such legislation.

Once the favored bankrupt railroads are bought and paid for by the U.S. Railway Association, they are turned over to that interesting entity known as the Consolidated Rail Corporation. The Consolidated Rail Corporation is the operational arm of the government-dominated railroad system. Its function is to operate the railroads turned over to it pursuant to the "final system plan" and to "improve" the railroad properties it holds.[92] Although the statute insists that Consolidated Rail is a "for-profit" corporation that is *not* an instrumentality of the federal government,[93] it is not likely to be either profitable or independent of government control. The prognosis is for ever-greater federal subsidies to the bankrupt railroads,[94] and so long as more than half of the Corporation's debts remain owed to or guaranteed by the U.S.

government, at least seven (and potentially eight) of the Corporation's fifteen-member board of directors are required to be presidential appointees.[95] Such is the prevailing fascist notion of "for-profit" nongovernmental economic activity. However, it is comforting to note that, like the U.S. Railway Association, the Consolidated Rail Corporation will see to it that "adequate and efficient rail services" are maintained.[96]

In addition to the enormous sums expended through the U.S. Railway Association, the Regional Rail Reorganization Act authorizes a broad program of railroad subsidies to be administered by the Secretary of Transportation.[97] The Act authorizes grants and loans to be made either to states or to local or regional transportation authorities.[98] The direct grants, appealingly called "rail service continuation subsidies," may be used to finance bankrupt railroads *not* designated for continuation under the final system plan, as well as certain state-supported rail services and rail services whose abandonment is hereafter authorized by the Interstate Commerce Commission.[99] In addition, the statute authorizes the Secretary of Transportation to direct the U.S. Railway Association to provide loans to willing states for the acquisition and modernization of railroads taken over by the Consolidated Rail Corporation, thereby negating any private market decision to abandon those rail services.[100] All the economic incentives established by the Regional Rail Reorganization Act thus encourage the preservation of local rail service that, while appealing to a few direct beneficiaries, is economically inefficient and extremely costly to the taxpayers forced to finance the venture.

Thus it is that the government has taken over the bankrupt railroads of the Northeast and the Midwest, compelling taxpayers to finance economic activity that paternalistic government officials deem "essential." Still maintaining characteristic fascist deference to the private enterprise it now controls, the government in the Regional Rail Reorganization Act again reveals its current unprecedented willingness actively to intervene when frustrated in indirect efforts to manipulate the economy.

All of this recent legislation represents attempts by lawmakers in an accelerating fascist economic system to tie up loose ends, consolidating existing economic power and acquiring authority previously beyond the government's reach. It has now become explicit in the laws as well as in the pronouncements of federal officials that the government's goal is the central one of a fascist economy: to manipulate a still nominally capitalistic economy to accomplish the government's will. Yet even as the measures implemented to impose the collective's wishes on theoretically "private" economic activities become increasingly oppressive, the vast majority of the public displays passive acquiescence to the government's expanding economic role. Undoubtedly, this is due in part to insufficient knowledge of the full scope of existing government power and unfamiliarity with the economic consequences of government activity. Nevertheless, more fundamental reasons for this acquiescence may be found in the economic and psychological effects of a fascist economy on individuals within such a system, as well as a unique development of America's economic structure which effectively co-opts opposition to prevailing policies.

IV. THE ILLUSORY ALIGNMENT OF SELF-INTEREST WITH FASCIST ECONOMIC POLICIES

The chief reason a fascist economic system such as that of the United States is able to maintain popular support for its programs is that, on a variety of levels, it makes people feel that their self-interest depends on the continuation of existing government policies and programs. This illusory linking of self-interest with preservation of the economic/political status quo operates both by promoting psychological and economic dependence on the government and, in America, by making the people believe that the governmental decisions that rule their economic lives somehow embody their personal values and wishes.

As does any collectivist system, a fascist economy stimulates psychological dependence by causing people to rely upon the government to perform the economic functions it has usurped. People gradually come to believe that these functions have *always* been performed by the government, making any alternative appear risky and threatening. In addition, many people understandably feel increasingly helpless to effect significant change as the government's shadow looms ever larger on the economic horizon. Ironically, this psychological impotence feeds on itself. The more psychologically dependent people feel, the more they want the government to function as omnipotent economic risk-bearer and social panacea, perceiving the government as the only tangible tool to fix all social and economic problems. The net result is psychological emasculation of individuals who feel inescapably dependent on the political hierarchy that governs their economic welfare.

By subjugating individuals to political control over economic matters, fascism also creates economic dependence on existing government policies and programs. While the increasing prevalence of government contracts is of extreme importance in achieving the economic subservience of businesses, other primary architects of economic dependence are government subsidies and welfare (transfer) payments. Although the public should perceive that taxation and inflation are the only means of financing these government expenditures, most people feel — or hope — that *as individuals* they receive more from the government than the government expropriates from them. Moreover, while the costs of subsidies and welfare payments are diffuse and difficult to conceptualize, the benefits are immediate and tangible. The dauntless human wish to acquire something for nothing is thus a valuable ally of any fascist economic system. Since to challenge the fascist economy is to threaten net financial benefits that people feel (however erroneously) they derive under the existing system, the money that the government lavishes upon special-interest groups does much to ensure fascism's survival.

Transfer payments as well as subsidies can be paid both to businesses and to individuals. The crucial distinction between the two is that unlike the transfer or welfare payment, which is an *unconditional* transfer of money, true subsidies require the recipient of government funds to perform a specific economic activity in return, to provide a *quid pro quo* to obtain the money.[101] One comprehensive study aptly defines a subsidy as

> the provision of Federal economic assistance, at the expense of others in the economy, to the private-sector producers or consumers of a particular good, service or factor of production. The Government receives no equivalent compensation in return, but *conditions the assistance on a particular performance by the recipient — a quid pro quo —* that has the effect of altering the price or costs of the particular good, service, or factor to the subsidy recipient, so as to encourage or discourage the output, supply, or use of these items and the related economic behavior.[102]

Thus subsidies are a particularly ideal tool of a fascist economy, the perfect device for getting "private" parties to undertake government-preferred economic activity without necessitating overt coercion to achieve compliance with the government's wishes. Since subsidies require recipients to engage in government-favored economic activity in order to "qualify" for federal benefits, they enable the government to manipulate a superficially private economy to do its bidding without the unpleasant visibility of active government economic intervention. Altering the market's economic signals through government bribes to private businesses and individuals, developed fascist economies rely heavily on the indirect technique of subsidization to achieve favored economic and political results.

The rapid expansion of U.S. subsidy programs provides a grim but accurate measure of the current acceleration of America's fascist econ-

278

omy. The U.S. government's inventive repertoire of subsidization techniques now runs the gamut, including direct cash payments, tax subsidies and penalties, credit (loan) subsidies, government sales at less than market prices (so-called benefit-in-kind subsidies), government purchases at above-market prices, regulatory subsidies, and subsidies created by import barriers.[103] Government subsidies presently influence such diverse economic activities as transportation, housing, education, agriculture, science, health care, forestry, outdoor recreation, and arts and entertainment. It is estimated that in 1970 federal subsidies reached an overall magnitude of $63 billion (not counting the vast cost of regulatory subsidies, benefit-in-kind subsidies, or subsidies to domestic industries implicit in import tariffs and quotas).[104] The enormous sums now spent on welfare payments (unconditional transfers of all kinds) must be added to this figure if one wishes to have anything resembling a complete picture of the government expenditures currently aimed at buying political support for the fascist economy.

Besides fostering economic dependence and inducing recipients to take requisite economic actions designated by law, subsidies and welfare payments have another virtue prized by supporters of a fascist economy. As with government contracts, the very magnitude of federal subsidies and welfare expenditures enables the government to use the threat of withholding these funds as a potent, arm-twisting lever to prompt "voluntary" responsiveness to its economic wishes, even if it lacks legal authority to require such compliance. Like previous fascist economies, the U.S. government has been unable to resist the overwhelming appeal of subsidization as an instrument for achieving economic dependence and manipulating "private" economic decision-making.

But the innovation of America's fascist economy designed to fuse superficially the individual's self-interest with the current economic/political system is a feature that may be labeled "participatory fascism." This refinement of previous fascist economic systems enables the U.S. government effectively to co-opt even those individuals and interest groups whose will is thwarted under existing economic controls.

The essence of participatory fascism is the ostensible inclusion of all potential dissident parties within the government's economic decision-making process. The usefulness of this technique in quelling opposition is manifest. First, it provides the appearance of fairness. For the vast majority of people who never directly confront or participate in the government's decision-making process, forming judgments on the basis of what the system *says* its rules are rather than the practical reality of those rules, it is sufficient that the government's procedure sounds fair and promotes the illusion that an individual can have an impact on the process if he so desires. Second, participatory fascism absorbs and dissipates the energies of those few individuals who do participate in and attempt to influence the government's economic decision-making. Even if certain of these participants lose regularly, the appearance of fairness and the release provided by self-expression tend to dispel opposition to the government's economic power.

America's economic legislation consistently embodies these characteristics of participatory fascism. In each statute, much care and attention are devoted to the formal trappings of due process, assuring the public that federal officials will listen carefully to diverse viewpoints before imposing the government's economic wishes on the people. Ironically, the bright facade of fair procedure blinds the public to the system's fundamental abrogation of individual economic freedom.

The subtle identification of individual self-interest with preservation of the fascist economy thus provides the key to understanding the average citizen's paradoxical acquiescence to a system that so drastically impairs both his economic liberty and his standard of living. This government-engineered distortion of the individual's self-interest explains how it is that the perpetuation and acceleration of America's fascist economic system need not be interpreted as a sinister product of conscious evil, but rather the consequence of citizens', politicians', and bureaucrats' efforts to maximize their well-being within the political/economic context of fascism.

By capitalizing on the government-fostered illusion linking self-interest to fascist economic policies, the United States government by 1975 has been able to establish fascist controls over virtually every aspect of economic life. Instinctively seeking the jugular vein of America's economy, U.S. lawmakers have mimicked previous fascist economies by imposing most stringent controls over those "vital" industries whose influence pervades all other economic activity. Key economic areas – agriculture, banking (the money supply), transportation, communications, energy, and information – one by one have fallen victim to the central government's drive to manipulate the "private sector" to implement politically formulated economic goals. That the flow of energy and the flow of information, the lifeblood upon which all other economic endeavor depends, have been recent targets of government takeover is perhaps the most ominous documentation to date of America's accelerating fascist economy. Only when people perceive both the extent of existing legal infringement of their economic liberty and the impairment of their living standard entailed in such government controls will these fascist economic policies be challenged.

280

Notes

Unless otherwise noted, emphasis in quoted
matter has been supplied by the author and
does not appear in the source material.

Chapter 1: Fascism's Economic Tenets

1. Ernst Basch (pseudonym, E. B. Ashton) was the first writer to identify the essence of fascism as *capitalistic collectivism,* in a work entitled *The Fascist – His State and His Mind* (New York: William Morrow & Co., 1937), pp. 32 et seq. That book is uniquely valuable because of Basch's superb ability to abstract and conceptualize the underlying principles governing fascism's economic, political, and philosophic structure and consequences.
2. See A. James Gregor, *The Ideology of Fascism* (New York: Free Press, 1969), pp. 184–85, 196.
3. For a discussion of fascism's "organic" concept of the state, see Basch, *op. cit.,* pp. 54 –56.
4. *Ibid.,* pp. 117–18.
5. Gregor, *op. cit.,* pp. 196, 322, 324.
6. See Basch, *op. cit.,* pp. 37, 56.
7. Gregor, *op. cit.,* pp. 304–5.
8. Max Ascoli and Arthur Feiler, *Fascism for Whom?* (New York: W. W. Norton, 1938), p. 95; Basch, *op. cit.,* pp. 97–98.
9. Michael T. Florinsky, *Fascism and National Socialism* (New York: Macmillan Company, 1936), pp. 190–91.
10. *The Program Manifesto of the Fascist Republican Party,* Italy, November 14, 1943, §11.
11. See George N. Halm, *Economic Systems: A Comparative Analysis,* 3d ed. (New York: Holt, Rinehart and Winston, 1968), pp. 182–84.
12. Ascoli and Feiler, *op. cit.,* p. 192; Basch, *op. cit.,* p. 87. See generally, John T. Flynn, *As We Go Marching* (Garden City, N.Y.: Doubleday, Doran and Co., 1944).
13. See Gregor, *op. cit.,* pp. 288–89.
14. See Basch, *op. cit.,* pp. 104–9.
15. Peter F. Drucker, *The End of Economic Man* (New York: John Day Company, 1939), p. 156; Florinsky, *op. cit.,* pp. 110, 215–16; Henri Lichtenberger, *The Third Reich* (New York: Greystone Press, 1937), pp. 251–52, 266.
16. Florinsky, *op. cit.,* pp. 147, 164.
17. Ascoli and Feiler, *op. cit.,* pp. 211–14; Florinsky, *op. cit.,* pp. 215–16; William L. Shirer, *The Rise and Fall of the Third Reich* (New York: Simon & Schuster, 1960), p. 260.
18. Lichtenberger, *op. cit.,* p. 248.
19. Arthur Schweitzer, *Big Business in the Third Reich* (Bloomington: Indiana University Press, 1964), pp. 308–9, 458–59; Florinsky, *loc. cit.;* Shirer, *loc. cit.* Schweitzer states that twelve billion mefo-bills were issued between 1934 and 1938. See also Ascoli and Feiler, *loc. cit.;* and Lichtenberger, *loc. cit.,* who terms Hitler's program of credit expansion "a draft on the future."
20. Ludwig von Mises, *Omnipotent Government* (New Rochelle, N.Y.: Arlington House, 1969), p. 225.
21. Shirer, *op. cit.,* p. 261.
22. Drucker, *op. cit.,* pp. 163, 165; Florinsky, *op. cit.,* p. 113; Schweitzer, *op. cit.,* pp. 460 –61.
23. Schweitzer, *op. cit.,* pp. 460–63.
24. Robert A. Brady, *The Spirit and Structure of German Fascism* (New York: Viking Press, 1937), pp. 340–42; Franz L. Neumann, *Behemoth* (New York: Oxford University Press, 1942), pp. 250–59; Schweitzer, *op. cit.,* pp. 184–96. See also William

Ebenstein, *The Nazi State* (New York: Farrar and Rinehart, 1943), pp. 255–56; and Drucker, *op. cit.*, pp. 146–48. A general freeze of wages and prices at the level prevailing on October 18, 1936, was imposed on November 26, 1936. Ascoli and Feiler, *op. cit.*, pp. 241, 244–45; Neumann, *op. cit.*, p. 251.

25. Florinsky, *op. cit.*, pp. 98–99; Gaetano Salvemini, *Under the Axe of Fascism* (London: Victor Gollancz, 1936), p. 418.
26. Ascoli and Feiler, *op. cit.*, p. 233; Florinsky, *op. cit.*, pp. 109–11.
27. Ebenstein, *op. cit.*, p. 246; Richard Grunberger, *The 12-Year Reich* (New York: Holt, Rinehart and Winston, 1971), p. 168.
28. Florinsky, *op. cit.*, p. 111; Grunberger, *loc. cit.*
29. Ascoli and Feiler, *op. cit.*, pp. 183–87.
30. Drucker, *op. cit.*, p. 148; Gregor, *op. cit.*, p. 288.
31. Von Mises, *op. cit.*, p. 56.
32. *The Program Manifesto of the Fascist Republican Party*, Italy, November 14, 1943, §14.
33. Drucker, *loc. cit.*
34. Shirer, *op. cit.*, p. 261.
35. Grunberger, *op. cit.*, pp. 162–63.
36. Basch, *op. cit.*, p. 114.
37. Armen A. Alchian and William R. Allen, *University Economics*, 2d ed. (Belmont, Calif.: Wadsworth Publishing Company, 1968), pp. 37, 320–21.
38. Ebenstein, *op. cit.*, p. 242.
39. Neumann, *op. cit.*, pp. 218–19; Shirer, *op. cit.*, p. 262.
40. Neumann, *op. cit.*, p. 218.
41. See Ascoli and Feiler, *op. cit.*, p. 260; Ebenstein, *op. cit.*, pp. 245–49.
42. Shirer, *op. cit.*, pp. 144–45.
43. Basch, *op. cit.*, pp. 88–91; Gregor, *op. cit.*, p. 298.
44. Lichtenberger, *op. cit.*, pp. 239; Florinsky, *op. cit.*, p. 108.
45. Ebenstein, *op. cit.*, pp. 276–78.
46. Gregor, *op. cit.*, pp. 177, 300.
47. Ebenstein, *op. cit.*, pp. 277–78.
48. Brady, *op. cit.*, pp. 292–358 and charts IV and V.
49. Salvemini, *op. cit.*, pp. 33–35.
50. Florinsky, *op. cit.*, pp. 120, 141–42.
51. Ascoli and Feiler, *op. cit.*, pp. 226–27; Lichtenberger, *op. cit.*, pp. 256–57.
52. Ascoli and Feiler, *op. cit.*, p. 228; Brady, *op. cit.*, pp. 342–43; Drucker, *op. cit.*, p. 148.
53. Von Mises, *op. cit.*, pp. 69–72.
54. Drucker, *op. cit.*, p. 182.
55. Lichtenberger, *op. cit.*, p. 255; Schweitzer, *op. cit.*, pp. 469–76.
56. Lichtenberger, *op. cit.*, pp. 273–75. See also Stephen H. Roberts, *The House That Hitler Built* (New York: Harper & Brothers, 1938), pp. 145–46.
57. Lichtenberger, *op. cit.*, p. 274.
58. See Von Mises, *op. cit.*, pp. 66, 76–77.
59. Ebenstein, *op. cit.*, pp. 253, 256–57.
60. *Ibid.*, pp. 246–47.
61. Drucker, *op. cit.*, p. 148.

Chapter 2: Unlimited Federal Power to Control the U.S. Economy

1. *Gibbons* v. *Ogden*, 9 Wheat. 1, 6 L. Ed. 23 (1824).
2. *Cooley* v. *Board of Wardens of the Port of Philadelphia*, 12 How. 299, 13 L. Ed. 996 (1851).
3. *The Daniel Ball*, 10 Wall. 557, 19 L. Ed. 999 (1871).
4. *Ibid.*, p. 1002.
5. *Stafford* v. *Wallace*, 258 U.S. 495, 516, 519 (1922).

6. *Houston, East and West Texas Ry.* v. *United States* (*Shreveport* case), 234 U.S. 342, 354–55 (1914).
7. *Ibid.*, p. 353.
8. *United States* v. *E. C. Knight Co.*, 156 U.S. 1 (1895).
9. *Hammer* v. *Dagenhart*, 247 U.S. 251, 272 (1918).
10. *Carter* v. *Carter Coal Co.*, 298 U.S. 238, 305 (1936).
11. See *Swift & Co.* v. *United States*, 196 U.S. 375 (1905); *Standard Oil Co.* v. *United States*, 221 U.S. 1 (1911); *United States* v. *American Tobacco Co.*, 221 U.S. 106 (1911).
12. *Coronado Coal Co.* v. *United Mine Workers*, 268 U.S. 295, 310 (1925).
13. *Carter* v. *Carter Coal Co.*, 298 U.S. 238, 303–4, 308 (1936).
14. *Gibbons* v. *Ogden*, 9 Wheat. 1, 6 L. Ed. 23, 70 (1824).
15. *Schechter Poultry Corp.* v. *United States*, 295 U.S. 495 (1935).
16. *Carter* v. *Carter Coal Co.*, 298 U.S. 238, 307–8 (1936).
17. *Lottery* case (*Champion* v. *Ames*), 188 U.S. 321, 355–56 (1903).
18. *Hammer* v. *Dagenhart*, 247 U.S. 251, 269–70 (1918).
19. *Child Labor Tax* case (*Bailey* v. *Drexel Furniture Co.*), 259 U.S. 20, 37–38 (1922).
20. *McCray* v. *United States*, 195 U.S. 27 (1904).
21. *Carter* v. *Carter Coal Co.*, 298 U.S. 238, 289 (1936).
22. *United States* v. *Butler*, 297 U.S. 1, 75 (1936).
23. *NLRB* v. *Jones & Laughlin Steel Corp.*, 301 U.S. 1, 37 (1936).
24. *Ibid.*, p. 40.
25. *Ibid.*, p. 41.
26. *United States* v. *Darby*, 312 U.S. 100, 116–17 (1941).
27. *NLRB* v. *Jones & Laughlin Steel Corp.*, 301 U.S. 1, 37 (1937).
28. *Ibid.*, pp. 36–37.
29. *Ibid.*, p. 37.
30. *Ibid.*, p. 41.
31. *Ibid.*
32. *United States* v. *Darby*, 312 U.S. 100, 114 (1941).
33. *Ibid.*, p. 124.
34. *Wickard* v. *Filburn*, 317 U.S. 111, 128 (1942).
35. *Ibid.*, p. 125.
36. *Heart of Atlanta Motel* v. *United States*, 379 U.S. 241, 255 (1964).
37. *Katzenbach* v. *McClung*, 379 U.S. 294, 304–5 (1964).
38. *Maryland* v. *Wirtz*, 392 U.S. 183, 194, 197 (1968).
39. *Ibid.*, 183, 204–5 (dissenting opinion, Justice Douglas).
40. *United States* v. *Darby*, 312 U.S. 100, 113, 114 (1941).
41. *Steward Machine Co.* v. *Davis*, 301 U.S. 548, 589 (1937).
42. *Ibid.*, p. 590.
43. *U.S. Constitution*, Art. VI, cl. 2.
44. *Ibid.*, Art. I, §8, cl. 17.
45. *Ibid.*, Art. I, §10, cl. 1.
46. See, e.g., *New York Central R.R.* v. *Winfield*, 244 U.S. 147 (1917).
47. See *Huron Portland Cement Co.* v. *Detroit*, 362 U.S. 440 (1960); *Pennsylvania* v. *Nelson*, 350 U.S. 497 (1956); *San Diego Building Trades Council* v. *Garmon*, 359 U.S. 236 (1959).
48. *San Diego Building Trades Council* v. *Garmon*, 359 U.S. 236 (1959).
49. See, e.g., *Huron Portland Cement Co.* v. *Detroit*, 362 U.S. 440 (1960).

Chapter 3: Centralized Control over Money and Banking
1. *Currency and Foreign Transactions Reporting Act*, 31 U.S.C.* §1051 (1970). [Hereafter cited as *Currency and Foreign Transactions Reporting Act.*]

* U.S.C. refers to the *United States Code*, which contains a compilation of all federal statutes currently in effect.

2. *Ibid.*
3. *Ibid.*, §1081.
4. *Ibid.*, §1052(e).
5. *Ibid.*, §1101(a).
6. *Ibid.*, §1101(b).
7. *Ibid.*, §1102(a).
8. *Ibid.*, §1103.
9. *Ibid.*, §1121(a).
10. *Ibid.*, §§1141, 1142 (Supp. III, 1973).
11. 12 U.S.C. §95a(1) (1970).
12. *Currency and Foreign Transactions Reporting Act*, §1055.
13. *Ibid.*, §1104.
14. *Ibid.*, §1121(a).
15. *Ibid.*, §1122.
16. Exec. Order No. 6560, January 15, 1934, *as amended by* Exec. Order No. 8389, 5 Fed. Reg. 1400 (April 10, 1940); Exec. Order No. 8405, 5 Fed. Reg. 1677 (May 10, 1940); Exec. Order No. 8493, 5 Fed. Reg. 2667 (July 25, 1940).
17. Exec. Order No. 11387, 33 Fed. Reg. 47 (January 1, 1968).
18. *Federal Reserve Bulletin*, Vol. 61, No. 3 (Washington, D.C.: Board of Governors of the Federal Reserve System, March 1975), p. A18.
19. 12 U.S.C. §95 (1970).
20. 12 U.S.C. §95a(1)(A) (1970).
21. *Federal Reserve Act*, 12 U.S.C. §221 *et seq.* (1970). [Hereafter cited as *Federal Reserve Act.*]
22. For a discussion of the nature and consequences of inflation, see Armen A. Alchian and William R. Allen, *University Economics*, 2d ed. (Belmont, Calif.: Wadsworth Publishing Company, 1968), pp. 649–56.
23. *Ibid.*, pp. 662–63.
24. *Federal Reserve Act*, §222.
25. *Ibid.*, §§241, 248, 461; Lester V. Chandler, *The Economics of Money and Banking*, 4th ed. (New York: Harper & Row, 1964), pp. 171–72.
26. *Federal Reserve Bulletin*, Vol. 61, No. 3 (Washington, D.C.: Board of Governors of the Federal Reserve System, March 1975), p. A18.
27. Chandler, *op. cit.*, pp. 167–69.
28. Alchian and Allen, *op. cit.*, pp. 585–86; Chandler, *op. cit.*, pp. 14–16.
29. Alchian and Allen, *op. cit.*, pp. 597–98.
30. Chandler, *op. cit.*, p. 23.
31. Alchian and Allen, *op. cit.*, p. 603.
32. *Federal Reserve Act*, § 263.
33. *Ibid.*, §461(c).
34. *Ibid.*, §461(b).
35. Chandler, *op. cit.*, pp. 95, 97.
36. Paul A. Samuelson, *Economics*, 6th ed. (New York: McGraw-Hill Book Company, 1964), pp. 296–305; Alchian and Allen, *op. cit.*, pp. 596–611.
37. Alchian and Allen, *op. cit.*, pp. 622–25; Chandler, *op. cit.*, p. 225.
38. Chandler, *op. cit.*, p. 227.
39. *Federal Reserve Act*, §§263(b), 355(2); Chandler, *op. cit.*, p. 173 (for the mechanics of the Federal Reserve's open market operations, see the same work, pp. 226–28).
40. Alchian and Allen, *op. cit.*, p. 625; Chandler, *op. cit.*, pp. 205–6, 227.
41. Chandler, *op. cit.*, pp. 94–95, 229.
42. *Ibid.*, pp. 206–7.
43. *Federal Reserve Act*, §355(1) (Supp. III, 1973). Another statute permits the President to direct the Secretary of the Treasury to conclude agreements with the Federal Reserve system for its purchase of an *additional* $3,000,000,000 worth of government securities directly from the Treasury Department whenever the President finds, to select one example among several equally elastic statutory pretexts,

that "an economic emergency requires an expansion of credit" — 31 U.S.C. §821 (1970).

44. Alchian and Allen, *op. cit.*, pp. 629–34; Chandler, *op. cit.*, pp. 524–68.
45. *Federal Reserve Act*, §357; Chandler, *op. cit.*, pp. 232–33.
46. Alchian and Allen, *op. cit.*, pp. 623–24.

Chapter 4: The American Cartels: Compulsory Government Licensing and Rate Making

1. Armen A. Alchian and William R. Allen, *University Economics*, 2d ed. (Belmont, Calif.: Wadsworth Publishing Company, 1968), pp. 320–23.
2. Paul A. Samuelson, *Economics*, 6th ed. (New York: McGraw-Hill Book Company, 1964), pp. 446–56, 477–83; Roger Sherman, *The Economics of Industry* (Boston: Little, Brown and Company, 1974), pp. 35–39, 45–46.
3. Alchian and Allen, *op.cit.*, pp. 325–26.
4. Sherman, *op. cit.*, pp. 53–55.
5. Alchian and Allen, *op.cit.*, pp. 262, 346–49.
6. *Part I of the Interstate Commerce Act*, 49 U.S.C. §1(18) (1970). [Hereafter cited as *Interstate Commerce Act — Railroads.*]
7. *Ibid.*
8. *Ibid.*, §1(20).
9. *Ibid.*, §1(21).
10. *Ibid.*, §§5(11), 5b(9).
11. *Ibid.*, §§5(1), 5(2).
12. *Ibid.*, §5(1).
13. *Ibid.*, §5(2)(b).
14. *Ibid.*
15. *Ibid.*, §5b(2).
16. *Ibid.*, §5b(4).
17. *Ibid.*, §15(3).
18. *Ibid.*, §5b(6).
19. Clair Wilcox, *Public Policies Toward Business*, 4th ed. (Homewood, Ill.: Richard D. Irwin, Inc., 1971), pp. 383–84.
20. *Interstate Commerce Act — Railroads*, §§20a, 20b.
21. *Ibid.*, §20a(2).
22. *Ibid.*, §6(1).
23. *Ibid.*, §§15(3), 15(6).
24. *Ibid.*, §15(7).
25. *Ibid.*, §§1(10), 1(14).
26. *Ibid.*, §1(14)(a).
27. *Ibid.*
28. *Ibid.*
29. *Ibid.*, §1(16).
30. *Ibid.*, §3(5).
31. *Ibid.*, §1(15).
32. *Ibid.*
33. *Ibid.*, §15(4).
34. *Ibid.*, §15(14).
35. *Ibid.*, §1(4).
36. *Ibid.*, §1(5).
37. *Ibid.*, §1(6).
38. *Ibid.*, §1(11).
39. *Ibid.*, §3(1).

40. *Part II of the Interstate Commerce Act,* 49 U.S.C. §§302(a), 302(b) (1970). [Hereafter cited as *Interstate Commerce Act — Motor Carriers.*]
41. *Ibid.,* §316(f).
42. *Ibid.,* §304(a)(4a)
43. *Ibid.,* §302(c).
44. *Ibid.,* §303(b).
45. *Ibid.,* §303(a)(14).
46. *Ibid.,* §303(a)(15).
47. *Ibid.,* §303(a)(17).
48. *Ibid.,* §§304(a)(1), 304(a)(2).
49. *Ibid.,* §304(a)(3).
50. *Ibid.,* §§306(a)(1), 303(c).
51. *Ibid.,* §307(a).
52. *Ibid.,* §308(a).
53. *Ibid.*
54. *Ibid.,* §§303(c), 309(a).
55. *Ibid.,* §309(b).
56. *Ibid.*
57. *Ibid.,* §§311(a), 303(a)(18).
58. *Ibid.,* §311(b).
59. *Ibid.,* §§316(a), 316(b), 316(d).
60. *Ibid.,* §§316(a), 316(b).
61. *Ibid.,* §316(e).
62. *Ibid.,* §316(g).
63. *Ibid.,* §316(i).
64. *Ibid.,* §318(a).
65. *Ibid.*
66. *Ibid.,* §318(b).
67. *Ibid.,* §318(a).
68. *Ibid.,* §304(b).
69. See discussion of ICC regulation of railroads, pp. 75-76 above.
70. *Interstate Commerce Act — Motor Carriers,* §310.
71. *Ibid.*
72. *Part III of the Interstate Commerce Act,* 49 U.S.C. §§903(b), 903(e)(2) (1970). [Hereafter cited as *Interstate Commerce Act—Water Carriers.*]
73. *Ibid.,* §904(c).
74. *Ibid.,* §§902(d), 902(e).
75. *Ibid.,* §902(e).
76. *Ibid.,* §909(a).
77. *Ibid.,* §909(c).
78. *Ibid.,* §909(d).
79. *Ibid.,* §909(g).
80. *Ibid.*
81. *Ibid.,* §905(a).
82. *Ibid.,* §§906(a), 906(b), 906(d).
83. *Ibid.,* §907(b).
84. *Ibid.,* §906(e).
85. *Ibid.,* §907(h).
86. *Ibid.,* §906(e).
87. *Part IV of the Interstate Commerce Act,* 49 U.S.C. §1002(a)(5) (1970). [Hereafter cited as *Interstate Commerce Act — Freight Forwarders.*]
88. *Ibid.*
89. *Ibid.,* §1006(f).
90. *Ibid.,* §1010(a)(1).
91. *Ibid.,* §1010(c).
92. *Ibid.,* §1010(e).
93. *Ibid.*

94. *Ibid.*, §1010(i).
95. *Ibid.*, §1004(a).
96. *Ibid.*
97. *Ibid.*, §1006(b).
98. *Ibid.*, §1018.
99. See discussion in section on railroad regulation, pp. 75-76, above.
100. *Interstate Commerce Act — Freight Forwarders*, §1009.
101. *Ibid.*, §1009(a).
102. *Ibid.*, §1009(b).
103. *Federal Communications Act of 1934*, 47 U.S.C. §301 *et seq.*, §307 (1970). [Hereafter cited as *Federal Communications Act.*]
104. *Ibid.*, §307(a).
105. *Ibid.*, §307(d).
106. *Ibid.*, §307(b).
107. *Ibid.*, §309(a).
108. *Ibid.*, §308(b).
109. *Ibid.*, §309(e).
110. *Ibid.*, §319.
111. *Ibid.*, §319(a).
112. *Ibid.*, §319(c).
113. *Ibid.*, §319(d).
114. *Ibid.*, §316(a).
115. *Ibid.*, §310(b).
116. *Ibid.*, §311(c)(3).
117. *Ibid.*, §317(d).
118. *Ibid.*, §326.
119. *Administrative Procedure Act*, 5 U.S.C. §706 (1970).
120. See Harry Kalven, "Broadcasting, Public Policy and the First Amendment," *Journal of Law and Economics* 10 (1967): 15 *et seq.*
121. See *Robinson* v. *FCC*, 334 F.2d 534 (1964), *certiorari denied*, 85 S.Ct. 84 (October 12, 1964); and *In Re Pacifica Foundation*, 136 F.C.C. 147 (1964).
122. 47 C.F.R.* §§73.699, 73.670 (1972).
123. *Ibid.*, §73.670 (1972).
124. *Ibid.*, §73.674 (1972).
125. *Ibid.*, §1.514(a) (1972).
126. *Ibid.*, §§1.533–1.550 (1972).
127. See FCC Form 301, §§IV–A and B, Parts I, II, and III; FCC Form 303, §§IV–A and B, Parts I, II, and III; 33 Fed. Reg. 12113 (1968).
128. *NBC* v. *United States*, 319 U.S. 190, 215–16 (1943).
129. *Ibid.*, pp. 216–17.
130. *Ibid.*, p. 226.
131. 47 C.F.R. §73.123 (1972).
132. *Red Lion Broadcasting Co.* v. *FCC*, 395 U.S. 367 (1969).
133. October 15, 1971, action by the Commission by letter, reported in *FCC News*, Report No. 10206, Broadcast Action, October 18, 1971-B.
134. *Red Lion Broadcasting Co.* v. *FCC*, 395 U.S. 367, 389–90 (1969).
135. *Fourth Report on Subscription Television*, 15 F.C.C. 2d 466, 595–97 (1968).
136. See DeVany, Eckert, Meyers, O'Hara, and Scott, "A Property System for Market Allocation of the Electromagnetic Spectrum: A Legal–Economic–Engineering Study," *Stanford Law Review* 21 (1969): 1499.
137. *Federal Power Act*, 16 U.S.C. §797(e) (1970). [Hereafter cited as *Federal Power Act.*]
138. *Ibid.*, §817.
139. *Ibid.*, §801.

* C.F.R. refers to the *Code of Federal Regulations*, which contains a compilation of all current rules and regulations promulgated by federal regulatory and administrative agencies.

140. *Ibid.*, §797.
141. *Ibid.*, §§799, 804.
142. *Ibid.*, §797(g).
143. *Ibid.*, §800(a).
144. *Ibid.*
145. *Ibid.*, §803(a).
146. *Ibid.*, §812.
147. *Ibid.*
148. *Ibid.*, §813.
149. *Ibid.*, §803(d).
150. *Ibid.*
151. *Ibid.*, §803(e).
152. Ibid., §803(f).
153. *Ibid.*, §807(a).
154. *Ibid.*
155. *Ibid.*, §808(b).
156. *Ibid.*
157. *Ibid.*, §814.
158. *Ibid.*, §824(a).
159. *Ibid.*, §824b.
160. *Ibid.*, §824b(a).
161. *Ibid.*, §824b(b).
162. *Ibid.*, §824f.
163. *Ibid.*, §824c(a).
164. *Ibid.*
165. *Ibid.*, §824a(b).
166. *Ibid.*
167. *Ibid.*, §824a(c).
168. *Ibid.*
169. *Ibid.*, §824d(a).
170. *Ibid.*, §824e(a).
171. *Ibid.*, §824d(b).
172. *Ibid.*, §824d(c).
173. *Ibid.*, §824d(e).
174. *Natural Gas Act*, 15 U.S.C. §717(a) (1970). [Hereafter cited as *Natural Gas Act*].
175. *Ibid.*, §717f(c).
176. *Ibid.*
177. *Ibid.*
178. *Ibid.*, §717f(b).
179. *Ibid.*
180. *Ibid.*, §717f(e).
181. *Ibid.*
182. *Ibid.*, §717d(a).
183. *Ibid.*, §717c(a).
184. *Ibid.*, §717c(c).
185. *Ibid.*, §717c(b).
186. *Ibid.*, §717c(e).
187. *Ibid.*, §717f(a).
188. *Ibid.*
189. *Ibid.*, §717b.
190. *Ibid.*, §717f(h).
191. *Federal Aviation Act of 1958*, 49 U.S.C §1371(a) (1970). [Hereafter cited as *Federal Aviation Act*.]
192. *Ibid.*, §1371(e).
193. *Ibid.*, §1371(d)(1).
194. *Ibid.*, §1371(e).
195. *Ibid.*, §1371(g).

196. *Ibid.*, §1371(h).
197. *Ibid.*, §1371(j).
198. *Ibid.*, §1348(a).
199. *Ibid.*, §§1348(a), 1348(e).
200. *Ibid.*, §§1422, 1301(7), 1430(a)(2).
201. *Ibid.*, §1422(b).
202. *Ibid.*, §§1423(a), 1301(11).
203. *Ibid.*, §1423(a)(2).
204. *Ibid.*, §§1423(a), 1423(b), 1423(c).
205. *Ibid.*, §1423(b).
206. *Ibid.*, §§1423(c), 1430(a)(1).
207. *Ibid.*, §§1424, 1430(a)(4).
208. *Ibid.*, §1424.
209. *Ibid.*, §1424(b).
210. *Ibid.*, §§1432, 1430(a)(8).
211. *Ibid.*, §1427.
212. *Ibid.*, §1426.
213. *Ibid.*, §1301(8).
214. *Ibid.*, §1349(a).
215. *Ibid.*, §1374(a).
216. *Ibid.*, §1373(a).
217. *Ibid.*, §1373(b).
218. *Ibid.*, §§1373(a), 1482(d), 1482(g).
219. *Ibid.*, §1482(d).
220. *Ibid.*, §§1482(h), 1482(i).
221. *Ibid.*, §1375(b).
222. *Ibid.*, §1376(a).
223. *Ibid.*, §1377(a).
224. *Ibid.*
225. *Ibid.*, §1377(d).
226. *Ibid.*, §§1378(a), 1378(b).
227. *Ibid.*, §1302.
228. *Ibid.*, §1302(d).

Chapter 5: Government Control over Product Quality

1. Armen A. Alchian and William R. Allen, *University Economics,* 2d ed. (Belmont, Calif.: Wadsworth Publishing Company, 1968), pp. 334–36.
2. Roger Sherman, *The Economics of Industry* (Boston: Little, Brown and Company, 1974), pp. 121–24.
3. *Consumer Product Safety Act,* 15 U.S.C. §2051 *et seq.* (Supp. II, 1972). [Hereafter cited as *Consumer Product Safety Act.*]
4. *Ibid.*, §2052(a).
5. The products excluded from the Consumer Product Safety Commission's authority include tobacco products, motor vehicles, boats, aircraft, insecticides, food, drugs, and cosmetics [*Consumer Product Safety Act,* §2052(a)(1)]. Federal regulation of aircraft is discussed in chapter four; government controls over insecticides, food, drugs, and cosmetics are described in the balance of chapter five. For the laws governing tobacco products, motor vehicles, and boats, excluded from the present discussion because of their narrow specificity, see: *Public Health Cigarette Smoking Act of 1969,* Pub. L. No. 91–222, 84 Stat. 87 (April 1, 1970); *National Traffic and Motor Vehicle Safety Act of 1966,* 15 U.S.C. §§1381–1431 (1970); *Federal Boat Safety Act of 1971,* 46 U.S.C. §§1451–89 (Supp. III, 1973).
6. *Consumer Product Safety Act,* §2056(a).

7. *Ibid.*, §§2056(a), 2058(c)(2)(A).
8. *Ibid.*, §2058(c)(2)(B).
9. *Ibid.*, §2062(a).
10. *Ibid.*, §2062(b).
11. *Ibid.*, §2057.
12. *Ibid.*, §§2061(a), 2061(b), 2071.
13. *Ibid.*, §2064.
14. *Ibid.*, §2065(b).
15. *Ibid.*, §§2069, 2070.
16. *Ibid.*, §2075(a).
17. *Ibid.*, §2075(c).
18. *Flammable Fabrics Act*, 15 U.S.C. §§1191–1204 (1970).
19. *Federal Hazardous Substances Act*, 15 U.S.C. §§1262–74 (1970).
20. *Consumer Product Safety Act*, §2079.
21. *Federal Food, Drug and Cosmetic Act*, 21 U.S.C. §§301–92 (1970). [Hereafter cited as *Federal Food, Drug and Cosmetic Act*.]
22. *Ibid.*, §347(a).
23. *Ibid.*, §347(b).
24. *Ibid.*, §347(c).
25. 21 U.S.C. §61(c) (1970).
26. *Ibid.*
27. *Ibid.*, §62.
28. *Federal Food, Drug and Cosmetic Act*, §341.
29. *Ibid.*
30. *Ibid.*, §343(h)(1).
31. *Ibid.*, §342(a).
32. *Ibid.*
33. *Ibid.*, §§346, 342(a)(2).
34. *Ibid.*, §§346a(c), 348(i), 360(j).
35. *Ibid.*, §§346a(b), 348(c), 360b(d).
36. *Ibid.*, §§346a(a), 348(a), 360b(a), 360b(d).
37. E.g., *ibid.*, §§346, 346a(b), 346a(c), 348(i).
38. *Ibid.*, §342(a)(3).
39. Alchian and Allen, *op. cit.*, p. 334.
40. *Federal Food, Drug and Cosmetic Act*, §§360(b), 360(h), 374.
41. *Ibid.*, §360(g)(4).
42. *Ibid.*, §351(a).
43. *Ibid.*
44. *Ibid.*, §355(a).
45. *Ibid.*, §321(p).
46. *Ibid.*, §355(i).
47. *Ibid.*
48. *Ibid.*, §§355(d)(1), 355(d)(2).
49. *Ibid.*, §355(d)(3).
50. *Ibid.*, §§355(d)(4), 355(d)(5).
51. *Ibid.*, §§321(w), 360b.
52. *Ibid.*, §§356, 357.
53. *Ibid.*, §§352(k), 352(l).
54. *Ibid.*, §357(c).
55. *Ibid.*, §361.
56. *Ibid.*, §375(b).
57. *Federal Insecticide, Fungicide, and Rodenticide Act*, chap. 125, 61 Stat. 163 (June 25, 1947).
58. *Federal Environmental Pesticide Control Act of 1972*, 7 U.S.C. §136a (Supp. III, 1973). [Hereafter cited as *Federal Environmental Pesticide Control Act*.]
59. *Ibid.*, §136a(5).
60. *Ibid.*, §136a(d)(1)(B).
61. *Ibid.*, §136a(d)(1)(C).

62. *Ibid.*, §136c.
63. *Ibid.*, §136k(b)(3).
64. *Ibid.*, §136e.
65. *Ibid.*, §135f(a).
66. *Ibid.*, §136w(b).
67. *Ibid.*, §136g(c)(3).
68. *Ibid.*, §136s(b).
69. *Ibid.*, §136r(b).
70. *United States Cotton Standards Act,* 7 U.S.C. §§52, 56 (1970) [hereafter cited as *Cotton Standards Act*]; *United States Grain Standards Act,* 7 U.S.C. §§76, 78 (1970) [hereafter cited as *Grain Standards Act*].
71. *Cotton Standards Act,* §58; *Grain Standards Act,* §79.
72. *Cotton Standards Act,* §§51b, 53; *Grain Standards Act,* §84.
73. *Cotton Standards Act,* §60; *Grain Standards Act,* §87b.
74. *Grain Standards Act,* §87.
75. *Ibid.*
76. *Ibid.*, §87c(b).
77. *United States Warehouse Act,* 7 U.S.C. §257 (1970).
78. *Ibid.*, §§243, 244.
79. *Ibid.*, §243.
80. *Ibid.*, §246.
81. *Ibid.*, §264.
82. *Ibid.*, §254.
83. *Ibid.*
84. *Ibid.*, §252.
85. *Ibid.*, §§256, 265.
86. *Agricultural Marketing Act of 1946,* 7 U.S.C. §1622(c) (1970).
87. *Ibid.*, §1626.
88. *Ibid.*, §1622(h).
89. *Ibid.*
90. *Poultry Products Inspection Act,* 21 U.S.C. §451 (1970) [hereafter cited as *Poultry Products Inspection Act*]; *Federal Meat Inspection Act,* 21 U.S.C. §602 (1970) [hereafter cited as *Meat Inspection Act*]; *Egg Products Inspection Act,* 21 U.S.C. §1031 (1970) [hereafter cited as *Egg Products Inspection Act*].
91. *Poultry Products Inspection Act,* §451; *Meat Inspection Act,* §602; *Egg Products Inspection Act,* §1031.
92. *Meat Inspection Act,* §602; *Egg Products Inspection Act,* §1031.
93. *Poultry Products Inspection Act,* §451; *Meat Inspection Act,* §602; *Egg Products Inspection Act,* §1031.
94. *Egg Products Inspection Act,* §§1034(a), 1034(d).
95. *Meat Inspection Act,* §§603, 604, 606.
96. *Poultry Products Inspection Act,* §455.
97. *Poultry Products Inspection Act,* §453(g)(3); *Meat Inspection Act,* §601(m)(3); *Egg Products Inspection Act,* §1033(a)(3).
98. *Poultry Products Inspection Act,* §453(g)(4); *Meat Inspection Act,* §601(m)(4); *Egg Products Inspection Act,* §1033(a)(4).
99. *Poultry Products Inspection Act,* §453(g)(1); *Meat Inspection Act,* §601(m)(1); *Egg Products Inspection Act,* §1033(a)(1).
100. *Poultry Products Inspection Act,* §460(c); *Meat Inspection Act,* §643.
101. *Poultry Products Inspection Act,* §460(b); *Meat Inspection Act,* §642; *Egg Products Inspection Act,* §1040.
102. *Poultry Products Inspection Act,* §465; *Meat Inspection Act,* §605; *Egg Products Inspection Act,* §1045.
103. *Poultry Products Inspection Act,* §456(a); *Meat Inspection Act,* §608; *Egg Products Inspection Act,* §1035(a). See also 21 U.S.C. §463(a) (1970).
104. *Poultry Products Inspection Act,* §456(a); *Egg Products Inspection Act,* §1035(a).
105. *Poultry Products Inspection Act,* §§464(c)(2), 464(c)(3).
106. *Egg Products Inspection Act,* §1044(a)(7).

107. *Poultry Products Inspection Act,* §462; *Meat Inspection Act,* §676(b); *Egg Products Inspection Act,* §1042.
108. *Egg Products Inspection Act,* §§1033(g)(3), 1033(g)(8), 1037(a)(1), 1037(a)(2).
109. *Meat Inspection Act,* §619.
110. *Fair Packaging and Labeling Act,* 15 U.S.C. §§1451–61 (1970).
111. *Ibid.,* §1453. Note that the *Consumer Product Safety Act* augments the objective labeling requirements of the *Fair Packaging and Labeling Act* by empowering the Consumer Product Safety Commission to require consumer products to bear the date of their manufacture as well as certification that the products conform to specifically identified consumer product-safety standards [15 U.S.C. §2063(c) (Supp. II, 1972)].
112. *Fair Packaging and Labeling Act,* 15 U.S.C. §1454(b) (1970).
113. *Ibid.,* §1454(c).
114. *Ibid.,* §1454(d).
115. *Ibid.*
116. *Ibid.,* §1454(e).
117. *Federal Food, Drug and Cosmetic Act,* §§343(a), 352(a), 362(a).
118. *Ibid.,* §§343(d), 352(i), 362(d).
119. *Ibid.,* §§343(f), 352(c), 362(c).
120. *Ibid.,* §§343(i), 343(k), 352(e).
121. *Federal Environmental Pesticide Control Act,* §§136(q), 136w(c)(3).
122. *Poultry Products Inspection Act,* §§453(h), 457.
123. *Meat Inspection Act,* §§601(n), 607.
124. *Egg Products Inspection Act,* §§1033(1), 1036.

Chapter 6: Stretching the President's Economic Power

1. Act of July 26, 1935, chap. 417, 49 Stat. 500, 44 U.S.C. §§1501–11 (1970).
2. See House Committee on Government Operations, 85th Cong., 1st sess., *Executive Orders and Proclamations: A Study of a Use of Presidential Powers* (Committee Print 1957), pp. 35–36, for a discussion of the historical uses of executive orders. [Hereafter cited as *Study—Executive Orders.*]
3. See *United States* v. *Midwest Oil Co.,* 236 U.S. 459 (1915).
4. See *Ex Parte Merryman,* 17 Fed. Cas. 144 (No. 9487) (C.C.D. Md., 1861).
5. *Study—Executive Orders,* p. 36.
6. Exec. Order No. 10340, 17 Fed. Reg. 3139 (1952).
7. *Youngstown Sheet & Tube Co.* v. *Sawyer,* 343 U.S. 579 (1952).
8. See Exec. Order No. 10210, 15 Fed. Reg. 1049 (1951), and Exec. Order No. 8802, 6 Fed. Reg. 3109 (1941).
9. See, e.g., Exec. Order No. 10925, 26 Fed. Reg. 1977 (1961), and Exec. Order No. 11114, 28 Fed. Reg. 6485 (1963).
10. Exec. Order No. 10479, 18 Fed. Reg. 4899 (1953).
11. Exec. Order No. 11063, 27 Fed. Reg. 11527 (1962), entitled *Equal Opportunity in Housing.*
12. See concurring opinion of Mr. Justice Jackson, *Youngstown Sheet & Tube Co.* v. *Sawyer,* 343 U.S. 579, 635–38 (1952).
13. *United States* v. *Curtiss-Wright Export Corp.,* 299 U.S. 304 (1936).
14. U.S. *Constitution,* Art. II, §1, cl. 1.
15. *Myers* v. *United States,* 272 U.S. 52 (1926).
16. *In Re Neagle,* 135 U.S. 1 (1890).
17. See William D. Neighbors, "Presidential Legislation by Executive Order," *University of Colorado Law Review* 37 (1964): 105, 108–9.
18. *United States* v. *Chemical Foundation, Inc.,* 272 U.S. 1 (1926).

19. Exec. Order No. 9066, 3 C.F.R. 1092 (Cum. Supp., 1943), upheld in *Korematsu v. United States*, 323 U.S. 214 (1944), and *Hirabayashi v. United States*, 320 U.S. 81 (1943). See also *Ex Parte Endo*, 323 U.S. 283 (1944).

20. *United States v. Curtiss-Wright Export Corp.*, 299 U.S. 304 (1936).

21. *United States v. Midwest Oil Co.*, 236 U.S. 459, 474 (1915).

22. *Contractors Assn. of Eastern Pa. v. Secretary of Labor*, 442 F.2d 159 (3d Cir., 1971).

23. Exec. Order No. 11246, 30 Fed. Reg. 12319 (September 24, 1965), *as amended by* Exec. Order No. 11375, 32 Fed. Reg. 14303 (October 13, 1967).

24. *Contractors Assn. of Eastern Pa. v. Secretary of Labor*, 442 F. 2d 159, 171 (3d Cir., 1971).

25. *Economic Stabilization Act of 1970*, Pub. L. 91–379, §§201–20, 84 Stat. 799, *as amended by* Pub. L. 91–558, 84 Stat. 1468 (December 17, 1970); Pub. L. 92–8, 85 Stat. 13 (March 31, 1971); Pub. L. 92–15, 85 Stat. 38 (May 18, 1971); and Pub. L. 92–210, 85 Stat. 743 (December 22, 1971). [Hereafter cited as *Economic Stabilization Act.*]

26. *Council on Wage and Price Stability Act of 1974*, Pub. L. 93–387 (August 1974).

27. For scholarly analysis of the economic consequences of wage-price controls, see Armen A. Alchian and William R. Allen, *University Economics*, 2d ed. (Belmont, Calif.: Wadsworth Publishing Company, 1968), pp. 91–99; and Paul A. Samuelson, *Economics*, 6th ed. (New York: McGraw-Hill Book Company, 1964), pp. 385–88.

28. *Economic Stabilization Act*, §203.

29. *Ibid.*, §204.

30. *Ibid.*, §203(i).

31. *Ibid.*, §202.

32. *Ibid.*, §203(f)(1).

33. *Ibid.*, §§203(a)(1), 203(b), 203(e).

34. *Ibid.*, §203(a).

35. *Ibid.*, §203(b).

36. *Ibid.*

37. *Ibid.*, §203(a).

38. *Ibid.*, §203(c).

39. *Ibid.*, §218.

40. *Ibid.*, §206.

41. *Ibid.*, §214.

42. *Ibid.*, §217.

43. *Ibid.*

44. *Ibid.*, §207(a).

45. *Ibid.*, §207(b).

46. *Ibid.*

47. *Administrative Procedure Act*, 5 U.S.C. §§554–57 (1970).

48. *Ibid.*, §553(b)(3)(B).

49. *Economic Stabilization Act*, §207(c).

50. *Ibid.*, §211(c).

51. *Ibid.*, §211(d)(1).

52. *Ibid.*, §211(d)(2).

53. Exec. Order No. 11640, 37 Fed. Reg. 1213 (January 26, 1972), *as amended by* Exec. Order No. 11660, 37 Fed. Reg. 6175 (March 23, 1972); and Exec. Order No. 11674, 37 Fed. Reg. 12913 (June 29, 1972). [Hereafter cited as *Executive Order—Wage and Price Controls.*]

54. *Ibid.*, §1.

55. *Ibid.*, §§7(b), 8(b).

56. *Ibid.*, §7(c).

57. *Ibid.*, §8(c).

58. *Ibid.*, §1(b).

59. *Ibid.*, §5.

60. *Ibid.*, §3(d).

61. *Ibid.*, §9(b).
62. *Ibid.*, §3(b).
63. *Ibid.*, §§4(a)(ii), 5.
64. *Ibid.*, §1(c).

Chapter 7: Government Dominion over Labor

1. For detailed descriptions of the legal mechanisms and bureaucratic structures through which fascist rulers in Italy and Germany controlled labor and management, see Robert A. Brady, *The Spirit and Structure of German Fascism* (New York, Viking Press, 1937), pp. 120–60; and William G. Welk, *Fascist Economic Policy* (Cambridge, Mass.: Harvard University Press, 1938), pp. 54–58, 74–105 (Italy).
2. Certain less comprehensive statutory provisions that empower the government to regulate subsidiary aspects of labor/management relations are omitted in the interest of clarity. Significant among these are:

   a. the *Employee Retirement Income Security Act of 1974* [Pub. L. No. 93–406, 88 Stat. 829 (September 2, 1974)], which gives the government broad powers to regulate private pension plans;

   b. legislation that establishes the United States Employment Service, authorizing the Secretary of Labor to develop a national system of governmentally supervised employment offices, nominally operated by individual states but actually funded and controlled by the federal government through national standards that states must emulate to obtain federal subsidies [29 U.S.C. §§49–49k (1970)]; and

   c. legislation that empowers the government to promulgate and promote standards controlling apprentice labor [29 U.S.C. §50 (1970)].
3. *Employment Act of 1946*, 15 U.S.C. §§1021–25 (1970).
4. *Ibid.*, §1021.
5. *Ibid.*, see also 15 U.S.C. §1023(e)(1) (1970).
6. 15 U.S.C. §1021 (1970).
7. *Ibid.*; §1023(c)(4).
8. *Ibid.*, §1026 (Supp. III, 1973).
9. Pub. L. 93–311, 88 Stat. 236 (June 8, 1974).
10. 15 U.S.C. §1026(a)(1) (Supp. III, 1973).
11. *Ibid.*
12. *Ibid.*, §1026(a)(3).
13. Pub. L. 93–311, §(a), 88 Stat. 236 (June 8, 1974).
14. *Ibid.*, §(f)(D).
15. 15 U.S.C. §1026(a)(2) (Supp. III, 1973).
16. *Ibid.*, §1026(a)(4).
17. *Ibid.*, §1026(c)(1)(B).
18. *Ibid.*, §1026(b)(4).
19. *Ibid.*, §1026(b)(3).
20. *Ibid.*, §1026(b)(1).
21. *Ibid.*
22. *Ibid.*, §1026(b)(4).
23. *Ibid.*, §1026(a)(4).
24. *Ibid.*, §1026(b)(4).
25. *Ibid.*
26. *Ibid.*, §1026(d)(1)(H).
27. Pub. L. 93–311 §(d)(1), 88 Stat. 236 (June 8, 1974).
28. *Occupational Safety and Health Act of 1970*, 29 U.S.C. §§651–78 (1970). [Hereafter cited as *Occupational Safety and Health Act*.]

29. *Ibid.*, §652(8).
30. *Ibid.*, §§651(3), 655.
31. *Ibid.*, §654.
32. *Ibid.*, §654(a).
33. *Ibid.*, §654(b).
34. *Ibid.*, §651.
35. *Ibid.*, §651(2).
36. *Ibid.*, §667(b).
37. *Ibid.*, §667(c)(2).
38. *Ibid.*
39. *Ibid.*, §655(d).
40. *Ibid.*, §657.
41. *Ibid.*, §657(c).
42. *Ibid.*, §651(13).
43. *Ibid.*, §656(a).
44. *Ibid.*, §656(b).
45. *Fair Labor Standards Act of 1938*, 29 U.S.C. §§201–19 (1970).
46. *Ibid.*, §202(a).
47. *Ibid.*
48. *Ibid.*, §211(c).
49. *Ibid.*, §207.
50. *Ibid.*, §206.
51. Armen A. Alchian and William R. Allen, *University Economics*, 2d ed. (Belmont, Calif.: Wadsworth Publishing Company, 1968), pp. 402–3.
52. *Ibid.*, p. 402.
53. *Fair Labor Standards Act of 1938*, 29 U.S.C. §§214(a), 214(b), 214(c), 214(d)(1).
54. *Ibid.*, §214(d)(1).
55. *Ibid.*, §206(d).
56. *Ibid.*, §206(d)(1).
57. *Ibid.*
58. For an excellent discussion of the economic consequences of the equal-pay-for-equal-work maxim, see Alchian and Allen, *op. cit.*, pp. 404–5.
59. *Ibid.*, pp. 387–88.
60. *National Labor Relations Act*, 29 U.S.C. §141 *et seq.* (1970), *as amended by* Pub. L. 93–360, 88 Stat. 395 (July 26, 1974). [Hereafter cited as the *National Labor Relations Act.*] The *National Labor Relations Act* is a composite of the 1935 *Wagner Act* [49 Stat. 449 (July 5, 1935)], and the 1947 *Taft-Hartley Act* [61 Stat. 136 (June 23, 1947)].
61. *National Labor Relations Act*, §141(b).
62. *Ibid.*
63. *Ibid.*, §151.
64. *Ibid.*, §159(a).
65. *Ibid.*, §159.
66. *Ibid.*, §§158(a)(5), 158(b)(3).
67. *Ibid.*, §158(d).
68. *Ibid.*, §159(b).
69. *Ibid.*, §159(a).
70. *Ibid.*, §157.
71. *Ibid.*, §158(a)(3).
72. *Ibid.*, §164(b).
73. *Ibid.*, §160(a).
74. *Ibid.*, §160(c).
75. *Ibid.*, §158(a)(2).
76. *Ibid.*, §158(a)(1).
77. *Ibid.*, §157.
78. *Ibid.*, §158(b)(1).
79. *Ibid.*, §151.
80. *Ibid.*, §163.

81. *Ibid.*, §151.
82. *Ibid.*, §141(b).
83. *Ibid.*, §151.
84. *Ibid.*, §141.
85. *Labor-Management Reporting and Disclosure Act of 1959*, 29 U.S.C. §401 *et seq.* (1970).
86. *Ibid.*, §431(a)(5).
87. *Ibid.*, §431(b).
88. *Ibid.*, §433.
89. Roger Sherman, *The Economics of Industry* (Boston: Little, Brown and Company, 1974), p. 332.
90. Economists' statistics indicate that strong unions are likely to increase workers' wages by five to fifteen percent (Sherman, *loc. cit.*).
91. *Ibid.*, p. 290.
92. For valuable discussions of the economic consequences of labor unions, see Alchian and Allen, *op. cit.*, pp. 408–10; and Sherman, *op. cit.*, pp. 287–91, 347–48 (and the works cited therein).
93. While a monopoly's demand for labor is less elastic than that of a nonmonopoly, even a monopoly has a negatively sloped labor demand curve.
94. Sherman, *op. cit.*, p. 290.
95. Alchian and Allen, *op. cit.*, p. 410.
96. 29 U.S.C. §171 *et seq.* (1970).
97. *Ibid.*, §171(a).
98. *Ibid.*, §§174(a)(3), 158(d)(3).
99. *Ibid.*, §171(b).
100. *Ibid.*, §173(c).
101. *Ibid.*, §§173(b), 173(d).
102. *Ibid.*, §173(c).
103. *Ibid.*, §176.
104. *Ibid.*, §§176–80.
105. *Ibid.*, §179(a).
106. *Comprehensive Employment and Training Act of 1973*, 29 U.S.C. §801 *et seq.* (Supp. III, 1973). [Hereafter cited as *Comprehensive Employment and Training Act.*]
107. *Ibid.*, §881(a).
108. *Ibid.*
109. *Ibid.*, §882(a).
110. *Ibid.*, §882(b).
111. *Ibid.*, §882(d).
112. *Ibid.*, §882(g).
113. *Ibid.*, §811(5).
114. *Ibid.*, §§841, 843, 844(c).
115. *Ibid.*, §981(a)(7).
116. *Ibid.*
117. *Ibid.*, §845(c)(8).
118. *Ibid.*, §845(c)(24).
119. *Ibid.*, §848(a)(1).
120. *Ibid.*, §881 *et seq.*
121. *Ibid.*, §881(b).
122. *Ibid.*, §883(c).
123. *Ibid.*
124. *Ibid.*
125. *Ibid.*, §§981(a)(11), 981(a)(12).
126. *Ibid.*, §811.
127. *Ibid.*, §812.
128. *Ibid.*, §814.
129. *Ibid.*, §817.
130. *Ibid.*, §§814, 817(b).

131. *Ibid.*, §§815, 816.
132. *Ibid.*, §951 *et seq.*
133. *Ibid.*, §951(a).
134. *Ibid.*
135. *Ibid.*, §953(1).
136. *Ibid.*, §952(a).
137. *Ibid.*, §952(a)(2).

Chapter 8: Federal Control over Agriculture

1. Hendrik S. Houthakker, *Economic Policy for the Farm Sector* (Washington, D.C.: American Enterprise Institute for Public Policy Research, 1967), p. 6; see especially fn. 2 on that page. Named after its discoverer, Ernst Engel, this principle is known as Engel's law.
2. *Ibid.* See also Paul A. Samuelson, *Economics*, 6th ed. (New York: McGraw-Hill Book Company, 1964), pp. 400–403.
3. Houthakker, *op. cit.*, p. 7.
4. *Ibid.*, pp. 7, 9; Samuelson, *op. cit.*, pp. 399–400.
5. Houthakker, *op. cit.*, pp. 7–8; Clair Wilcox, *Public Policies Toward Business*, 4th ed. (Homewood, Ill.: Richard D. Irwin, Inc., 1971), pp. 741–42.
6. Wilcox, *op. cit.*, pp. 754–55.
7. *Ibid.*, pp. 757–58.
8. John A. Schnittker, "Changes Needed in Farm Legislation," Joint Economic Committee Print, *The Economics of Federal Subsidy Programs*, 93d Cong., 1st sess. (Washington, D.C.: U.S. Government Printing Office, 1973), p. 855.
9. Wilcox, *op. cit.*, pp. 740–41.
10. Samuelson, *op. cit.*, p. 403.
11. Wilcox, *op. cit.*, p. 741.
12. Houthakker, *op. cit.*, p. 14; Wilcox, *op. cit.*, p. 738.
13. On the economics of price-takers' markets, see Armen A. Alchian and William R. Allen, *University Economics*, 2d ed. (Belmont, Calif.: Wadsworth Publishing Company, 1968), pp. 104–6, esp. p. 106, fn. 1. For definition of perfect competition, see Samuelson, *op. cit.*, pp. 451–52.
14. For discussion of the role of the commodity futures trader, see Samuelson, *op. cit.*, pp. 415–23.
15. Samuelson, *op. cit.*, pp. 408–9.
16. Alchian and Allen, *op. cit.*, pp. 340–41.
17. Wilcox, *op. cit.*, pp. 750–51.
18. Alchian and Allen, *op. cit.*, p. 342.
19. Houthakker, *op. cit.*, pp. 41–43.
20. Russell Lidman, "The Distributional Implications of Agricultural Commodity Programs," Joint Economic Committee Print, *The Economics of Federal Subsidy Programs*, 93d Cong., 1st sess. (Washington, D.C.: U.S. Government Printing Office, 1973), pp. 893–95.
21. Wilcox, *op. cit.*, p. 755.
22. Lidman, *op. cit.*, pp. 893, 912.
23. *Ibid.*
24. Houthakker, *op. cit.*, pp. 16–17.
25. Lidman, *op. cit.*, pp. 902–4.
26. *Ibid.*, p. 911.
27. *Agricultural Marketing Act of 1946*, 7 U.S.C. §§1621–30 (1970).
28. *Ibid.*, §§1621, 1622.
29. *Ibid.*, §§1621, 1622(b), 1622(m).
30. *Ibid.*, §1622(i).
31. *Ibid.*, §1621.

32. *Ibid.*, §1622(a).
33. *Agricultural Adjustment Act of 1938*, 7 U.S.C. §1304 (1970).
34. *Ibid.*, §§1311, 1321, 1331, 1341, 1351.
35. *Ibid.*, §1331.
36. *Ibid.*, §1304; see also §1331.
37. *Ibid.*, §1321.
38. *Ibid.*, §1331.
39. *Ibid.*, §§1311, 1351(b).
40. *Ibid.*, §§1311(c), 1331.
41. *Ibid.*, §§1321, 1331, 1341, 1351; *Agricultural Marketing Act of 1946,* 7 U.S.C. §§1621, 1622(b) (1970).
42. *Agricultural Adjustment Act* (1933), 7 U.S.C. §602 (1970).
43. Pub. L. No. 88–354, 78 Stat. 269 (July 3, 1964), *as amended by* Pub. L. No. 89–20, 79 Stat. 111 (May 15, 1965).
44. *Ibid.*, §§4(3), 4(4).
45. 7 U.S.C. §§451–57 (1970).
46. *Agricultural Act of 1949*, 7 U.S.C. §1428(b) (1970).
47. 7 U.S.C. §291 (1970).
48. *Ibid.*, §292.
49. *Ibid.*, §455.
50. *Ibid.*, §§453(b)(5), 453(b)(6).
51. *Agricultural Adjustment Act* (1933), 7 U.S.C. §601 *et seq.* (1970).
52. *Ibid.*, §608b.
53. *Ibid.*
54. *Ibid.*, §608c.
55. *Ibid.*, §608c(6).
56. *Ibid.*, §608c(9).
57. *Ibid.*, §608c(12).
58. *Ibid.*, §608c(14).
59. *Ibid.*, §608d.
60. *Ibid.*, §608a(5).
61. Schnittker, *op. cit.*, pp. 860–62.
62. Samuelson, *op. cit.*, pp. 403–5; Wilcox, *op. cit.*, p. 747.
63. See sec. I of this chapter.
64. *Agricultural Adjustment Act* (1933), 7 U.S.C. §602(1) (1970). The statutory formula for computing parity prices appears in the *Agricultural Adjustment Act of 1938*, 7 U.S.C. §1301(a)(1) (1970).
65. *Agricultural Adjustment Act* (1933), 7 U.S.C. §608(3) (1970).
66. *Ibid.*, §612c.
67. *Ibid.*
68. *Agricultural Adjustment Act of 1938*, 7 U.S.C. §1303 (1970).
69. *Agricultural Act of 1949,* 7 U.S.C. §1421 *et seq.* (1970).
70. *Ibid.*, §§1421(b), 1422, 1423, 1441, 1447.
71. *Ibid.*, §1425.
72. *Federal Crop Insurance Act*, 7 U.S.C. §§1501–19 (1970).
73. *Ibid.*, §1508(a).
74. *Agricultural Adjustment Act of 1938*, 7 U.S.C. §1281 *et seq.* (1970).
75. *Agricultural Act of 1949*, 7 U.S.C. §§1421(c), 1445a(b) (1970).
76. *Agricultural Adjustment Act of 1938*, 7 U.S.C. §1331 (1970).
77. *Ibid.*, §§1332(a), 1332(b).
78. *Ibid.*, §1336.
79. *Ibid.*, §§1330(2), 1330(3), 1340(2), 1340(3).
80. *Ibid.*, §1336.
81. Alchian and Allen, *op. cit.*, p. 343.
82. *Agricultural Adjustment Act of 1938*, 7 U.S.C. §1333 (1970).
83. *Ibid.*
84. *Ibid.*, §1334.
85. Alchian and Allen, *loc. cit.*

86. *Agricultural Adjustment Act of 1938,* 7 U.S.C. §§1334(a), 1334(b), 1334(c) (1970). See also §1379c(a) of the same statute, *as amended by* the *Agriculture and Consumer Protection Act of 1973,* Pub. L. No. 93–86, §9 (August 10, 1973).
87. *Agricultural Adjustment Act of 1938,* 7 U.S.C. §1334(c) (1970).
88. *Ibid.,* §1379c(a)(4), *as amended by* the *Agriculture and Consumer Protection Act of 1973,* Pub. L. No. 93–86, §9 (August 10, 1973).
89. *Ibid.*
90. *Ibid.,* §1334(g).
91. *Ibid.,* §§1334(a), 1334(b). See also §§1379c(a)(1), (2), (3), and (4) of the same statute, *as amended by* the *Agriculture and Consumer Protection Act of 1973,* Pub. L. No. 93–86, §9 (August 10, 1973).
92. *Ibid.,* §§1334(c)(1), 1334(c)(4), 1339(b).
93. *Ibid.,* §1379b(b), *as amended by* the *Agriculture and Consumer Protection Act of 1973,* Pub. L. No. 93–86, §9 (August 10, 1973).
94. *Ibid.,* §1379c(f).
95. *Soil Conservation and Domestic Allotment Act,* 16 U.S.C. §590-l(b)(1970).
96. *Agricultural Adjustment Act of 1938,* 7 U.S.C. §1339 (1970).
97. *Ibid.,* §1379b(c), *as amended by* the *Agriculture and Consumer Protection Act of 1973,* Pub. L. No. 93–86, §9 (August 10, 1973).
98. *Agricultural Adjustment Act* (1933), 7 U.S.C. §§608(2), 611 (1970).
99. *Soil Conservation and Domestic Allotment Act,* 16 U.S.C. §§590a–590q (1970).
100. 16 U.S.C. §§1501–10 (Supp. Ill, 1973).
101. *Soil Conservation and Domestic Allotment Act,* 16 U.S.C. §590a (1970).
102. *Ibid.,* §§590b, 590j.
103. *Ibid.,* §590g(a) (Supp. Ill, 1973).
104. *Ibid.,* §590h(b).
105. *Ibid.,* §590g(a).
106. 16 U.S.C. §§1501–10 (Supp. Ill, 1973).
107. *Ibid.,* §§1501, 1503(b).
108. *Ibid.,* §1502.
109. *Ibid.,* §1505.
110. *Ibid.*
111. 7 U.S.C. §§1741, 1742 (1970).
112. *Public Law 480,* 7 U.S.C. §1701 *et seq.* (1970).
113. *Ibid.,* §1701.
114. *Ibid.,* §1702.
115. Houthakker, *op. cit.,* pp. 23–24; Wilcox, *op. cit.,* pp. 750–51.
116. 7 U.S.C. §1721 (1970).
117. *Ibid.*
118. *Public Law 480,* 7 U.S.C. §1703(e) (1970).
119. *Ibid.,* §1707(a).
120. 7 U.S.C. §1734 (1970).
121. *Ibid.,* §1859.
122. *Ibid.,* §1743(a).
123. *Agricultural Act of 1949,* 7 U.S.C. §1427 (1970).
124. *Ibid.,* §1431.
125. *Ibid.*
126. 7 U.S.C. §1744(b) (1970).
127. *Ibid.,* §1851.
128. *Agricultural Act of 1949,* 7 U.S.C. §1427 (1970).
129. *Ibid.*

Chapter 9: Fascist International Economic Policies: Import/Export Controls, Protectionism, and Autarky

1. For discussion of fundamental principles of international economics, see Armen A.

Alchian and William R. Allen, *University Economics*, 2d ed. (Belmont, Calif.: Wadsworth Publishing Company, 1968), chaps. 33–36; Lester V. Chandler, *The Economics of Money and Banking*, 4th ed. (New York, Harper & Row, 1964), sec. V, "International Monetary Relations"; Paul A. Samuelson, *Economics*, 6th ed. (New York: McGraw-Hill Book Company, 1964), pt. V, "International Trade and Finance"; and Delbert A. Snider, *Introduction to International Economics*, 3d ed. (Homewood, Ill.: Richard D. Irwin, Inc., 1963), esp. pt. IV, "Public and Private Barriers to Trade."

2. *Tariff Act of 1930*, 19 U.S.C. §1301 *et seq.* (1970), as amended.
3. *Trade Act of 1974*, Pub. L. No. 93–618, 88 Stat. 1978 (January 3, 1975), §171.
4. *Tariff Act of 1930*, 19 U.S.C. §§1336(a), 1336(b) (1970).
5. *Ibid.*, §1336(g).
6. *Ibid.*, §§1336(a), 1336(b).
7. *Trade Act of 1974*, Pub. L. No. 93–618, 88 Stat. 1978 (January 3, 1975).
8. *Ibid.*, §101(a). These trade agreements become legally effective only upon congressional passage of implementing legislation. See §§102(c), 102(d), and 102(e).
9. *Ibid.*, §101(a)(2).
10. *Ibid.*, §125(c).
11. *Ibid.*, §122(a).
12. *Ibid.*
13. *Ibid.*, §122(d)(2).
14. *Ibid.*
15. *Ibid.*, §122(e).
16. *Ibid.*
17. *Ibid.*, §§201, 202, 203.
18. *Ibid.*, §§203(a), 203(h)(3). The trade barriers may be imposed initially for a five-year period, which may be extended by the President for three years if he declares the extension to be in the "national interest."
19. *Ibid.*, §201(b)(1).
20. *Ibid.*, §201(b)(2)(B).
21. *Ibid.*, §201(b)(2)(A).
22. *Ibid.*, §201(b)(2)(C). Similarly, after stating in §406(a) and §406(b) that "market disruption" is sufficient grounds for increasing tariffs on products imported from communist countries, another provision of the *Trade Act of 1974* states:

Market disruption exists within a domestic industry whenever imports of an an article, like or directly competitive with an article produced by such domestic industry, are increasing rapidly, either absolutely or relatively, so as to be a significant cause of material injury, or threat thereof, to such domestic industry. [*Ibid.*, §406(e)(2).]

23. *Ibid.*, §201(b)(4).
24. *Ibid.*, §201(a)(1).
25. *Ibid.*, §§404, 405. See also §407.
26. *Ibid.*, §§405(b)(3), 406(e)(2).
27. *Ibid.*, §§501–5.
28. *Ibid.*, §§502, 503.
29. *Ibid.*
30. *Ibid.*, §501(3).
31. *Ibid.*, §§221–74.
32. *Ibid.*, §284.
33. *Ibid.*, §§271, 272.
34. *Ibid.*, §§254, 273.
35. *Ibid.*, §§231–33.
36. *Ibid.*, §236.
37. *Ibid.*, §237.
38. *Ibid.*, §238.
39. *Ibid.*, §251(c). See also §§222, 271(c).

40. *Ibid.*, §§222, 251(c), 271(c).
41. *Ibid.*, §§252(c), 253.
42. *Tariff Act of 1930*, 19 U.S.C. §§1337(a), 1337(g) (1970), *as amended by* the *Trade Act of 1974*, Pub. L. No. 93–618, 88 Stat. 1978 (January 3, 1975), §341.
43. *Ibid.*, §1337(d).
44. *Ibid.*, §1337.
45. 15 U.S.C. §72 (1970).
46. *Ibid.*
47. *Tariff Act of 1930*, 19 U.S.C. §1338(a) (1970).
48. *Ibid.*, §1338(b).
49. *Ibid.*, §1338(e).
50. *Ibid.*, §1338(f).
51. See sec. II of this chapter, entitled "Government Control over Exports."
52. *Tariff Act of 1930*, 19 U.S.C. §1303(a) (1970), *as amended by* the *Trade Act of 1974*, Pub. L. No. 93–618, 88 Stat. 1978 (January 3, 1975), §331.
53. *Trade Act of 1974*, Pub. L. No. 93–618, 88 Stat. 1978 (January 3, 1975), §301(a). The President's retaliatory actions under §301(a) may be overturned by Congress except when applied to a "country or instrumentality whose restriction, act, policy, or practice was the cause for taking such action" [§§302(a), 302(b)].
54. *Ibid.*, §301(a).
55. *Ibid.*, §§301(a)(1), 301(a)(3).
56. *Ibid.*, §301(a)(2).
57. *Ibid.*, §301(a)(4).
58. See sec. VI of this chapter, entitled "Spiraling Protectionism."
59. 15 U.S.C. §75 (1970).
60. *Ibid.*, §76.
61. *Ibid.*
62. *Ibid.*
63. *Consumer Product Safety Act*, 15 U.S.C. §2056(a) (Supp. II, 1972).
64. *Ibid.*, §2057.
65. *Ibid.*, §§2066(a), 2068(a)(1), 2068(a)(2).
66. *Ibid.*, §2069.
67. *Ibid.*, §2070.
68. *Agricultural Adjustment Act* (1933), 7 U.S.C. §624(a) (1970).
69. *Ibid.*, §624(b).
70. *Ibid.*
71. 7 U.S.C. §1854 (1970).
72. *Ibid.*
73. *Agricultural Adjustment Act* (1933), 7 U.S.C. §608a(1)(A)(i) (1970).
74. *Ibid.*, §608e–1.
75. 21 U.S.C. §§41–50 (1970), esp. §§41, 43.
76. *Agricultural Adjustment Act of 1938,* 7 U.S.C. §1380–1 (1970).
77. *Natural Gas Act*, 15 U.S.C. §717b (1970).
78. *Export Administration Act of 1969*, 50 U.S.C. App. §2404(b) (1970), *as amended* (Supp. II, 1972).
79. *Ibid.*, §2403(b).
80. *Ibid.*, §§2403(d), 2403(i), incorporating §2402 by reference, *as amended by* the *Export Administration Amendments of 1974*, Pub. L. No. 93–500, 88 Stat. 1552 (October 29, 1974), §§2, 7, 10, 11.
81. *Ibid.*, §2402(7), added by the *Export Administration Amendments of 1974*, Pub. L. No. 93–500, 88 Stat. 1552 (October 29, 1974), §11.
82. *Ibid.*, §2402(2)(A), *as amended by* the *Export Administration Amendments of 1974*, Pub. L. No. 93–500, 88 Stat. 1552 (October 29, 1974), §2.
83. *Ibid.*
84. *Ibid.*, §2402(1).
85. *Ibid.*, §2403(b)(1).
86. *Ibid.*, §2403(b)(2).

87. Exec. Order No. 11533, 35 Fed. Reg. 8799 (June 4, 1970).
88. *Export Administration Act of 1969*, 50 U.S.C. App. §2405 (1970), *as amended* (Supp. II, 1972).
89. *Natural Gas Act*, 15 U.S.C. §717b (1970).
90. *Ibid.*
91. 15 U.S.C. §65 (1970).
92. See sec. III of this chapter, which discusses foreign exchange controls.
93. Douglas R. Bohi, "Export Subsidies and U.S. Exports: An Analysis of the U.S. Eximbank," Joint Economic Committee Print, *The Economics of Federal Subsidy Programs*, 92d Cong., 2d sess. (Washington, D.C.: U.S. Government Printing Office, 1972), p. 162.
94. *International Economic Policy Act of 1972*, 22 U.S.C. §2845(6)(C) (Supp. II, 1972), *as amended by* Pub. L. No. 93–121 (October 4, 1973).
95. 15 U.S.C. §1026(c)(1)(E) (Supp. III, 1973).
96. *Agricultural Adjustment Act of 1938*, 7 U.S.C. §1292(g) (1970).
97. Exec. Order No. 11420, 33 Fed. Reg. 10997 (July 31, 1968).
98. Exec. Order No. 11753, 38 Fed. Reg. 34983 (December 21, 1973).
99. *Agricultural Adjustment Act* (1933), 7 U.S.C. §612c (1970).
100. 7 U.S.C. §1707(a) (1970).
101. 15 U.S.C. §§714c, 714b(1) (1970).
102. See *The Economics of Federal Subsidy Programs: A Staff Study*, Joint Economic Committee Print, 92d Cong., 1st sess. (Washington, D.C.: U.S. Government Printing Office, 1972), pp. 142–44.
103. *International Economic Policy Act of 1972*, 22 U.S.C. §2845(6) (Supp. II, 1972), *as amended by* Pub. L. No. 93–121 (October 4, 1973).
104. *Ibid.*, §2846(5).
105. 15 U.S.C. §1026(b)(5) (Supp. III, 1973).
106. *Consumer Product Safety Act*, 15 U.S.C. §§2066(a), 2067 (Supp. II, 1972).
107. *Export Administration Act of 1969*, 50 U.S.C. App. §2402(5) (1970), *as amended* (Supp. II, 1972).
108. 15 U.S.C. §62 (1970).
109. *Agricultural Adjustment Act* (1933), 7 U.S.C. §§617, 615(e) (1970). Although still retained in the *United States Code*, the cited provisions may be obsolete by virtue of the U.S. Supreme Court's 1936 holding that the "processing tax" structure established by the 1933 Agricultural Adjustment Act was unconstitutional. See *United States* v. *Butler*, 297 U.S. 1 (1936), discussed in Chapter 2 at pages 38-39.
110. 12 U.S.C. §95a (1970).
111. *Ibid.*, §95a(1).
112. *Ibid.*, §95a(1)(B).
113. *Ibid.*, §95a(1).
114. These include (1) an excerpt from Pub. L. No. 1, 73d Cong., 1st sess. (1933), which ratified President Roosevelt's March 1933 declaration of national emergency; (2) Truman's Proclamation No. 2914, 15 Fed. Reg. 9029 (December 16, 1950); (3) Nixon's Proclamation No. 3972, March 23, 1970; and (4) Nixon's Proclamation No. 4074, August 15, 1971. See Senate Report of the Special Committee on the Termination of the National Emergency, 93d Cong. 1st sess., *Emergency Powers Statutes: Provisions of Federal Law Now in Effect Delegating to the Executive Extraordinary Authority in Time of National Emergency* (Committee Print, 1975) [hereafter cited as *Senate Emergency Powers Statutes Report*], pp. 594–97.
115. Exec. Order No. 6560 (January 15, 1934). See *Senate Emergency Powers Statutes Report, op. cit.*, p. 187.
116. Exec. Order No. 6560 (January 15, 1934), §1.
117. *Ibid.*
118. Exec. Order No. 8389, 5 Fed. Reg. 1400 (April 10, 1940).
119. Exec. Order No. 11387, 88 Fed. Reg. 47 (January 1, 1968).
120. An explicit provision so stating is included in the statute that creates and controls the Export-Import Bank. See *Export-Import Bank Act of 1945*, 12 U.S.C.

§635(b)(1)(B) (1970), *as amended by* the *Export-Import Bank Amendments of 1974,* Pub. L. No. 93–646, 88 Stat. 2333 (January 4, 1975).
121. *Export-Import Bank Act of 1945,* 12 U.S.C. §635(a)(1) (1970), *as amended* (Supp. II, 1972).
122. *Ibid.*
123. *Ibid.,* §635(b)(2), *as amended by* the *Export-Import Bank Amendments of 1974,* Pub. L. No. 93–646, 88 Stat. 2333 (January 4, 1975).
124. *Ibid.,* §§635(a)(1), 635(c)(1).
125. *Ibid.,* §635(b)(4).
126. *Ibid.,* §635(b)(1).
127. *Ibid.,* §635j(a).
128. *Ibid.,* §635(a)(2).
129. *Ibid.*
130. *Ibid.,* §635d.
131. *Ibid.,* §635k.
132. *Ibid.,* §635e.
133. Bohi, *op. cit.,* p. 165.
134. *International Economic Policy Act of 1972,* 22 U.S.C. §§2841–49 (Supp. II, 1972), *as amended by* Pub. L. No. 93–121 (October 4, 1973).
135. *Ibid.,* §§2842, 2843.
136. *Ibid.,* §2841.
137. *Ibid.,* §2845(2).
138. *Ibid.,* §2845(6).
139. *Export Administration Act of 1969,* 50 U.S.C. App. §2404(a) (1970), *as amended* (Supp. II, 1972).
140. *Ibid.,* §2404(6).
141. 15 U.S.C. §713a–13 (1970); see also 15 U.S.C. §714c (1970).
142. *Export Administration Act of 1969,* 50 U.S.C. App. §2402(6) (1970), *as amended* (Supp. II, 1972).
143. *Ibid.,* §2404(c).
144. *Ibid.,* §2403(a)(2).
145. *Ibid.,* §2408.
146. *Export-Import Bank Act of 1945,* 12 U.S.C. §635a(d) (1970), *as amended* (Supp. II, 1972).
147. *Trade Act of 1974,* Pub. L. No. 93–618, 88 Stat. 1978 (January 3, 1975), §135(a).
148. *Ibid.,* §282.
149. *Export Administration Act of 1969,* 50 U.S.C. App. §2402(2)(A) (1970), *as amended by* the *Export Administration Amendments of 1974,* Pub. L. No. 93–500, 88 Stat. 1552 (October 29, 1974).
150. *Ibid.,* §2403(c)(1).
151. *Ibid.,* §2403(c)(2).
152. *Trade Act of 1974,* Pub. L. No. 93–618, 88 Stat. 1978 (January 3, 1975), §608(b).
153. *Tariff Act of 1930,* 19 U.S.C. §1484(e) (1970), *as amended by* the *Trade Act of 1974,* Pub. L. No. 93–618, 88 Stat. 1978 (January 3, 1975), §608(a).
154. *Trade Act of 1974,* Pub. L. No. 93–618, 88 Stat. 1978 (January 3, 1975), §411.
155. *Ibid.,* §410.
156. *Ibid.,* §411(a).
157. *Ibid.,* §411(b).
158. *Federal Energy Administration Act of 1974,* Pub. L. No. 93–275 (May 7, 1974), §25(a).
159. *Ibid.*
160. *Agriculture and Consumer Protection Act of 1973,* Pub. L. No. 93–86 (August 10, 1973), §27.
161. *Trade Act of 1974,* Pub. L. No. 93–618, 88 Stat. 1978 (January 3, 1975), §283.
162. See chap. 1.
163. *Trade Act of 1974,* Pub. L. No. 93–618, 88 Stat. 1978 (January 3, 1975), §108(a).
164. *Ibid.,* §301(a)(4).

303

165. *Export Administration Act of 1969*, 50 U.S.C. App. §2401(5) (1970), *as amended by* the *Export Administration Amendments of 1974*, Pub. L. No. 93–500, 88 Stat. 1552 (October 29, 1974).
166. *Ibid.*, §2402(5)(C).
167. *Ibid.*, §2402(7).
168. *Ibid.*, §2403(d).

Chapter 10: America's Accelerating Fascist Economy
1. *National Commission on Supplies and Shortages Act of 1974*, Pub. L. No. 93–426, 88 Stat. 1166 (September 30, 1974).
2. *Regional Rail Reorganization Act of 1973*, 45 U.S.C. §§701–93 (Supp. III, 1973).
3. *Federal Energy Administration Act of 1974*, Pub. L. No. 93–275, 88 Stat. 96 (May 7, 1974).
4. *Federal Nonnuclear Energy Research and Development Act of 1974*, Pub. L. No. 93–577, 88 Stat. 1878 (December 31, 1974). [Hereafter cited as *Nonnuclear Energy Act.*]
5. *Emergency Petroleum Allocation Act of 1973*, 15 U.S.C. §§751–56 (Supp. III, 1973), *as amended by* Pub. L. No. 93–511, 88 Stat. 1608 (December 5, 1974).
6. George N. Halm, *Economic Systems*, 3d ed. (New York: Holt, Rinehart and Winston, 1968), pp. 275, 280–81.
7. *Standard Reference Data Act*, 15 U.S.C. §§290–290f (1970).
8. *National Commission on Supplies and Shortages Act of 1974*, Pub. L. No. 93–426, 88 Stat. 1166 (September 30, 1974).
9. *Ibid.*, §720(g).
10. *Ibid.*, §720(d).
11. *Ibid.*, §§720(b)(3), 720(b)(4).
12. *Ibid.*, §§720(b)(1), 720(b)(2).
13. *Ibid.*, §§720(b)(3), 720(b)(4), 720(b)(5).
14. *Ibid.*, §720(b)(3).
15. *Ibid.*, §720(c).
16. *Ibid.*, §720(b)(4).
17. *Ibid.*, §720(g).
18. *Ibid.*, §§720(g)(1), 720(g)(2).
19. *Ibid.*, §720(g)(3).
20. *Defense Production Act Amendments of 1974*, Pub. L. No. 93–426, 88 Stat. 1166 (September 30, 1974).
21. S. 3523, 93d Cong., 2d sess. (1974), summarized in *U.S. Code Congressional and Administrative News*, September 15, 1974, 93d Cong., 2d sess., pp. xi–xiii.
22. *U.S. Code Congressional and Administrative News*, November 15, 1974, 93d Cong., 2d sess., pp. 4806–12, esp. pp. 4809–10.
23. See *ibid.*, September 15, 1974, pp. xi-xiii.
24. *National Commission on Supplies and Shortages Act of 1974*, Pub. L. No. 93–426, 88 Stat. 1166 (September 30, 1974), §720(h).
25. *Standard Reference Data Act*, 15 U.S.C. §§290–290f (1970).
26. *Ibid.*, §290b.
27. *Ibid.*, §290a(a).
28. *Ibid.*
29. This trend is further reflected in the Federal Trade Commission's recent move, through what are called "line of business reporting" requirements, to compel disclosure of the cost, sales, and profits of some 345 of America's largest firms. Only about sixty of the 345 are challenging this move. See *U.S. News & World Report*, March 3, 1975, p. 73.

30. *Federal Energy Administration Act of 1974*, Pub. L. No. 93–275, 88 Stat. 96 (May 7, 1974).
31. *Emergency Petroleum Allocation Act of 1973*, 15 U.S.C. §§751–56 (Supp. III, 1973).
32. *Nonnuclear Energy Act*, Pub. L. No. 93–577, 88 Stat. 1878 (December 31, 1974).
33. *Federal Energy Administration Act of 1974*, Pub. L. No. 93–275, 88 Stat. 96 (May 7, 1974), §§5(b)(5), 5(b)(10), 18(a).
34. *Ibid.*, §2(a).
35. *Ibid.*
36. See chap. 6.
37. *Federal Energy Administration Act of 1974*, Pub. L. No. 93–275, 88 Stat. 96 (May 7, 1974), §§6(a)(1), 6(b).
38. *Ibid.*, §22(a).
39. *Ibid.*, §5(b)(1).
40. *Ibid.*, §5(a); see also §2(a).
41. *Ibid.*, §5(b)(6).
42. *Ibid.*, §§5(b)(2), 5(b)(4), 5(b)(5).
43. *Ibid.*, §5(b)(5).
44. *Ibid.*, §5(a).
45. *Ibid.*, §5(b)(7).
46. *Ibid.*, §13(b); see also §§12(b), 12(c).
47. *Emergency Petroleum Allocation Act of 1973*, 15 U.S.C. §§751–56 (Supp. III, 1973).
48. *Ibid.*, §751(a).
49. *Ibid.*, §751(a)(3).
50. *Ibid.*, §753(a).
51. *Ibid.*, §753(d).
52. *Ibid.*, §753(g).
53. Exec. Order No. 11748, 38 Fed. Reg. 33575 (December 4, 1973).
54. *Nonnuclear Energy Act*, Pub. L. No. 93–577, 88 Stat. 1878 (December 31, 1974).
55. *Energy Reorganization Act of 1974*, Pub. L. No. 93–438, 88 Stat. 1233 (October 11, 1974).
56. *Nonnuclear Energy Act*, §§2(a), 2(b).
57. *Ibid.*, §2(d).
58. *Ibid.*, §§4(b), 6(a), 6(b)(1).
59. *Ibid.*, §4(e).
60. *Ibid.*, §§3(b)(3), 6(b)(3).
61. *Ibid.*, §§4(c), 7(a).
62. *Ibid.*, §7(a), esp. §7(a)(4).
63. *Ibid.*, §§7(a)(1), 7(b), 7(b)(7)(B).
64. *Ibid.*, §7(b)(2).
65. *Ibid.*, §7(b)(3).
66. *Ibid.*
67. *Ibid.*
68. *Ibid.*, §9(a).
69. *Ibid.*, §§9(c), 9(d), 9(e).
70. *Ibid.*, §§9(f), 9(g), 9(h).
71. *Ibid.*, §§9(g)(1) and 9(h), esp. 9(h)(5), 9(h)(6), and 9(h)(7).
72. *Ibid.*, §12(a).
73. *Rail Passenger Service Act*, 45 U.S.C. §§501–645 (Supp. III, 1973), *as amended by the Amtrak Improvement Act of 1974*, Pub. L. No. 93–496, 88 Stat. 1526 (October 28, 1974). Government control is achieved through a government-managed corporation called the National Railroad Passenger Corporation, commonly referred to as Amtrak.
74. George W. Hilton, "The Costs to the Economy of the Interstate Commerce Commission," Joint Economic Committee Print, *The Economics of Federal Subsidy Programs*, 93d Cong., 1st sess. (Washington, D.C.: U.S. Government Printing Office, 1973), pp. 707–33.
75. *Regional Rail Reorganization Act of 1973*, 45 U.S.C. §§701–93 (Supp. III, 1973). [Hereafter cited as the *Regional Rail Reorganization Act.*]

76. *Ibid.*, §§771–79, esp. §775(b) and 775(c).
77. *Ibid.*, §716, esp. §716(c).
78. *Ibid.*, §§741–42.
79. *Ibid.*, §§720, 721, 762, 763.
80. *Ibid.*, §§701(b)(1), 716(a)(2); see also §715(d)(1).
81. *Ibid.*, §701(a).
82. *Ibid.*, §701(a)(6).
83. *Ibid.*, §711.
84. *Ibid.*, §§712(a)(1), 716.
85. *Ibid.*, §716(c).
86. *Ibid.*, §791(a)(2).
87. *Ibid.*, §716(a)(5).
88. *Ibid.*, §720(b).
89. *Ibid.*
90. *Ibid.*, §721(a).
91. *Ibid.*, §712(f).
92. *Ibid.*, §742.
93. *Ibid.*, §741(b).
94. In early March 1975 President Ford signed bills appropriating additional subsidies totaling $472 million for bankrupt Northeast and Midwest railroads (*Seattle Times*, March 2, 1975, p. A5; see also *U.S. News & World Report*, March 3, 1975, p. 77).
95. *Regional Rail Reorganization Act*, §741(d).
96. *Ibid.*, §742(d).
97. *Ibid.*, §§761, 762, 763.
98. *Ibid.*, §§762, 763.
99. *Ibid.*, §762(c), *as amended by* Pub. L. No. 93–488, 88 Stat. 1464 (October 26, 1974), §(d).
100. *Ibid.*, §§763, 744(c).
101. *The Economics of Federal Subsidy Programs: A Staff Study*, Joint Economic Committee Print, 92d Cong., 1st sess. (Washington, D.C.: U.S. Government Printing Office, 1972). p. 18.
102. *Ibid.*
103. *Ibid.*
104. *Ibid.*, p. 4.

Index

Aviation. *See* Air carriers

Bailey v. Drexel Furniture Co. See Child Labor Tax Case

Balance of payments, 221–222, 237–238

Banking system: fascism's attitude toward, 18–19, 27; U.S. government's "emergency" powers over, 57–59. *See also* Federal Reserve Act; Federal Reserve system

Broadcasting: FCC's regulatory power, 91–98; license applicant's character and programming scrutinized, 92, 94; free speech threatened by regulation, 93–94; potential censorship, 93–97; program content control by FCC, 94–97; "fairness" doctrine, 95–96; pay television suppressed, 97; property rights in airwaves opposed, 97–98

Capitalism: nominal economic system of fascist state, 16–17

Capitalistic collectivism, 14–17

Cartels: German, Italian, Japanese, 21; characteristic of fascism, 21–22, 25; in United States, authorized by law, 70–112; government as enforcer of collusive agreements, 71–73; agricultural, government-sponsored, 196–199; U.S. international cartels authorized, 242. *See also* Licensing; Price fixing, governmental

Carter v. Carter Coal Co., 34, 35–36, 38, 41

Censorship. *See* Broadcasting

Champion v. Ames. See Lottery Case

Child Labor Tax Case (*Bailey v. Drexel Furniture Co.*), 37–38

Civil Aeronautics Board: economic regulation of air carriers, 108–109, 111–112

Co-optation. *See* Participatory fascism; Subsidies

Collective bargaining, 171–175. *See also* Labor/management relations

Collectivism, 14–17

Collusion: in unregulated market, 71–72; government's role in enforcing, 71–73. *See also* Cartels

Commerce Clause. *See* Interstate Commerce Clause

Commodity Credit Corporation, 201–202, 209–211, 240, 249–250

Commodity futures trader: role in stabilizing agricultural supply and price, 188–189

Communism, 15, 16–17

Comparative advantage, 17, 214, 215–216, 218, 220, 238, 239–240, 241, 244, 246

Comprehensive Employment and Training Act of 1973, 162, 177–183

Consolidated Rail Corporation, 273–276

Consumer Product Safety Act, 117–120, 230–232, 241

Consumer Product Safety Commission, 117–119, 230–232, 241

Consumer sovereignty: destroyed by fascism, 17–18; characteristic of market economy, 17–18, 70–71; undermined by government licensing and price fixing, 73–74; superseded by product-quality laws, 115, 123, 132, 133–134, 136, 137, 139; reduced by wage-price controls, 148, 150; threatened by National Commission on Productivity and Work Quality law, 164; effect of labor unions, 175; effect of subsidized employment, 180–181; undercut by government's agricultural programs, 191; eroded by import/export controls, 248–249; threatened by National Commission on Supplies and Shortages Act, 260–266; foreclosed in matters of energy production, 267–268; curtailed by government takeover of railroads, 274

Cost of Living Council, 158–160

riculture, control of, 18, 21; inflation, 18–19; money supply and banking system, control of, 18–19, 27; wage-price controls, 19–20, 28; product quantity and quality controls, 20; compulsory licensing, 20, 27; production decrees, 20–21; cartelization, 21, 25; favors big business, 21–22, 27; labor and management, attitude toward, 22–24; mandatory economic associations, 23–24; strikes and lockouts, hostility toward, 24; import/export controls, 24–26; international trade policies, 24–27; autarky, advocacy of, 26–27; government contracts, 27–28; economic and psychological dependence, 27–29; politicizing economic risk, 28–29

Federal Aviation Administration: safety regulation of air carriers, 108–111

Federal Communications Act of 1934, 91–98

Federal Communications Commission: regulation of broadcasting, 91–98

Federal Crop Insurance Act, 202, 206

Federal Energy Administration Act of 1974, 253, 261, 267–269

Federal Environmental Pesticide Control Act of 1972, 127–129

Federal Food, Drug and Cosmetic Act, 120–127

Federal Hazardous Substances Act, 120

Federal Meat Inspection Act, 132–136

Federal Mediation and Conciliation Service, 162, 175–176

Federal Nonnuclear Energy Research and Development Act of 1974, 261, 267, 269–273

Federal Power Act. *See* Federal Power Commission

Federal Power Commission: water project regulation, 98–102; electric utility regulation, 102–105; natural gas regulation, 105–108, 234, 236

Federal Register Act, 141

Federal Reserve Act: control over money supply and banking system, 54, 59; indirect nature of monetary controls, 59, 60, 65, 67–68; relationship between Federal Reserve and Treasury Department, 67. *See also* Federal Reserve system

Federal Reserve system: government's "emergency" powers over, 58; structure, 61, 63; Board of Governors, 61, 63, 64, 69; demand deposits as instrument of inflation, 62–63; Federal Open Market Committee, 63, 65, 69; required reserves, inflationary role of, 64–65; inflation of money supply, mechanics of, 64–68; open market purchases of government bonds, inflationary role of, 65–68; legal reserves as "high-powered money," 66; discount rates, inflationary role of, 68. *See also* Federal Reserve Act

Federal Trade Commission, 236

Financial transactions: compulsory reporting of, 55–57; government's "emergency" powers to regulate, 57–59

Flammable Fabrics Act, 120

Food: government controls pertaining to. *See* Agriculture; Federal Food, Drug and Cosmetic Act; Product-quality controls

Foreign exchange: government's "emergency" control over, 58, 242–244; function of, 237

Foreign resources: U.S. demand for "access" to, 229, 251, 254–257

Freight forwarders: ICC's regulatory powers, 88–91

German fascism, 13, 18–19, 20–21, 22–23, 24, 25, 26–27, 28, 166, 184, 255

Gibbons v. Ogden, 34–35, 46

Government-industry corporations:

for production of nonnuclear energy, 271–272; directing "reorganized" Northeast and Midwest railroads, 275–276

Grain Standards Act, United States, 130

Hammer v. Dagenhart, 33, 37, 41, 48

Health, Education and Welfare, Secretary of: powers under Federal Food, Drug and Cosmetic Act, 122–127

Heart of Atlanta Motel v. United States, 46–47

Hitler, Adolf: mentioned, 13, 20, 22, 28, 184

Import/export controls: characteristic of fascism, 24–26, 213; autarky, 213, 218–219, 223, 226, 238, 257–259; importance of international trade, 214; comparative advantage, 214, 215–216, 218, 220, 238, 239–240, 241, 244, 246; international trade barriers, economic effects of, 215–219; political corruption encouraged by, 216; emotional appeal of, 216–219; equalizing production costs, harmful effects of, 217–218, 220–221; retaliation as rationale for, 218, 227–230; imports, U.S. laws restricting, 219–234; tariffs, 219–223, 232–234; quotas, 222–223; "most-favored-nation" status, 223; "adjustment assistance," authorized by Trade Act of 1974, 224–225; exclusion of imports, 225–227, 230–234; "access" to foreign nations' resources demanded, 229, 251, 254–257; agricultural products, 232–234, 242; exports, U.S. laws governing, 234–242; export licenses and license fees, 235–236; subsidies to export industries, 239–241, 244, 247–248; foreign exchange controls, 242–244; Export-Import Bank, 244–248; disarming the op-

position, 250–251; monitoring international trade, 251–254

Imports. *See* Import/export controls

Inflation: characteristic of fascism, 18–19; Federal Reserve Act as legal basis for, 59; indirect government techniques, 59, 60, 65, 67–68; defined, 59–60; economic consequences, 59–60; causes, 60–61; demand deposits' role in, 62; legal reserves, role of, 64–65; Federal Reserve purchase of government bonds as means of, 65–68; Federal Reserve discount rates as means of, 68

International Economic Policy Act, 239, 241, 249

International trade: U.S. regulation of. *See* Import/export controls

International Trade Commission, 220–221, 225–226, 232, 252–253

Interstate Commerce Act. *See* Interstate Commerce Commission

Interstate Commerce Clause: original purpose, 30–31; constitutional basis for government economic regulation, 30–50; early expansion of judicial interpretation, 31–33; "substantial relation" to interstate trade as basis for national control, 33, 40–41, 42–43, 44; production and trade (transportation) differentiated, 33–34, 35, 40–42; employment relation (wages, hours, working conditions), national regulation of, 33–34, 40–42, 47–48; antitrust cases, 34, 42; direct versus indirect effects on interstate commerce, 34–36, 42–48; government *prohibition* of commerce, 36–37, 48; taxation as means of regulation, 37–39, 48–50; post-1937 interpretation, 39–50; *intrastate* economic activity deemed subject to national regulation, 45–48

Interstate Commerce Commission: regulation of railroads, 74–79; regulation of motor carriers, 79–86; regulation of water carriers, 86–88; regulation of freight forwarders, 88–91

Italian fascism, 13, 16, 18, 19, 20–21, 23, 24, 166, 184

Johnson, Lyndon B.: foreign exchange controls, 243–244

Katzenbach v. McClung, 47
Kennedy, John F.: use of executive orders, 142

Labor/management relations: fascism's attitude toward, 22–24; constitutional basis of government control, 33–34, 40–42, 47–48; National Labor Relations Act, 40–42, 161, 171–174; Fair Labor Standards Act of 1938, 41–42, 44, 47–48, 168–171; fascist themes in U.S. laws, 161–163; Employment Act of 1946, 163; National Commission on Productivity and Work Quality, 163–166; Occupational Safety and Health Act of 1970, 166–168; minimum wages, 168–169; Equal Pay Act of 1963, 169–171; National Labor Relations Board, 171–174, 176; unions and collective bargaining, 171–175; Labor-Management Reporting and Disclosure Act of 1959, 174; unions, economic effects of, 174–175; Federal Mediation and Conciliation Service, 175–176; government monitoring of labor market, 177–179; Comprehensive Employment and Training Act of 1973, 177–183; use of subsidies to control distribution of labor, 179–181

Labor-Management Reporting and Disclosure Act of 1959, 161, 174
Legal reserves. *See* Federal Reserve system
Licensing: characteristic of fascism,

20, 27; economic and political effects, 72–74; of railroads, 74–75; of motor carriers, 82–83; of water carriers, 86–87; of freight forwarders, 88–90; of television and radio broadcasters, 91–93; of water projects, 98–100; of natural-gas sellers and distributors, 105–106; of air carriers, 108–111

Lincoln, Abraham: use of executive orders, 141

Lottery Case *(Champion v. Ames),* 36–37, 48

McCray v. United States. See Oleomargarine Tax Act Case

Market economy: characteristics, 17–18; consumer sovereignty in, 17–18, 70–71; producers' and consumers' roles in, 70–71; function of prices, 71–72, 148, 150, 151; suppressed by Economic Stabilization Act of 1970, 147–148, 151–160; effects of controlling wages and prices, 148–151; discourages racial and sexual discrimination, 150; characteristics of agriculture in, 185–186, 187–189; threatened by National Commission on Supplies and Shortages Act, 262–266. *See also* Consumer sovereignty

Maryland v. Wirtz, 47–48
Minimum wages, 168–169
Money: characteristics of, 62
Monitoring, economic. *See* Surveillance, economic
Monopoly power: created by government licensing and price fixing, 73–74; created by tariffs and quotas, 216. *See also* Cartels
Motor carriers: ICC's regulatory power, 79–86; limits on ICC's power, 80–82; common carriers and contract carriers distinguished, 81
Motor vehicles. *See* Motor carriers
Mussolini, Benito: mentioned, 13, 20, 184